SHI^cI DOCTRINE, MU^cTAZILI THEOLOGY

To my parents

SHIᶜI DOCTRINE, MUᶜTAZILI THEOLOGY

AL-SHARĪF AL-MURTAḌĀ AND IMAMI DISCOURSE

◆ ◆ ◆

HUSSEIN ALI ABDULSATER

EDINBURGH
University Press

Edinburgh University Press is one of the leading university presses in the UK. We publish academic books and journals in our selected subject areas across the humanities and social sciences, combining cutting-edge scholarship with high editorial and production values to produce academic works of lasting importance. For more information visit our website: edinburghuniversitypress.com

Edinburgh University Press Ltd
The Tun – Holyrood Road
12 (2f) Jackson's Entry
Edinburgh EH8 8PJ

Typeset in 10/12.5pt JaghbUni by
Servis Filmsetting Ltd, Stockport, Cheshire

A CIP record for this book is available from the British Library

ISBN 978 1 4744 0440 2 (hardback)
ISBN 978 1 4744 0441 9 (webready PDF)
ISBN 978 1 4744 2531 5 (epub)

CONTENTS

Acknowledgements vii

Introduction 1
The ambivalent relation between Imami Shiᶜism and Muᶜtazilism 2
Analysing the ambivalent relation 3
Three masters on Imamism and Muᶜtazilism 6
The present study 7

1 Life and Works 16
Historical setting 16
Biography 18
Oeuvre 22
Magna opera 23
Sources and classification 28
Murtaḍā's bibliography 28

2 God and the World 52
Epistemological sketch: knowledge, investigation, reason and proofs 53
Ontological sketch: entities, attributes and causality 60
Theological sketch: God's existence, attributes and the theory of states 66
Conclusion 79

3 Moral Theory and Divine Justice 87
Moral theory 88
Desert 97
God as moral agent 98
Consequences as deserved treatments 104

Rational and revelational morality 116
Conclusion 119

4 Humans and the Origins of Religious Experience 128
The human being 129
Creation and moral obligation 135
Conclusion 143

5 The Imama and the Need for Moral Leadership 151
Theoretical model 154
The test of history 160
Inconvenient outcomes 167
Conclusion 172

6 Prophethood and the Value of Divine Guidance 182
Theoretical model 183
Historical disclosure 189
Inconvenient outcomes 199
Conclusion 203

Conclusion 211
Theology, doctrine and influence 213
Divine assistance as a theology of history 215

Bibliography 222
Index 242

ACKNOWLEDGEMENTS

I would like to express my deep gratitude to many people whose help has been essential in writing this book. First and foremost, I am indebted to my advisors: Gerhard Böwering for his great support and informative comments, and Hossein Modarressi for his precious advice and meticulous feedback. Their criticism, counsel, patience and encouragement were all indispensable in finishing the doctoral dissertation and, later, in applying the changes that made the present book a totally different work.

Since my undergraduate years Maher Jarrar has been an exceptional mentor. Likewise, I could not be more indebted to Vahid Behmardi for his outstanding guidance and support. I am also grateful to Dimitri Gutas for his illuminating seminars, to Tarif Khalidi for his insightful remarks on history and literature, to Ebrahim Moosa for his enriching view of Islamic ethics, and to Nader El-Bizri, who made me more aware of the contemporary relevance of many *kalām* debates.

The support of many friends made this work possible through their valuable suggestions at various stages of work. I have benefited greatly from Matthew Melvin-Koushki's (occult) feedback, Mushegh Asatryan's knowledge of Shiᶜi extremism, Mahmud Younes' philosophical view of *kalām*, Tarek Idris' stringent theological arguments and Toufic Salloum's remarkable outside perspective. I would also like to thank my many teachers and friends in traditional circles of learning for their instructive comments, often in the context of heated conversations and sometimes amidst accusations of Occidentosis. Because of our differences, my father's critique has always been most educating, as has his personal library. I am also grateful to the anonymous readers chosen by Edinburgh University Press for their suggestions, and to Nicola Ramsey and Ellie Bush for their support during the publication process. The writing of this book, in its various stages, would not have been possible without Nermine el-Horr.

Finally, I credit these esteemed individuals with the merits of the book. Any shortcoming is solely my responsibility.

INTRODUCTION

وجُمْلةُ الأمْر إنَّ المذاهبَ يجبُ أن تُؤخذَ من أفواهِ قائليها وأصحابِهم المختصّين بهم ومَنْ
هو مأمونٌ في الحكايةِ عنهم ولا يُرجع فيها إلى دعاوى الخصوم؛ فإنه إنْ يُرجعْ إلى ذلك في
المذهبِ اتَّسعَ الخرْقُ وجَلَّ الخطْبُ ولم نثقْ بحكايةٍ في مذهبٍ ولا استنادِ مقالة.[1]
الشريف المرتضى

It is perhaps paradoxical, following this epigraph by the Imami Shiᶜi al-Sharīf al-Murtaḍā (d. 1044), to invoke the tangential comments on Imami Shiᶜism made by al-Jāḥiẓ (d. 869), the great *littérateur* and also a *sui generis* Muᶜtazili theologian.[2] Revelling as usual in scathing sarcasm, he remarked that the Rāfiḍis had been narrowing down the line of legitimate claimants to the Imama. This would eventually lead them to argue that an incumbent Imam must live forever; for if the Imam lacked issue and died or was killed by want of prudence, the consistency of their theory would be undermined. The attack was a hypothetical scenario that Jāḥiẓ proposed to cruelly mock a childless ᶜAbbāsid bureaucrat whose bad fortune had made him the object of Abū ᶜUthmān's merciless satire.[3] In response, the bureaucrat argued that Jāḥiẓ's incredible gift for spreading pure falsehood must also indicate his absolute inability to tell the truth; but these protests were in vain.[4]

His penchant for excessive polemics and hyperbole aside, Jāḥiẓ's comments reflect the harshness of the Imamis' opponents in judging their beliefs in a reductionist manner and caricaturing their standpoint. This was still material for complaint even two centuries later, as echoed in the words of al-Sharīf al-Murtaḍā quoted at the beginning. Jāḥiẓ's elliptical remarks, however, are illuminating for what they reveal: first, familiarity with the conditions under which the Imams were living; second, awareness of developments in the Imami position over time; third, knowledge of Imami investment in developing a coherent theory of the Imama; and fourth, appreciation of the sensitivity of history for Imami beliefs, on which Jāḥiẓ based both his negative judgement on their reasoning and his expectation of future refinements in the theory. Given Jāḥiẓ's court connections as a friend of both the grand judge Aḥmad b. Abī Duʾād (d. 854) and the vizier Muḥammad b. ʿAbd al-Malik al-Zayyāt (d. 847), these remarks reflect the strength of the interaction between Muʿtazilism and Imami Shiʿism in high intellectual and political circles. It is also worth noting that these remarks were made at a time when the Wāqifiyya had been, for around four decades, awaiting the return of the Seventh Imam (in Imami reckoning, which will be used throughout this book), Mūsā b. Jaʿfar al-Kāẓim (d. 799), who they believed had gone into hiding. The Imamis were not particularly impressed by such beliefs;[5] their later authorities, however, argued that their rejection of these beliefs at the time was not driven by the improbable age of the presumptive hidden Imam but by the fact that his death had been proven beyond doubt.[6]

The ambivalent relation between Imami Shiʿism and Muʿtazilism

This book examines the critical turn that shaped Imami Shiʿism in the tenth to eleventh centuries, particularly as seen in the work of the theologian, *littérateur*, jurist and community leader Abū al-Qāsim ʿAlī b. al-Ḥusayn al-Mūsawī, better known as al-Sharīf al-Murtaḍā. The book argues that the main tasks facing Imami theology were the systematisation of its scattered responses to various challenges and the preservation of established distinguishing beliefs. I show that both tasks were largely accomplished in Murtaḍā's work, which reflects his deep engagement with Muʿtazilism. Nevertheless, this accomplishment came with a significant modification of some ideological positions, which proved irreversible.

From a wider historical perspective, the relation between Imami Shiʿism and Muʿtazilism has been subject to much debate since its early appearance in Islamic polemical and heresiographical literature. The two schools of thought concur on key questions, some of which stirred immense contention, such as the divine essence and attributes, the origination of the Qurʾān and the existence of free will as opposed to determinism. Generally speaking, two theses have been proposed to explain this concurrence.

According to the first thesis, it was the Imamis who appropriated Muʿtazili positions on these questions; before that, they had been apathetic to these discussions, ignorant of their true nature or adherents of different views on them. The proponents of this understanding of the Imami–Muʿtazili relation are mainly preoccupied with identifying the Imami individuals responsible for the adoption of the Muʿtazili positions and determining the time period of this process. This view is dominant in traditional non-Imami heresiographies[7] and in recent scholarship in both Arabic[8] and Western languages.[9]

The common denominator among the proponents of the second thesis is the independence of Imami positions from Muʿtazilism, despite the substantive concurrence.[10] Some of these proponents further dispute the first thesis by proposing alternative explanations of the roots of this phenomenon. They either point to early traditions from the Imams that could serve as the theoretical basis of the Imami position on these questions without the need to invoke any factor external to the Imami context,[11] or rely on the considerably independent judgement of early Imami theologians, with whom this trend started.[12] Others go a step further to suggest that it was the Muᶜtazilis who fell under the influence of Imami teachings, drawing on the similarity between Imamism and Baghdadi Muᶜtazilism in contrast to Basran Muᶜtazilism and relating it to the sizable Imami population in Baghdad compared with Basra.[13] Many proponents of this thesis are Imami scholars, whether writing in the traditional mode or more recently in a scholarly fashion. In a tone akin to that of the epigraph, they voice complaints against the first thesis, stressing that it issues from rival accounts in traditional literature, which has also shaped the presentation of Imamis in modern scholarship.[14]

Analysing the ambivalent relation

A useful entry point into this debate is to follow a common practice of authors in various disciplines of Islamic scholarship and Arabic literature: that is, to explain the choice of title in the introduction.[15] In the particular case of the present monograph, such explanation is not a mere bow to tradition; rather, it helps to address the relation between Imamism and Muᶜtazilism by clarifying the terms of the debate. Three points need to be covered in this regard; first, the parties to this relation, Imamism and Muᶜtazilism; second, its subject, theology; and third, its nature, influence.

Imamism and Muᶜtazilism

Shiᶜism served as a most powerful stimulus for historical writing in Islam.[16] The concern with history that was prompted by the Shiᶜi involvement in the political controversy over the succession to the Prophet was paralleled by a kindred attention to the religious character of Shiᶜism, attested in beliefs, law and a specific body of traditions. This complex character of Shiᶜism, further complicated by the fundamental changes that it underwent over time, caused much confusion regarding its origins, development and internal dynamics.[17] Of the various Shiᶜi groups, the Imamis had developed a distinct identity already by the early eighth century, as evidenced by their legal practice.[18] Nevertheless, the boundaries separating the Imami community[19] from the larger Muslim collective were perforated,[20] and tension always existed between the needs to assert difference and to accept sameness.[21]

Muᶜtazilism, on the contrary, 'tended to become a tradition of socially and politically disembodied intellection',[22] representing an allegiance to abstract positions, a specific method of argumentation about God's attributes and an objectivist view of moral theory. As such, it was not restricted to any religious community, and it was accepted by many Shiᶜis and Sunnis of different affiliations (Ḥanafi, Zaydi, Imami) as well as by non-Muslims, as the Jewish tradition shows.[23] In fact, Muᶜtazilis never developed a solid agreement on political matters.[24] Muᶜtazilism was, therefore, too cold, no matter how heated the theoretical disputes, to make for a communal identity, inasmuch as the latter is intimately related to the realm of the concrete, that of the particular and the historical.

Theology and doctrine

Muʿtazilism and Imamism are thus incommensurable. The former has no veritable communal identity, despite some ephemeral exceptions; the latter is a community substantially defined by the legal and the historical specificities. The relation between the two was thus bound to centre on the theoretical aspect, given the lack of exclusively Muʿtazili ritual practices and historical narrative and the presence of specifically Imami beliefs. The theoretical aspect that constitutes the subject of this relation is usually referred to as theology, although further qualifications are necessary pertaining both to the form/matter distinction and to major subfields of theology.

Concerning the form/matter distinction, the term theology, in this context, is a translation of *ʿilm al-kalām*. Although not an exact translation because of the lack of an English equivalent, theology is the best possible rendering, for *ʿilm al-kalām* does serve an essential function as 'the fundamental science of Islam'.[25] However, *ʿilm al-kalām* is a composite concept, covering both a method of reasoning and the content that this method treats. These correspond to the form and matter of *ʿilm al-kalām*, respectively. Going back to the problem of translation, 'theology' seems to emphasise method more than content, form more than matter: it strongly indicates a particular system or theory.[26] Of course, method is not pure form, for it must at least contain its basic premises and hold them as contents of belief. Nevertheless, there are questions that are not integral to method as such but are rather views arrived at through the application of a particular method. Moreover, theology cannot be defined 'by [a] specific content of belief' but rather must be seen as

> the product of a rational reflection, accompanied by premises of belief, on the content of a given religious tradition, and on the instructions concerning salvific activity that are to be deduced from that content, when the latter is legitimised by previous initiation and by consent of leading supporters of a community of belief.[27]

The content, which seems to be invariably the object of theological treatment, is semantically similar to doctrine inasmuch as the latter is 'that which is taught'.[28] Therefore, doctrine is associated more with matter than with form; it 'assumes a community that defines itself through the establishment of orthodox thinking and correct conduct. The authority of doctrine may be founded on charisma or on formal policies'.[29] But this emphasis on content in the case of doctrine need not connote rigidity and irrationality, for these pejorative features have been historically associated with dogma.[30] The fact that doctrine implies reference to a community can also distinguish it from theology, which seeks to explore ideas without necessarily committing to them.[31] These distinctions between form and method, on the one hand, and matter and content, on the other, will prove useful in analysing the relation between Imamism and Muᶜtazilism to the extent to which it concerns *ᶜilm al-kalām*.

Theologians (*mutakallimūn*) typically divide their subject matter into two major subfields known as grand (*jalīl*) theology and subtle or fine (*daqīq*, *laṭīf*) theology. The former subfield encompasses questions that belong to religion proper (such as the attributes of God, determinism and prophethood), whereas the latter is mainly concerned with questions of natural philosophy (such as atoms, accidents and motion), although their significance for religious questions is never absent. In light of their contents, and echoing the aforementioned form-matter compositeness of *ᶜilm al-kalām*, the subfields are sometimes termed *kalām al-dīn* and *kalām al-falsafa*, respectively.[32] Discussions of subtle theology are thus better read in relation to interests that extend beyond the strictly religious questions; their importance lies in the light they shed on the epistemology of theologians and the premises on which they build their competing systems.[33] Therefore, they usually take a back seat in defining a group's identity; a theologian would feel justified in considering them marginal to the fundamentals of Islam.[34] For religious purposes, subtle theology is significant only inasmuch as it constitutes the fine print of theological manifestos: it is crucial only if one intends to chase unlikely interpretations of the body text or unearth its assumptions. For example, if one argues that language is divinely inspired, one must postulate that God created in people a prior knowledge of language before He could reveal His will, given that His will is known through His word. This, in turn, means that God compelled people to understand His word, for they were not given enough time to use their reason to understand it by learning language (which would have created the possibility of mistakes). However, such compulsion would undermine their freedom of choice, the essence of divine justice – which would be an invalid conclusion. Therefore, language, according to this line of reasoning, must be a matter of human convention, not divine inspiration.[35]

The foregoing discussion leaves open two questions concerning the subject of relation, that is, whether it is about form or matter, and whether it falls under grand or subtle theology. It suffices here to note that communal identity depends more on matter than on form, and more on grand theology than on subtle theology. For disembodied intellection, the situation is more complex: grand theology is also more important than subtle theology, but the significance of matter is mostly dependent on providing the indispensable premises that enable the form to remain systematic. Thus, in the study of the relation between Imamism and Muᶜtazilism, grand theology is the more central subject from the Muᶜtazili perspective, whereas doctrine is more significant for Imamism.[36]

Influence

It is difficult to qualify a relation as influence when it comes to affiliation of ideas. This difficulty is caused by methodological considerations, as well as by the connotations of the term concerning the respective parties to this relation. Methodologically, no exact rules can be devised to establish the reality of influence with certainty. In general, external and internal evidence is necessary. For external evidence, one has to examine chronological developments and local concurrences to verify the possibility of interaction between different authors and traditions credited with particular ideas. As for internal evidence, one needs to study conceptual similarities and textual affinities to exclude, to the extent possible, the likelihood of resemblances being mere coincidences.[37] But even when these considerations are properly addressed, the question is not put to rest. For influence connotes having power over another; it thus leaves an inescapable sense of imbalance in power which translates, intellectually, into a claim of originality versus imitation, genuineness versus spuriousness. This discomfort, naturally, is the problem of the presumptive influenced party; it breeds what has been dubbed 'anxiety of influence'. Nevertheless, influence need not be construed as a monolithic category that necessitates the enslavement of the later to the earlier. It can be analysed based on the many ways in which later authors and traditions treat past material to formulate their specific contributions. These ways can be conceived of as 'revisionary ratios' in that they reflect the creation of distinct ideas that, nevertheless, are enriched by awareness of precedents.[38]

In the case of Imamism and Muᶜtazilism, the prevalent theory is the first thesis outlined above. Given the connotations of influence, it generally puts Imamism in the position of the passive party, ascribing agency and activity to Muᶜtazilism. Even if the methodological requirements of arguing for the reality of influence have been secured, this theory leaves much to be said in terms of the revisionary ratios that may qualify it. In addition, the foregoing distinctions concerning the subject of influence are not adequately employed, although they might also be consulted in approaching the question of influence at large.

Three masters on Imamism and Muᶜtazilism

Al-Shaykh al-Mufīd (d. 1022), the senior religious authority of the Imami community in Baghdad, was asked to author a book detailing the difference between Imamism and Muᶜtazilism. His answer rested on defining Shiᶜism in light of a historical narrative and applying a more restrictive theological measure for Imamism: only those who accept ᶜAlī as the Prophet's immediate successor are Shiᶜa; and only those who accept the line of succession down to the Eighth Imam, ᶜAlī al-Riḍā (d. 819), are Imamis, as long as they also believe in the necessity of the Imama and the infallibility of the Imam.[39] By contrast, he defined Muᶜtazilism as belief in 'the station between the two stations' (*al-manzila bayn al-manzilatayn*), even if accompanied by disagreement with other Muᶜtazilis on other points.[40] Mufīd's position thus maintained a static view of the significance of the term and an unflattering one of its origin, for he took the term to have originated in a dispute in the circle of Ḥasan al-Baṣrī (d. 728) and still considered it to denote anyone who concurred with the group on this single question. This stance agreed only partly with the view of the leading Muᶜtazili theologian Abū al-Qāsim al-Kaᶜbī al-Balkhī (d. 931), who was keen to indicate, with cautious acceptance, that the original meaning of the term had been supplanted by a broader significance that made everyone who believed in divine unicity and justice a Muᶜtazili.[41] Mufīd's older contemporary, the leading scholar of Muᶜtazilism al-Qāḍī ᶜAbd al-Jabbār (d. 1024), attacked the Imamis for their views on the Imama while admitting that they had recently elaborated a more cogent argument to support their claims. While accusing the majority of Imamis of being extremists (*ghulāt*) in their beliefs concerning the nature and status of the Imams,[42] he also ascribed to many prominent Imamis views that he found objectionable on fundamental religious questions, such as anthropomorphism and determinism.[43] For his part, al-Sharīf al-Murtaḍā, Mufīd's student, denied that earlier and contemporary Imamis really accepted these beliefs. He presented their argument for the Imama differently, accusing ᶜAbd al-Jabbār of misunderstanding their positions or even mischaracterising them.[44]

These exchanges, which took place within a single generation, are telling: they indicate that Imamism and Muᶜtazilism were being conceptually confused, at least in some high circles, and that neither party was happy with this confusion. The elaborateness of Mufīd's answer, a book entitled *Awāʾil al-maqālāt*, suggests the dire need of Imamis to assert their separate identity in the face of accusations that they were indistinct from Muᶜtazilis. In prioritising the historical over the conceptual and stressing grand over subtle theology in defining Shiᶜism, Mufīd emphasised the primacy of the communal over the intellectual, of doctrine over theology – though without dismissing the latter. ᶜAbd al-Jabbār's approach shows that even for a scholar who had privileged library access and wide social exposure given his status as the grand judge of Rayy, the Imami theory was still nebulous. ᶜAbd al-Jabbār was aware of changes that were making it more sophisticated, and he thus felt obliged to dedicate a double-length volume of his *summa*, *al-Mughnī*, to arguing against Imamism. The tone of the youngest of the three scholars, al-Sharīf al-Murtaḍā, betrays confidence that ᶜAbd al-Jabbār's understanding of the Imami theory is outdated. His four-volume *al-Shāfī fī al-imāma*, intended as a refutation of ᶜAbd al-Jabbār's criticism, leaves the impression that he aimed to show his opponent's arguments to be more irrelevant than ineffectual. He further claimed that it was common practice for everyone to employ arguments that were not perfectly coherent, even on topics as sensitive as God's unicity.[45] Students of both ᶜAbd al-Jabbār and al-Sharīf al-Murtaḍā continued this debate on behalf of their teachers, and later generations kept it alive for centuries.[46]

The present study

Themes and emphasis

This book analyses individual key components of Murtaḍā's theological system in the context of both Imamism and Muᶜtazilism. Such analysis allows for a broad understanding of the consolidation of Imami identity when these components are presented in relation to each other, with emphasis on the interdependence of their theological functions.

In addition, the book studies the intellectual-historical aspect of this turn, detecting the major influences behind Murtaḍā's thought and tracing his legacy in the subsequent tradition. It presents the intellectual context of his theology against the backdrop of sociopolitical changes that proved beneficial to Imami Shiᶜism, with Murtaḍā's status as a senior political figure positioning him to benefit from these changes.

Therefore, the book occupies a station between two stations. It is not focused on the social development of Imami identity in light of rituals and charisma;[47] nor is it primarily concerned with critique and analysis of Muᶜtazili theology from a philosophical standpoint from within or without the broader Islamic tradition.[48] Rather, it studies the specific formation of Imami identity reflected in Murtaḍā's theology in the context of the inevitable encounter with Muᶜtazilism. This specific formation may be described as a discourse, 'a particular way of talking about and understanding the world (or an aspect of the world)'.[49] The tension between discourse as a collective body of knowledge and the individual as both an enactor and a subject of discourse makes it especially difficult to read Murtaḍā's position. This difficulty is due to his various functions as political actor, community leader, public intellectual and religious authority. The complexity is evident when discourse is analysed as a system of statements, for it 'is this character of an "ordered system" which is constitutive of statements, rather than the intentionality of individuals in situations'.[50] In this regard, Murtaḍā's case reveals the paradox of privilege: inasmuch as it emphasises agency, it exposes the privileged to a torrent of influence that erodes individuality. The effect of this paradox on this study is also paradoxical: it makes Murtaḍā's works more accessible as a corpus, but not his ideas as their author. Following the analogy of discourse as an image of reality, we can see this study as a picture of an image. As in photography, pictures bring some things to the fore and keep others in the background: parts of the picture are in high resolution, depicting their objects in extreme detail; others are blurred, showing only the rough contours of that which is pictured. The former parts, usually the concern of the photographer, are the distinctive features of the scene, whereas the latter represent its well-known aspects. If discourse is defined simplistically as 'a particular way of seeing',[51] then this monograph is one in a double sense: it offers a particular way of seeing Murtaḍā's particular way of seeing Imami theology.

These considerations, in addition to restrictions of space, dictate the selection and uneven treatment of various elements in Murtaḍā's theology and doctrines. Thus, only theological themes that are either fundamental to his system (for example, epistemology, divine attributes and the Imama) or doctrines characteristically related to Imami identity (for example, the Imama – again – and divine pardon) are covered. Moreover, particular attention is given to elements of his theology, whether doctrines or arguments, that reveal his originality in relation to both Imami and Muᶜtazili traditions (as in – once more – the Imama and his detailed theory on the inimitability of the Qurʾān). For the same considerations, as well as for reasons related to its reception in the Imami tradition, his contribution to jurisprudence, though substantively important and historically significant, is addressed only as far as it concerns theology; the reader is referred to another venue for a more elaborate discussion of the matter.[52]

Context and authors

Pursuant to the methodological considerations regarding the affiliation of ideas, this book concentrates on the main theologians who are known to have interacted with Murtaḍā in both Imami and Muᶜtazili contexts and whose extant works can serve as material to verify affiliation and to analyse the nature of influence. Among the Imamis, the work of Mufīd is of utmost importance, as is that of Murtaḍā's most famous student Muḥammad b. al-Ḥasan al-Ṭūsī (d. 1067), later known in the Imami tradition as 'Shaykh al-Ṭāʾifa' (the Master of the [Imami] Community). Among the Muᶜtazilis, ᶜAbd al-Jabbār, the head of the Basran Muᶜtazila at the time, and his circle of students constitute the axis of Murtaḍā's engagement with Muᶜtazili thought: Ibn Mattawayh (fl. eleventh century),[53] Mānkdīm (d. 1034)[54] and Abū Rashīd al-Naysābūrī (d. before 1076?)[55] transmitted their teacher's output, expounding on many of his positions and modifying others. In addition to citing Imami and Muᶜtazili figures of previous generations,[56] Murtaḍā either mentions these scholars[57] or is referenced by them.[58] Despite the availability of ample and helpful secondary literature on the teaching of ᶜAbd al-Jabbār's circle and on Mufīd, the book also draws on primary sources to highlight textual affinities on the level of details.

Outline of the book

This book consists of six chapters. Its ordering proved somewhat problematic, mainly because of the atomistic nature of classical theological discussions in the Islamic tradition and their thematic discontinuities, which forced me to systemise evidence and not only to gather it.[59] Or, as Murtaḍā himself noted in his largest work on theology, the *Dhakhīra*, these discussions are so intertwined (*tadākhul*) and mingled (*tamāzuj*) that eventually one needs to cover the relevant topics without investing too much effort in fixing an order (*wa-lā iᶜtibār bi-taqdīm wa-taʾkhīr*).[60] A bird's eye view of the order of topics reveals that Chapter 1 provides the historical setting. Chapters 2, 3 and 4 investigate Murtaḍā's depiction of the universals of his thought, dissociated from the particulars of history. Chapters 5 and 6, by contrast, centre on the historical experience as the concretisation of the universals; therefore, the introduction to Chapter 5 serves as a theoretical prelude to both. What follows is a more detailed description of the chapters' contents.

Chapter 1 presents an overview of Murtaḍā's historical context and family background and a detailed account of his life. It traces his career as a politician, student, teacher and religious authority. His biography is followed by a survey of his most important writings, intended to acquaint readers with each work's general objectives and specific contribution. The last section of this chapter is dedicated to an exhaustive annotated bibliography of Murtaḍā.

Chapter 2 explains the conceptual framework of Murtaḍā's system by detailing his views of God and the natural world. It presents a discussion of the major epistemological tools needed to construct an understanding of existence, followed by a study of the basic ontological claims that govern both divine and natural realms. The last part of the chapter concentrates on God's attributes, with emphasis on Murtaḍā's efforts to create a coherent system to satisfy various conceptual requirements. His agreement with Muᶜtazili theology is at a maximum here, although he still preserves earlier Imami doctrines.

Chapter 3 examines Murtaḍā's moral theory and its compatibility with divine justice. The first part of the chapter analyses the theoretical foundations of moral judgements, investigating the nature of desert as a connection between acts and consequences. The next part investigates God's acts from the standpoint of justice, whether He extends divine assistance or causes evil. The following section covers the elaborate taxonomy of deserved treatments accruing from human worldly acts, tracing the pervasive moral classification of otherworldly outcomes. The complex question of divine pardon of sinners is given special attention. Finally, I analyse the relationship between rational and revelational morality.

Chapter 4 investigates the position of human beings in this theological system. Its point of departure is an elaborate discussion of the definition of the human being, from which I develop an understanding of human agency in relation to God and the world. I also highlight the importance of divine assistance as the bridge between human autonomy and divine sovereignty. What follows is a lengthy description and analysis of religious experience: its origins, justification, relevant parties, responsibilities and characteristics. The concept of moral obligation is shown to be the cornerstone of Murtaḍā's theory on religion.

Chapter 5 covers Murtaḍā's changes to the theology of the Imama, which proved permanent. The chapter elucidates the theoretical aspects of the Imama, understood as an expression of divine assistance: definition, justification, and charismatic qualifications. This analysis establishes the theory's two core principles: the necessity of the Imama and the infallibility of the Imam. Prophets being also Imams, the theoretical aspects that the two offices have in common allow this section of the chapter to provide the broad framework to the next chapter also. The discussion then turns to an examination of applications of the theory to particular Imams, introducing a sacred-historical outlook. The next part treats two major challenges arising from inopportune historical developments: the Imami view of Muḥammad's companions and the occultation of the Twelfth Imam. The chapter closes with a brief discussion of miscellaneous controversial questions related to the ontological status of the Imams and the metaphysical dimensions of the Imama.

Chapter 6 studies the notion of prophethood as the pinnacle of human perfection. In the theory section, emphasis is placed on prophethood as the channel of divine assistance that communicates sacred laws, and on miracles in their relation to Murtaḍā's occasionalist view on causality. In the application section, the focus is on Murtaḍā's peculiar view, heretofore unstudied, on the miraculous nature of the Qurʾān. Next, I provide an exposé of his attempts to resolve contradictions between theory and application in light of narratives concerning particular prophets, likewise from a sacred-historical perspective. This exposé is followed by a discussion of the conflict between different religious laws, examined in light of the belief in the progressive revelation of God's word. This chapter, like the preceding one, closes with a brief discussion of miscellaneous controversial questions concerning the finality of Muḥammad's prophethood and the nature of revelation.

The Conclusion brings together the individual conclusions of the previous chapters. It seeks to read Murtaḍā's contributions in light of the different kinds of influence as a relation between Muᶜtazilism and Imamism.

Style and translation

Given the conceptual horizon and terminological pool of classical Islamic theology, one is faced by the challenge of maintaining a balance between the original usage of terms in these texts and the need to present them in an up-to-date manner. This balancing act becomes more sensitive still when it involves translation. Through one's choice of specific styles and translations, one has to decide whether to invest in making the texts relevant to current discussions on ontology and morality[61] or to strictly observe their fashion of presenting their topics, which is almost opaque to modern sensibilities. My decision was made easier in this case by the book's objective; for I do not treat Murtaḍā's theology as a closed holistic system that is analysed to assess its interpretative power in comparison with his contemporaries or ours. Rather, I explain his selected theological positions in the extent of detail needed to show their interrelations within his system, their relations to the contributions of the aforementioned scholars and their connections with his communal identity. The peculiar *kalām* style of argument has, for the most part, been preserved, since it is inseparable from the underlying logic. Nevertheless, full passages in which such arguments are found have not been translated, given the twists and turns of their phrasing. Only key expressions have been translated; in these cases, the original is usually given in transliteration.

For the translation of technical theological terms, the disagreement of the scholarly community is indeed a form of grace. It provides many existing options to choose from and facilitates the suggestion of new ones. Such cases of disagreement are noted, as are the venues of alternative translations. But given that these are terms of art, the quest for exact or near-exact equivalents is better replaced by consistent common usage that can eventually effect the required semantic shift in the corresponding English terms. Nevertheless, it is important at this point to address one critical term. Rationalism has a particularly interesting history in modern literature on Islam, for it has been usually employed as a positive judgement and associated with the Muᶜtazila, in both academic scholarship[62] and the more general intellectual reformist writings, whether in Sunni or Shiᶜi milieus.[63] In the present book, 'rational', 'reason' and 'rationality' are all intended as translations of the term *ᶜaql* and its derivatives in Murtaḍā's usage; they are characterisations issuing from within his system. Only 'rationalist' and 'rationalism' are used as characterisations of his system from without. But in either case, the terms do not indicate agreement with his definition of reason, let alone with the assumption that reason – whatever its definition – is the foundation of religious experience, or even that it is better for religiosity to be rationalist than otherwise.

Finally, a word on the usage of 'doctrine' and 'theology'. In traditional circles of Islamic education, it is often said of certain terms that they are different when conjoined and synonymous when disjoined (*idhā ijtamaᶜā iftaraqā wa-idhā iftaraqā ijtamaᶜā*), the proverbial example being *miskīn* and *faqīr*.[64] A similar rule applies to the usage of doctrine and theology throughout this book. In the default case, theology is employed as a translation of *kalām*, that is, to cover both method and content. But when contrasted with doctrine, it refers more specifically to method, whereas doctrine indicates content; hence *Shiᶜi Doctrine, Muᶜtazili Theology*.

Notes

1. *Shāfī*, 1:85. See the beginning of the Bibliography for conventions of citation.
2. For an overview of his theology, see van Ess, *Theologie und Gesellschaft*, 4:96–118, who notes (pp. 106, 111) that Jāḥiẓ wrote unsystematically, paying more attention to style than content. This, however, underlies the unique richness of his writings as a source for both intellectual and social history. It also explains Murtaḍā's great interest in them, himself being a *littérateur* and a theologian as well.
3. Jāḥiẓ, 'Risālat al-tarbīᶜ', 102; Jāḥiẓ, *Tarbīᶜ*, 42, 73, 76, 97; cf. Jāḥiẓ, *Ḥayawān*, 1:308–11. Jāḥiẓ's text was written between 841 and 845; van Ess, *Theologie und Gesellschaft*, 4: 96.
4. See Tawḥīdī, *Hawāmil*, 320, the only source in which excerpts from the response are preserved.
5. See Modarressi, *Crisis*, 60–1, for examples of how the Imamis referred to the Wāqifiyya.
6. Mufīd, *al-Masāʾil al-ᶜashr*, 112.
7. For example, Khayyāṭ, *Intiṣār*, 6; Ashᶜarī, *Maqālāt*, 35; Shahrastānī, *Milal*, 1:145, 166; Ibn Taymiyya, *Minhāj*, 1:31, 2:7, 24. Dhahabī speaks of the friendship between Muᶜtazilism and Rāfiḍism since 979 (Dhahabī, *Siyar*, 17:507 and *Mīzān*, 3:149); while agreeing on Dhahabī's main premise, Ibn Ḥajar, *Lisān*, 4:248, dates it back to the reign of al-Maʾmūn (d. 833).
8. For example, Amīn, *Ḍuḥā*, 3:267–8; Nashshār, *Nashʾat al-fikr*, 1:414–15; Jadᶜānī, *Ṣila*, 1: *jīm–dāl*, 371–2; Madan, *Taṭawwur*, 64–5.
9. See Sourdel, 'L'Imamisme', 233–4, on the Muᶜtazili influence on Imamism; McDermott, *Theology*, 4–5; McDermott, 'Debate', 223, where the author states that Imamis, even before Mufīd, had some Muᶜtazili-leaning theologians. See also Madelung, 'Imāmism', 15, 17, 25, 28; Jafri, *Origins*, 305–6 (speaking of the early Imami theologian Zurāra b. Aᶜyan); Lambton, 'Political theory', 93; Kohlberg, *Shiᶜism*, xxiv; Bar-Asher, *Scripture*, 11; Bayhom-Daou, *Shaykh*, 23; Clarke, 'Faith', 103; Schmidtke, 'al-ᶜAllāma', 154, 156; Gleave, 'Recent research', 1600–2; Amir-Moezzi, 'Shīᶜī doctrine' (though only talking about a particular theological trend in Imami Shiᶜism); Halm, *Shiᶜism*, 49–50; Momen, *Introduction*, 79–82; Yann, *Shiᶜite Islam*, 5–6; Newman, *Formative Period*, 20, 26.

10. Kharsān, *Nashʾa*, 77; Amīn, *Aʿyān*, 1:22, 41, 52, 68, 127, 172, 2:134, 3:53, 104, 338, 384, 389, 5:8, 12, 56, 393, 398, 6:95, 160, 7:248, 410, 8:255, 10:22, 290; Āghā Buzurg, *Dharīʿa*, 1:39, 5:44–5, 8:56; Amīn, *Mustadrakāt*, 1:127; Amīnī, *Ghadīr*, 4:66–7; Niʿma, *Hishām*, 23–5; Gorjī, 'Shiʿism', 43–7; Ḥājj, *Shaykh*, 134.
11. Akhtar, in 'al-Shaykh al-Ṣadūq', 102–15, tries to trace the roots of Islamic theology to the traditions of the Imams, going as far back as ʿAlī b. Abī Ṭālib (d. 661). See also Khamenei, 'Place', particularly 199–210, where the author strongly protests the ascription of Imami theology to Muʿtazili influence. He nonetheless admits that such an influence existed among some individuals who were unaware of the incompatibility of Imami Shiʿism with Muʿtazili thought. Amīn, *Aʿyān*, 1:342; Mughniyya, *Shiʿa*, 110–11; Niʿma, *Falāsifa*, 39–41; Ḥasanī, *Shiʿa*, 14–15, 279–84; Amīnī, *Ṣirāʿ*, 24–5; Ṭabāṭabāʾī, *Mīzān*, 5:78–80; Ṭabāṭabāʾī, *Shiʿa*, 86; Muhajirani, 'Twelve-Imām thought', 179, 181; ʿAbd al-Ghaffār, *Kulaynī*, 423; Jaʿfarī, 'al-Kalām', 164–5; Abrahamov, 'Attitude', 208.
12. For example, Modarressi, *Crisis*, 115–16; Ali, *Imamite Rationalism*, 9–10, who also provides an overview of the relevant literature; see also Dāwūd's introduction to Muẓaffar's *ʿAqāʾid*, 19–22.
13. Jaʿfarī, 'al-Kalām', 231–9; Subḥānī, *ʿIṣma*, 13–19.
14. For example, Ṣadr, *Shiʿa*, 33, 165; Mughniyya, *Shiʿa*, 121–2; Ḥasanī, *Shiʿa*, 14–15, 285–6; Shams al-Dīn, *Dirāsāt*, 63–8; Wāʾilī, *Huwiyya*, 69–70; Ḥusaynī's introduction to Mufīd, *Ḥikāyāt*, 18–31; Anṣārī's introduction to al-Sharīf al-Murtaḍā's *Mulakhkhaṣ*, 19–26.
15. For examples of this practice, see Kulaynī, *Kāfī*, 1:8; Iskāfī, *Tamḥīṣ*, 28–9; Masʿūdī, *Murūj*, 1:26; al-Qāḍī al-Nuʿmān, *Daʿāʾim*, 1:2–3; Ibn Qūlawayh, *Kāmil*, 37–8; Kalābādhī, *Taʿarruf*, 20; Ṣadūq, *Muqniʿ*, 5; Ṣadūq, *Man lā yaḥḍuruhu al-faqīh*, 2; Tanūkhī, *Faraj*, 1:52–5 (with justification for borrowing the title of previous works); Raḍī, *Nahj*, 1:13; Thaʿālibī, *Fiqh*, 19; *Dharīʿa*, 32; Bakrī, *Muʿjam*, 1:1; Jishumī, *Tanbīh*, 16.
16. Khalidi, *Arabic Historical Thought*, 40.
17. Halm, *Shiʿism*, 1; Takim, *Heirs*, 79.
18. Haider, *Origins*, 251–2.
19. Caution is needed in employing the term 'sect', given its particular Christian baggage and negative connotations; on the problems of applying Western sociological typology to religious groups in the Islamic context, see Kenny, 'Politics', particularly 140–2. Because it can eventually gain a different connotation, sect may still be used to refer to some religious groups in Islam, but such use is beyond the needs of the present study, for which 'community' suffices as a term that admits of social boundaries of different strengths; see Zinser, 'Group, religious'. Only the adjectival form 'sectarian' will be used because it applies exactly to contexts in which separation is emphasised over unity.
20. Dakake, *Charismatic Community*, 241.
21. Haider, *Shīʿī Islam*, 2.
22. Cook, *Commanding Right*, 195, where the author also shows how this peculiar situation dictates certain organisational choices in the study of the positions of various Muslim communities on a given question.
23. For examples of Muʿtazilis from different religious communities and traditions, see

Erder, 'Karaites', 778; editors' introduction in Adang, Madelung and Schmidtke, *Baṣran Muʿtazilite Theology*, 2–3; Ansari and Schmidtke, 'Muʿtazili and Zaydī reception', 90.

24. Van Ess, *Theologie und Gesellschaft*, 2:270.
25. Frank, 'Science', 37; the article discusses elaborately the problem of translating *kalām* on pp. 9–12; see also the brief comments in Holtzman, 'Islamic theology', 56; and van Ess, 'Early development', 175–6, for discussion of *kalām* as a technique.
26. *Oxford English Dictionary*, 2nd edn, s.v. 'Theology'.
27. Von Stietencron, 'Theology'.
28. *Oxford English Dictionary*, 2nd edn, s.v. 'Doctrine'.
29. Wiegers, 'Doctrine'.
30. Although it is based on the understanding of these terms in the Roman Catholic tradition, McGrath, *Genesis*, 8–10, is useful for understanding the difference between dogma and doctrine.
31. McGrath, *Genesis*, 10–15; the Roman Catholic frame of reference probably makes the insistence on individuality in theology more significant, as it is seen against the background of central ecclesial authority.
32. Jāḥiẓ, *Ḥayawān*, 2:134, 140. Throughout this book, the term 'philosophy' refers exclusively to *falsafa* and the term 'philosophers' to its practitioners; they are not used in their more general sense. But in this single instance, the term *falsafa* is retained to preserve Jāḥiẓ's concentration on the subject matter of study and his inclusion of other modes of intellectual activity under this label.
33. Dhanani, *Physical Theory*, 3; Vasalou, *Moral Agents*, 18.
34. See, for example, *Mawsūʿa*, 5:523; Mufīd, *Awāʾil*, 102; this is contrary to the view of Jāḥiẓ, *Ḥayawān*, 2:134, who argues that a master theologian should be able to integrate both discussions while still maintaining the said hierarchy of significance elsewhere; Jāḥiẓ, 'Fī Kitāb al-Futyā', 319.
35. Naysābūrī, *Masāʾil*, 158–9.
36. Similarly, Ali, *Imamite Rationalism*, 77, points out a distinction between what he calls 'formal-rationalism' and 'material-rationalism' in his analysis of a text by Ṣadūq (d. 991) and the critical commentary by Mufīd.
37. See the brief theoretical discussion and case study in Hourani, 'Islamic and non-Islamic origins', 61–84.
38. See Bloom, *Anxiety*, 1–16, for an overview of the problem of influence in poetry. Bloom's work is, however, still useful in thinking about influence in general, and it is occasionally consulted in this book.
39. Mufīd, *Awāʾil*, 33.
40. Mufīd, *Awāʾil*, 38.
41. See the discussion in van Ess, *Theologie und Gesellschaft*, 2:335–42.
42. ʿAbd al-Jabbār, *Mughnī*, 20{1}:11–15.
43. ʿAbd al-Jabbār, *Mughnī*, 20{1}:37–8.
44. See, for example, *Shāfī*, 1:38, 45, 50, 57, 63, 65, 67, 150.
45. *Shāfī*, 4:6–7.
46. See Chapter 1, under Magna Opera, *al-Shāfī fī al-imāma*.

47. As, for example, in Haider, *Origins*, and Dakake, *Charismatic Community*, respectively.
48. As, for example, in Frank, *Being*, and Wolfson, *Philosophy*, respectively.
49. Philips and Jørgensen, *Discourse*, 1.
50. Diaz-Bone et al., 'Field of Foucaultian discourse', 11.
51. See Lockman, *Contending Visions*, 184–90, for a definition and a case study.
52. In addition to Chapter 1 on Murtaḍā the jurist, see Abdulsater, *Climax*, 403–84, particularly on the question of traditions and of the relation between moral theory and legal reasoning in Murtaḍā's jurisprudence.
53. On Ibn Mattawayh's dependence on ᶜAbd al-Jabbār's work, and particularly on his *Majmūᶜ* as a critical commentary on ᶜAbd al-Jabbār's *Muḥīṭ*, see Schmidtke, 'Ibn Mattawayh'.
54. On Mānkdīm's critical paraphrase (*taᶜlīq*) of ᶜAbd al-Jabbār's *Sharḥ al-uṣūl al-khamsa* and the problem of attribution in the available edition, see Heemskerk, *Suffering*, 3–4, 60–2.
55. See Ansari and Schmidtke, 'Muᶜtazilism', 244, for Abū Rashīd's dependence on ᶜAbd al-Jabbār's *Mughnī*.
56. See, for example, *Dhakhīra*, 114 (Naẓẓām and the Banū Nawbakht), 132 (the Baghdadi Muᶜtazilis), 140–1 (the two Jubbāʾīs), 166 (Jāḥiẓ), 464 (Ibn Mītham); *Sharḥ Jumal*, 105 (Muᶜammar and Ibn al-Ikhshīd); *Shāfī*, 1:83–4 (Hishām b. al-Ḥakam), 2:126 (Ibn Qiba); *Rasāʾil*, 1:136–7 (Kaᶜbī).
57. Aside from the *Shāfī*, in the *Dhakhīra*, 138, Murtaḍā refers to ᶜAbd al-Jabbār as *ṣāḥib Kitāb al-Mughnī*. The books entitled *al-Fuṣūl al-mukhtāra* and *al-Ḥikāyāt* are selections by Murtaḍā from Mufīd's work (see Murtaḍā's bibliography in Chapter 1); *Rasāʾil*, 4:309 (Naysābūrī).
58. For example, see Ṭūsī, *ᶜUdda*, 1:4 (see also below for other instances); Mānkdīm, *Sharḥ*, 620–62. Ibn Mattawayh often discusses Murtaḍā's position verbatim, though without mentioning his name; see, for example, Ibn Mattawayh, *Majmūᶜ*, 3:342–6; cf. *Dhakhīra*, 295–8.
59. Vasalou, 'Subject', 268–9.
60. *Dhakhīra*, 105.
61. As in Hourani's pioneering *Islamic Rationalism*, which studies the human but not the divine side of ᶜAbd al-Jabbār's ethics (pp. 14–17), and which compares his ethics to British Intuitionism and judges them as a third stage between ancient Greece and the modern West (pp. 144–8).
62. For a critical appraisal of scholarship on *ᶜaql* and an analysis of the concept's role in mischaracterisation of the debate between the Muᶜtazila and their opponents, see Reinhart, *Before Revelation*, 151–5, 167–71; see also Martin, *Defenders*, 12, who compares the Muᶜtazila to philosophers of the Enlightenment; Abrahamov, *Islamic Theology*, 52–3, argues that there are degrees of rationalism in Islamic theology but not a clear-cut distinction, although the Muᶜtazila admittedly are the most rationalist of theologians.
63. See Hildebrandt, *Neo-Muᶜtazilismus*, 79–80, for the different categories of intellectuals who might be identified as neo-Muᶜtazilis in the modern Arab world. See, for example, Hashas, 'Abdolkarim', 163, for a comparable case in the Iranian context.
64. See, for example, Ālūsī, *Tafsīr*, 28:18; Anṣārī, *Makāsib*, 2:48.

CHAPTER

1

LIFE AND WORKS

Historical setting

The arrival of the Shiᶜi Būyids in Baghdad in 945 represented a historic turning point for the Imami community; for although the new dynasty may have been originally of another Shiᶜi affiliation, the Būyids of Baghdad favoured the Imamis over other Shiᶜis.[1] The ᶜAbbāsid caliphate had been weakened by mercenaries and had lost the iron grip under which Imamis had lived, but their participation in authority was limited to a few notable families whose members held bureaucratic offices.[2] The death of the Eleventh Imam, Ḥasan al-ᶜAskarī, in 874 had left Imamis for the first time without a present Imam, generating a major crisis that compelled the community to devise new forms of management to sustain itself. The effects of this crisis, later known as the 'Minor Occultation' (*al-ghayba al-ṣughrā*) and taken to have ended in 941, were still very much in evidence when the Būyids arrived. Their advent and the ensuing improvement in the Imamis' political position alleviated the strain that the Imamis were experiencing. The Būyids were to maintain control of Baghdad for a long century, to be replaced by the Saljuqs only in 1055.

The Būyid age was marked by tolerance and constituted a heyday of intellectual activity. Termed both 'the Shiᶜi century'[3] and 'the renaissance of Islam',[4] the period witnessed some of the greatest masters of philosophy, theology, language and literature of medieval Islam; these were the days of Ibn Sīnā (d. 1037), Qāḍī al-Quḍāt ᶜAbd al-Jabbār, Ibn Jinnī (d. 1001), al-Tawḥīdī (d. 1023) and al-Mutanabbī (d. 965), to name but a few. Probably owing to both their sectarian status as members of a minority and their non-Arab origins, the Būyids showed exceptional acceptance of religious and cultural diversity.[5] Accordingly, debates on various matters, including doctrinal questions, were often held at the monarch's court and in his presence.[6] Many members of the ruling elite were men of learning, especially the viziers, some of whom, such as Ibn al-ᶜAmīd (d. 970)[7] and al-Ṣāḥib b. ᶜAbbād (d. 995), were among the great belletrists of Islam.[8] These influential political figures, in turn, had their own courts, where they hosted the leading intellectuals of the time, sometimes in competition with their masters. The Būyids also paid considerable attention to the pre-Islamic Iranian heritage, reviving the Persian title Shāhānshāh and some aspects of Sasanid rule while respecting the Islamic nature of government by nominally preserving allegiance to the caliph.[9]

Alongside their support for the religious scholars of other Muslim communities, the Būyids showed great respect for Imami scholars, who had never before won government favour. The Būyid age represented the first period in Islamic history when not only were the Imamis free to practise publicly, but their religious leaders also enjoyed the patronage of political authorities, be it in Rayy or in Baghdad.[10] Extant sources record famous debates between Imami scholars and other scholars in the presence of Būyid princes in which they openly challenged other schools and creeds.[11] The relationship was a win-win situation: the Būyids needed popular support to balance the Sunni support for the caliph; the Imamis, now without their Imam and therefore politically unthreatening, needed political cover.[12] This situation stands in sharp contrast, in retrospect, to the subsequent plight of the Imamis in the aftermath of the Būyid downfall.[13]

On the economic level, however, Būyid policies appear not to have been as successful. Their reign witnessed drought and inflation, with poverty afflicting most of the quarters of Baghdad for long periods despite the attempts of some rulers to introduce reforms.[14] The economic downturn was further exacerbated by the recurrent wars between Būyid princes, which brought disasters upon the populace, especially in southern Iraq and southwestern Iran, where the battles between the Būyids of Baghdad and those of Shiraz often took place.[15]

Būyid society was hierarchical and complex. It allowed individuals many opportunities but at the same time exerted even greater demands on them. Relations were knit into an intricate network of acquired loyalties that were founded on diverse grounds; these grounds reflected the spirit in which the Būyids administered the empire, as they mainly relied on people's indebtedness to those who had helped them climb the social ladder. Although inborn 'merit' retained some significance, many of the most distinguished men of the age were self-made individuals whose success was owed to their acquired loyalties. There were also ever-growing categories of loyalty based on sectarian bonds, professions and regional affiliations – these being frequently combined.[16] Belief in the need to respect these loyalties went beyond merely social aspects and found expression in theological convictions about the value of patrons and beneficiaries in dictating the course of events for a moral purpose.[17] The *ᶜulamāʾ* class matured during this period, and the Būyids showed them respect, not least because of the scholars' influence in a society whose majority did not share the Būyids' beliefs. The increasing numbers of the ᶜAlid and ᶜAbbāsid branches of the Banū Hāshim made them into a separate class, with an officially appointed syndic (*naqīb*) for each line.[18] Given his status as a descendant of the Prophet and given the Shiᶜi sympathies of the new dynasty, the syndic of the ᶜAlids was often extremely influential.

Among the syndics of the Ṭālibids, Abū Aḥmad al-Ḥusayn b. Mūsā (d. 1009), known as al-Ṭāhir al-Awḥad and Dhū al-Manāqib, played an important role in public life over the half-century until his death. He combined religious prestige and political stature, owing both to his lineage and to his connections – if these could ever be separated. An ᶜAlid, he was a scion of Mūsā al-Kāẓim.[19] In his days of success, he acted as a peacemaker between the Būyids of Baghdad and the Ḥamdānids of Mosul in 969[20] and 973.[21] This prominence, however, did not mean he always enjoyed the grace of the dynasty. The powerful Būyid king ᶜAḍud al-Dawla (d. 983) confiscated his property and exiled him to Fārs in 979, where he was imprisoned.[22] He was restored to favour a few years later at the hands of Sharaf al-Dawla (d. 989), ᶜAḍud al-Dawla's son.[23] In addition to these recurrent political engagements, he served as the chief syndic of the Ṭālibids for five terms.[24] He was also in charge of the pilgrims (*amīr al-ḥājj*) and took responsibility for the department of grievances (*wilāyat al-maẓālim*).[25] Given the original Zaydi affiliation of the Būyids, Abū Aḥmad's position must have been enhanced by his marriage to one of the descendants of the Zaydi Imam al-Ḥasan al-Uṭrūsh (d. 917), the third ruler of the Zaydi dynasty of Ṭabaristān and eastern Gīlān (864–1126) under the title al-Nāṣir al-Kabīr.[26]

The cultured public figure, a common Būyid theme as attested by the examples of individuals such as Ibn al-ᶜAmīd and al-Ṣāḥib b. ᶜAbbād, was also represented in Abū Aḥmad's life and career. But it is without doubt his two sons, whose rise to prominence Abū Aḥmad witnessed in his lifetime, who embody this theme in a much more exemplary fashion. Although both shared their father's involvement in public matters and government work, they were also active in intellectual life and made significant contributions to it; so much so that their primary historical image is not that of politicians but of intellectuals, each in his own right. The younger son, Muḥammad (d. 1016), known as al-Sharīf al-Raḍī,[27] was a renowned poet who is sometimes considered the most gifted poet in the entire history of the tribe of Quraysh.[28] In the Imami tradition, however, he owes his fame to his compilation of the sayings, sermons and letters of ᶜAlī b. Abī Ṭālib. This collection, entitled *Nahj al-balāgha*, is highly regarded for its literary value, although its religious significance and authenticity have long been called into question outside Imami circles.[29] But it is the life and contributions of the older son, ᶜAlī, that constitute the subject of our study.[30]

Biography

Abū al-Qāsim ᶜAlī b. al-Ḥusayn al-Mūsawī, better known as al-Sharīf al-Murtaḍā, was born in July 965[31] to a family of Basran descent.[32] Although mainly known as a scholar, Murtaḍā was deeply engaged in political life from a young age, starting in 990 when he and his brother Raḍī were appointed deputies to their father as chief syndic before being dismissed along with him four years later.[33] His circle of friends and acquaintances included caliphs and Būyid kings in addition to other members of the ruling elite. A few examples suffice to show the strength of these relations:

he was entrusted with executing the marriage contract (*ᶜaqd*) of Musharrif al-Dawla (d. 1025), the youngest son of Bahāʾ al-Dawla (d. 1012), and the daughter of the Kakuyid ᶜAlāʾ al-Dawla (d. 1041) in 1024;[34] poems in his *Dīwān* reflect his close friendships with many viziers, especially Fakhr al-Mulk (d. 1016);[35] and he composed a poem on behalf of the vizier Abū ᶜAlī Ḥasan b. Ḥamad (d. 1037) in praise of Bahāʾ al-Dawla.[36] However, Raḍī, who harboured ambitious political aspirations, applied himself more vigorously to that domain and acquired most of the titles and responsibilities of their father in 1012,[37] although Murtaḍā – out of religious considerations – had led the funeral prayer upon the father's death.[38] The death of Raḍī at the age of forty-five was a severe emotional crisis for Murtaḍā,[39] but it left him the syndic of the Ṭālibids and the occupant of his brother's social and political offices for the three decades until the end of his own life.[40] Later, the death of his teacher al-Shaykh al-Mufīd made Murtaḍā also the leader of the Imami community in Baghdad. Although Mufīd was a more senior scholarly authority, Murtaḍā's family connections gave him enormous leverage, even during his master's lifetime.[41]

Despite his portrayal mainly as an intellectual, Murtaḍā's diplomatic skills appear to have exceeded those of both his father and his brother. His father's troubles with the Būyids have already been noted; Raḍī, for his part, had strained relations with the ᶜAbbāsid caliph al-Qādir (d. 1031), caused by both his personal ambitions[42] and his evident sympathy for the Fāṭimids in word and deed.[43] Murtaḍā, by contrast, maintained excellent relations with both the Būyids and the ᶜAbbāsids. He acted as a broker between the Turkish mercenaries and the vizier Abū al-Qāsim al-Maghribī in 1024, thus ending a crisis that was about to force the vizier out of office.[44] That same year he was present when the mercenaries paid allegiance to Musharrif al-Dawla.[45] In 1029, Murtaḍā headed a delegation of the notables of Karkh, asking the caliph for permission to resume Friday prayers in the Burāthā mosque after they had been suspended following sectarian strife.[46] The following year he helped mitigate tensions by ordering the residents of Karkh to do away with mourning signs that stoked sectarian conflict between Sunnis and Shiᶜis around the day of ᶜĀshūrā.[47] He also took part in the negotiations between the Būyid king Jalāl al-Dawla (d. 1044) and his Turkish generals in 1028.[48] Murtaḍā's house was vandalised during the riots of 1025,[49] 1031[50] and 1033.[51] In the first instance, his house was set on fire and he had to move to another house while Musharrif al-Dawla dispatched a group of his own guards to prevent the looting of Murtaḍā's property.[52] Also in the riots of 1026, the whole quarter was pillaged and Murtaḍā sought refuge in the caliphal palace. He returned to his house after its renovation, with a caliphal decree that he be escorted there by the generals of the army and the notables.[53] In 1031 Murtaḍā attended a ceremony in which a mutual oath of allegiance was sworn by the caliph and Jalāl al-Dawla.[54] In 1032 rebellious mercenaries forced Jalāl al-Dawla to flee his palace; the king moved his family members to Murtaḍā's residence on the other side of the Tigris and joined them later. Murtaḍā then acted as a broker between the two parties; the success of the mission was announced when the king rode from this house of Murtaḍā to another.[55] A similar incident took place in 1035, but this time Jalāl al-Dawla stayed in Murtaḍā's house for a short while before leaving Baghdad for Tikrit.[56] Earlier that year Murtaḍā had been given custody of the vizier Ibn Mākūlā (d. 1038) following the latter's arrest.[57] In 1033, following the death of al-Burjumī, the chief *ʿayyār* in Baghdad,[58] Murtaḍā was commissioned with receiving repentant *ʿayyārūn* in his house and granting them governmental pardon.[59] Finally, Murtaḍā's prominence is vividly illustrated by his role after the death of the caliph al-Qādir when he was the first to pay allegiance to the new caliph, al-Qāʾim (d. 1075),[60] an act of immense symbolic importance in view of what it reveals about Murtaḍā's standing and its relation to the legitimacy of the new caliph.

Murtaḍā's titles are also indicative of his intimacy with senior politicians. In a decree dated 1006, the Būyid king Bahāʾ al-Dawla bestowed on him the title 'al-Murtaḍā Dhū al-Majdayn', apparently alluding to both his noble ancestry and his personal qualities; Raḍī was given the title 'al-Raḍī Dhū al-Ḥasabayn'.[61] Murtaḍā is also often called 'al-Sayyid', especially in the Imami tradition. One of the most famous of his titles is 'ʿAlam al-Hudā'; although it was a common appellation for him already in his lifetime,[62] only late sources associate it with the story of a dream that the vizier Muḥammad b. Ḥusayn b. ʿAbd al-Raḥīm (d. 1047) had in 1029 in which ʿAlī b. Abī Ṭālib referred to Murtaḍā by this title.[63]

Murtaḍā's enormous wealth enabled him to allocate considerable resources to his studies. His annual income was estimated at 24,000 *dīnārs*,[64] apparently the revenue of irrigated land on the banks of the Euphrates, as he was said to have owned eighty farms between Baghdad and Karbalāʾ.[65] It was reported that his library contained around 80,000 volumes, in addition to the many books that he presented to his friends and students.[66] The Dār al-ʿIlm (Abode of Knowledge) was an institution that he administered, dedicated to study and teaching.[67] It was probably there and at his house that he would receive his students and other scholars, convene meetings (*majālis*) and hold debates (*munāẓarāt*) between adherents of different schools.[68] The stipends that he distributed to his students were quite generous; in addition, he placed his vast library at their disposal and provided them with paper.[69] Despite this, it appears that he was known for broadmindedness more than for generosity.[70] Among his close friends were intellectuals of varying sectarian and religious affiliations; being a descendant of the Prophet, the leader of a religious community and a prominent Muslim scholar did not discourage him from eulogising the famous Sabaean *littérateur* Abū Isḥāq al-Ṣābī (d. 994), with whom he had a close friendship.[71] He is also reported to have maintained a friendship with the poet Abū al-ʿAlāʾ al-Maʿarrī, famously accused of holding heretical views.[72] The encounter between Murtaḍā and Maʿarrī survives in many anecdotes, some portraying it in a negative light, others in a positive one.[73] The fact remains that Maʿarrī's references in poetry to Murtaḍā and his family members are highly positive.[74] In terms of the 'distinctions of level' that defined one's position in the social hierarchy, it may be said that Murtaḍā in the second half of his life combined *ḥasab* (merit), *nasab* (lineage), leadership among the *ʿulamāʾ*, *riyāsa* (prominence) of a region, being one of the *aʿyān* and mastery in *adab* – all among the most celebrated values of Būyid times.[75] Given his aristocratic lineage, Murtaḍā's status was even higher than that of patrician families whose prestige and power derived from landholding, trade and/or religion;[76] this explains his enormous influence in Baghdad and beyond.

Murtaḍā died on 19 October 1044 in Baghdad; his body was washed by the famous biblio-biographer Abū al-ᶜAbbās al-Najāshī (d. 1058), his student Sallār (Sālār) al-Daylamī (d. 1057?) and Abū Yaᶜlā al-Jaᶜfarī (d. 1071).[77] He was first buried in his house, then most probably moved to Karbala to be buried next to the Third Imam, Ḥusayn b. ᶜAlī (d. 680).[78] After him the office of syndic fell to his nephew Abū Aḥmad ᶜAdnān b. Muḥammad (d. 1057–8).[79] His line continued through his son Muḥammad, but it apparently came to an end with the genealogist Abū al-Qāsim ᶜAlī b. Ḥasan in the early thirteenth century.[80]

Given the favourable social setting, it was only natural that Murtaḍā should have had access to the prominent scholars of the time. It suffices here to list some of his more famous teachers.[81] Murtaḍā studied language and rhetoric with the famous poet Ibn Nubāta al-Saᶜdī (d. 1014),[82] poetry and *adab* with al-Marzubānī (d. 994),[83] grammar with the grammarian and Muᶜtazili theologian al-Rummānī (d. 994),[84] and *ḥadīth* with Ḥusayn b. ᶜAlī Ibn Bābawayh[85] and Mufīd, with whom he also studied theology and jurisprudence (*uṣūl al-fiqh*).[86] The studentship of Murtaḍā and Raḍī under Mufīd is associated with an anecdote that shows the enormous influence of their mother and her prestigious position.[87] It is unclear whether he studied with ᶜAbd al-Jabbār, but if he did, he must have done so only for a short period.[88] Most of these figures had a strong influence on Murtaḍā in their respective specialist fields, as the examination later in this book of his views on various theological themes and of his contribution to literature shows. This influence is evidenced either in the concurrence between his views and theirs or in his explicit reference to them in the course of presenting his positions.

The list of Murtaḍā's students is indicative of the influence of his thought in Imami Shiᶜism, even if those students did not fully endorse their teacher's positions. His most prominent student – also a younger colleague, for they both studied under Mufīd – was undisputedly Muḥammad b. al-Ḥasan al-Ṭūsī. Besides his major contributions to Qurʾānic exegesis and jurisprudence, Ṭūsī is the author of two of the four most authoritative collections of traditions for Imamis, namely, *Tahdhīb al-aḥkām* and *al-Istibṣār fī mā ikhtalafa min al-akhbār*.[89] Also among Murtaḍā's most prominent students were Abū al-Ṣalāḥ al-Ḥalabī (d. 1055),[90] Abū al-Fatḥ al-Karājikī (d. 1057),[91] Sallār al-Daylamī[92] and Ibn al-Barrāj (d. 1088).[93] This number of prominent students, in addition to their diversity in terms of social status and geographical origin, suggests that the Imami community in Murtaḍā's time had reached a point at which it was able to produce a class 'of people for whom religious learning was a normal and highly respected aspect of life'.[94] In addition to the strong bond between masters and disciples in the traditional Islamic world of learning, Murtaḍā's finances must have guaranteed him the 'acquired loyalty' of his students thanks to the concept of due gratitude for benefit rendered (*shukr al-niᶜma*).[95]

Oeuvre

Murtaḍā was a prolific author whose oeuvre spanned many Islamic disciplines. This comprehensiveness is attested by his substantial contributions in theology, jurisprudence, law and literature – both as a critic and as a poet. In addition, he appears to have been interested in philosophy more than were other theologians of the age,[96] although – like most of them – he was averse to it.[97] His works in each of these fields exerted quite different levels of influence on the later tradition. It may be said that his literary works had the most favourable reception and his works on jurisprudence the least favourable, his theological works being somewhere in between, as illustrated by the following brief exposé of his contributions.

The littérateur

Murtaḍā was known as a distinguished poet already during his lifetime.[98] His poetry is frequently compared with that of his brother, the judgement being unanimously in favour of the latter;[99] in an exaggeration typical of hagiographic accounts, it is said that Murtaḍā's only shortcoming in poetry was being Raḍī's brother.[100] As a critic, his thematic anthologies of Arabic poetry and the comments scattered throughout his works, especially in his *Amālī* (Dictations), show a vast knowledge of the poetic tradition and of both linguistic questions (the fields of *naḥw*, *ṣarf* and *gharīb al-lugha*) and rhetorical ones (*balāgha*). It is even said that no work by an Imami ever received more praise from non-Imamis than did Murtaḍā's *Amālī*.[101] The work's significance is reflected in the fact that the vast majority of published Arabic literature on Murtaḍā is concerned exclusively or primarily with this aspect of his oeuvre.[102] The reason may also be that his literary output could be considered unstained by his sectarian affiliation, and it thus appealed more easily to diverse groups.

The jurist

Murtaḍā's contribution to jurisprudence, by contrast, was short-lived. Although he appears to have dedicated much effort to the study of *ḥadīth*,[103] his approach was primarily characterised by his rejection of non-prevalent traditions (*akhbār al-āḥād*) as a source of legal rulings.[104] This position was probably the reason for the rejection of his jurisprudential work by subsequent scholars, especially given Murtaḍā's extreme formulation of this principle,[105] which had been abandoned by most Muʿtazilis even before Murtaḍā's time.[106] In fact, it was mostly the work of his student Ṭūsī that rendered Murtaḍā's jurisprudential views on this question obsolete.[107] Murtaḍā's radical position was, on the one hand, accurately seen as depriving jurists of one of the richest potential sources of legal knowledge and, on the other, perceived as being overly hostile to traditionists (and traditionalists), whose work it would effectively have invalidated.[108] Even within the Imami juristic tradition, then, his contribution seems to have only barely survived him, despite an abortive attempt to revive it more than a century later.[109]

The theologian

Murtaḍā's theology appears to have been his most influential contribution to the religious sciences. This significance is attested by the fact that many of his biographers describe him as a theologian before listing his other scholarly activities.[110] Murtaḍā produced a theological system distinct from that of Mufīd. His influence was tremendous, as his system would come to constitute mainstream Imami theology – at least until its Aristotelian turn at the hands of Naṣīr al-Dīn al-Ṭūsī (d. 1274).[111] The success of his system may be seen in the fact that it found currency beyond Imami circles, in Zaydi[112] and Jewish[113] theological works.

Murtaḍā remained solidly in the Imami camp theologically, but many of his Sunni biographers described him either as a prominent and erudite Muᶜtazili (*raʾs, mutabaḥḥir fī al-iᶜtizāl*)[114] or as pro-Muᶜtazili (*yamīl ilā al-iᶜtizāl*),[115] though also noting his Imami convictions. Shiᶜi biographers often expressed dismay at this assessment, ascribing it to Sunni unfamiliarity with Imami theology.[116] But this leaves open the question why Mufīd and Ṭūsī are usually not as readily qualified as Muᶜtazilis in the same Sunni biographical dictionaries,[117] nor are they listed in Muᶜtazili biographical dictionaries whereas Murtaḍā is.[118] The answer to this question may be found in a detailed comparison of the views of these three scholars. Mufīd's views have been thoroughly documented and analysed in a separate study,[119] so the remaining task is to examine Murtaḍā's positions and compare them to Ṭūsī's positions on the same questions. The latter's theological contributions, however, are relatively unknown; in addition, his thought probably underwent change as a result of the influence of the prominent Muᶜtazili Abū al-Ḥusayn al-Baṣrī (d. 1044).[120] With this caveat in mind, the challenge consists of scrutinising Murtaḍā's theology in light of the inner Imami context and the broader Imami–Muᶜtazili framework.

Magna opera

For the purposes of this monograph, five books by Murtaḍā represent his most significant works: *Ghurar al-fawāʾid wa-durar al-qalāʾid*, better known as *al-Amālī*; *al-Dhakhīra fī ᶜilm al-kalām* and *al-Mulakhkhaṣ fī uṣūl al-dīn*, which are treated as a single book for reasons explained below; *al-Dharīᶜa ilā uṣūl al-sharīᶜa*; *al-Shāfī fī al-imāma*; and *Tanzīh al-anbiyāʾ wa-l-aʾimma*. The reason for this selection is that these works present the most reliable and comprehensive statements of Murtaḍā's views on theology. His other works, consulted throughout this study, are also helpful, but to a lesser extent. No survey of them is presented here because some of them are of little or no relevance to theology. Of those that do deal with theology, many are correspondences that have been lost completely or partially, represent earlier views that Murtaḍā later abandoned according to his own declarations, or constitute summaries of positions presented in full detail in these five works, to which he himself refers his readers for more extensive discussion.

al-Amālī

Although the *Amālī* is not a work on theology or law per se but rather belongs to the *amālī* genre in Arabic literature, it is replete with theological discussions. The eighty meetings, in addition to the sizable 'Takmila' (appendix), offer a wealth of information on theology, language, rhetoric, poetry, biographies and miscellaneous *adab* questions. The original text was completed on Tuesday, 29 August 1022,[121] and the 'Takmila' was added later. An old manuscript of the text was recently discovered, which is probably based on a copy that Murtaḍā himself had written.[122]

Each meeting usually discusses the interpretation of a Qurʾānic verse or a Prophetic tradition that poses a challenge to Murtaḍā's theology, contains a rare linguistic occurrence to be explained or presents an interesting stylistic case. In each instance, Murtaḍā lists different views on the question, especially from theologians and linguists. Among theologians, his main sources are the Muʿtazilis, with special emphasis on the school's classical figures, such as Ibrāhīm al-Naẓẓām (d. between 825 and 835), Abū al-Hudhayl (d. 841?) and Jāḥiẓ; of the later period the most frequently mentioned authority is Abū al-Qāsim al-Balkhī. As for linguists, his teacher Marzubānī is quoted most frequently, alongside renowned authorities such as Abū ʿUbayd (d. 838). Murtaḍā appears to disagree with them most of the time, providing a vivid picture of scholarly debate as pursued during this period and of his independent scholarly personality in the maturity of his career.

Throughout these discussions, Murtaḍā often digresses to cite lines of poetry that support his interpretation. In the course of quoting poetry, he provides information on the poet's biography, his religious affiliation and how it manifests itself in his output. Poems and proverbs on the same theme are also presented. It is not uncommon for linguistic discussion to lead to an examination of different definitions of theological concepts, from which Murtaḍā then starts a new presentation of his views in a similar vein.

The importance of the book may also be estimated statistically: it contains interpretation of more than 140 Qurʾānic verses, thirty *ḥadīth*s, thirty-one proverbs and 1,349 lines of poetry in addition to biographical information on sixty-five individuals.[123]

al-Dhakhīra *and* al-Mulakhkhaṣ

The *Dhakhīra* is Murtaḍā's most comprehensive – and fortunately extant – work on theology, and its structure reflects its peculiar compilation process. Initially, Murtaḍā had embarked on a detailed work on theology entitled *al-Mulakhkhaṣ fī uṣūl al-dīn* but then decided to abandon the project sometime before 1026, as attested by the bibliography of Murtaḍā's works in his licence (*ijāza*) for Muḥammad al-Buṣrawī (d. 1051).[124] By contrast, the *Dhakhīra* was initially intended to be a succinct text on theology.[125] But at some point in the process of writing, Murtaḍā changed his plan and undertook an exhaustive treatment of theological questions. The last passage in the *Dhakhīra* justifies the change. He had started writing the *Dhakhīra* while writing the *Mulakhkhaṣ*; having abandoned the latter, he decided to make up for it in the rest of the *Dhakhīra*, which explains the variance in style between the early chapters and the later ones.[126] For present purposes, and following Murtaḍā's usage, I deal with both as one work, although I cite them separately throughout the monograph since each of the two books is published independently.

The work provides a systematic treatment of the main theological debates. Its structure echoes that of Muᶜtazili works common at the time and is significantly different from that of earlier works,[127] which suggests Murtaḍā was more dependent on his contemporaries than on previous works. The *Mulakhkhaṣ* discusses ontological questions related to subtle theology, God's existence, His essence (*dhāt*) and attributes (*ṣifāt*), divine justice (*ᶜadl*) and human acts (*fiᶜl*). The *Dhakhīra* continues this last theme, then proceeds to cover moral obligation (*taklīf*), the obligated party (*mukallaf*) and the human being (*insān*),[128] investigation (*naẓar*), resurrection (*iᶜāda*), divine assistance (*luṭf*),[129] humans' best interest (*al-aṣlaḥ*), pain (*alam*), compensation (*ᶜiwaḍ*), due term (*ajal*), provision (*rizq*), commodity prices (*asᶜār*), reward and punishment (*al-thawāb wa-l-ᶜiqāb*), prophethood (*nubuwwa*), the inimitability (*iᶜjāz*) of the Qurʾān, the Imama, the threat of divine punishment (*waᶜīd*), commanding the right and forbidding the wrong, and God's names. On each of these topics, especially towards the end, that is, in the *Dhakhīra*, Murtaḍā touches on known views and offers his critique of them before stating his own position. Most of the positions he enumerates are Muᶜtazili views, making the *Dhakhīra* a source on the Baghdadi–Basran Muᶜtazili debate as well as on the Imami positions.

The presentation of each chapter follows the standard organisation and method of detailed theological works of the time: it begins with a definition of the chapter's topic, usually with an emphasis on language, and then provides the technical definitions given by various theologians. Concepts pertaining to the point in question are also defined to familiarise the reader with its various aspects prior to the main discussion. Possible objections and questions are answered in an attempt to exhaust the question before moving on to another. Throughout the work, the main mode is dialectic, following the traditional formula of theologians: 'if it is said, we say' (*fa-in qīla qulnā*).

The main problem with the book is its corrupt text, which is probably due to the lack of interest in Murtaḍā's theology following the turn towards philosophy in Imami theology; with few readers, the few extant manuscripts, mostly incomplete, were left in a bad condition. The problem is particularly acute in the case of the *Mulakhkhaṣ*, of which only one, incomplete manuscript survives. The significance of the book for the broader Muᶜtazili movement can nevertheless be gleaned from the fact that there are fragments of it written in Hebrew script that probably date to the eleventh or twelfth century.[130]

al-Dharīᶜa

In the introduction to the *Dharīᶜa*, Murtaḍā states that the book is unprecedented because his views on jurisprudence are not fully shared by any author. The *Dharīᶜa* must be a compilation of Murtaḍā's lectures and his earlier shorter treatises on jurisprudential questions; the material was combined into a book after Ṭūsī compiled his *ᶜUdda*, which explains why some scholars consider Ṭūsī's work the first Imami work on jurisprudence.[131] The *Dharīᶜa* is a systematic work that argues against the non-Imami understanding of the sources of the law and provides a jurisprudential framework consistent with Imami doctrines. As such, the book is a lengthy polemic that often enumerates the views of non-Imami jurists in great detail, probably mainly responding to ᶜAbd al-Jabbār's *ᶜUmad*.[132] It was completed on Friday, 6 July 1039.[133]

The book deals with issues such as the legal significance of the Qurᵓānic text, the requirement of certainty in law, the types of reports, the probativeness of consensus (*ijmāᶜ*), and the validity of analogical reasoning (*qiyās*). For each of these, Murtaḍā names the proponents and opponents of the point of contention and then proceeds to argue elaborately for his own perspective. Interestingly, it may be noted that a Ḥanafi Muᶜtazili, Ibn Abī al-Ḥadīd (d. 1258), authored a detailed commentary on the *Dharīᶜa* entitled *Iᶜtibār al-Dharīᶜa*.[134] A few commentaries were likewise produced by Imami scholars, including one by al-ᶜAllāma al-Ḥillī (d. 1325).[135]

al-Shāfī fī al-imāma

Initially written as a refutation of ᶜAbd al-Jabbār's discussion of the Imama in his *Mughnī*, the text of the *Shāfī* is many times longer than that of ᶜAbd al-Jabbār's work, including as it does lengthy excerpts from the latter. As in the *Dhakhīra*, the later parts of the work are more detailed, since Murtaḍā had originally intended to write an abridged book but subsequently changed his mind.[136]

Since the *Shāfī* is a response, its structure is determined by that of the *Mughnī*. Murtaḍā thus closely follows the arguments of ᶜAbd al-Jabbār. Three major arguments – rational, scriptural and historical – pervade the content. The foci of the rational argument are the necessity of the Imama in any community at any time and the qualifications of the Imam, such as infallibility (*ᶜiṣma*), superior knowledge, virtue and so on. The scriptural argument deals primarily with Qurᵓānic verses and Prophetic traditions that Murtaḍā takes to refer to ᶜAlī's right to succeed Muḥammad directly. The historical argument seeks to demonstrate the illegitimacy of the first three caliphs by pointing out inconsistencies in the transition of power and flaws in their administration, especially in attending to the religious obligations of the caliphate. As for the caliphate of ᶜAlī, Murtaḍā is keen to reject the specific reasons proposed by ᶜAbd al-Jabbār for accepting ᶜAlī's status.

According to Murtaḍā, ᶜAbd al-Jabbār's methodology suffers from an unfair, inaccurate, uninformed[137] or even impolite presentation of Imami views,[138] although Murtaḍā's own statements are not immune against the same attacks.[139] Another problem, according to Murtaḍā, is ᶜAbd al-Jabbār's use of sources, as he seems either to misunderstand the authors' intentions or, worse, to deliberately manipulate (*taḥrīf*) the quoted text.[140] Also, his terminology is imprecise.[141] Ironically, Ibn Abī al-Ḥadīd, studying the arguments of both sides, pointed out similar flaws in Murtaḍā's handling of ᶜAbd al-Jabbār's positions.[142]

The *Shāfī* is probably Murtaḍā's most substantial and far-reaching contribution to Imami theology, given the centrality of the Imama doctrine in the Imami *Weltanschauung*. It survives also in Ṭūsī's recension, *Talkhīṣ al-Shāfī*. Ṭūsī's excisions are themselves very indicative of the aspects of Murtaḍā's theology that did not stand the test of time in the tradition. Abū al-Ḥusayn al-Baṣrī is credited with a refutation of the *Shāfī*,[143] which was in turn countered by Murtaḍā's student Sallār al-Daylamī[144] and apparently partially by Karājikī.[145] In his *Sharḥ Nahj al-balāgha*, Ibn Abī al-Ḥadīd preserved substantial parts of both ᶜAbd al-Jabbār's and Murtaḍā's works, together with elaborate comments assessing their opposing arguments. Other abridgements (*mukhtaṣar*) and supercommentaries (*ḥāshiya*) of the book have also been made, the latest in the eighteenth century.[146]

Tanzīh al-anbiyāᵓ

Two aspects of infallibility are subjects of debate in Islamic theology: its definition and the individuals supposed to be endowed with it. Defence of the infallibility of prophets is a well-known genre in Islamic theology, regardless of sectarian affiliation. Murtaḍā's *Tanzīh* is among the early works of this genre, and it seems to have influenced later scholarship on the question.[147] In the book, Murtaḍā presents a brief statement of various positions on the issue followed by his own view, together with a stringent refutation of possible objections – which in this case happen to be many; Murtaḍā's position seems to have been singled out as extreme in the later tradition.[148]

Murtaḍā's discussion on the infallibility of prophets concentrates almost exclusively on explaining away the numerous Qurᵓānic verses that seem to contradict his position. The *Tanzīh* is thus a trove of Muᶜtazili views on Qurᵓānic exegesis concerned with infallibility, especially the views of the two Jubbāᵓīs, Abū ᶜAlī (d. 915–16) and his son Abū Hāshim (d. 933), and the commentary by Abū Muslim Muḥammad b. Baḥr al-Iṣfahānī (d. 934).[149] Murtaḍā's discussion of the Imami position of extending infallibility to the Imams is mostly historical; he discusses certain incidents that could be construed as impinging on the infallibility of some Imams. A particularly detailed discussion is dedicated to Naẓẓām's critique of Imam ᶜAlī's legal views, although it is not clear whether Murtaḍā was relying directly on Naẓẓām's text or working on the basis of an intermediate one.

Given the Imami preoccupation with the question of infallibility in general and the Imams' infallibility in particular, Murtaḍā's work is considered an indispensable reference for Imami doctrine.[150]

Sources and classification

In terms of form, Murtaḍā's works fall into several categories: books, some of which he did not complete; responses (*jawābāt, ajwiba*) to questions (*masāʾil*) posed by followers or students; short treatises; and meetings as well as commentaries on poems and Qurʾānic verses.

For compiling a bibliography of Murtaḍā's works, the responses are the most problematic. Owing to the scattered nature of the extant collections of responses, some of the responses have often been left out by uninterested copyists, compromising the collections' integrity. Moreover, many of the responses have been taken out of context and given titles based on the copyists' personal discretion. In addition, even Murtaḍā's earliest bibliographies mention that he answered more than 100 unconnected questions (*masāʾil mufradāt*) on miscellaneous topics.[151] This situation has resulted in the same text often being published and discussed under different titles, frequently unrelated to each other. The many sporadic extant responses may thus be part of collections that have been lost, fully or partially; alternatively, they may belong among the many loose questions he answered. Also, some of the lost discussions may have been neglected because Murtaḍā dealt with the same question elsewhere, as he himself admits doing in the late *Dharīᶜa*;[152] this replication is reflected in the disarray of the surviving manuscripts.[153]

The earliest and most reliable list of Murtaḍā's works appears in his licence to Buṣrawī, which is dated September 1026 and explicitly permits Buṣrawī to add Murtaḍā's later works.[154] In addition to Buṣrawī's, the earliest and most reliable of Murtaḍā's bibliographies are those of Najāshī and Ṭūsī. Any work that appears in these three sources is indicated by (**B**), (**N**) and (**Ṭ**), respectively. If a work makes its first appearance in later sources, this is mentioned in the notes. Of particular importance are the published collections of Murtaḍā's short works, entitled *Rasāʾil al-Sharīf al-Murtaḍā* (henceforth *Rasāʾil*),[155] *Masāʾil al-Murtaḍā* (henceforth *Masāʾil*)[156] and *Mawsūᶜat turāth al-Sayyid al-Murtaḍā* (henceforth *Mawsūᶜa*).[157] The bibliography below lists the editions used in this monograph and refers to other available editions in the endnotes. For ease of reference, the titles used are the ones provided by the editors. In cases in which a different title appears in the bibliographies of Murtaḍā's works or in other editions of the same work, I point out the discrepancy. The titles of texts that are not published and that cannot be confirmed extant are neither italicised nor placed between quotation marks, as it is not possible to classify them as books or as shorter texts. The list is ordered alphabetically.

Murtaḍā's bibliography

1. 'ᶜAdam wujūb ghasl al-rijlayn fī al-ṭahāra', in *Rasāʾil*, 3:159–73.
2. 'Aḥkām ahl al-ākhira', in *Rasāʾil*, 2:131–43.[158]
3. *ᶜAjāʾib al-aghlāṭ*. Attributed to Murtaḍā in Āghā Buzurg, *Dharīᶜa*, 2:216,

15:218. The book has been published and is in fact *al-Ta*c*ajjub* by Murtaḍā's student Abū al-Fatḥ al-Karājikī.[159]

4. 'Ajwiba min masā'il mutafarriqa fī al-ḥadīth wa-ghayrihi', in *Rasā'il*, 3:121–51.
5. 'Ajwibat al-masā'il al-Qur'āniyya', in *Rasā'il*, 3:83–120.[160]
6. 'Alfāẓ al-ṭalāq', in *Rasā'il*, 4:321–2.[161] The text was written in February 1036.
7. *Amālī al-Murtaḍā: Ghurar al-fawā'id wa-durar al-qalā'id*. Edited by Muḥammad Abū al-Faḍl Ibrāhīm. Cairo: Dār Iḥyā' al-Kutub al-cArabiyya, 1954 (reprint, Qum: Dhawī al-Qurbā, 2008).[162] **(B, N, Ṭ)**
8. 'Aqāwīl al-carab fī al-jāhiliyya', in *Rasā'il*, 3:221–31.
9. 'Aqsām al-manāfic', in *Masā'il*, 118–21.[163]
10. *al-Āyāt al-nāsikha wa-l-mansūkha*. Published as Murtaḍā, *al-Āyāt al-nāsikha wa-l-mansūkha*. Edited by cAlī Jihād al-Ḥassānī. Beirut: Dār al-Balāgh, 2000. Sometimes referenced as *Risālat al-Muḥkam wa-l-mutashābih*. This work is not authentic, as a study of its content and chain of transmission has shown.[164]
11. 'Dafc shubha li-l-barāhima fī bacth al-anbiyā'', in *Rasā'il*, 4:346–9.[165]
12. 'al-Dalīl calā anna al-jawāhir mudraka', in *Rasā'il*, 4:346.[166]
13. 'al-Dalīl calā anna al-jawhar laysa bi-muḥdath', in *Rasā'il*, 4:342–3.[167]
14. 'Dawr al-caql wa-l-samc fī al-nawāfil', in *Rasā'il*, 4:345–6.[168]
15. *al-Dhakhīra fī cilm al-kalām*. Edited by Aḥmad al-Ḥusaynī. Qum: Mu'assasat al-Nashr al-Islāmī, 1990. **(B, N, Ṭ)**
16. *al-Dharīca ilā uṣūl al-sharīca*. Qum: Mu'assasat al-Imām al-Ṣādiq, 2009.[169] The final passage indicates the book was finished on Friday, 6 July 1039. **(N, Ṭ)**
17. *Dīwān al-Sharīf al-Murtaḍā*. Edited by Rashīd al-Ṣaffār. Cairo: Dār Iḥyā' al-Kutub al-cArabiyya, 1958 (reprint, Beirut: Dār al-Balāgha, 1998).[170] **(B, Ṭ)**
18. 'al-Farq bayn najis al-cayn wa-najis al-ḥukm', in *Rasā'il*, 4:328–9.[171]
19. *al-Fuṣūl al-mukhtāra*. Edited by cAlī Mīr Sharīfī. Beirut: Dār al-Mufīd, 1993. The book was solicited from Murtaḍā; it consists of selections from Mufīd's *al-cUyūn wa-l-maḥāsin* that Murtaḍā completed during Mufīd's lifetime, as the wording of the introduction indicates.
20. *al-Ḥikāyāt*. Edited by Muḥammad Riḍā al-Ḥusaynī al-Jalālī. Beirut: Dār al-Mufīd, 1993. This book seems to be originally part of *al-Fuṣūl al-mukhtāra*, but it was printed separately because it has been referenced and collated in different ways in the tradition.[172]
21. 'al-Ḥudūd wa-l-ḥaqā'iq', in *Rasā'il*, 2:259–89. The text is inauthentic, as indicated by a detailed analysis of its contents.[173]
22. 'Ibṭāl muddacī al-ru'ya' [sic], in *Masā'il*, 115–17.[174]
23. 'Ibṭāl qawl inna al-shay' shay' li-nafsihi', in *Rasā'il*, 4:343.[175]
24. 'Iḍāfat al-awlād ilā al-jadd iḍāfa ḥaqīqiyya', in *Rasā'il*, 4:327–8.[176]
25. Inkāḥ Amīr al-Mu'minīn ibnatahu min cUmar.[177]
26. 'Inqādh al-bashar min al-jabr wa-l-qadar', in *Rasā'il*, 2:175–247.[178] Inauthentic, as evidenced by a study of the text.[179]
27. *al-Intiṣār fī mā infaradat bihi al-Imāmiyya*. Qum: Mu'assasat al-Nashr al-Islāmī, 1990. = Kitāb al-Intiṣār li-mā ajmacat calayhi al-Imāmiyya = Masā'il

al-infirādāt fī al-fiqh = Kitāb Masāʾil infirādāt al-Imāmiyya wa-mā ẓunna infirāduhā bihi. **(B, N, Ṭ)**

28. *Irshād al-ᶜawāmm*. In his 'al-Sharīf al-Murtaḍā' Brockelmann mentions this book as a work of Murtaḍā's, referring the reader to E. G. Browne, *A Year amongst the Persians*, 554. But Browne ascribes the book to its author Muḥammad Karīm Khān (d. 1871).[180]
29. 'Istiḥqāq madḥ al-bārī ᶜalā al-awṣāf', in *Rasāʾil*, 4:331–5.[181] The text was written in December 1035.
30. 'Istimrār al-ṣawm maᶜ qaṣd al-munāfī lahu', in *Rasāʾil*, 4:322–7.[182]
31. 'Jawāb ahl al-Ḥijāz'. The text first appears in Majlisī, *Biḥār*, 17:122–9, whose author rules that it is most likely by Mufīd. The original title of the text is 'Jawāb ahl al-Ḥāʾir', as attested in its last paragraph. It is attributed to Murtaḍā or Mufīd by Āghā Buzurg, *Dharīᶜa*, 5:175–6, who eventually argues that it is by neither because of its excessively harsh language concerning Ṣadūq and because of the fact that no such work is ascribed to either of them in earlier sources. The author denies that the prophet might fall into inadvertence even in minor matters; this position contradicts Murtaḍā's view but agrees with that of Mufīd. Also, the text is replete with second-person discourse, introduced by 'O brother' (*ayyuhā al-akh*), which Murtaḍā does not usually use even in correspondence. In any case, the text has been edited and published as a work by Mufīd.[183]
32. 'Jawāb al-masāʾil al-Tabbāniyyāt', in *Rasāʾil*, 1:3–96.[184] These are answers by Murtaḍā to the questions of his student Abū ᶜAbdullāh Muḥammad b. ᶜAbd al-Malik al-Tabbān (d. 1028). **(B, N)**
33. 'Jawābāt al-masāʾil al-Dimashqiyya' = 'Jawābāt al-masāʾil al-Nāṣiriyya', in *Rasāʾil*, 3:135–9. Total number of responses unknown; at least one is extant.[185] **(B)**
34. 'Jawābāt al-masāʾil al-Mawṣiliyyāt al-thālitha', in *Rasāʾil*, 1:199–267. A total of 110 responses, all extant. These are answers to questions that were received in March 1029, as the opening passage indicates.[186] **(Ṭ)**
35. 'Jawābāt al-masāʾil al-Mawṣiliyyāt al-thāniya', in *Rasāʾil*, 1:167–98. A total of nine responses, as Murtaḍā himself states, all extant.[187] **(B, Ṭ)**
36. 'Jawābāt al-masāʾil al-Mayyāfāraqiyyāt', in *Rasāʾil*, 1:269–306.[188] According to Buṣrawī's list, this collection contains 100 questions; Ibn Shahrāshūb (d. 1192) states that it contains sixty-five.[189] The published edition includes sixty-six questions, and later scholars confirm the published number.[190] The published text concludes with a closing remark and does not seem to have been interrupted. **(B)**
37. 'Jawābāt al-masāʾil al-Miṣriyyāt', in *Rasāʾil*, 4:15–35.[191] Responses to twenty-two questions (6th–27th) remain extant out of an unknown total. The text does not match any of the 'al-Masāʾil al-Miṣriyyāt' mentioned by Buṣrawī, Najāshī and Ṭūsī, either in terms of the number of questions or in terms of content. The opening passage, which seems to be a later addition to the text, speaks about

questions coming from al-Nīl. This does not necessarily indicate Egyptian provenance, as the term can also denote other places; in addition, the wording does not seem to refer to a river but to a place,[192] and thus it probably refers to the town by the name of al-Nīl that is located on the outskirts of Kūfa.[193] The first question concerns a position ascribed to the early Muᶜtazili Thumāma b. Ashras (d. 828).[194] The language and content are similar to those of Murtaḍā's works; as such, this text may in fact be one of Murtaḍā's lost miscellaneous responses.

38. 'Jawābāt al-masāᵓil al-Rassiyya al-thāniya', in *Rasāᵓil*, 2:381–91.
39. 'Jawābāt al-masāᵓil al-Rassiyya al-ūlā', in *Rasāᵓil*, 2:313–79. These are responses to questions posed by one al-Muḥassin b. Muḥammad b. al-Nāṣir al-Ḥusaynī al-Rassī.[195] The text was completed on 21 October 1037.
40. 'Jawābāt al-masāᵓil al-Rāziyya', in *Rasāᵓil*, 1:99–132. The published text includes fifteen responses, which matches the figure mentioned by Baḥr al-ᶜUlūm (d. 1797) and Āghā Buzurg (d. 1970), but according to Ibn Shahrāshūb the collection contains only fourteen responses.[196]
41. 'Jawābāt al-masāᵓil al-Sallāriyya'. The text includes eight responses,[197] and it was written by Murtaḍā as answers to questions posed by his student Sallār al-Daylamī. Six are extant (numbers 2nd–7th), and scattered excerpts of them have been published. They treat the following topics: (2) the relationship between power and its substrate, published in *Mawsūᶜa*, 1:211–13; (3) the relationship between life and its substrate, in *Mawsūᶜa*, 1:213; (4) the relationship between the agent's intention and his creation of accidents in a specific substrate (*maḥall*), in *Mawsūᶜa*, 2:522–3; (5) astrological predictions, in *Mawsūᶜa*, 1:469–73;[198] (6) 'Masᵓala fī al-manāmāt', in *Rasāᵓil*, 2:7–14;[199] and (7) how knowledge is generated by investigation, in *Mawsūᶜa*, 1:496–8.[200] The whole text is being edited for publication.[201]
42. 'Jawābāt al-masāᵓil al-Ṭabariyya'. See *Masāᵓil al-Nāṣiriyyāt* below.
43. 'Jawābāt al-masāᵓil al-Ṭarābulusiyyāt al-thālitha', in *Rasāᵓil*, 1:357–443. The sources provide different accounts of the number of questions, but most likely there are twenty-three.[202] The collection published under this title is complete, as evidenced by the text and by the reference to it in the collection published as 'Jawābāt al-masāᵓil al-Ṭarābulusiyyāt al-thāniya'. But this is not sufficient evidence to establish that it has been correctly identified. See also 'Jawābāt al-masāᵓil al-Ṭarābulusiyyāt al-thāniya'. **(B)**
44. 'Jawābāt al-masāᵓil al-Ṭarābulusiyyāt al-thāniya', in *Rasāᵓil*, 1:307–56.[203] These are twelve responses, a number corroborated by one source only; other sources specify ten responses.[204] They refer (p. 331) to the collection published as 'Jawābāt al-masāᵓil al-Ṭarābulusiyyāt al-thālitha', which proves that they were written later and, as such, are misidentified in the publication. The collection nevertheless seems complete, so it cannot be the 'Jawābāt al-masāᵓil al-Ṭarābulusiyyāt al-rābiᶜa', which is supposed to comprise twenty-five responses. A possible solution to the problems posed by this collection and the

preceding one is to reverse their order. This way, the titles would reflect the chronological order of the works' writing as indicated by the references in the text, and the number of responses in each collection would still correspond to the respective number mentioned in the sources. The main challenge confronting this solution is that it assumes that the mistake of one collection for the other dates back to our earliest source and survived undetected in later works. **(B, Ṭ)**

45. 'Jawābāt al-masāʾil al-Wāsiṭiyyāt', in *Rasāʾil*, 4:37–44.[205] Originally containing 100 responses, of which eight (numbers 5th–12th) are extant. **(B)**
46. Jawāz al-wilāya min jihat al-ẓālimīn. **(B)**
47. 'al-Jism lam yakun kāʾinan bi-l-fāʿil', in *Rasāʾil*, 4:337–8.[206] The text was written in January 1036.
48. 'Jumal al-ʿilm wa-l-ʿamal', in *Rasāʾil*, 3:5–81.[207] The success of this short work is evidenced by the fact that the Karaite theologian Sahl b. al-Faḍl (fl. second half of the eleventh century) was asked to model a book of his after Murtaḍā's *Kitāb al-Jumal*.[208] **(B, N, Ṭ)**
49. Kitāb al-Barq.[209] **(B, Ṭ)**
50. Kitāb al-Fiqh al-malakī.[210]
51. Kitāb al-Khilāf fī uṣūl al-fiqh[211] = Masāʾil al-khilāf fī uṣūl al-fiqh. Incomplete. **(B, N, Ṭ)**
52. Kitāb al-Miṣbāḥ fī al-fiqh. Incomplete.[212] **(B, N, Ṭ)**
53. Kitāb al-Naqḍ ʿalā Ibn Jinnī fī al-ḥikāya wa-l-maḥkī. **(Ṭ)**
54. Kitāb al-Waʿīd. **(N)**
55. Kitāb fī al-taʾkīd = Masʾala fī al-taʾkīd. Judging by the title and content, this is probably the text published as 'Masʾala fī wajh al-takrār fī al-āyatayn' in *Rasāʾil*, 2:73–6.[213] **(B, N)**
56. Kitāb fī dalīl al-khiṭāb = Masʾala fī dalīl al-khiṭāb. **(B, N)**
57. Kitāb Sharḥ Masāʾil al-khilāf fī al-fiqh = al-Masāʾil al-mustakhrajāt. Incomplete. Ṭūsī mentions a Kitāb Masāʾil al-khilāf fī al-fiqh, which is probably the same text, since the book and its autocommentary may count as one item given Ṭūsī's concern with large works. **(B, N, Ṭ)**
58. Kitāb Taqrīb al-uṣūl. Murtaḍā wrote this book for a certain al-Aʿazz. The title of the work and Buṣrawī's phrasing (*ʿamilahu li-l-Aʿazz*) suggest that it is preliminary and short. There is a catechism among Murtaḍā's published works, which might itself be this text: 'Muqaddima fī al-uṣūl al-iʿtiqādiyya', in *Nafāʾis al-makhṭūṭāt*, 2:79–82. Edited by Muḥammad Ḥasan Āl Yāsīn. Baghdad: Maṭbaʿat al-Maʿārif, 1952. **(B, N)**
59. Kitāb Tatabbuʿ al-abyāt allatī takallama ʿalayhā Ibn Jinnī fī [abyāt] al-maʿānī li-l-Mutanabbī.[214] **(Ṭ)**
60. 'Majmūʿa fī funūn min ʿilm al-kalām', in *Nafāʾis al-makhṭūṭāt*, 5:61–90. Edited by Muḥammad Ḥasan Āl Yāsīn. Baghdad: Maṭbaʿat al-Maʿārif, 1952.
61. 'Manʿ kawn al-ṣifa bi-l-fāʿil', in *Rasāʾil*, 4:341–2.[215]

62. 'al-Man^c min al-^camal bi-akhbār al-āḥād', in *Rasā^oil*, 4:335–7.[216] The text was written in January 1036.
63. 'Ma^cnā al-naf^c fī al-ḍarar', in *Rasā^oil*, 4:349–53.[217]
64. 'Ma^cnā qawl al-Nabī man ajbā fa-qad arbā', in *Rasā^oil*, 4:353–4.[218]
65. al-Masā^oil al-Bādarayyāt.[219] These are supposedly twenty-four responses; their titles are given in Buṣrawī's list. Three of them resemble extant discussions: (5) 'Mā yajib fīhi al-khums', a typical legal discussion that Murtaḍā covers in *Intiṣār*, 225–7; (12) 'Wa-lā yazālūna mukhtalifīna illā man raḥima rabbuka', found in *Amālī*, 1:70–5; and (20) 'Innī mukhallif^un fīkum mā in tamassaktum bihimā lan taḍillū kitāb Allāh wa-^citratī', a classic of Shi^ci polemic, elaborately covered in *Shāfī*, 3:122–33. **(B, N)**
66. al-Masā^oil al-Barmakiyya = al-Ṭūsiyya. Supposedly five responses; incomplete. In 'Jawābāt al-masā^oil al-Rassiyya al-ūlā' (*Rasā^oil*, 2:329), Murtaḍā refers to an argument that he advanced only in al-Barmakiyyāt. The extant works of his do not include a text in which such an argument is made. **(B, Ṭ)**
67. al-Masā^oil al-Daylamiyya.[220] **(Ṭ)**
68. al-Masā^oil al-Ḥalabiyya al-thālitha. Supposedly thirty-three responses. Ṭūsī mentions the first and last questions from Aleppo, which could be a reference to either 'al-Masā^oil al-Ḥalabiyya al-thālitha' or 'al-thāniya'; the latter has been chosen here (hence the next reference) to minimise conjecture, but he could well have meant the 'thālitha' since it is much larger than the 'thāniya'. **(B)**
69. al-Masā^oil al-Ḥalabiyya al-thāniya. Supposedly three responses. **(B, Ṭ)**
70. al-Masā^oil al-Ḥalabiyya al-ūlā. Supposedly three responses.[221] **(B, Ṭ)**
71. al-Masā^oil al-Jurjāniyya.[222] Given that Jurjān was considered part of Ṭabaristān,[223] and in light of the discussion of *Masā^oil al-Nāṣiriyyāt* (see below), it is likely that 'al-Masā^oil al-Jurjāniyya' is the text published as 'Jawābāt al-masā^oil al-Ṭabariyya', in *Rasā^oil*, 1:133–66, for these are questions that came from Ṭabaristān.[224] **(Ṭ)**
72. al-Masā^oil al-Mawṣiliyyāt = 'al-Masā^oil al-Mawṣiliyyāt al-ūlā' and 'Jawāb ahl al-Mawṣil'.[225] Supposedly three responses; all titles are given in the three early bibliographies. These were written during the 990s[226] and were extremely elaborate.[227] Murtaḍā's later discussions of analogical reasoning (*qiyās*)[228] and the threat of divine punishment (*wa^cīd*)[229] in major works of his must have relied on these early texts, which in turn made them obsolete, whether he changed his mind or not. The third question concerns pressure (*i^ctimād*), which – like most subjects of subtle theology – was of little interest to the subsequent tradition. **(B, N, Ṭ)**
73. al-Masā^oil al-Miṣriyya al-thālitha. See 'al-Masā^oil al-Ramliyya'.
74. al-Masā^oil al-Miṣriyya al-thāniya. Supposedly nine responses. Ṭūsī mentions the first and last questions from Egypt, which could be a reference to either 'al-Masā^oil al-Miṣriyya al-thālitha' or 'al-thāniya'; I have taken it to mean the latter to minimise conjecture, especially given that the 'thālitha' were probably known as 'al-Ramliyya'. See 'al-Masā^oil al-Ramliyya'. **(B, Ṭ)**

75. al-Masāʾil al-Miṣriyyāt al-uwal. Supposedly five responses; their titles are given in Buṣrawī's list.[230] **(B, N, Ṭ)**
76. 'al-Masāʾil al-Muḥammadiyyāt'. Four questions (numbers 1st, 2nd, 4th and 5th) are extant of the original five: (1) 'Wa-la-qad bawwaʾnā li-Ibrāhīm', in *Rasāʾil*, 3:117–20; (2) 'Mā maᶜnā an yuqāl ᶜinda istilām al-ḥajar amānatī addaytuhā ... ilā ākhir al-kalām' = 'Masʾala fī istilām al-ḥajar', in *Rasāʾil*, 3:273–7; (4) 'Anbiʾūnī bi-asmāʾ hāʾulāʾi', in *Rasāʾil*, 3:111–15; and (5) 'Fa-talaqqā Ādam min rabbihi kalimāt', in *Rasāʾil*, 3:115–17. See also 'The third *masʾala* of "al-Masāʾil al-Muḥammadiyyāt"'. **(B, N)**
77. *Masāʾil al-Nāṣiriyyāt* [sic]. Edited by Markaz al-Buḥūth wa-l-Dirāsāt al-ᶜIlmiyya. Tehran: Rābiṭat al-Thaqāfa wa-l-ᶜAlāqāt al-Islāmiyya, 1997. Although not mentioned in either version of Buṣrawī's list under this name, this collection is probably what he refers to as 'al-Masāʾil al-Ṭabariyya'. This thesis is confirmed by a few observations. First, Murtaḍā's introduction to *Masāʾil al-Nāṣiriyyāt* (p. 61) shows that the work was written as responses to questions. Second, a late Imami scholar states that these two titles refer to the same work.[231] Third, Buṣrawī's list specifies that 'al-Masāʾil al-Ṭabariyya' consists of 207 questions, an unusually large figure that corresponds to the number contained in *Masāʾil al-Nāṣiriyyāt*. Fourth, the interest in the details of al-Nāṣir's legal opinions indicates that the questions came from an area in which they were prominent, which would justify calling them 'al-Masāʾil al-Ṭabariyya'. Fifth, Ṭūsī qualifies Murtaḍā's 'al-Masāʾil al-Nāṣiriyya' as a work on law. On the other hand, Buṣrawī states that the item he calls 'al-Masāʾil al-Nāṣiriyya' is also 'al-Masāʾil al-Dimashqiyya'; but the latter collection treats not law but theology, judging by an extant question.[232] This discrepancy shows that Buṣrawī and Ṭūsī use 'al-Masāʾil al-Nāṣiriyya' to refer to different works. **(B, Ṭ)**
78. 'al-Masāʾil al-Ramliyya' = 'al-Masāʾil al-Miṣriyya al-thālitha'. Originally seven responses; three are extant. The second is published, unidentified, in *Rasāʾil*, 3:150–1. The last two are identified and published in *Rasāʾil*, 4:45–50.[233] The wording of Buṣrawī's list indicates that 'al-Masāʾil al-Ramliyya' is also known as 'al-Masāʾil al-Miṣriyya al-thālitha'. This is confirmed by Baḥr al-ᶜUlūm[234] and is further supported by the fact that Murtaḍā's prominent Egyptian student, Karājikī, was a resident of Ramla,[235] which makes it probable that the questions addressed to Murtaḍā by the Egyptian Imami community came from Ramla. However, a comparison of the contents of the two extant versions of 'al-Masāʾil al-Ramliyya' with the references to this work made by later scholars reveals that these scholars were actually referring to 'al-Masāʾil al-Mawṣiliyyāt al-thālitha' under the title 'al-Masāʾil al-Miṣriyya al-thālitha'.[236] **(B, N)**
79. al-Masāʾil al-Ṣaydāwiyya. It is not clear whether the title refers to the city in modern-day Lebanon, to the clan of the Banū Asad with the same name[237] or to a person belonging to either who solicited answers from Murtaḍā.[238] **(Ṭ)**

80. ‘al-Masāʾil al-Ṭarābulusiyya al-ūlā’. This collection contains supposedly seventeen responses; sixteen are extant. Scattered excerpts from most of them have been published: (1) excerpts from a discussion concerning the necessity of designation (*naṣṣ*) as a means to identify the legitimate Imam, in *Mawsūʿa*, 1:342, 2:35, 66, 244, 3:3, 45, 468–73; (2) a discussion concerning the illegitimacy of choosing the Imam by the community, in *Mawsūʿa*, 1:386–7; unless Murtaḍā is copying himself, the excerpts of the discussion concerning the means to identify the Imam’s view, identified as part of ‘al-Masāʾil al-Ṭarābulusiyya’ in *Mawsūʿa*, 1:104–7, 185–6 (where the text becomes corrupt), are in fact part of the published ‘Jawāb al-masāʾil al-Tabbāniyyāt’, in *Rasāʾil*, 1:11–26; (3) a discussion concerning the legitimacy of the Imama of the less excellent (*mafḍūl*), in *Mawsūʿa*, 1:368–9; (4) a discussion concerning the origination of atoms and bodies in *Mawsūʿa*, 2:4–5;[239] (5) ‘al-Masʾala al-khāmisa li-l-Zaydiyya’, in *Mawsūʿa*, 1:52–3; (6) ‘al-Masʾala al-sādisa fī al-ʿiṣma’, in *Mawsūʿa*, 2:524–5;[240] (7) a commentary on a tradition from Imām Riḍā concerning prophetic miracles in *Mawsūʿa*, 3:157–8; (8) ‘Masʾala fī al-dharr’, in *Mawsūʿa*, 1:33–5; (9) ‘al-Kalām fī al-akhbār al-wārida ʿan madḥ ajnās min al-ṭayr wa-l-bahāʾim wa-l-maʾkūlāt wa-l-araḍīn wa-dhamm ajnās minhā’, in *Mawsūʿa*, 1:138–41;[241] (10) a detailed discussion concerning the integrity of the text of the Qurʾān in *Mawsūʿa*, 3:142–55, 271–3; (11) ‘Khabar muʾākhāt al-Nabī bayn Salmān al-Fārisī wa-Abī Dharr wa-mā qīla fī dhālik’, in *Amālī*, 2:329–30, as part of the ‘Takmila’; (12) a discussion concerning the human being (*insān*), in *Mawsūʿa*, 1:394–400; (14) a discussion concerning the greatness of rewards for good deeds, in *Mawsūʿa*, 1:197, 3:235; and (15) a discussion concerning the status of whoever vilifies ʿAlī, in *Mawsūʿa*, 1:420. The whole extant text is being edited for publication.[242] **(B, Ṭ)**
81. Masʾala ʿalā Yaḥyā ayḍ^{an} fī ṭabīʿat al-mumkin = al-Radd ʿalayhi fī masʾala sammāhā ṭabīʿat al-muslimīn.[243] Murtaḍā provides a very short summary of the content of the text in *Mulakhkhaṣ*, 128–9. **(B, N)**
82. ‘Masʾala fī al-ʿamal maʿ al-sulṭān’, in *Rasāʾil*, 2:87–97.[244] The text was solicited by the vizier al-Maghribī in August 1024. **(B, N)**
83. ‘Masʾala fī al-ḥusn wa-l-qubḥ al-ʿaqlī’, in *Rasāʾil*, 3:175–80.
84. ‘Masʾala fī al-ijmāʿ’, in *Rasāʾil*, 3:199–205.
85. Masʾala fī al-imāma. **(B)**
86. ‘Masʾala fī al-ʿiṣma’. See ‘al-Masāʾil al-Ṭarābulusiyya al-ūlā’.
87. ‘Masʾala fī al-istithnāʾ’, in *Rasāʾil*, 2:77–81.[245]
88. ‘Masʾala fī al-iʿtirāḍ ʿalā man yuthbitu ḥudūth al-ajsām min al-jawāhir’. See ‘al-Masāʾil al-Ṭarābulusiyya al-ūlā’.
89. Masʾala fī al-kurr.[246] **(B)**
90. ‘Masʾala fī al-manʿ min tafḍīl al-malāʾika ʿalā al-anbiyāʾ’, in *Rasāʾil*, 2:167–74 = Masʾala ʿalā man taʿallaqa bi-qawlihi taʿālā wa-la-qad karramnā banī Ādam al-āya ʿalā anna al-malāʾika afḍal min al-anbiyāʾ ʿalayhum al-salām[247] = al-Kalām ʿalā man taʿallaqa bi-qawlihi taʿālā wa-la-qad karramnā banī Ādam wa-ḥamalnāhum fī al-barr wa-l-baḥr. **(B, N)**

91. 'Masᵓala fī al-manāmāt'. See 'Jawābāt al-masāᵓil al-Sallāriyya'.
92. 'Masᵓala fī al-masḥ ᶜalā al-khuffayn', in *Rasāᵓil*, 3:181–5.[248]
93. Masᵓala fī al-radd ᶜalā Yaḥyā b. ᶜAdī al-Naṣrānī fī mā yatanāhā wa-lā yatanāhā[249] = al-Radd ᶜalā Yaḥyā b. ᶜAdī. Najāshī does not give a full title, but comparing his list to Buṣrawī's establishes the identity of these two titles. The work argues against the Christian philosopher Yaḥyā b. ᶜAdī (d. 975); Murtaḍā provides a brief summary of the content of the text in *Mulakhkhaṣ*, 60–2. **(B, N)**
94. 'Masᵓala fī al-ruᵓya bi-l-abṣār', in *Masāᵓil*, 111–14.[250]
95. Masᵓala fī al-tawba. This is very similar to the discussion in *Amālī*, 1:628–30. **(B, N)**
96. Masᵓala fī dalīl al-ṣifāt.[251] **(B)**
97. 'Masᵓala fī ḥukm al-bāᵓ fī qawlihi taᶜālā wa-imsaḥū bi-ruᵓūsikum', in *Rasāᵓil*, 2:65–71.[252]
98. 'Masᵓala fī ibṭāl al-ᶜamal bi-akhbār al-āḥād', in *Rasāᵓil*, 3:307–13.[253]
99. 'Masᵓala fī ᶜillat imtināᶜ ᶜAlī ᶜan muḥārabat al-ghāṣibīn li-ḥaqqihi baᶜd al-Rasūl', in *Rasāᵓil*, 3:315–21.
100. 'Masᵓala fī ᶜillat khidhlān Ahl al-Bayt wa-ᶜadam nuṣratihim', in *Rasāᵓil*, 3:207–20.
101. 'Masᵓala fī ᶜillat mubāyaᶜat Amīr al-Muᵓminīn Abā Bakr', in *Rasāᵓil*, 3:241–7.
102. 'Masᵓala fī irth al-awlād', in *Rasāᵓil*, 3:255–66.
103. 'Masᵓala fī jawāb al-shubuhāt al-wārida li-Khabar al-Ghadīr', in *Rasāᵓil*, 3:249–54.
104. Masᵓala fī kawnihi ᶜālim^an^. **(B, N)**
105. 'Masᵓala fī khalq al-afᶜāl', in *Rasāᵓil*, 3:187–97.
106. 'Masᵓala fī man yatawallā ghasl al-imām', in *Rasāᵓil*, 3:153–7.
107. 'Masᵓala fī muᶜjizāt al-anbiyāᵓ', in *Rasāᵓil*, 4:277–99.[254]
108. 'Masᵓala fī nafy al-ḥukm bi-ᶜadam al-dalīl ᶜalayhi', in *Rasāᵓil*, 2:99–104.[255]
109. 'Masᵓala fī nafy al-ruᵓya', in *Rasāᵓil*, 3:279–84.
110. 'Masᵓala fī nikāḥ al-mutᶜa', in *Rasāᵓil*, 4:301–6.[256] The text was written in November 1035. **(B, N)**
111. 'Masᵓala fī qawl al-Nabī niyyat al-muᵓmin khayr^un^ min ᶜamalihi', in *Rasāᵓil*, 3:233–9.[257]
112. Masᵓala fī qawlihi taᶜālā inna Allāh lā yaghfiru an yushraka bihi. **(B)**
113. 'Masᵓala fī tafḍīl al-anbiyāᵓ ᶜalā al-malāᵓika', in *Rasāᵓil*, 2:153–65.[258]
114. 'Masᵓala fī taḥdīd nisbat al-awlād ilā al-ābāᵓ', in *Rasāᵓil*, 4:328.
115. 'Masᵓala fī tawārud al-adilla'. See 'Jawābāt al-masāᵓil al-Sallāriyya'.
116. 'Masᵓala fī wajh al-ᶜilm bi-tanāwul al-waᶜīd kāffat al-kuffār', in *Rasāᵓil*, 2:83–6.[259]
117. 'Masᵓala fī wajh al-takrār fī al-āyatayn'. See 'Kitāb fī al-taᵓkīd'.
118. Masᵓala radda bihā ayḍ^an^ ᶜalā Yaḥyā b. ᶜAdī fī iᶜtirāḍihi dalīl al-muwaḥḥidīn fī ḥudūth al-ajsām. **(B, N)**
119. 'Masᵓalat ᶜadam takhṭiᵓat al-ᶜāmil bi-khabar al-wāḥid', in *Rasāᵓil*, 3:267–72.
120. *al-Mūḍiḥ ᶜan jihat iᶜjāz al-Qurᵓān wa-huwa al-kitāb al-maᶜrūf bi-l-Ṣarfa.*

Edited by Muḥammad Riḍā Anṣārī Qummī. Mashhad: Mujammaᶜ al-Buḥūth al-Islāmiyya, 2003. = *Kitāb al-Ṣarfa fī iᶜjāz al-Qurᵓān.* **(B, N, Ṭ)**

121. *al-Mulakhkhaṣ fī uṣūl al-dīn.* Edited by Muḥammad Riḍā Anṣārī Qummī. Tehran: Kitābkhāna-yi Majlis-i Shūrā-yi Islāmī, 2000. **(B, N, Ṭ)**
122. 'Munāẓarat Abī al-ᶜAlāᵓ al-Maᶜarrī'. Attributed to Murtaḍā in Āghā Buzurg, *Dharīᶜa*, 22:286. Its earliest appearance is in Ṭabrisī, *Iḥtijāj*, 2:329–36. The account is clearly legendary, written in a pedantic style full of allusions that serve to show both men's wit and Murtaḍā's superiority due to his religious knowledge.
123. 'Munāẓarat al-khuṣūm wa-kayfiyyat al-istidlāl ᶜalayhim', in *Rasāᵓil*, 2:115–30.[260]
124. 'Muqaddima fī al-uṣūl al-iᶜtiqādiyya', in *Nafāᵓis al-makhṭūṭāt*, 2:79–82. See 'Kitāb Taqrīb al-uṣūl'.
125. *al-Muqniᶜ fī al-ghayba.* Edited by Muḥammad ᶜAlī al-Ḥakīm. Qum: Muᵓassasat Āl al-Bayt, 1995. **(B, N, Ṭ)**
126. Naḍḍ al-īḍāḥ. Attributed to Murtaḍā in Brockelmann, *GAL*, SI: 706. No such book is mentioned elsewhere as a work of Murtaḍā. The book is probably *Naḍd al-īḍāḥ*, a work on *rijāl* by Muḥammad b. Muḥammad Muḥsin b. Murtaḍā al-Kāshānī (d. early eighteenth century), also known as ᶜAlam al-Hudā.[261]
127. 'Naqd al-Naysābūrī fī taqsīmihi li-l-aᶜrāḍ', in *Rasāᵓil*, 4:307–15.[262]
128. 'al-Naẓar qabl al-dilāla', in *Rasāᵓil*, 4:338–9.[263]
129. 'al-Nisba bayn al-afᶜāl wa-mā huwa luṭfᵘⁿ minhā', in *Rasāᵓil*, 4:343–5.[264]
130. 'al-Risāla al-bāhira fī al-ᶜitra al-ṭāhira', in *Rasāᵓil*, 2:249–57. The text appears first in Ṭabrisī, *Iḥtijāj*, 2:336–40. The beginning seems to be missing some parts. The argumentative method in the first part of the extant text is similar to Murtaḍā's method in his other works. The author also refers to 'al-Masāᵓil al-Tabbāniyyāt' and *Kitāb al-Intiṣār* as his own works and relies on them in his argument. Nevertheless, the writing style and argumentative method in the second part are very different from Murtaḍā's, especially in the excessive use of rhyming prose (*sajᶜ*) and the passionate tone that is uncharacteristic of Murtaḍā – for example, when he singles out the people of Khurāsān as 'known for their deviation from this way' (that is, Shiᶜism), yet paying enormous respect at the shrine of the Eighth Imam, ᶜAlī al-Riḍā. Unless Murtaḍā decided to write the text in a literary style that responds to the needs of a varied audience and goes beyond the usual standard in his theological works, there is the possibility that the surviving text comprises some original arguments by him and additional modification by a later author. This possibility is corroborated by the fact that Ṭabrisī seems to have copied it from the same source as the aforementioned 'Munāẓarat Abī al-ᶜAlāᵓ al-Maᶜarrī', whose style matches its problematic content.
131. 'Risāla fī al-radd ᶜalā aṣḥāb al-ᶜadad', in *Rasāᵓil*, 2:15–63 = Jawāb al-Karājikī fī fasād al-ᶜadad. Though without specifying a particular text, Ṭūsī mentions that Murtaḍā answered many questions on this theme.[265] **(B, Ṭ)**

132. 'Risāla fī ghaybat al-ḥujja', in *Rasāʾil*, 2:291–8.[266]
133. *al-Shāfī fī al-imāma*. Edited by ᶜAbd al-Zahrāʾ al-Ḥusaynī al-Khaṭīb. Tehran: Muʾassasat al-Ṣādiq, 1986. **(B, N, Ṭ)**
134. 'al-Shahāb fī al-shayb wa-l-shabāb', in *Rasāʾil*, 4:141–275[267] = Kitāb al-Shayb wa-l-shabāb. The book was completed in December 1030. **(B, Ṭ)**
135. 'Sharḥ al-Qaṣīda al-Mudhahhaba', in *Rasāʾil*, 4:51–139 = Tafsīr Qaṣīdat al-Sayyid al-Bāʾiyya = Tafsīr Qaṣīdat al-Sayyid al-Ḥimyarī al-Mudhahhaba. **(B, Ṭ)**
136. *Sharḥ Jumal al-ᶜilm wa-l-ᶜamal*. Edited by Yaᶜqūb al-Jaᶜfarī al-Marāghī. Tehran: Dār al-Uswa, 1998. There are doubts concerning the authenticity of this autocommentary,[268] but these do not suffice to discredit it as a source of Murtaḍā's views.
137. 'Ṣīghat al-bayᶜ', in *Rasāʾil*, 4:319–21.[269] The text was written in November 1035.
138. 'al-Tāʾ fī kalimat al-dhāt laysat li-l-taʾnīth', in *Rasāʾil*, 4:339–40.[270]
139. 'Tafsīr al-āyāt al-mutashābiha min al-Qurʾān', in *Rasāʾil*, 3:285–305.[271]
140. 'Tafsīr al-Khuṭba al-Shiqshiqiyya', in *Rasāʾil*, 2:105–14 = al-Khuṭba al-Muqammaṣa.[272] **(B)**
141. Tafsīr al-Qaṣīda al-Mīmiyya min shiᶜrihi = Tafsīr qaṣīdatihi.[273] **(B, N)**
142. 'Tafsīr qawlihi taᶜālā laysa ᶜalā alladhīna āmanū', in *Amālī*, 2:312–16. **(B, N)**
143. 'Tafsīr qawlihi taᶜālā qul taᶜālaw atlu mā ḥarrama rabbukum', published as part of 'Ajwibat al-masāʾil al-Qurʾāniyya', in *Rasāʾil*, 3:97–101.[274] **(B)**
144. Tafsīr sūrat al-Ḥamd wa-miʾa wa-khams wa-ᶜishrīn āya min sūrat al-Baqara = Tafsīr sūrat al-Ḥamd wa-qiṭᶜa min sūrat al-Baqara. **(B, N)**
145. 'Takmilat Amālī al-Murtaḍā', in *Amālī*, 2:253–333.[275]
146. 'Tanajjus al-biʾr thumma ghawr māʾihā', in *Rasāʾil*, 4:329–31.[276]
147. *Tanbīh al-ghāfilīn ᶜan faḍl al-Ṭālibiyyīn*. Murtaḍā is mentioned, with hesitation, as one of the possible authors in Āghā Buzurg, *Dharīᶜa*, 4:446. The work is in fact by al-Ḥākim al-Jishumī (d. 1101) and has been published.[277]
148. *Tanzīh al-anbiyāʾ wa-l-aʾimma*. Edited by Fāris Ḥassūn Karīm. Qum: Maktab al-Iᶜlām al-Islāmī, 2002[278] = Kitāb al-Tanzīh. **(B, N, Ṭ)**
149. *Ṭayf al-khayāl*. Edited by Ḥasan Kāmil al-Ṣayrafī. Cairo: ᶜĪsā al-Bābī al-Ḥalabī, 1962 = Kitāb al-Ṭayf wa-l-khayāl. **(B, Ṭ)**
150. The third *masʾala* of 'al-Masāʾil al-Muḥammadiyyāt' = 'Mā ruwiya ᶜan al-Nabī ᶜalayhi wa-ālihi al-salām inna al-qulūb ajnādᵘⁿ mujannada … al-khabar'. **(B, N)**

Notes

1. The particular Shiᶜi community to which the Būyids belonged has still not been fully determined. It may be said, however, that those members of the family who were in Baghdad showed a stronger inclination towards Imami Shiᶜism than did their relatives elsewhere, and that the second- and third-generation Būyids gravitated towards Imamism whereas the first-generation Būyids were Zaydis. Their profession of the

Isma^cili creed, a claim found only in Isma^cili sources, must have been very circumscribed and shortlived, if it ever took place. See the discussion and summary of scholarship in Ali, *Imamite Rationalism*, 50–1.

2. For a succinct survey of the prominent Shi^ci families and their respective relations, see Newman, *Formative Period*, 19–26.
3. Al-Qāḍī, 'Abū Ḥayyān al-Tawḥīdī', passim, which describes the Shi^ci colour of the era as seen by a Sunni intellectual.
4. For a discussion of the appellation, see Kraemer, *Humanism*, 1–5.
5. Kraemer, *Humanism*, 75–80.
6. Kraemer, *Humanism*, 275.
7. Cahen, 'Ibn al-^cAmīd', no. 1.
8. See the two recently edited parts of treatises written by him in Madelung and Schmidtke, *al-Ṣāḥib*; see Pomerantz, 'Political biography', for his public career.
9. Madelung, 'Assumption', 181–3.
10. For the distinctly favourable treatment of Imamis, see Busse, *Chalif*, 605–6.
11. See, for example, the debate in the presence of Rukn al-Dawla (d. 976) between Ṣadūq and an individual who denied the existence of the Twelfth Imam; Ṣadūq, *Kamāl*, 87–8.
12. Cahen, 'Buwayhids'.
13. See, for example, Ibn al-Jawzī, *Muntaẓam*, 16:16; Ibn al-Athīr, *Kāmil*, 9:638; Dhahabī, *Siyar*, 18:335.
14. Busse, *Chalif*, 607–8; Kraemer, *Humanism*, 46–52.
15. See, for example, Madelung, 'Assumption', 169, 173, 174, 175.
16. Mottahedeh, *Loyalty*, 79–96, 158–67.
17. See the reactions to cases of a prominent Mu^ctazili judge at the time in Bray, 'Practical Mu^ctazilism', 119–21.
18. On the responsibilities and authorities of the office, see Māwardī, *Aḥkām*, 96–9; Abū Ya^cla, *Aḥkām*, 90–5; Havemann, 'Naḳīb al-ashrāf'.
19. For his lineage up to ^cAlī b. Abī Ṭālib Ibn al-Farrā^c, see Najāshī, *Rijāl*, 270; Ṭūsī, *Fihrist*, 98.
20. Ibn al-Athīr, *Kāmil*, 8:594.
21. Ibn al-Athīr, *Kāmil*, 8:630.
22. Ibn al-Athīr, *Kāmil*, 8:710; Ibn Abī al-Ḥadīd, *Sharḥ*, 1:32; Ibn ^cInaba, *^cUmda*, 204.
23. According to Ibn al-Athīr, *Kāmil*, 9:50, this took place in 986 following Sharaf al-Dawla's entry to Baghdad. Ibn al-Jawzī presents two dates: 986, when everyone's property was restored (Ibn al-Jawzī, *Muntaẓam*, 14:317–18), and 987, when he mentions the name of Abū Aḥmad al-Mūsawī (Ibn al-Jawzī, *Muntaẓam*, 14:322). But the first date is more probable given Abū Aḥmad's close association with Sharaf al-Dawla, who released him from prison promptly and whom Abū Aḥmad accompanied in his march to Baghdad to unseat his brother Ṣamṣām al-Dawla (d. 988), who appears to have shared his father's dislike of Abū Aḥmad; Ibn al-Athīr, *Kāmil*, 9:23.
24. Ibn al-Jawzī, *Muntaẓam*, 14:161, 205, 237, 268, 344, 15:43, 72; Ibn al-Athīr, *Kāmil*, 8:565–6, 710, 9:77–8, 105, 182, 219.
25. See Nielsen, 'Maẓālim'.

26. On him, see Strothmann, 'Ḥasan al-Uṭrūsh'.
27. On him see Djebli, 'al-Sharīf al-Raḍī'.
28. Thaʿālibī, *Yatīma*, 3:155.
29. The controversy existed already before the great commentary on *Nahj al-balāgha* by Ibn Abī al-Ḥadīd was written; Djebli, 'Encore', 33–56.
30. This biography is based on the following sources: Thaʿālibī, *Yatīma*, 5:69–72; Najāshī, *Rijāl*, 270–1; Ṭūsī, *Fihrist*, 98–101; Khaṭīb Baghdādī, *Tārīkh*, 11:401; Ibn Shahrāshūb, *Maʿālim*, 104–6; Ibn al-Jawzī, *Muntaẓam*, 15:294–300; Yāqūt, *Muʿjam al-udabāʾ*, 4:1728–33; Ibn Khallikān, *Wafayāt*, 3:313–16; Dhahabī, *Siyar*, 17:588–90; Ṣafadī, *Wāfī*, 20:231–4; Afandī, *Riyāḍ*, 4:14–65; Shīrāzī, *Darajāt*, 458–66; Khʷānsārī, *Rawḍāt*, 4:284–301; Amīn, *Aʿyān*, 8:213–19.
31. Ṭūsī, *Fihrist*, 100; Khaṭīb Baghdādī, *Tārīkh*, 11:401; Ibn Shahrāshūb, *Maʿālim*, 104.
32. Ṣafadī, *Wāfī*, 13:49.
33. Ibn al-Jawzī, *Muntaẓam*, 9:23, 14:344; Ibn al-Athīr, *Kāmil*, 9:77–8, 105.
34. Ibn al-Athīr, *Kāmil*, 9:341; see also Murtaḍā's *Dīwān*, 2:298–300.
35. *Dīwān*, 1:330–2, 508–10.
36. *Dīwān*, 1:208–11.
37. Ibn al-Jawzī, *Muntaẓam*, 15:89; Ibn al-Athīr, *Kāmil*, 9:263.
38. Ibn al-Jawzī, *Muntaẓam*, 15:72; Ibn al-Athīr, *Kāmil*, 9:219.
39. Ibn al-Jawzī, *Muntaẓam*, 15:119; Ibn al-Athīr, *Kāmil*, 9:261–2; see Murtaḍā's *Dīwān*, 1:577–81.
40. Ibn al-Jawzī, *Muntaẓam*, 15:294; Ibn al-Athīr, *Kāmil*, 9:263.
41. Madelung, 'ʿAlam al-Hodā'.
42. Djebli, 'al-Sharīf al-Raḍī'; see also his poem upon Qādir's ascension to power in Ibn Abī al-Ḥadīd, *Sharḥ*, 1:33–4.
43. He is credited with a poem praising the 'ʿAlid' (that is, Fāṭimid) caliph of Egypt, a blatant challenge to the ʿAbbāsid policy of not acknowledging the Fāṭimid claim of ʿAlid ancestry. In addition, he refused to sign the document on this question promulgated by Qādir in 1011; Ibn al-Jawzī, *Muntaẓam*, 15:117–19; Ibn al-Athīr, *Kāmil*, 8:24–5, 9:236; Ibn Abī al-Ḥadīd, *Sharḥ*, 1:37–9.
44. Ibn al-Athīr, *Kāmil*, 9:335.
45. Ibn al-Jawzī, *Muntaẓam*, 15:163.
46. Ibn al-Jawzī, *Muntaẓam*, 15:200–1; Ibn al-Athīr, *Kāmil*, 9:393–4.
47. Ibn al-Jawzī, *Muntaẓam*, 15:204.
48. Ibn al-Jawzī, *Muntaẓam*, 15:190–1.
49. Ibn al-Jawzī, *Muntaẓam*, 15:171; see the related poem in *Dīwān*, 1:190–3.
50. Ibn al-Jawzī, *Muntaẓam*, 15:214.
51. Ibn al-Athīr, *Kāmil*, 9:438.
52. See the poem in Murtaḍā's *Dīwān*, 2:170–3.
53. Ibn al-Jawzī, *Muntaẓam*, 15:175; see the poem in the *Dīwān*, 1:505–6.
54. Ibn al-Jawzī, *Muntaẓam*, 15:227.
55. Ibn al-Jawzī, *Muntaẓam*, 15:235–6; Ibn al-Athīr, *Kāmil*, 9:431.
56. Ibn al-Jawzī, *Muntaẓam*, 15:253–5; Ibn al-Athīr, *Kāmil*, 9:446.

57. Ibn al-Jawzī, *Muntaẓam*, 15:253.
58. The *ᶜayyārūn* had more complex social functions than can be captured by a simple translation; see Tor, 'ᶜAyyār'.
59. Ibn al-Jawzī, *Muntaẓam*, 15:241.
60. Ibn al-Jawzī, *Muntaẓam*, 15:217; Ibn al-Athīr, *Kāmil*, 9:417–18, with a few lines of Murtaḍā's poem on the occasion.
61. Ibn al-Jawzī, *Muntaẓam*, 15:54; Ibn al-Athīr, *Kāmil*, 9:189, where he has the date as 1005; see Murtaḍā's poem thanking the king for the title in his *Dīwān*, 1:403–6.
62. As in Ṭūsī, *Fihrist*, 99.
63. Al-Shahīd al-Awwal, *Arbaᶜūn*, 51–2; Afandī, *Riyāḍ*, 4:19–20; Khʷānsārī, *Rawḍāt*, 4:285. In the earliest of these sources, al-Shahīd al-Awwal Muḥammad b. Makkī (d. 1385) reports that he copied this story from a personal record written by Ṣafī al-Dīn Muḥammad b. Maᶜadd al-Mūsawī (d. 1223).
64. Yāqūt, *Muᶜjam al-udabāʾ*, 4:1731.
65. Afandī, *Riyāḍ*, 4:30; Khʷānsārī, *Rawḍāt*, 4:286.
66. Ibn ᶜInaba, *ᶜUmda*, 206; Afandī, *Riyāḍ*, 4:22; Khʷānsārī, *Rawḍāt*, 4:286.
67. This institution was basically a library founded by the Būyid vizier Abū Naṣr Sābūr b. Ardashīr (d. 1025) either in 991 or 993; see Sourdel, 'Dār al-ᶜIlm'.
68. Ibn al-Jawzī, *Muntaẓam*, 15:294; Afandī, *Riyāḍ*, 4:22.
69. Afandī, *Riyāḍ*, 4:21, 30; Khʷānsārī, *Rawḍāt*, 4:285.
70. Ibn Abī al-Ḥadīd, *Sharḥ*, 1:37–9; Ibn ᶜInaba, *ᶜUmda*, 206; Afandī, *Riyāḍ*, 4:21–2; contrast with his poem in the *Dīwān*, 2:89–91 (1st edn).
71. *Dīwān*, 2:209–12; see de Blois, 'Ṣābiʾ', no. 7.
72. Smoor, 'al-Maᶜarrī'.
73. Ṭabrisī, *Iḥtijāj*, 2:326–9; Afandī, *Riyāḍ*, 4:21. Madelung, 'ᶜAlam al-Hodā', gives some credit to the reports about an unfriendly encounter but maintains that those reports were 'anecdotically transformed'.
74. Maᶜarrī, *Saqṭ*, 31–8.
75. Mottahedeh, *Loyalty*, 99–157.
76. See Bulliet, *Patricians*, 20–7, for what constituted a patriciate in Naysābūr during these centuries.
77. First-person account in Najāshī, *Rijāl*, 271. See Afandī, *Riyāḍ*, 4:14, for other dates.
78. Ibn ᶜInaba, *ᶜUmda*, 206; Afandī, *Riyāḍ*, 4:30; Khʷānsārī, *Rawḍāt*, 4:286. Thus the mausoleum in Baghdad near Kāẓim's, commonly believed to be Murtaḍā's, is probably someone else's; see Muṣṭafā Jawād's introduction to Murtaḍā's *Dīwān*, 28–32.
79. Ibn al-Jawzī, *Muntaẓam*, 15:292; Ibn al-Athīr, *Kāmil*, 9:526.
80. Ibn ᶜInaba, *ᶜUmda*, 206; the abovementioned Abū al-Qāsim is credited with *Dīwān al-nasab*, infamous for doubting the ancestry of many proclaimed ᶜAlids; Kohlberg, *Medieval Muslim Scholar*, 145–6.
81. See the editors' introductions to his *Amālī* and *Dīwān* for a more comprehensive list.
82. On him, see Ibn Khallikān, *Wafayāt*, 3:190–3.
83. Sellheim, 'al-Marzubānī'.
84. Kulinich, 'Beyond theology'; Flanagan, 'al-Rummānī'.

85. Ṭūsī, *Rijāl*, 434; he is the brother of Ṣadūq, on whom see Najāshī, *Rijāl*, 68; Khūʾī, *Muᶜjam*, 7:47–8.
86. On Mufīd's life, see McDermott, *Theology*, 8–22; see also Murtaḍā's eulogy of Mufīd in his *Dīwān*, 2:438–40.
87. Ibn Abī al-Ḥadīd, *Sharḥ*, 1:41.
88. Jishumī, 'Sharḥ', 383, and Ibn al-Murtaḍā, 'Ṭabaqāt', 117 (the latter apparently copying from the former), report that Murtaḍā studied under ᶜAbd al-Jabbār, Jishumī adding that it was in Baghdad upon ᶜAbd al-Jabbār's return from pilgrimage; Madelung, 'ᶜAlam al-Hodā', dates the encounter to 999. If this is true, the brevity of the acquaintance might have been the reason why other biographers of Murtaḍā do not count ᶜAbd al-Jabbār among his teachers. Nonetheless, Murtaḍā's brother Raḍī was a student of ᶜAbd al-Jabbār, as stated by Raḍī himself in his *Majāzāt*, 48, 180, 362. It is possible that Jishumī is confusing the two brothers, since he fails to mention Raḍī, whose encounter with ᶜAbd al-Jabbār is documented. In addition, Murtaḍā himself never alludes to such a connection in the *Dhakhīra*, where he engages explicitly with the Qāḍī's views (the *Shāfī* was probably finished before their presumed meeting). Another explanation is that Jishumī is trying to connect Murtaḍā to the Muᶜtazili tradition as a student of a Muᶜtazili master, since Murtaḍā was more of a theologian than was Raḍī.
89. Amir-Moezzi, 'al-Ṭūsī'; Brown, *Hadith*, 131; Amīn, *Aᶜyān*, 9:159–67; Khūʾī, *Muᶜjam*, 16:257–62.
90. Ibn Shahrāshūb, *Maᶜālim*, 66; Amīn, *Aᶜyān*, 3:634–5; Khūʾī, *Muᶜjam*, 4:283.
91. Ibn Shahrāshūb, *Maᶜālim*, 53–4; Amīn, *Aᶜyān*, 9:400–1; Khūʾī, *Muᶜjam*, 17:357–8.
92. Ibn Shahrāshūb, *Maᶜālim*, 169–70; Amīn, *Aᶜyān*, 7:70–2; Khūʾī, *Muᶜjam*, 9:177.
93. Ibn Shahrāshūb, *Maᶜālim*, 115; Amīn, *Aᶜyān*, 8:18; Khūʾī, *Muᶜjam*, 11:42–3.
94. As Bulliet, *Conversion*, 136–7, notes in relation to various regions of the Muslim world.
95. Mottahedeh, *Loyalty*, 72–8.
96. McDermott, *Theology*, 376.
97. Madelung, 'ᶜAlam al-Hodā'.
98. As in the excerpts and comments in Thaᶜālibī, *Yatīma*, 5:69–72.
99. See Ṣafadī, *Wāfī*, 20:234; Ibn Ḥajar, *Lisān*, 5:141.
100. Khʷānsārī, *Rawḍāt*, 4:300; Amīn, *Aᶜyān*, 8:217.
101. Khʷānsārī, *Rawḍāt*, 4:292.
102. In addition to editions of his works, see Maᶜtūq, *Sharīf*, 354–61.
103. Najāshī, *Rijāl*, 270.
104. Modarressi, *Introduction*, 43. The translation of *akhbār al-āḥād* is problematic, as there are different definitions of the term. In Murtaḍā's usage, it refers to all reports that are not *mutawātir*; so he defines such traditions by negation. In any case, the translation depends on that of *tawātur*, for which 'prevalence' has been selected here. Other possible translations include recurrence (Hallaq, *Introduction*, 17) and massive transmission (Brown, *Hadith*, 104).
105. Calder, 'Doubt', 61; Madelung, 'ᶜAlam al-Hodā'.
106. Ansari and Schmidtke, 'Muᶜtazilī and Zaydī reception', 93.
107. Modarressi, *Introduction*, 45.

108. Calder, 'Doubt', 62, is inclined to see Ṭūsī's rejection of this principle as symptomatic of a desire to expand and preserve the area of clerical authority.
109. Modarressi, *Introduction*, 46.
110. Najāshī, *Rijāl*, 270; Ṭūsī, *Fihrist*, 99; Ibn Khallikān, *Wafayāt*, 3:313.
111. Madelung, 'ʿAlam al-Hodā'.
112. See the references in Ansari and Schmidtke, 'Muʿtazilism', 230–1.
113. Erder, 'Karaites', 786.
114. Dhahabī, *Tārīkh*, 29:434; Dhahabī, *Siyar*, 17:589; Ṣafadī, *Wāfī*, 20:231; Ibn Ḥajar, *Lisān*, 4:223.
115. Ibn al-Jawzī, *Muntaẓam*, 9:294.
116. Afandī, *Riyāḍ*, 4:56; Amīn, *Aʿyān*, 1:41.
117. For Sunni biographies of Mufīd, see Khaṭīb Baghdādī, *Tārīkh*, 3:449–50; Ibn al-Jawzī, *Muntaẓam*, 15:157; Ibn Ḥajar, *Lisān*, 5:368. The only exception is Dhahabī's reference to Mufīd's acceptance of Muʿtazilism; Dhahabī, *Siyar*, 17:344. On Ṭūsī's case, see Dhahabī, *Siyar*, 18:334–5; Ibn Ḥajar, *Lisān*, 5:135.
118. As in Jishumī, 'Sharḥ', 383, and Ibn al-Murtaḍā, 'Ṭabaqāt', 117, both adding that Murtaḍā is an Imami.
119. McDermott, *Theology*.
120. Ansari and Schmidtke, 'al-Shaykh al-Ṭūsī', 483–8.
121. See the editor's introduction to *Amālī*, 18.
122. Ansari, 'Nuskha-ʾī kuhansāl'.
123. Maʿtūq, *Sharīf*, 114–15.
124. On him, see Khaṭīb Baghdādī, *Tārīkh*, 3:355–6; Amīn, *Aʿyān*, 9:404; Khūʾī, *Muʿjam*, 15:323.
125. See the last passage of *Jumal al-ʿilm wa-l-ʿamal* in *Rasāʾil*, 3:81.
126. *Dhakhīra*, 607. See a more detailed discussion about the relationship between the two texts in Schmidtke, 'Jewish reception'. Ansari, 'Kitāb-i al-Taʿlīq', and Naẓarī, 'Nikātī', disagree on the exact structural connection between the two texts, depending on whether the original *Dhakhīra* begins with the section on investigation (Naẓarī's position) or with a section on divine unicity that was later elided upon Murtaḍā's suggestion (Ansari's position); see also Naẓarī, 'Piyvast'. It seems that Murtaḍā's student Sallār al-Daylamī authored a completion (*tatmīm*) of the *Mulakhkhaṣ*; Schwarb, 'Short communication', 77n8.
127. See the editors' introduction in Adang, Madelung and Schmidtke, *Baṣran Muʿtazilite Theology*, 7, for this change in structure.
128. In translating *mukallaf* and other terms that refer to the human being as agent, there is a tension between the moral/legal and ontological/existential aspects; compare, for example, Vasalou, *Moral Agents*, 50 (subject of the Law); Reinhart, *Before Revelation*, 12 (the one made-responsible); Austin, 'Some key words', 55–6 (slave preferred to servant). Except in the more technical sections discussing parties to moral obligation, I use the term 'individual' both for stylistic reasons and because it is more consistent with the common Muslim view on responsibility.
129. See Heemskerk, *Suffering*, 149 for a discussion of the translation of *luṭf*.

130. Schwarb, 'Short communication', 76–7. See the helpful studies by Ḥamīd Naẓarī where he points out many problems in the current publications, eventually suggesting that a new edition may be needed for both; Naẓarī, 'Luzūm', and 'Luzūm (2)', for *Dhakhīra* and *Mulakhkhaṣ*, respectively.
131. In the introduction to his *ᶜUdda*, 1:3–4, Ṭūsī states that Murtaḍā has not written a work on jurisprudence despite his treatment of its questions; however, he quotes Murtaḍā's views on certain points in great detail, in wording that is identical to that of the *Dharīᶜa*; Ṭūsī, *ᶜUdda*, 2:455–62, 470–81, 669–719. Ṭūsī either refrains from specifying his source for Murtaḍā's views or refers the reader to texts other than the *Dharīᶜa*, although in other cases he often mentions his sources for Murtaḍā's statements (as in *ᶜUdda*, 1:82–8, and *Ghayba*, 12, where he states that he is quoting the *Dhakhīra*). Thus, Murtaḍā's jurisprudential system was elaborated earlier than Ṭūsī's, although the latter's *ᶜUdda* was put into circulation as an independent work before the *Dharīᶜa*. Akhtar, 'al-Ṭūsī', 156 proposed the possibility that the *Dharīᶜa* was put together after Murtaḍā's death. In addition to being an unnecessary assumption, this hypothesis cannot account for the book's concluding paragraph, in which Murtaḍā states that the book (*kitāb*) was completed (*itmām*) on the date provided; *Dharīᶜa*, 561. In light of this statement, it makes more sense to assume that the work was compiled in his lifetime, though after Ṭūsī's *ᶜUdda*. This assumption explains why Baḥr al-ᶜUlūm, *Fawāʾid*, 3:144, still considers Murtaḍā's work the earliest.
132. Murtaḍā seems not to have been aware of Abū al-Ḥusayn al-Baṣrī's *al-Muᶜtamad fī uṣūl al-fiqh*, although in their introductions to the *Muᶜtamad* and the *Dharīᶜa*, respectively, Baṣrī and Murtaḍā express similar complaints about the methodology of ᶜAbd al-Jabbār's *ᶜUmad* (Murtaḍā, however, refrains from mentioning names in this context); *Dharīᶜa*, 29–31; cf. Baṣrī, *Muᶜtamad*, 1:7–8. A comparison of Murtaḍā's and Baṣrī's discussions of the same topic supports the assumption that Murtaḍā was not familiar with Baṣrī's work, as the former's arguments do not generally correspond to the latter's positions. See, for example, the discussions on non-prevalent reports and analogical reasoning in *Dharīᶜa*, 366–86, 465–81; cf. Baṣrī, *Muᶜtamad*, 2:583, 607, 724–53.
133. *Dharīᶜa*, 561.
134. Ibn Abī al-Ḥadīd, *Sharḥ*, 1:18, 290, 20:34. Beyond his staunch Muᶜtazilism, Ibn Abī al-Ḥadīd's affiliation is hard to determine, although his pro-ᶜAlid proclivities are explicit. Afsaruddin, *Excellence*, 78, describes him as ᶜAlid-Muᶜtazili; al-Qāḍī, 'Early Fāṭimid political document', 89, considers him Shiᶜi and Muᶜtazili.
135. Āghā Buzurg, *Dharīᶜa*, 10:25.
136. *Shāfī*, 1:33–4, 4:365–6.
137. *Shāfī*, 1:43, 73, 86–7, 96–8, 137, 167–8, 179, 210, 215, 318, 3:72, 4:117; cf. ᶜAbd al-Jabbār, *Mughnī*, 20{1}:18, 31–5, 37–8, 56, 69–70, 75, 79, 91–2, 181, 336.
138. *Shāfī*, 1:38, 90; cf. ᶜAbd al-Jabbār, *Mughnī*, 20{1}:13.
139. See, for example, *Shāfī*, 1:90–6.
140. *Shāfī*, 2:247, 321, 4:249, 256, 347; cf. ᶜAbd al-Jabbār, *Mughnī*, 20{1}:138–9, 155–6, {2}:50, 89.
141. *Shāfī*, 4:216, 236; cf. ᶜAbd al-Jabbār, *Mughnī*, 20{2}:20–6, 45–7.

142. See, for example, Ibn Abī al-Ḥadīd, *Sharḥ*, 12:204, 249, 17:186.
143. Ibn al-Murtaḍā, *Ṭabaqāt*, 119.
144. Āghā Buzurg, *Dharīʿa*, 10:179–80.
145. Ansari and Schmidtke, 'al-Shaykh al-Ṭūsī', 478.
146. Āghā Buzurg, *Dharīʿa*, 4:423, 6:104–5, 15:49.
147. For example, the editor of Fakhr al-Dīn al-Rāzī's (d. 1209) classic on the question, *ʿIṣmat al-anbiyāʾ*, expresses discomfort with the similarity between Rāzī's work and Murtaḍā's *Tanzīh*; see Rāzī, *ʿIṣma*, 34–5. See also the editor's introduction to *Tanzīh al-anbiyāʾ* by Ibn Ḥimyar (fl. twelfth century) for other books of this genre with a similar title.
148. Ibn Abī al-Ḥadīd, *Sharḥ*, 17:162.
149. On him, see Ziriklī, *Aʿlām*, 6:50; Sarmadī, 'Abo Moslem Eṣfahānī Mofasseri'; Rabbānī, 'Abo Moslem Eṣfahānī'. His commentary, *Jāmiʿ al-taʾwīl li-muḥkam al-tanzīl*, is lost, but fragments from it were collected and published in 1921 in India.
150. The debate on infallibility in the 1990s gave rise to heated exchanges, and the various sides appealed to Murtaḍā's position to defend their own. The contemporary Imami scholar Jaʿfar Subḥānī singled out Murtaḍā's contribution to this discussion in the Shiʿi tradition; Subḥānī, *ʿIṣma*, 6, 35–6, 55–7. Another scholar, responding to confessional enquiries on the question, referred community members to the *Shāfī* and the *Tanzīh*; Gulpaygānī, *Risālatān*, 114. See examples of the very detailed discussion in Zayn al-ʿĀbidīn, *Murājaʿāt*, 118, 178, 255 and 346.
151. Ṭūsī, *Fihrist*, 100.
152. *Dharīʿa*, 31.
153. See Modarressi, *Introduction*, 101–2, for some of the manuscripts of the collected miscellaneous responses.
154. The earliest appearance of this list is in Afandī, *Riyāḍ*, 4:34–9, where the author claims to be copying from a manuscript with both Buṣrawī's and Murtaḍā's handwriting. Another published version is based on Ḥusayn Maḥfūẓ's copy of a manuscript; it appears in Muḥyī al-Dīn, *Adab*, 164n1, and is reprinted in the introduction to Murtaḍā's *Dīwān*, 1:126–32. Maḥfūẓ's and Afandī's versions are very similar, with minor differences probably due to misreading. I usually prefer Afandī's version in this bibliography, but I note differences between the two. Whenever I cite Maḥfūẓ's and Afandī's versions, I do so in reference to their readings of this list.
155. *Rasāʾil al-Sharīf al-Murtaḍā*. Edited by Aḥmad al-Ḥusaynī. Qum: Dār al-Qurʾān al-Karīm, 1985–90. Not to be confused with the earlier but shorter collection of Murtaḍā's works under the same title and by the same editor: *Rasāʾil al-Sharīf al-Murtaḍā*. Edited by Aḥmad al-Ḥusaynī. Najaf: Maṭbaʿat al-Ādāb, 1966. The latter is referred to below as *Rasāʾil* (1966). As with *Dhakhīra* and *Mulakhkhaṣ*, Naẓarī, 'Nigarishī (3)', points out many of the deficiencies of the edited text, even offering a taxonomy of these mistakes.
156. *Masāʾil al-Murtaḍā*. Edited by Wafqān Khuḍayr Muḥsin al-Kaʿbī. Beirut: Muʾassasat al-Balāgh, 2001.
157. *Mawsūʿat turāth al-Sayyid al-Murtaḍā fī ʿilm al-kalām wa-radd al-shubuhāt*. Najaf: al-Markaz al-Islāmī li-l-Dirāsāt al-Istrātījiyya, 2015.

158. Also published in *Rasāʾil* (1966), 39–50.
159. For more on this misattribution, see the editor's introduction to Karājikī, *Taʿajjub*, 19–21.
160. Probably the work referred to as 'Masāʾil āyāt' in Ibn Shahrāshūb, *Maʿālim*, 105.
161. Entitled 'Aḥkām al-ṭalāq bi-lafẓ wāḥid' in *Masāʾil*, 33–5.
162. Also published as *Amālī al-Sayyid al-Murtaḍā*. Edited by Muḥammad Badr al-Dīn al-Naʿsānī al-Ḥalabī. Cairo: Maṭbaʿat al-Saʿāda, 1907.
163. Also in *Amālī*, 1:72–4.
164. Abdulsater, 'Resurgence'.
165. Part of the text, entitled 'Fī al-jawāhir al-mudraka', is also found in *Masāʾil*, 193–7.
166. Entitled 'Fī anna al-jawāhir mudraka' in *Masāʾil*, 81–3.
167. Entitled 'al-Jawhar lā yakūn muḥdath[an]' in *Masāʾil*, 98.
168. Entitled 'Aḥkām al-nawāfil' in *Masāʾil*, 63–5.
169. Previously published as *al-Dharīʿa ilā uṣūl al-sharīʿa*. Edited by Abū al-Qāsim Gurjī. Tehran: Tehran University Publications, 1967.
170. Also published as *Dīwān al-Sharīf al-Murtaḍā*. Edited by Muḥammad al-Tūnjī. Beirut: Dār al-Jīl, 1997.
171. Entitled 'al-Farq bayn najis al-ʿayn wa-l-ḥukm' in *Masāʾil*, 59–60.
172. See the editor's introduction, 32–6.
173. Abdulsater, *Climax*, 61–71.
174. Also in *Amālī*, 1:61–3.
175. Entitled 'Waṣf al-shayʾ li-nafsihi' in *Masāʾil*, 201.
176. Entitled 'Ḥukm wild al-bint min ḥaythu al-siyāda' in *Masāʾil*, 47–8.
177. The earliest source to mention this is Ibn Shahrāshūb, *Maʿālim*, 105. This is probably what Ibn al-Jawzī, *Muntaẓam*, 15:295–9, transmits under the same theme from Murtaḍā. Nevertheless, the text published as 'Inkāḥ Amīr al-Muʾminīn ibnatahu' under 'Ajwiba min masāʾil mutafarriqa fī al-ḥadīth wa-ghayrihi' in *Rasāʾil*, 3:148–50, is significantly shorter than Ibn al-Jawzī's and is probably one of the miscellaneous loose questions answered by Murtaḍā.
178. Also in the earlier collection, *Rasāʾil* (1966), 51–124. Also under the same title in the collection of treatises *Rasāʾil al-ʿadl wa-l-tawḥīd*. Edited by Muḥammad ʿAmāra. Cairo: Dār al-Shurūq, 1988, 1:283–342.
179. Abdulsater, 'Theological Treatise'.
180. Āghā Buzurg, *Dharīʿa*, 1:515.
181. Entitled 'al-Qadīm lā yafʿal al-qabīḥ', in *Masāʾil*, 122–7.
182. Entitled 'al-ʿAzm ʿalā al-ifṭār ghayr mufṭir', in *Masāʾil*, 40–6.
183. Mufīd, al-Shaykh Muḥammad b. Muḥammad. *ʿAdam sahw al-Nabī*. Edited by Muḥammad Riḍā Ḥusaynī Jalālī. Beirut: Dār al-Mufīd, 1993.
184. There is much confusion around this work. Maḥfūẓ (d. 2009) states that it consists of ten questions; according to Afandī (d. 1718) it consists of three. The published text has ten sections (*fuṣūl*) that address the same argument, which supports Maḥfūẓ's reading. Murtaḍā's own references to his responses to al-Tabbān match the published text in terms of content; *Intiṣār*, 81; *Rasāʾil*, 3:202. Nevertheless, Najāshī, *Rijāl*, 271, seems to

hold that there are three responses, in agreement with Afandī's version, and that they are related to the king (*sulṭān*). However, caution is required, because Najāshī's wording is slightly ambiguous: it leaves room for the possibility that he is referring to two separate entries and not qualifying the first one, which is 'al-Tabbāniyyāt'. Following a certain reading of Najāshī's remarks, Āghā Buzurg, *Dharīʿa*, 2:78–9, suggests that there are two such answers by Murtaḍā: the published one, named after al-Tabbān and written in ten sections; and a second one, which includes three questions and is possibly called 'al-Masāʾil al-Tubāniyyāt', after the city of Tubān (Yāqūt, *Muʿjam al-buldān*, 2:10). Āghā Buzurg, *Dharīʿa*, 2:84, further calls it 'al-Asʾila al-Sulṭāniyya', on the assumption that the king of Tubān asked these questions of Murtaḍā. The main question that needs to be answered, in this case, is the reason for Ṭūsī's omission of the text published as 'Jawāb al-masāʾil al-Tabbāniyyāt' from his list, despite its size and importance. One possibility is that the discussion is also covered in the *Dharīʿa*, which he mentions.

185. The identity of 'Jawābāt al-masāʾil al-Dimashqiyya' and 'Jawābāt al-masāʾil al-Nāṣiriyya' is stated in Buṣrawī's list, on which Baḥr al-ʿUlūm, *Fawāʾid*, 3:148, is probably basing his similar assertion while still being aware of another work entitled 'al-Nāṣiriyyāt'.

186. See also Āghā Buzurg, *Dharīʿa*, 5:235. Baḥr al-ʿUlūm, *Fawāʾid*, 3:145, 154–5, reverses the order of 'al-Masāʾil al-Mawṣiliyyāt al-thāniya' and 'al-Masāʾil al-Mawṣiliyyāt al-thālitha'. Although it is difficult to determine their original order, it seems that Āghā Buzurg's list is more in line with Murtaḍā's tone in *Intiṣār*, 81, 99 and 452, and the text of the two questions, for the text of the shorter one does not invoke Murtaḍā's lengthy argument against analogical reasoning and non-prevalent traditions, even when the occasion arises; *Rasāʾil*, 1:179. Thus, it is probable that the lengthy argument appearing in the longer text was written later. Ṭūsī's silence on 'Jawābāt al-masāʾil al-Mawṣiliyyāt al-thāniya' may be due to his explicit commitment to larger works.

187. *Intiṣār*, 452.

188. See Modarressi, *Introduction*, 101, for the manuscripts.

189. Ibn Shahrāshūb, *Maʿālim*, 105.

190. In the published text, the nineteenth and twentieth questions are exceedingly similar and could be considered one question, which might explain the discrepancy in the count. Baḥr al-ʿUlūm, *Fawāʾid*, 3:148–9, states that he has seen different manuscripts of this work and they all contain sixty-six questions. Strangely, he notes that all of them are questions on law, which does not correspond to the current collection. Cf. Āghā Buzurg, *Dharīʿa*, 5:238, who also states that there are sixty-six questions. Afandī's version reads *miʾat masʾala*, whereas Maḥfūẓ's reads *miʾa*. It is possible that the *miʾat masʾala* in Afandī's version is a misreading of *sitt wa-sittūn*.

191. Entitled 'Ajwibat al-masāʾil al-Nīliyyāt' in *Masāʾil*, 132–53.

192. The editor of *Masāʾil* takes the title to refer to a river in Raqqa with the name al-Nīl.

193. Yāqūt, *Muʿjam al-buldān*, 5:334; cf. Murtaḍā's contemporary Muqaddisī, *Aḥsan*, 123, who calls it a city and the earlier view of Jāḥiẓ, 'al-Awṭan', 142, who considers it a village.

194. The published text reads ‘qawluhu [zīda] bahāʾuhu’, but it is most probably ‘qawl Thumāma’. See similar statements ascribed to Thumāma (reading ‘Ashras’ for ‘Asrash’) in Ibn al-ʿArabī, *ʿAwāṣim*, 1:97; Jurjānī, *Sharḥ*, 8:178.
195. Baḥr al-ʿUlūm, *Fawāʾid*, 3:149–50.
196. Baḥr al-ʿUlūm, *Fawāʾid*, 3:150; Āghā Buzurg, *Dharīʿa*, 5:221; Ibn Shahrāshūb, *Maʿālim*, 105.
197. Ibn Ṭāwūs, *Faraj*, 43.
198. Also in *Amālī*, 2:319–25, as part of the ‘Takmila’. Published as ‘al-Radd ʿalā al-munajjimīn’, in *Rasāʾil*, 2:299–312. See Kohlberg, *Medieval Muslim Scholar*, 260 (no. 378), for other published editions of the text.
199. Also, under the same title, in *Masāʾil*, 288–97; the text is also found in *Amālī*, 2:325–8, as part of the ‘Takmila’, but without the opening sentence.
200. Published as ‘Masʾala fī tawārud al-adilla’, in *Rasāʾil*, 2:145–52.
201. See Ansari, ‘Āthār (2)’.
202. Maḥfūẓ states that the collection contains twenty-five questions, without any mention of ‘Jawābāt al-masāʾil al-Ṭarābulusiyyāt al-rābiʿa’. But according to Afandī’s version and to Baḥr al-ʿUlūm, *Fawāʾid*, 3:153, there are twenty-three questions.
203. Entitled ‘Ajwibat al-masāʾil al-Ṭarābulusiyya al-thāniya’ in *Masāʾil*, 220–87.
204. Baḥr al-ʿUlūm, *Fawāʾid*, 3:153, contrary to Maḥfūẓ and Afandī.
205. Entitled ‘Baʿḍ al-masāʾil al-Wāsiṭiyyāt’ in *Masāʾil*, 49–58.
206. Entitled ‘al-Jism maʿ al-ṣifa’ in *Masāʾil*, 128–9.
207. Also available as an earlier, separate publication by the same editor: *Jumal al-ʿilm wa-l-ʿamal.* Edited by Aḥmad al-Ḥusaynī. Najaf: Maṭbaʿat al-Ādāb, 1967.
208. Erder, ‘Karaites’, 786.
209. Afandī mentions this work as ‘al-Burūq’. Ibn Shahrāshūb, *Maʿālim*, 105, is the earliest to call it ‘al-Marmūq fī awṣāf al-burūq’. Āghā Buzurg, *Dharīʿa*, 20:315, suggests also ‘al-Mawmūq fī awṣāf al-burūq’. But these titles do not seem to appear in other early bibliographies. Given Afandī’s text and bearing in mind that some of Murtaḍā’s works came to be known already early on by a short title other than their original long one (such as *al-Ṣarfa*), it can be assumed that the book’s title is actually that included in Ibn Shahrāshūb’s or Āghā Buzurg’s list. The terms *marmūq* and *mawmūq* both appear in Murtaḍā’s writing and are plausible for the title, so it is hard to determine which of the two possible readings is more probable.
210. The earliest source to mention this work is Ibn Shahrāshūb, *Maʿālim*, 105, who says it is short. Interestingly, later scholars always cite the book on one specific question, namely, whether Friday prayers can be held without the permission of the Imam. In these discussions they seem not to have consulted the book itself but relied on the work of a much later scholar, al-Shahīd al-Thānī (d. 1558); al-Shahīd al-Thānī, *Rasāʾil*, 1:194; Khājūʾī, *Rasāʾil*, 1:493; see also Jaʿfarian, *Davāzdah*, 245.
211. In Afandī it is ‘Kitāb Masāʾil al-khilāf fī al-uṣūl’, which – in light of Murtaḍā’s terminology – gives the impression that the book is on theology, although by Afandī’s time *ūṣūl* had come to mean primarily jurisprudence. Nevertheless, the readings of both Najāshī and Ṭūsī support Maḥfūẓ’s reading, listed in the main as the first choice.

212. Buṣrawī's list, in addition to Ṭūsī's, affirm that Murtaḍā did not complete this book. Baḥr al-ᶜUlūm, *Fawāᵓid*, 3:145, reports, disapprovingly, that someone claimed to have seen a complete text of the work.
213. Included under the same title in *Masāᵓil*, 334–5, and in *Amālī*, 2:258, as part of the 'Takmila'.
214. Reading 'abyāt' for 'ithbāt'.
215. Entitled 'Kawn al-ṣifa bi-l-fāᶜil' in *Masāᵓil*, 191–2.
216. Entitled 'Masᵓala fī al-manᶜ min al-ᶜamal bi-khabar al-wāḥid' in *Masāᵓil*, 81–3.
217. Entitled 'al-Alam wa-wajh al-ḥusn fīhi' in *Masāᵓil*, 202–7.
218. Entitled 'Maᶜnā al-ijbāᵓ fī al-lugha' in *Masāᵓil*, 331–3.
219. This is how the title appears in Maḥfūẓ's edition. In Afandī's, it reads al-mubādariyyāt. However, the reference is probably to Bādarāyā, which supports Maḥfūẓ's reading; Yāqūt, *Muᶜjam al-buldān*, 1:317–18.
220. Ibn Shahrāshūb, *Maᶜālim*, 105 (and, copying him, Baḥr al-ᶜUlūm, *Fawāᵓid*, 3:149), states that these are questions on law; he also mentions 'al-Masāᵓil al-Rāziyya', stating that the latter consists of fourteen questions on various subjects. Āghā Buzurg, *Dharīᶜa*, 5:221 and 20:347, considers 'al-Masāᵓil al-Daylamiyya' and 'al-Masāᵓil al-Rāziyya' to be the same text. Unless Ibn Shahrāshūb had seen a copy of 'al-Masāᵓil al-Daylamiyya', the possibility advanced by Āghā Buzurg is very likely, especially given that Ṭūsī does not mention 'al-Masāᵓil al-Rāziyya' in the first place.
221. Maḥfūẓ copies it as 'al-Jabaliyya' but still proposes 'al-Ḥalabiyya' as a second reading. The latter is the only option in Afandī's version. However, a nineteenth-century work on jurisprudence quotes it under the title 'al-Masāᵓil al-Ḥalabiyyāt', Tustarī, *Kashf*, 128. In addition, in the context of praising Abū al-Ṣalāḥ al-Ḥalabī, Afandī, *Riyāḍ*, 4:17 reports that Murtaḍā, upon receiving questions from Aleppo, would refer people to the former.
222. Later sources (Baḥr al-ᶜUlūm, *Fawāᵓid*, 3:149; Āghā Buzurg, *Dharīᶜa*, 5:217, 20:342) seem to copy Ṭūsī.
223. Yāqūt, *Muᶜjam al-buldān*, 4:13.
224. See the notes at http://www.hadithcongresses.ir/Article.aspx?id=968.
225. Mentioned as 'Jawābāt al-masāᵓil al-Mawṣiliyya al-ūlā' in Ṣafadī, *Wāfī*, 21:8, 20:232; Amīn, *Aᶜyān*, 8:219 and Āghā Buzurg, *Dharīᶜa*, 1:70.
226. *Rasāᵓil*, 1:204.
227. *Shāfī*, 4:160; *Dharīᶜa*, 31; *Rasāᵓil*, 1:131.
228. *Dharīᶜa*, 453–536.
229. *Dhakhīra*, 295–320, 504–52.
230. Though not providing the titles, Ṭūsī states that these responses are concerned with subtle theology (reading *al-laṭīf* for *al-ṭayf*). This remark corresponds with the titles in Buṣrawī's list.
231. Baḥr al-ᶜUlūm, *Fawāᵓid*, 3:145.
232. *Rasāᵓil*, 3:135–9.
233. Entitled 'al-Masāᵓil al-Ramliyyāt' in *Masāᵓil*, 35–9.
234. Baḥr al-ᶜUlūm, *Fawāᵓid*, 3:151–2.
235. Afandī, *Riyāḍ*, 4:17; see also the editor's introduction to Karājikī, *Taᶜajjub*, 13.

236. See, for example, Ḥillī, *Mukhtalaf*, 1:316; al-Shahīd al-Awwal, *Dhikrā*, 1:204; Baḥrānī, *Ḥadāʾiq*, 4:207 (cf. *Rasāʾil*, 1:223); also Ḥillī, *Mukhtalaf*, 2:115, 151; Baḥrānī, *Ḥadāʾiq*, 8:145 (cf. *Rasāʾil*, 1:220); Ḥillī, *Mukhtalaf*, 3:157 (cf. *Rasāʾil*, 1:224).
237. Samʿānī, *Ansāb*, 5:571–3.
238. A scholar by the name of Abū al-Fatḥ al-Ṣaydāwī is mentioned among the students of Murtaḍā's student Ibn al-Barrāj, but very little is known about him. Amīn, *Aʿyān*, 2:393, suggests that this person could be Abū al-Fatḥ al-Karājikī.
239. Also in *Amālī*, 2:289–91, as part of the 'Takmila'; also published as 'Masʾala fī al-iʿtirāḍ ʿalā man yuthbit ḥudūth al-ajsām min al-jawāhir', in *Rasāʾil*, 3:329–34, and, missing some paragraphs, in *Masāʾil*, 184–6.
240. Also in *Amālī*, 2:291–3, as part of the 'Takmila'; as 'Masʾala fī al-ʿiṣma' in *Rasāʾil*, 3:323–7; and under the same title in *Masāʾil*, 187–90.
241. Also in *Amālī*, 2:293–7, as part of the 'Takmila'.
242. See Ansari, 'Paydā Shudan', where the titles are provided.
243. This is how the title appears in Najāshī's list, but it is probably a mistake.
244. Under the same title in *Masāʾil*, 65–78; also edited and translated in Madelung, 'Treatise', 22–9.
245. Under the same title in *Masāʾil*, 342–4.
246. In Maḥfūẓ's version, the title reads 'Masʾala fī ركدى'. In Afandī's, it reads ركذت. Professor Hossein Modarressi suggested that the word could be *al-kurr*. This is a classic discussion in law that Murtaḍā covers in *Intiṣār*, 85, and *Masāʾil al-Nāṣiriyyāt*, 68.
247. Also in *Rasāʾil* (1966), 31–8. This title reflects Afandī's reading. Maḥfūẓ breaks the title after *al-āya* and inserts *masʾala*, giving the impression these are two separate questions.
248. Under the same title in *Masāʾil*, 21–5.
249. The last phrase 'wa-lā yatanāhā' is missing from Maḥfūẓ's version.
250. Also in *Amālī*, 1:49–51.
251. Maḥfūẓ's version reads 'Masʾala fī al-imāma fī dalīl al-ṣifāt', as if this were the title of one question. The correction is based on Afandī's version.
252. Entitled 'Masʾala fī ḥukm al-bāʾ' in *Masāʾil*, 336–41.
253. The manuscript is referenced by Baḥr al-ʿUlūm, *Fawāʾid*, 3:144–5.
254. Entitled 'Munāqashat raʾy al-mujbira wa-l-mushabbiha' in *Masāʾil*, 162–83.
255. Entitled 'Masʾala fī aṣl al-barāʾa wa-nafy al-ḥukm bi-ʿadam al-dalīl ʿalayhi' in *Masāʾil*, 105–8.
256. Entitled 'Masʾala fī jawāz nikāḥ al-mutʿa' in *Masāʾil*, 26–9.
257. Also in *Amālī*, 2:267–70.
258. Also in *Rasāʾil* (1966), 17–29, and in *Amālī*, 280–5.
259. Repeated as 'al-Lafẓa al-dālla ʿalā al-istighrāq' in the same publication, 4:354–5; entitled 'Masʾala fī wajh al-ʿilm bi-tanāwul al-waʿīd kāffat al-kuffār' in *Masāʾil*, 218–19.
260. Entitled 'Ṭarīq al-istidlāl ʿalā furūʿ al-Imāmiyya' in *Masāʾil*, 84–104. This is probably what Baḥr al-ʿUlūm, *Fawāʾid*, 3:144, mentions as 'Risāla fī ṭarīqat al-istidlāl'.
261. Āghā Buzurg, *Dharīʿa*, 24:186. On the author, see Amīn, *Aʿyān*, 10:46; Amīnī, *Ghadīr*, 11:362–3.

262. Entitled 'al-Kalām fī al-aᶜrāḍ' in *Masāʾil*, 208–17, and 'Tatimmat anwāᶜ al-aᶜrāḍ min jamᶜ Abī Rashīd al-Naysābūrī' in Ibn Shahrāshūb, *Maᶜālim*, 105–6.
263. Entitled 'Awwal al-wājibāt al-naẓar' in *Masāʾil*, 130–1.
264. Entitled 'al-Afᶜāl maᶜ al-luṭf' in *Masāʾil*, 199–200.
265. Baḥr al-ᶜUlūm, *Fawāʾid*, 3:146, confirms that Murtaḍā was responding to material that Karājikī had collected.
266. Entitled 'Masʾala fī al-ghayba' in *Masāʾil*, 154–61; the same text, but missing the last two sentences, is entitled 'Masʾala wajīza fī al-ghayba' in *Nafāʾis al-makhṭūṭāt*, 4:9–13. Edited by Muḥammad Ḥasan Āl Yāsīn. Baghdad: Maṭbaᶜat al-Maᶜārif, 1955.
267. Also published separately as al-Sharīf al-Murtaḍā, *al-Shahāb fī al-shayb wa-l-shabāb*. Beirut: Dār al-Rāʾid al-ᶜArabī, 1982.
268. See Ansari, 'Taᶜlīq'.
269. Entitled 'Ḥukm al-ījāb wa-l-qubūl fī al-muᶜāmalāt' in *Masāʾil*, 30–2.
270. Entitled 'Masʾalat al-tāʾ min qawlihi dhāt al-qadīm' in *Masāʾil*, 301–30, where the text is mostly a commentary by the editor.
271. Mentioned by Baḥr al-ᶜUlūm, *Fawāʾid*, 3:146, as 'Risāla mukhtaṣara fī mutashābihāt al-Fātiḥa wa-l-Ḥurūf al-Muqaṭṭaᶜa'.
272. The earliest source to mention 'al-Khuṭba al-Muqammaṣa' is Ibn Shahrāshūb, *Maᶜālim*, 106. The opening passage of 'Tafsīr al-Khuṭba al-Shiqshiqiyya' makes it clear that these two titles refer to the same text.
273. There is no clear indication as to which poems are meant. Of the poems rhyming in *mīm*, a particularly fitting one is Murtaḍā's lengthy eulogy of Ḥusayn; *Dīwān*, (*yā dāru dāra al-ṣuwwam*), 3:264–8 (1st edn). The editor of Baḥr al-ᶜUlūm, *Fawāʾid*, 3:147n2, specifies another poem, but reference to Murtaḍā's *Ṭayf*, 98, does not provide justification for his choice.
274. Also in *Amālī*, 2:297–300.
275. The earliest source to mention this is Ibn Shahrāshūb, *Maᶜālim*, 105. It is also referenced by Ibn Abī al-Ḥadīd, *Sharḥ*, 1:305.
276. Entitled 'Ḥukm māʾ al-biʾr baᶜd al-jafāf' in *Masāʾil*, 61–2.
277. Jishumī, al-Ḥākim al-Muḥassin b. Karāma. *Tanbīh al-ghāfilīn ᶜan faḍl al-Ṭālibiyyīn*. Edited by Ibrāhīm al-Darsī. Ṣaᶜda, Yemen: Markaz Ahl al-Bayt, 2000.
278. Published also as *Tanzīh al-anbiyāʾ*. Beirut: Dār al-Aḍwāʾ, 1989.

CHAPTER

2

GOD AND THE WORLD

To understand the conceptual framework of classical Muslim theologians, we must be mindful of both God and the world. Although God, in His self-sufficiency, does not depend on this world, the latter is the necessary point of departure for our knowledge of Him, be it of His existence or His other attributes. But to perfect our knowledge of the whole religious experience,[1] a return to the world is needed once the reasoning about God has been completed; this reasoning allows us to understand how He manages the affairs of this world, of paramount importance among them the salvation of the human being.

With this consideration in mind, this chapter examines the major premises of Murtaḍā's theological system. It opens with a brief inventory to take stock of his terms, definitions and argumentative methods. This is followed by a discussion of the proof for the existence of God, inseparable from subsequently learning of His attributes and acts. These were topics of heated debate in Islamic history, and the very involvement in such discussions brought the wrath of traditionalists upon theologians, regardless of their affiliation.[2] But even among theologians themselves, much ink was spilt on merciless accusations; a label no less grave than that of polytheism always loomed over the discussion of the relationship between divine essence and attributes, given the danger of accepting real multiplicity in the divine;[3] talk of God's corporeality was closely associated with the slander of anthropomorphism,[4] whereas that of His speech led to the famous inquisition (*miḥna*) instituted by the caliph al-Maʾmūn.

In these discussions Murtaḍā comes very close to the teachings of the Basran Muʿtazili school, to the point of endorsing most of its positions. This agreement is occasioned by the fact that these debates do not involve concepts that contradict staple Imami doctrines – in contrast to discussions of divine justice (in connection with which the Basran Muʿtazili understanding of intercession can pose a real problem), the Imama (on which both the historical/political and theological aspects of the common Mu^c^tazili position are incompatible with Imami doctrine) and prophethood (regarding which the Muᶜtazili view of religious law may dispense with the necessity of the Imama). Nevertheless, his agreement with the teachings of the Basran Muᶜtazilis, in addition to his belief that the fundamentals of religion must be acquired through the intellect and his dismissal of non-prevalent traditions, leaves little room for the specificity of Imami doctrine in Murtaḍā's corpus. The need to assert his distinct Imami identity is probably what gives rise to a paradoxical situation: although he rarely invokes authority in his theology, it is here – in discussions that are usually least dependent on revelation – that he claims that the origins of theological thinking about God's unicity and justice are to be found in the words of ᶜAlī and the other Imams. By firmly grounding the content of belief in the authority of the Imams, Murtaḍā is consolidating the connection between theology and doctrine: his choice of individuals and episodes is an unmistakable statement of identity. For although it is common for Muᶜtazilis to count some of the Imams among their ranks,[5] Murtaḍā goes on to include other Imams who are not usually claimed by Muᶜtazilis. In addition, he relates an episode that is intended to show Kāẓim's miraculous knowledge, not only his adherence to precepts acceptable to and claimed by Muᶜtazilis.[6]

Epistemological sketch: knowledge, investigation, reason and proofs

The major components of Murtaḍā's epistemology are knowledge (*ᶜilm*), investigation (*naẓar*), reason (*ᶜaql*) and evidence (*dilāla, dalīl*). Although these components do not operate on the same level of precedence, they are all united by the assumption that the world can be fully explored using human epistemic tools. This section presents a succinct treatment of these components, with particular emphasis on their interconnections and synergy. As such, it will serve as a prelude to understanding Murtaḍā's theological system.

Knowledge

The cornerstone of Murtaḍā's epistemology is the concept of knowledge, since it functions as the constituent unit of reason (see below), the teleological product of investigation and the criterion to test the validity of evidence. Knowledge is defined as a conviction (*iᶜtiqād*) about something that entails authentic confidence (*sukūn al-nafs*) in the soul of the knower and is congruous with the reality of the object of conviction.[7] Thus the subjective aspect of knowledge – that is, the authentic confidence of the knower – is considered, in no equivocal words, prior to the objective aspect – that is, the correspondence of this conviction with external reality. This definition has stirred much controversy in Muslim theology, since it seems to leave unanswered the challenge posed by the cases of sceptics or mistaken individuals whose confidence in their conviction is no less authentic than that of knowing individuals. ᶜAbd al-Jabbār's laborious attempts to address this problem eventually led him to adopt a 'practical' criterion whereby he compares the consequences of actions undertaken by knowing agents with those done by other agents with whom they share authentic confidence. As such, ᶜAbd al-Jabbār's solution amounts to an implicit admission of the impossibility of contenting oneself with the subjective criterion while also deeming a purely theoretical objective criterion implausible, conclusions that make the practical alternative more attractive. This practical solution, investing in consequences, is also adopted by Murtaḍā in his statement that a knowing individual will act in full accordance with his knowledge, as in the case of someone seeing a beast and avoiding it. Nevertheless, his extant corpus does not betray equal awareness of the complexity of the problem as compared to ᶜAbd al-Jabbār, for he resorts to ad hominem attacks on his adversaries, accusing them of dimwittedness (*qillat al-fiṭna*).[8]

There are two types of knowledge: necessary (*ḍarūrī*) and acquired (*muktasab*). Necessary knowledge is that which a knowing person cannot disavow. It is divided into two main categories: that which occurs initially (*ibtidāʾ*) and that which occurs following its determinant (*sabab*). Examples of the first category are basic theoretical rules (such as the impossibility of being in two places at the same time and of a middle ground between affirmation and negation – the excluded third according to the philosophers). Examples of the second category are knowledge that must (*yajib*) occur following its determinant (such as knowledge acquired through perception) and knowledge that occurs following its determinant due to a norm (*ṭarīquhu al-ᶜāda*), that is, not as an effect of the causal function of its determinant but as an effect of God's norm, whether this norm is uniform (as in knowledge that accrues from hearing prevalent traditions, for those who deem such knowledge necessary) or not (as in memorisation accruing from repeated study, which varies for different people).[9] As will be seen throughout the discussion of Murtaḍā's various positions, the concept of necessary knowledge is crucial for him as an argumentative tool. It also provides a major insight into his view on causality, discussed later. At this point, it may be noted that the distinction between what must occur following its determinant and what occurs due to God's norm – despite the existence of its determinant – is critical for our understanding of the nature of connections between events, on the one hand, and the limits of possibility and reasonability, on the other, in Murtaḍā's thought. For the inevitability of knowledge acquired through perception is separated from God's norm in a manner strongly suggestive of an unbreakable connection between the event of perception and the knowledge accruing from it, without any hint of divine intervention to make it possible. By contrast, when God's norm is needed in addition to the determinant, the conclusion to be drawn is that Murtaḍā admits some sort of connection between the two consecutive events but stipulates that divine intervention is necessary to allow the connection to take effect. The flip side of this latter position is that divine intervention can also suspend this effect from taking place. As Murtaḍā eloquently puts it: 'There is no inevitability in that which is established through God's norm' (*lā wujūb fī mā ṭarīquhu al-ᶜāda*).[10]

Acquired knowledge, in turn, is knowledge that a knowing person can disavow by subjecting it to the challenge of a problematic question (*shubha*). It is also divided into two categories: that which is generated (*mutawallid*) by investigation and that which is not. An example of the latter category is retrieving knowledge that has been established by investigation, whether one still remembers its details or just remembers that one has studied it and acquired knowledge of it in the past (such as one's renewed knowledge of theological matters upon waking up from sleep, without having to reconstruct the whole argument). Another example of this category is matching a general principle to a particular case (such as knowing that injustice is vile [*qabīḥ*] and knowing an act to be unjust so as to judge it vile).[11] As for the former category, that of knowledge established through investigation, a definition of investigation is required for any discussion of it.

Investigation is thinking (*fikr*) about whether or not the object of thought is qualified by a certain attribute (*hal al-manẓūr fīhi ᶜalā al-ṣifa aw laysa ᶜalayhā*). For investigation to work properly, the investigating person must be uncertain about the answer to the question; this uncertainty may take the form of doubt (*shakk*), conjecture (*ẓann*) or a present random conviction (*tabkhīt*). Investigation depends on the demonstrative power of evidence, and thus the investigating person must be aware of the way in which evidence leads to its conclusions. Only then does investigation generate knowledge. Once it does, it ceases to exist, as the investigating person no longer has a motive to investigate.[12] The connection between investigation and the knowledge generated through it is both inevitable and exclusive: inevitable in that knowledge must be generated from investigation once all conditions are met; exclusive in that only knowledge, and no other type of conviction, is generated from it.[13]

Here one encounters a position on inevitability similar to that expressed in the discussion of necessary knowledge. Upholding the power of investigation takes Murtaḍā as far as counting its outcomes among the inevitable effects that need not depend on divine intervention. Moreover, any attempt to question this inevitability amounts to distrusting generation (*tawlīd*), which is an important explanation of causality; for knowledge proceeds from investigation by way of generation.[14] Therefore, the main difference between necessary and acquired knowledge is that the former is not an act of the knower but is rather effected in him by other agents (as in God creating such knowledge in the knower's mind), whereas the latter arises from the knower's motives and purposes that make him investigate matters.[15] As seen later, faults in necessary knowledge lead the faulty out of the pale of rational beings (sing. *ᶜāqil*), especially when it comes to the basic theoretical rules of thought. But deficiencies in acquired knowledge can always be mended by reconstructing the process of investigation to generate knowledge, as long as necessary knowledge is not faulty.[16]

Murtaḍā's sketch of necessary knowledge is similar to ᶜAbd al-Jabbār's, except for the position on knowledge acquired through perception, which ᶜAbd al-Jabbār deems to be created initially by God, not following its determinant. But the consequences of the disagreement are minimal, since ᶜAbd al-Jabbār holds that this creation is inevitable, basing his position on a foundational epistemic principle shared with Murtaḍā.[17] The element of inevitability therefore makes ᶜAbd al-Jabbār's position on

God's initial creation of knowledge practically indistinct from Murtaḍā's belief in its occurrence due to God's norm. In the discussion of acquired knowledge Murtaḍā is in full agreement with ᶜAbd al-Jabbār and his circle both in understanding investigation as the root cause of acquired knowledge and in allowing divine intervention to replace acquired knowledge with necessary knowledge by creating such knowledge in the mind of the agent. Mufīd, by contrast, sides with the Baghdadi Muᶜtazilis in rejecting the second thesis regarding the replaceability of acquired with necessary knowledge through divine power.[18] Ṭūsī, for his part, agrees with Murtaḍā, at times copying him verbatim in his own discussion on knowledge and its types.[19]

Reason

Knowledge, in its function as the constituent unit in Murtaḍā's epistemology, provides the definition of reason inasmuch as the lack of necessary knowledge – particularly the basic theoretical rules – renders a person irrational. Nevertheless, reason is also defined in a more positive light based on the purpose of knowledge, which justifies calling its possessor a rational being. Faithful to his teleological approach to human experience, Murtaḍā rules reason to comprise types of knowledge whose goal is to help a person learn his religious duties and perform them as ordained. Seen from this vantage point, reason is revealed as nothing more than the toolbox required by humans to achieve the end of their journey as conceived by Murtaḍā and like-minded theologians. Therefore, the fundamentals of reason include premises needed to construct arguments and establish evidence (for example, the proposition that bodies can be either in motion or at rest), together with the tools that can help in establishing the veracity of particular religious calls (for example, recognising a true miracle) and the moral standards that function as the justification of one's calculated actions (for example, aspects of blameworthiness and their fearful consequences). All of these features are required of an individual if he is to be considered a rational being.[20] As such, rational beings constitute a doubly imaginary group: on the one hand, the status of reason as moral arbiter was far from unanimously acknowledged even within the Muslim community, and on the other, the claim that its judgements are universal stemmed from its proponents' exaggerated optimism concerning the limits of their own reasoning. Nevertheless, these fundamentals fit perfectly within Murtaḍā's salvific model of the purpose of human existence: the first set represents the most basic givens of human thinking; the second is more pertinent to what is acquired through life experience; and the third assumes that the human being's most natural motive is avoiding harm. Reason is thus taken in a purely utilitarian sense, which reveals the primacy of the theological over the epistemological: what matters is its function in driving humankind to its pre-planned goal, and not its status as humans' distinct characteristic. This hierarchy is neatly expressed when Murtaḍā dismisses an ontological discussion for its marginal relevance to theology proper (*uṣūl al-dīn*).[21]

The tension is obvious between the view of reason as a bulk of principles subsumed under necessary knowledge, on the one hand, and the urgent need to cater to theological considerations, on the other. What heightens the tension is Murtaḍā's inability, given his fundamental commitments, to degrade reason – already a slogan used against traditionalists and Ashᶜaris – to a position in which it would fall under the absolute sway of revelation and lead to problematic positions on human rationality and, consequently, human beings' responsibility as moral agents. But if one is to uphold reason in its minimal sense of accounting for both the basic rules of thought and sense data, the problem arises from the superfluous inclusion of moral standards – let alone requirements whose sole purpose is the eventual detection of miracles – in the definition of reason. The need to elevate the conclusions of certain arguments to the level of simple truths must also have dictated the inclusion of moral standards; dissent on issues such as the need to reward those who do good is not tolerated as a mistake that needs further investigation to be rectified, but rather is seen as a sign that the dissenter is voicing a view contrary to what he already believes, making futile any attempt to pursue the debate. This problematic situation is the price Murtaḍā's theology has to pay to avoid the pitfalls of the position that would make reason fully subordinate to revelation but render indefensible much of the moral justification of religion and explanation of everyday experience. Moreover, as an Imami he was no doubt more compelled to opt for this compromise than were ᶜAbd al-Jabbār and his circle: his doctrine still needed miracles to be possible after the Prophetic era for the Imam to be recognised, and it rested on the Imam's moral superiority as a rational justification for his leadership of the community.

Murtaḍā, Mufīd, Ṭūsī and ᶜAbd al-Jabbār all agree on a certain teleological approach to reason that makes reason aimed at supporting religious doctrines. The difference between them concerns the question whether reason, unaided by revelation, can be relied on to produce knowledge at any level. Mufīd clearly expresses doubts about reason's independent ability, both about its given assumptions and about its conclusions. But the disagreement is driven primarily by the paramount consideration of establishing revelation as an indispensable source of knowledge, for the absence of revelation is a purely hypothetical scenario in the first place.[22] ᶜAbd al-Jabbār makes his position clear in explaining the Qurʾānic declaration that God perfected (*akmala*) religion, stating that revelation must follow knowledge established by unaided reason.[23] Ṭūsī provides a lengthy discussion on the question of what a person knows prior to any revelation, ruling that such a person is capable of knowing God and affirming prophethood, thereby siding with Murtaḍā.[24]

Evidence

For investigation to generate knowledge, a road map is required, which is primarily a prescription of the proper methods to apply in order to guard against wrong conclusions. The Arabic terms *dalīl* and *dilāla* are frequently encountered in the discussion of these proper methods, but far from being proofs of the sort used in Aristotelian logic, they are more like evidence: they signify 'sign' or 'indication' as the means of transition (*dalīl, istidlāl*) from the investigation's point of departure to the knowledge generated in its conclusion.[25]

Two common situations require extreme caution in the use of evidence due to their pervasive effect and usage in Murtaḍā's corpus. The first is when one affirms (*yuthbit*) a judgement (*ḥukm*)[26] about a particular essence; the second is when an affirmed (*thābit*) judgement is applied to an unknown situation. The first is logically prior to the second, but the latter is more theologically relevant in the sense that it features in most discussions pertinent to human knowledge of God. In both situations, however, a foundational principle operates: 'The way in which a certain thing is affirmed must be the only method to affirm its states and attributes' (*kull shayʾ thabata min ṭarīq fa-minhu tathbutu aḥwāluhu wa-ṣifātuhu*).[27] Accordingly, if colours are to be affirmed relying on visual perception, any attribute of colours (for example, intensity and resemblance to each other) must be likewise affirmed. Thus, whether one is attempting to arrive at an affirmation of a judgement on a known essence or to apply such an affirmation to an unknown essence, it is mandatory to stick to the same method (*ṭarīq*) that allowed one to learn whatever is known about this essence in the first place. Bearing this in mind, we may now focus on the first of the two situations, that is, when one affirms a judgement about a particular essence.

Any judgement, whether negative or affirmative, needs to be made by relying on evidence.[28] Murtaḍā bases his refutation of affirmative judgements on dismissing evidence. But with negative judgements his position is more problematic: if one is to reject a negative based on its insufficient evidence, then the negative judgement is not brought under the burden of proof; rather, the cornerstone of this position is an *argumentum ex silentio*. However, there is more to be taken into consideration at points at which this seems to be Murtaḍā's approach.

The abovementioned foundational principle rests on two underlying assumptions: first, the limitedness of methods to know anything, and second, the impossibility of the presumed object of knowledge existing without these methods conveying knowledge about it. Thus in reality, Murtaḍā's approach is not an *argumentum ex silentio*; rather, it is based on exhaustive division and elimination. The first assumption allows one to establish that 'evidence for such-and-such does not exist'; the second allows the more critical transition to 'such-and-such is shown not to exist'. The burden of proof thus falls on both affirmative and negative judgements. The difference is that for negative judgements, one only has to show that their object belongs to the second assumption and to refute any evidence to the contrary. For affirmative judgements, on the other hand, one must construct the evidence for their content. In both judgements, if the content fails to pass the scrutiny of these two assumptions, it is not simply dismissed because of insufficient evidence; rather, it is categorically negated (*qaṭaʿnā ʿalā intifāʾ al-ḥukm*).[29]

This approach – 'the Method of Negation' – is extremely influential in shaping both Murtaḍā's ontology and his theology. The ontological significance is conspicuously reflected in the sparseness of his ontology, which does not offer a populous list of items but rather resorts to multiple configurations of them to explain the diversity of existence. As for the method's theological importance, this appears forcefully in the context of discussing the nature of the divine, where the Method of Negation dictates the admissible attributes of God.[30] In adopting this method, Murtaḍā is being faithful to the characteristic feature of Muslim theology, at least as criticised by philosophers, namely, conflating the establishment of a true position with the refutation of a false one.[31]

Having treated the method that Murtaḍā proposes for developing proper affirmations about known essences, we may now address the second situation, that is, when an affirmed judgement is applied to an unknown situation. A ubiquitous form of evidence in Murtaḍā's theology is evidencing from the known to the unknown (*al-istidlāl bi-l-shāhid ʿalā al-ghāʾib*).[32] This move allows a smooth transition from the application of an already affirmed judgement on that which is known to the application of a similar judgement on that which is not known, therefore conveying information about the latter. The utility of this form of evidence is owed mainly to the endeavour of learning about God from what is known with certainty, that is, necessary knowledge; but it also derives much of its appeal from its efficacy in non-theological matters, where it proves useful. Therefore, the centrality of evidence – together with the grave risk involved in its mistaken application in matters pertaining to the divine – justifies Murtaḍā's exposition of its various elements and conditions.

The first element to be examined is the basis from which the evidence is adduced, that is, the known. Although what is meant by the known mostly refers to sensory experiences, the concept's scope is wider than that. Not only does it encompass knowledge obtained through both sense experience and abstract thinking, but it also extends to include hypothetical scenarios as long as their presumed occurrence can produce knowledge (*yuthmiru ʿilm^an^*), as long as such hypotheses do not entail an absurdity, that is, they do not contradict the theoretical rules of thought. Therefore, any essence, whether actually originated (*fiʿl*) or hypothetical (*yataqaddaru bi-taqdīr al-fiʿl*), can function as evidence.[33] The investment in these theoretical rules of thought is most obvious in Murtaḍā's assertion that there are some acts that God cannot do, not because of his lack of power, but due to their intrinsic impossibility. Therefore, even God's ability is bound to the possibilities of human understanding in the sense that whatever humans cannot comprehend cannot possibly exist. The inviolable line between doable (*maqdūr*) and impossible (*mustaḥīl*) things is one on which epistemology and ontology concur.[34] The locus of miracles is the doable, not the impossible.[35]

The procedure of evidencing from the known to the unknown may take four forms. First, it may depend on the way in which a certain qualification of an essence is evidenced (for example, knowing that a human agent who can act is able allows us to evidence that any agent who can act is able). Second, if the cause (*ʿilla*) of some qualification is known, then it must be evidenced that the qualification exists whenever that cause does (for example, if the cause of our acts' dependency on us is their origination, then whatever is originated depends on its originator). Third, if certain characteristics are known to be concomitants of certain attributes, then the existence of these attributes is evidenced from that of the characteristics (for example, a person's being commanding is a concomitant of his being willing, from which it is evidenced that God is willing since we know Him to be commanding). Fourth, there is evidence based on a fortiori arguments (for example, if we know certain acts to be good even when based on conjecture, then they must be good when based on certitude).[36]

Evidencing, therefore, is an exercise in explication, that is, seeking to understand underlying causes. It operates on two levels: understanding the causes of events in the ontological structure of the world, and understanding the connections between beliefs in a manner that preserves the coherence of human knowledge. If we keep in mind that investigation generates knowledge and that evidence is the tool of investigation par excellence, it becomes easier to understand situations in which the failure to explain is considered unacceptable. Within a framework that trusts a particular definition of reason and pins salvific hopes on it, the inability to successfully resolve a problem must be treated firmly lest it backfire on the whole edifice. Taken to its logical end, the direst form of this scenario is one in which no causes or justifications can be found to explain a particular phenomenon. The key to solving such situations is to allow investigative reason to recline on the comfortable cushion of necessary knowledge: 'Being necessary precludes justification/seeking a cause' (*al-wujūb yamnaᶜu min al-taᶜlīl*),[37] or, more modestly, 'We should not abandon our necessary knowledge [...] when we are ignorant of the cause [that leads to a situation that seemingly contradicts this knowledge]' (*wa-laysa yajibu idhā lam naᶜlam al-ᶜilla* [...] *an narjiᶜa ᶜammā ᶜalimnāhu wa-tabayyannāhu ᶜalā al-ḍarūra*).[38] This necessary knowledge assumes its warranting role in two garbs: first, when investigation seeks to justify a phenomenon where no specificity can be detected to set it apart from other similar phenomena (for example, why a particular accident of green inheres in a tree and not another, similar accident, although both of them would result in the same colour), and second, when investigation may lead to contradiction, as in attempting to justify essential attributes that cannot, by definition, be justified (for example, why black is black as opposed to white). This corroborates the observation that the theologians employed necessary knowledge as evidence in their profound quest for certainty, despite their fondness for arguments.[39] Therefore, whatever can exist is subject to investigation, justification and ultimately knowledge. The line of distinction between what is possible and what is reasonable – inasmuch as it can be investigated – fades.

Ontological sketch: entities, attributes and causality

Entities

Murtaḍā's world is not populated by numerous types of beings; as such, his ontology proves 'sparse', like that of Basran Muᶜtazilis.[40] But from these few types, a complex ontological system arises, which he then utilises heavily – in tandem with epistemological tools – to support his theological positions.

Two types of essences (sing. *dhāt*) make up the created world: atoms (sing. *jawhar*) and accidents (sing. *ᶜaraḍ*). For Murtaḍā, the different arrangements of and interactions between these two types are sufficient to explain various phenomena. The main difference between the two is that whereas atoms occupy space (*mutaḥayyiz*), accidents inhere (*taḥillu*) in atoms – except for the accident of annihilation (*iᶜdām*), which destroys atoms. A body (*jism*) is an essence composed (*muᵓallaf*) of atoms; it has length (*ṭūl*), width (*ᶜarḍ*) and depth (*ᶜumq*).[41] These atoms are the substrates in which accidents inhere – but that is not to say that accidents are not corporeal, since accidents can only exist by inhering in atoms. Thus, every created thing is corporeal in that it has a physical existence and must be bound to a particular location (*jiha*).

While this classification is based on the simple atom–accident juxtaposition, Murtaḍā's terminology reflects different perspectives in considering these essences. Complexity is encountered in reference to the origination (*ḥudūth*) of originated essences that are termed 'acts' (sing. *fiᶜl*) inasmuch as they are caused by the acts of other agents – a notable and confusing departure from the grammatical sense of *fiᶜl*.[42] Complexity also arises in explaining the diversity caused by the inherence of accidents in atoms. In the case of atoms being joined to each other, the term 'body' suffices to describe the product of such composition, and atoms seem to be construed only in their function as constituent parts. But when accidents inhere in atoms they have more complex functions and more diverse effects than do atoms in a body; the attributes (sing. *ṣifa*) that qualify bodies usually depend on the inherence of accidents. In the physical furniture of the world, a particular item, the entity (*maᶜnā*),[43] has proved very useful for theologians, for it is 'something indefinable but individual and perceptible',[44] although it gave rise to confusion because of the Muᶜtazili tendency to use it synonymously with 'thing' (*shayᵓ*).[45] Accident and entity are coextensive but intensionally different: 'accident' is mostly employed as a classificatory term denoting the ontological status of the essence as opposed to atoms, whereas 'entity' is more concerned with the function of the essence as a cause that allows the predication of a contingent attribute of atoms.[46]

Extant writings do not offer a justification for Murtaḍā's support of atomism, which leaves open the question about theologians' preference for it over other physical theories.[47] However, it can be inferred that his atomism was 'strong' (seeing atoms as indivisible parts of matter, space and motion), in the line of Abū ᶜAlī al-Jubbāᵓī, Mufīd and ᶜAbd al-Jabbār, as opposed to the 'weak' atomism (which saw atoms as indivisible parts of material but not of space or motion) proposed by Abū Hāshim.[48] But when it comes to classification of accidents, Murtaḍā appears to have sided with Abū Hāshim, as is evident from his critique of Abū Rashīd al-Naysābūrī's taxonomy;[49] Ṭūsī followed Murtaḍā's suit.[50] Nevertheless, atomism was eventually abandoned in the Imami tradition, mainly thanks to the efforts of Naṣīr al-Dīn al-Ṭūsī.[51]

Attributes

Having established an inventory of basic ontological types, we can turn our attention to how these types give rise to the diversity of beings in Murtaḍā's thought. Diversity arises first and foremost from different qualifications of essences; nevertheless, a problem on both terminological and conceptual levels is immediately encountered. Murtaḍā uses the term *ṣifa* – in the sense of 'attribute' – to denote all qualifications, although many of the so-called attributes seem hardly to share a conceptual aspect that would allow their subsumption under one such category. For example, the attributes include contradictories such as existence (*wujūd*) and inexistence (*ʿadam*), pre-eternality (*qidam*) and origination (*ḥudūth*); qualifications of essences such as able (*qādir*), knowing (*ʿālim*) and living (*ḥayy*); and qualifications related to doing an act, such as being creating (*khāliq*) and rewarding (*muthīb*). But a closer examination of what each of these attributes signifies, that is, their characterisation (*ḥukm*) of the qualified essence, sheds more light on the differences between them and allows a better grasp of their role within Murtaḍā's system, where they are far from mere descriptions of an essence or its relation to its acts, as the word *ṣifa* might indicate. Although still significant in ontology and cosmology, the complicated functions of such attributes are best detected in theology proper – particularly the discussion on divine essence and attributes.

On the most basic level, attributes can refer to what would be understood as the essence's identity with itself, as when an atom is qualified as being an atom (*kawn al-jawhar jawhar^{an}*). This attribute is termed the 'attribute of essence' (*ṣifat al-dhāt*) and is the only attribute that unconditionally qualifies all essences – even inexistent (sing. *maʿdūm*) essences. The root of such interest in qualifying inexistent essences is theological: they may thus be referred to as things (sing. *shayʾ*) and be objects of God's knowledge, which encompasses even inexistent beings. The remaining attributes, however, apply only to existent essences. Therefore, existence, though considered an attribute, is a condition for the actualisation of other attributes (*muṣaḥḥiḥ*), even the most essential of them – only an existing atom can occupy space.[52] On this point Murtaḍā is in agreement with the Basran Muʿtazili position, as is Ṭūsī;[53] Mufīd approaches the issue of how inexistent entities can be referenced on the level of language, considering it a matter of metaphorical usage in speaking of inexistent beings.[54]

Yet another level of qualification, also referred to by the term 'attribute', is that corresponding to pre-eternality and origination. In contrast to other attributes, these qualify not the essence but rather the existence of the attribute itself; a pre-eternal essence is one whose existence never ceased to be, as opposed to an originated essence whose existence has been preceded by inexistence. It is thus that pre-eternality and origination are concomitants of the mode (*kayfiyya*) of the essence's existence. These modes are necessity (*wujūb*) and contingency (*jawāz*). Pre-eternality is a concomitant of the first, since necessary existence must be pre-eternal; origination is a concomitant of the second, since contingent existence must have a beginning in time.[55]

The introduction of the theory of states (*aḥwāl*, sing. *ḥāl*) by Abū Hāshim in relation to divine essence and attributes stirred great controversy in the theological tradition. States, which proponents of the theory use instead of attributes in relation to the divine, cause both conceptual and terminological problems.[56] Conceptually, the problem arises from the distinction between the referents of the terms 'attribute' and 'state'. For example, when an agent is described as able, there is not necessarily an accident of power inherent in the agent's body by which the agent becomes able; rather, a certain state of the agent's essence justifies describing him as able. The term 'attribute' has broader significance: it functions as a description of the agent, whether to denote his essence being in a certain state (in which case it covers the semantic field of *ḥāl*) or to convey that he is doing a certain act (which falls outside that field). Hence, agency (*fiᶜliyya*) is not a state;[57] for example, a striker is one who strikes, and he can only be known as such following the knowledge that he did the act of striking. On the level of terminology, defenders of this theory still prefer to use the term *ṣifa* and corresponding substantive constructions more often than not, scarcely alerting the reader to the terminological discrepancy. In addition to the controversy surrounding the terminological legitimacy of the term *ḥāl*, part of the problem is stylistic; it would be awkward to use phrases such as 'the able agent's being able' (*kawn al-qādir qādir^an^*) every time one wants to refer to this state,[58] a reflection of the fact that their position is better expressed in the form of 'x-as-F' and not 'x is F'.[59] Instead, using a single word, 'his power' (*qudratuhu*), allows a much smoother presentation, but at the same time it is more prone to obfuscation in that it leaves little room to preserve the distinction between this word and *kawnuhu qādir^an^* as it does not clearly limit its referent to the essence being qualified. Thus, throughout this chapter, the term 'attribute', although a translation of *ṣifa*, is used in its restricted sense to denote a state of the essence, unless otherwise noted.

At this point we may touch on the debate about the place of *kalām* as an alternative to the system of Hellenistic philosophers within the Muslim tradition and beyond.[60] At the core, this debate concerns the function of theology proper within *kalām*: the more weight is given to theology, the more *kalām* looks like a primarily apologetic discipline and, as such, a secondary one. A closer look at the considerations driving the ontology of *kalām* provides helpful insight: the more complicated discussions all branch out from theological concerns. The debate about the status of inexistent beings is intimately related to divine knowledge; the discussion of the modes of existence is implied by reflections on eternality; and the theory of states is centred on the tension between simplicity and multiplicity. In succinct phrases, Murtaḍā affirms that all states of created beings are grounded in spatial extension, directly or indirectly,[61] and that the idea of an essence that is neither a body nor an atom nor an accident is incomprehensible.[62] This leaves little doubt about the parameters of the ontology of *kalām* when the divine is not part of the discussion; a more materialistic ontology can hardly be imagined. A middle-ground conclusion thus suggests itself: subtle theology is mostly independent from theology proper, although it is teleologically subservient to it. Nevertheless, the fact that the intricate theories of *kalām* ontology were dictated by theological considerations need not lead to dismissing the *kalām* philosophical system on account of its apologetic nature, since many of its ontological positions can be analysed independently of their theological origins.

Causality

Causality is one of the main points of contention between *kalām* and philosophy. The general view is that most theologians rejected causality in the ontological structure of the world and interpreted its regular occurrences as God's norm (*ᶜāda*). This position on causality led to a kindred attitude towards necessity (*ḍarūra*) when it comes to the physical world. Occasionalism, therefore, was the dominant position among the classical theologians, even before Ghazālī's famous elaboration of this position against the philosophers.[63]

Murtaḍā's positions do not reveal dissent from the prevalent attitude of his fellow theologians. Nevertheless, in a few places it is possible to detect a more nuanced position, which allows for necessary connections between physical events without explicitly grounding them in God's norms. For him, there are two models of causality, the cause (*ᶜilla*) and the determinant (*sabab*). The cause, which necessarily and simultaneously causes its effect, is restricted to making an essence be qualified by a state (*awjab[at] li-ghayrihā ḥāl^an^*); for example, knowledge (*ᶜilm*) inherent in a person's heart/mind (*qalb*) causes him to be knowing (*ᶜālim*), that is, in a state of knowingness. As such, the effect is not an ontological parameter but a conceptual one.[64] This connection between the cause and its effect is discerned rationally, and thus the cause is called a rational cause (*ᶜilla ᶜaqliyya*). An essence, be it an atom or an entity, cannot be caused by a cause. When it comes to legal matters, the term 'legal cause' (*ᶜilla sharᶜiyya*) is used only in a restricted sense to indicate a connection between a ruling and a context based on revelation and not on reason, although it has no connotation of real causality or necessity.[65]

The model of causality defined with reference to the determinant is related to the physical world; it deals with the ontological structure as well as conceptual categories. However, the determinant's effect need not be simultaneous with it, and there may be conditions that impede its functioning, including both accompanying conditions and ones arising in the time lapse between the determinant and its presumed effect. Thus, with generated acts that depend on a determinant, something might occur that prevents the materialisation of the effect; for example, the accident of knowledge may not be generated from investigation due to some preconceived false conviction.[66] This is why the determinant model is not considered a real necessity-based (*mūjib ḥaqīqī*) model of causality. In sum, three main differences between the cause and determinant models of causality can be identified. First, the former is not concerned with the ontological structure of the world; second, only the former functions unconditionally; and third, only in the former are the cause and the effect simultaneous.[67]

Given the above, Murtaḍā rejects necessary causality in the ontological structure of the world, opting for the preposition 'upon' (*ᶜind*) instead of 'by' (*bi-*) in order to steer clear of the strong causative connotations of the latter. Thus, God's norm explains the apparent effect of medications, magnets, impregnation and nourishment.[68] Nevertheless, there are some events that cannot but take place following certain occurrences. In a digression, Murtaḍā offers a peculiar conjunction: providing examples that, he says, must not be considered God's norm lest norms and inevitabilities be confused (*khalṭ al-ᶜādāt bi-l-wājibāt*), he mentions that black and white must be mutually exclusive, causes must necessitate their effects (*ījāb al-ᶜilla li-l-maᶜlūl*) and life must be annulled when a person is beheaded.[69] This last example pertains to connections between physical occurrences, and it might at first seem that Murtaḍā is allowing for a sort of natural law that cannot be broken. But the explanation is better sought within his epistemological framework, not his ontological system.

It appears that the reason for this last reference is that it is something learnt from evidence and – unlike norms – not from observation; since investigation generates knowledge, the decapitated must die, or there can be no way to establish proper evidence. This demonstration follows a discussion on life as an accident that can inhere only in a substrate with a specific structure (*binya makhṣūṣa*) of a particular composition. This inherence is the cause (*ᶜilla*) for the being alive of the totality, as opposed to the mere physical connections between different organs: hair and nails, for example, are not alive despite their physical connection to the living body.[70] Here we again face the question of a cause functioning on the conceptual level, although the strong connection with the physical world makes the necessity of the conceptual cause trickle into the ontological structure in the form of inevitability. With beheading, the substrate is no longer conducive to (*yaḥtamilu*) the inherence of life, since the specific structure and its composition are both destroyed. If life, the accident, can no longer inhere in the substrate, then it can no longer make it living, since life's function as a cause is impeded. There is no affirmation of necessary causality between natural phenomena, only between an existent cause and its conceptual effect. Nevertheless, the belief in an inevitable connection – though not a causal one in the technical sense – cannot be mistaken. Murtaḍā's position, just as when he asserts a connection between agents and acts,[71] is dictated by an epistemological concern and not by a view on cosmology. The tendency to prioritise epistemology might be understood in light of his keenness to close possible doors to scepticism since the latter could undermine the connection between the conceptual and ontological worlds, thereby threatening Murtaḍā's theological edifice.

Another problematic question arises in the discussion of contagion (*ᶜadwā*). To be consistent with the rejection of necessary causality in the physical world and faithful to some Prophetic traditions, Murtaḍā – in agreement with many theologians at the time – denies the reality (*ḥaqīqa*) of contagion.[72] Thus, it is not possible to claim that contagion is God's norm, nor a matter of causality in any perceivable manner. To complicate matters even further, it is not possible to consider the sick infecting the healthy an act of God, since that would entail an admission of God's responsibility for evil. Finally, Murtaḍā holds that objects of this world have no natures (*ṭibā^c*) acting as causes from which fixed effects could flow as if they were natural laws,[73] which appears to rule out all possible candidates for the agency of contagion. Although Murtaḍā claims that contagion does take place fortuitously (*ittifāq^an*), this should not be taken as belief in randomness. It merely absolves the sick from blame due to the absence of intention.

In this position on necessary causality, Murtaḍā concurs with the Basran Mu^ctazili school. The only occasions on which necessities are allowed in his system are when they must be adopted to protect certain theoretical considerations, not as a consequence of the natures of interacting objects; as such, they are inevitabilities rather than necessities. This position is contrary to that of Mufīd, who stood with the Baghdadi Mu^ctazilis in allowing a certain unconditional necessary causality in the ontological structure of the world and accepting that bodies have natures that make them acquire certain depositions.[74]

After this brief inventory of Murtaḍā's terminological and conceptual framework, it is time to consider how he utilises it in constructing his theological system.

Theological sketch: God's existence, attributes and the theory of states

Arguments for the existence of God were a matter of contention in the Islamic tradition: the need to intellectually prove His existence was frowned on by many traditionalists who considered the belief in God an innate given of human nature, as well as by mystics who preferred an experiential approach. Among the ranks of theologians and philosophers, disagreements as to which argument is the strongest resulted in the refinement, rejection and replacement of many of these arguments, which fall into three main categories: cosmological, teleological and ontological. The cosmological argument, together with its later revisions, grew to become an article of faith in catechisms.[75]

Being first and foremost a theologian, Murtaḍā proposes his own version of the argument, which, unsurprisingly, is in line with the available cosmological arguments. Murtaḍā's argument establishes the origination of existing bodies, which necessitates the existence of an originator (*muḥdith*) who, given the impossibility of infinite regression, is pre-eternal (*qadīm*). Although Murtaḍā relies on the classical cosmological argument, his work reveals awareness on his part of a problem that later became the compelling reason for the introduction of the revised cosmological argument in the *kalām* tradition, that is, the problem of infinite regression.

Succinctly put, the classical cosmological argument postulates that the origination of bodies is based on the existence of certain entities inhering in these bodies; these entities are themselves originated, and bodies are permanently correlated with them. The fact that bodies cannot be devoid of originated beings necessitates that they also be originated. The entity that best serves the purpose of this argument is spatial presence (*kawn*), since it inheres in bodies that must all occupy space and be in a location. The change of the body's location indicates that spatial presence is originated: it ceases to exist in the previous location, and a new entity of spatial presence originates to inhere in the body as it comes to be in the new location.[76] Having established the origination of bodies, the argument then proceeds to establish the existence of an originator, following the premise that what is originated requires an originator. This claim also has to start from entities – in the form of acts such as writing and knitting – and then apply the same logic to bodies. These originated acts depend on us because they must occur following our states and motives (*dawāʿī*), just as a starving individual who has unrestricted access to food will eat it without fail. Since the acts are originated by their agents, origination must be the cause of the acts' dependency on their agents; this is because that whose existence comes into being (*yatajaddadu*) following the agents' motives and states is the acts' origination. Applying the same logic to bodies, it is reasoned that the origination of bodies necessitates their dependency on an originator.[77]

Once more, Murtaḍā adopts ʿAbd al-Jabbār's formulation of the argument regarding the dependency of acts on their agents.[78] It should be noted, however, that what this argument, usually presented as one for the 'existence' of God, actually establishes is the assertion (*ithbāt*) of God, that is, the concept of such a being. Since the inexistent is a thing in Murtaḍā's conceptual framework, God's existence is taken to be an attribute of His that can be evidenced only from the existence of His object of power, that is, the created world. The full force of the argument for the existence of God must therefore be recognised after God's power as the Creator has been established.[79]

Before addressing the more intricate problem of infinite regression, it is important to consider what might seem a secondary debate pertinent to the argument for the existence of God, since its importance is reflected within the moral restrictions of the conceptual framework of *kalām*. This debate concerns the question whether the knowledge that bodies are originated – which is the fourth principle in the classical cosmological argument as phrased by Abū Hāshim – is necessary or acquired knowledge.[80] On the one hand, classifying it as necessary knowledge would render useless the effort expended to prove it. In addition, it would lead to a problematic theological position, since in the view of Basran Muʿtazilis knowledge of God, which is a very small step from the debate about the origination of bodies in the classical cosmological argument, cannot be necessary. On the other hand, considering such knowledge acquired might start a harmful sequence of challenges that would, eventually, bring into question the proposition itself, therefore undermining the whole argument. Murtaḍā's position is that it is necessary knowledge as a universal statement (whatever does not precede the originated must also be originated) and acquired inasmuch as it applies to particular bodies; this can be compared to the distinction between the knowledge that injustice is vile (which is necessary knowledge) and the judgement of a particular act as unjust (which is acquired). However, Murtaḍā is keen to point out that such knowledge, although acquired, is not established by evidence, since once one observes bodies, this knowledge must emerge, even without any investigation;

the point of the whole discussion regarding it is merely to alert (*tanbīh*) individuals to its content. Therefore, no rational being who has knowledge of the bodies' permanent correlation with spatial presence can be ignorant of their origination.[81] This solution seems more practical than consistent: it acknowledges the theological rationale of investing in the discussion while still pre-empting the risk of bringing such a crucial point into the unsafe arena of contention dominated by acquired knowledge. Murtaḍā is aware of the challenge represented by the example of Ibn al-Rāwandī (d. 860 or slightly after 912), who did accept the origination of entities but nonetheless held that bodies, although never devoid of them, are pre-eternal; his thesis, similar to that of the philosophers, is that entities have been correlating with bodies since pre-eternity. Murtaḍā's response is that Ibn al-Rāwandī's divergence is in fact due to his rejection of the proposition that entities are originated, although he verbally concedes it. Again, this answer is identical to that of ᶜAbd al-Jabbār,[82] but it misses Ibn al-Rāwandī's point, which is that an infinite series of originated entities has been correlating with bodies since pre-eternity – a point that should be addressed within the framework of the rejection of infinite regression.

The problem of the possibility of infinities was much debated in the Islamic tradition, with positions varying between total rejection and total endorsement, in addition to positions that distinguished between actual and temporal infinities. The problem of actual and temporal infinities in the context of the argument for the existence of God is acutely felt in the cosmological component of Ibn Sīnā's argument, which, unlike the classical cosmological argument, allows an infinite regression of originated beings but rejects the actual infinity of existents.[83]

Murtaḍā deals with the question in more than one place in his corpus, although apparently without distinguishing actual and temporal infinities, which compromises his treatment of the subject. Any originated being must be finite (*mutanāhī*); otherwise, its originator could not be done with originating it, since there would always be something left to finish. Because all originated beings are finite, every one of them must have both a beginning and an end (*lā budda min an yakūna lahu awwal wa-ākhir*); otherwise, there would always be something in it whose existence is yet to come, precluding that it be actualised and contradicting the definition of the originated being. Therefore, Murtaḍā's concern in his treatment of the subject is obviously with actual infinities, and his rejection of them is based on a definition of finitude that requires the completion of the work of the originator, as attested in his claim that 'the existence of infinite known [things] is not possible' (*lā yajūzu wujūd mā lā nihāya lahu min al-maᶜlūm*).[84] In another place, Murtaḍā does not establish the necessity of originated beings having a beginning based on their finitude as construed from their definition. Rather, he argues that doing an act infinitely necessitates that at any point in time the agent has already done that act infinitely before any time in which he does it, which is impossible; for example, if someone claims that he will enter a house only after having entered an infinite number of houses, his statement must become false the moment he enters a house. The impossibility is thus independent of past, present and future, all of which are mere descriptions of time (*min awṣāf al-zamān*). Since an infinitely done act cannot exist, every originated being must be finite and thus have a beginning.[85]

It seems that Murtaḍā took finitude and the need to have a beginning to go hand in hand with each other. True, he does make a distinction in the sense that the two concepts are not used synonymously. However, he proposes that finitude necessitates a beginning, precluding the possibility that something be finite but with no such beginning. The root of the confusion lies in his practice of extending the ruling of each particular case to include the collective of such cases, so if every originated being is finite and has a beginning, the collective must share these characteristics – a position whose weakness comes from its failure to address the scenario of an infinite number of these finite beings. This position ignores precisely the challenge of infinite regression; Murtaḍā's cornerstone in establishing the origination of the world is its necessary finitude, that is, the impossibility of an actual infinity. When he proposes the impossibility of doing an act infinitely, his preoccupation is not with the regressive aspect of the problem (that of infinite regression), but with the actual aspect (that there cannot be an actual infinity). Therefore, the other alternative (that there be an infinite regression in time of finite originated beings) is ignored, as evident in the inadequacy of his example of entering a house when it comes to dealing with the regressive aspect of the act.

Murtaḍā thus conflates the two distinct concepts of beginninglessness and infinitude together with their application to particulars and collectives, despite his presumed endorsement of the distinction.[86] In his attempt to prove the impossibility of infinite regression, Murtaḍā is in fact dealing with the impossibility of actual infinity. The same problem is encountered in his attempted answer to the objection that bodies can be originated without the need to posit an originator.[87] Murtaḍā is equally unwilling to engage with philosophical categories in his handling of the proposition that the world originates from primary matter (*hayūlā*), analysing it based on the principles of Basran Muᶜtazili theology while protesting the incomprehensibility of philosophical discourse and the arrogance of philosophers.[88] It is against the inadequacy of such responses that Abū al-Ḥusayn al-Baṣrī first proposed his revised argument, within which he offered another argument for the impossibility of infinite regression.[89]

The Imami tradition before Murtaḍā seems to have accepted the need to argue for the existence of God, relying on the classical argument of *kalām*, as shown in the work of Ṣadūq.[90] In Mufīd's extant work no argument for the existence of God survives, although there is good reason to assume that he did engage in this discussion.[91] In the later tradition, Ṭūsī's treatment of the discussion depends heavily on Murtaḍā – as he himself admits, adhering to the latter's version of the argument.[92] Whether Murtaḍā's source was the Muᶜtazili teachings or the Imami tradition, his awareness of the problem of infinite regression does not seem to have been shared by contemporary Imami theologians, despite his unsatisfactory handling of the question.

Divine essence and attributes

In the reflection on divine essence and attributes, the core of the debate is the tension between simplicity and multiplicity in the Godhead. The similarities between these debates and earlier Christological debates present a challenge concerning the origins of the discussion, although the problem can be expected to arise in any context upholding the existence of a personal omnipotent God – even if the details of the treatment reveal strong affinities.[93] Nevertheless, from early times treatments of the question were polarised around two positions. The first was the anti-Attributist position spearheaded by the Muʿtazilis: in its strongest form, it denied the ontological reality of divine attributes, viewed them in absolute unity with the essence and considered the various scriptural descriptions of God to be mere words. The second was the Attributist position represented by proto-Sunni traditionalists, which took these scriptural descriptions to signify real, existing and pre-eternal attributes of God, such as His knowledge, life and power. The proto-Sunni traditionalist position regarding the reality of attributes was later adopted by the Ashʿaris, who also advanced speculative arguments in support of their views, although disagreements as to the exact understanding of the significance of each attribute persisted within the Attributist camp, especially between Ḥanbalis and Ashʿaris.[94]

Presentations of the Imami position seem to have been ambivalent from the earliest times, as seen in heresiographical literature. Whereas many non-Imami heresiographies ascribe to early Imamis views that are either anthropomorphic or corporealist,[95] the mainstream view of later Imami theologians was to repudiate these early individuals and denounce them as extremists or, failing this, to blame the heresiographers for what the Imamis deemed an inaccurate presentation of their views. Therefore, the Imami position gradually came to be expressed in strong anti-Attributist terms, with dissident voices marginalised in the manner just described. An exemplary case is that of Hishām b. al-Ḥakam (d. 795), whose views posed a particular challenge given both his prominence and his disagreement with other Imamis on divine essence and attributes. While acknowledging the authenticity of some of his reported views, later Imamis concentrated their efforts on interpreting them in a manner that would place him within the pale of acceptable disagreement, that is, not as expressions of divine corporeality or imperfect knowledge.[96]

With time, both the Attributist and anti-Attributist positions – though still commanding numerous followers – were modified by some of their respective adherents. The effect of such modifications was either to mellow down the strict conceptualist understanding of attributes (in the case of later Muʿtazilis) or to posit some sort of priority for the divine essence over the attributes (in the case of later Ashʿaris). Among the most important of these modifications was the theory of states, introduced to the anti-Attributist camp as an attempt to solve the tension between unicity and multiplicity in divine essence without totally sacrificing the reality of attributes or compromising the simplicity of the divine. Although it was mocked by many, even among the ranks of Muʿtazilis, it seems to have gained majority acceptance among Basran Mu^c^tazilis and even in a few non-Mu^c^tazili, particularly Ash^c^ari, circles, after being reworked to fit within their doctrinal framework.[97] The theory of states thus achieved a dual purpose in discussing the divine essence: on the one hand, it does not propose real diversity in the essence, but on the other, it precludes a purely conceptualist understanding of attributes that reduces them to a condition of our minds as we speak of God. Thus, when one speaks of God's knowledge, the referent is not an entity that – though eternal – is superadded to the divine essence, as is the case in the Attributist position; nor is the referent the divine essence itself conceived in its knowing capacity in the mind of the speaker, as argued in the original anti-Attributist position. Rather, one refers to the divine essence in a state of knowledge; that is, the divine essence can give rise to different states without this entailing the existence of multiple entities in which these states are grounded. This phenomenon is significant in that it reveals the debating parties' awareness that the complexity of the question called for more sophisticated answers than those available. Nevertheless, the question had – for both parties – become more a matter of ideological indoctrination than a debate open to new possibilities.[98]

Murtaḍā's thinking on the question betrays a line of development within the anti-Attributist camp from upholding its original position to accepting the theory of states. This development appears to have coincided with his passage from studentship under Mufīd to the formulation of his own, independent intellectual identity: in his early reports of Mufīd's debates with non-Imamis, Murtaḍā transmits acerbic comments by Mufīd to the effect that the theory of states is incomprehensible and even 'worse' (ironically, *aswa*ʾ *ḥāl*^an^) than the Ashʿari Attributist position.[99] Murtaḍā's silence on this comment is characteristic of his attitude in the *Ḥikāyāt*, although many of Mufīd's reported opinions contradict Murtaḍā's later views in matters of both subtle and grand theology. In later works Murtaḍā uses the term 'state' (*ḥāl*) in the context of discussing divine attributes in a manner that accords with Abū Hāshim's theory and even explicitly argues against the view of the Baghdadi Mu^c^tazilis espoused by Mufīd.[100]

As for the particulars of Murtaḍā's theory, the aforementioned epistemological maxim, 'The way in which a certain thing is affirmed must be the only method to affirm its states and attributes', is his starting point to argue that since God's existence is affirmed through His acts, so must all the divine attributes be: the occurrence of these acts indicates His being able (*qādir*), their design His being knowing (*^c^ālim*), and their particular manner His being willing (*murīd*) or averse (*kārih*). His being living (*ḥayy*) and existing (*mawjūd*) are evidenced from the attributes as their necessary prerequisites; His being perceiving (*mudrik*) is entailed by being living and actualised by the presence of the object of perception. This rationale, combined with his definition of states, leads Murtaḍā to develop a conceptual apparatus in order to classify God's attributes. But his first task is to present an explanation of the mode in which these attributes are predicated of God, since such an explanation can serve as the basis for subsequent classification. Some attributes of God are pre-eternal, such as His being able, knowing and living. Were He not deserving of these attributes by virtue of His self, the only alternative would be that He deserve them by virtue of pre-eternal entities. But pre-eternal entities preclude any distinction between attributes that are deserved by virtue of His self and those deserved by virtue of entities; they could also lead to positing multiple pre-eternal entities with – or within – God. Therefore, these attributes must be predicated of God necessarily and pre-eternally by virtue of His self.[101]

Based on the mode in which the attributes are predicated of God, one can classify divine attributes into five categories. First, there are attributes that do not cause the agent to be in a state but are purely conveying his agency; an example is God's being provisioning (*rāziq*), which describes Him only upon His doing the act of providing for His living creation. These are the attributes of act (*ṣifāt al-fiᶜl*). Second, there are attributes that refer to the agent being in a state at all times; an example is God's being knowing, which is predicable of God since pre-eternity and is entailed by God's essence. These are the essential attributes (*al-ṣifāt al-nafsiyya, al-ṣifāt al-dhātiyya*),[102] and their distinctive sign (*amāra*) is pre-eternality.[103] Third, there are attributes that also refer to the agent being in a state, but this state is not essential; it is not pre-eternal and has some connection to a cause (*ᶜilla, maᶜnā*) other than God Himself. An example of this type is His being willing: like in attributes of the first category, an act of willing has been done, but unlike in them, there is also a state of being willing that every agent knows of himself, independent of his knowledge of doing the act of willing. Fourth, there are attributes that are neither essential nor entailed by a cause (*lā li-l-nafs wa-lā li-l-ᶜilal*) but that do refer to a state of the agent; an example is His being perceiving, which is a concomitant of His being living, given the presence of perceived objects. Finally, there are attributes that are mere negations, such as His being self-sufficient, which in fact is a negation of need. These are the attributes of negation (*ṣifāt al-nafī*).[104] Thus, the states of God are His being able, knowing, living, existing, pre-eternal, perceiving (including hearing and seeing), and willing (and averse).[105] Of those, only the first five are essential, given their mode of predication of God.

Murtaḍā's treatment of the seven divine attributes that were most central to classical theological debates (able, living, knowing, hearing, seeing, willing and speaking)[106] differs from those of both Mufīd (see below) and ᶜAbd al-Jabbār. The latter, though accepting the theory of states, considers only the first four attributes on Murtaḍā's list to be essential. As for pre-eternality, ᶜAbd al-Jabbār subsumes it under the attribute of existence and conflates the two, even when he discusses the former separately.[107] The theory of states represents Murtaḍā's major disagreement with Mufīd on the question of divine attributes and essence. Mufīd upholds the original anti-Attributist position: his list of God's essential attributes includes only power, life and knowledge. He either assumes that two of Murtaḍā's list of five attributes are not attributes but rather grounds for the actuality of attributes (as in existence) or a mode of existence (as in pre-eternality), or, more likely, he relies on the fact that these two attributes (*mawjūd* and *qadīm*) do not appear in the Qurʾān – giving rise to a new point of disagreement concerning the use of language with respect to divine attributes. As for God's being perceiving, Mufīd's position is probably dictated by his view that perception is subsumed under knowledge, in agreement with Baghdadi Muᶜtazilis.[108] These positions, he asserts, are a matter of unanimous agreement among the Imamis,[109] which means most likely that Murtaḍā was responsible for introducing the theory of states into Imami theology. As for Ṭūsī, he seems to have hesitantly accepted the theory of states, as attested by his tone in using the term,[110] which explains some indirect indications that he later changed his position on the question.[111]

This general overview of Murtaḍā's positions on divine essence and attributes is followed by separate discussions of three pertinent questions that have a special place in Islamic history. God's pre-eternality and will each merit a special discussion given the complicated answers that the later tradition developed to the challenges posited by them, especially in light of the rise of the philosophical tradition as a rival and potential replacement of *kalām*. The issue of God's being speaking can be considered the question that signalled – mainly thanks to the inquisition – the birth of the theological identity of proto-Sunni traditionalism. The era of debates on this issue was later judged, in Sunni Islam, to represent the period of perseverance that led to the triumph of orthodoxy over heterodoxy.

Pre-eternality

Being a direct concomitant of necessity when it comes to the divine, pre-eternality qualifies other essential attributes. As such, pre-eternality is sometimes referred to as the most peculiar (*akhaṣṣ*) attribute of God, that is, the one by which He is distinguished from all beings; all other attributes (such as being knowing, living and able) are more or less shared by other beings.[112] But in spite of – or due to – this peculiarity, terminological and conceptual problems surrounded the usage of the term pre-eternal (*qadīm*).

Terminologically, the confusion caused by the term *qadīm* grew as the argument for the existence of God was increasingly challenged by the problem of infinite regression, especially in the Attributist camp. The classical cosmological argument does not work unless one takes 'pre-eternal by virtue of its self' (*qadīm li-nafsihi*) and 'originated by virtue of its self' (*muḥdath li-nafsihi*) to be contradictory rather than contrary, since this is why the classical argument presumes that any being that is not originated must be pre-eternal by virtue of its self. When it was argued that originated beings cannot regress infinitely (despite the deficient handling of the question), evidence was adduced of a pre-eternal being that would stop the regression; but any pre-eternal being that is not such by virtue of its self cannot bring the regression to an end, since it also depends on another being, and thus the argument falls apart. On the other hand, assuming that any of the pre-eternal attributes could bring the sequence to an end would lead to the grave problem of equating each one of them with God. Therefore, for Attributists, a new category had to be introduced to avoid undermining the argument, namely, 'pre-eternal by virtue of other-than-its-self' (*qadīm li-ghayrihi*), which, in the context of this argument, serves as 'originated by virtue of its self'. This category allows for some dependency of attributes on the divine essence, which alone stops the infinite regression. This solution was, however, still found unsatisfactory, so the term 'necessary existent' (*wājib al-wujūd*) replaced 'pre-eternal' (*qadīm*). The new term, free from its elaborate ontological distinctions, had been circulating in Mu^ctazili circles for several decades before Ibn Sīnā's usage made it popular.[113] Murtaḍā's usage of the term *qadīm* does not reveal any awareness on his part of the intricacies surrounding the question. This is consistent with the absence of the term *wājib al-wujūd* from his discussion.

Conceptually, the peculiarity of God's pre-eternality invited reflection on what constitutes God's Attribute of Essence, that is, His identity with His self. The most obvious candidate was pre-eternality, given its metaphysical priority over other attributes, and this position was adopted by some scholars based on a particular reading of ^cAbd al-Jabbār's position.[114] However, since the Attribute of Essence denotes God's identity with His self, one expects it to be that which causes Him to be necessarily qualified by all His essential attributes since pre-eternity. God's pre-eternality was accepted by these theologians, including ^cAbd al-Jabbār in the relevant passage, as His most peculiar essential attribute, not in the sense of it being His Attribute of Essence, but in the sense of it being the distinctive concomitant of the Attribute of Essence – which is not enough to consider it the said attribute. The distinction is made clear in contexts in which pre-eternality is counted among the essential attributes by which a being differs from all others, a category that ^cAbd al-Jabbār, as well as Murtaḍā, discusses,[115] as well as in contexts in which pre-eternality is explicitly judged as a mode of qualifying God's existence.[116]

This conception of God's pre-eternality makes it possible to understand why Murtaḍā speaks of pre-eternality or that which undergirds it (*mā tastanidu ilayhi*) as God's most peculiar attribute.[117] This understanding may also be seen in Murtaḍā's discussion of what each attribute of God signifies, in which he lists pre-eternality among the attributes, stating that it means only that God cannot be described by any of the attributes of originated beings, such as corporeality; thereafter, he dedicates a separate article to the Attribute of Essence.[118] Murtaḍā's analogy of an atom's being an atom and God's essential attributes must not be read to mean that any of the essential attributes – including pre-eternality – is analogous to the atom's attribute of essence, unless one is willing to take every one of them as God's Attribute of Essence to complete the analogy, which is exactly what the theory of states was proposed to avoid.[119] Rather, the atom's being an atom is invoked because it is the only attribute that must be unconditionally predicated of the atom, since all its other attributes are conditioned by existence, which does not apply to God who cannot cease to exist.

It may be said, therefore, that for someone like Murtaḍā who holds the Attribute of Essence to undergird all others, all the essential attributes are entailed by the Attribute of Essence (*muqtaḍā ṣifat al-nafs*).[120] However, this position is bound by the insistence on the functional utility of this attribute within the theological system: there is no way to prove the existence of any attribute that has no consequence whatsoever for God's acts and cannot be subsumed under any of the essential attributes, since its existence and inexistence would make no difference. In a passage strikingly similar to ᶜAbd al-Jabbār's, Murtaḍā argues that proposing the existence of such an attribute would lead to absurdities (*jahālāt*); thus the existence of divine quiddity (*māhiyya, māʾiyya*), inscrutable and independent from His acts, must be rejected on a conceptual basis, let alone for its inappropriate terminology.[121] Mufīd's extant works do not contain a discussion of the Attribute of Essence. This absence must be due to his strong anti-Attributist position, which dispenses with the distinction between the essence and attributes altogether and makes the discussion of such an attribute meaningless. Ṭūsī's position on the question agrees with that of Murtaḍā.[122]

Being willing

Based on a semantic discussion of will, in which he equates it with liking (*maḥabba*),[123] Murtaḍā argues that every person knows necessarily of himself that he has states of being willing and averse that are distinct from his other states.[124] Although an agent may do an act of willing, it is not his doing the act that makes him willing; rather, the will itself is what necessitates the state of willing in him, even if this will were created in him by other agents.[125] In addition to God's acts that must concur with His will, it is a matter of consensus that He has commanded, declared and prohibited certain things,[126] and these serve to establish willingness as one of His attributes.

The exact classification of His being willing proved extremely problematic: on the one hand, the distinction between the state and the act of willing precluded subsuming it under attributes of act, but on the other, it could not be considered an essential attribute since God may or may not be willing. This led to the notorious and much-criticised position of Basran Muᶜtazilis on God's will, namely, the proposition that it exists in no substrate (*lā fī maḥall*). They must have been cornered to make this claim based on an elimination informed by their understanding of human psychology in relation to physiology that they then extrapolated to the divine using the technique of evidencing from the known to the unknown. Murtaḍā shares this position, while clearly being aware of its weakness as attested by the excess of defensive remarks he makes on it. God's being willing is not an essential attribute, for He can be unwilling. But the accident of God's will cannot inhere in a body (*jism*), unlike that of human will, which inheres in the heart/mind (*qalb*). Since God is incorporeal, His will need not be correlated with Him in such a manner, and it must thus remain without a substrate.[127] The outcome of this elimination is positing an incorporeal existent independent of bodies and atoms, a claim that is totally at odds with Muᶜtazili atomist physics, which has no place for incorporeal beings except for God, who is not an accident. As such, God's will is a unique being in Basran Muᶜtazili ontology, and its function and place in the system were subject to many later alterations, probably on account of the uncanniness of this position.

The unique nature of God's being willing is best exemplified by its function as the necessary connection between essential attributes and the attributes of act: God must will every act of His, and at the same time, each act must be rooted in His being able and knowing. Murtaḍā diverges here from Mufīd's teaching, since the latter opts for the position that God's will and His acts are one and the same for divine acts and that God's will is a mere metaphor for a command (*amr*) when it comes to His will that people carry out prescribed acts. For Mufīd, will is thus an attribute of act and not one of essence, since his yardstick for the distinction between the two is whether the attribute in question must always be predicable of God.[128] However, Murtaḍā is concerned with states and not essential attributes: although God does the act of willing, He also has a state of being willing independent from this act.[129] Murtaḍā's awareness of this situation is well illustrated in his *Sharḥ Jumal*, where he discusses will and aversion in the context of essential attributes, that is, preceded by discussion of His power, pre-eternality and perception and followed by discussion of the mode of existence of each of these attributes. Nonetheless, he opens the section on will and aversion with the pre-emptive phrase 'although they are by virtue of an entity' (*wa-in kānatā ᶜan ᶜilla*) to distinguish them from essential attributes that share the same context.[130] Mufīd states that his view on will is that of all Imamis, except those who have recently dissented.[131] Given that Mufīd contrasts his position with that of the Basran Muᶜtazilis, the last remark indicates that the dissent must have occurred no more than one generation before Mufīd's writing his work; Murtaḍā was thus among the early exponents of this notion, which was later endorsed by Ṭūsī.[132] The recent Imami scholar Muḥammad Ḥusayn Ṭabāṭabāʾī (d. 1981) comments that for philosophers and most theologians, God's will, when it comes to His own acts, is an attribute of essence, but that some theologians (he singles out Mufīd) judged it an attribute of act.[133] This assertion, though late, further complicates the question of how early Imami theologians' presentation of the community's views should be handled, and it also indicates the course of development of the discussions of divine will in the Imami tradition. This trajectory serves to situate the view of al-ᶜAllāma al-Ḥillī, who, following the influence of Abū al-Ḥusayn al-Baṣrī, defines God's being willing as an attribute of essence subsumed under His being knowing, thus dismissing the views of both Murtaḍā and Mufīd.[134] The transition from considering the attribute of will a pure attribute of act (as does Mufīd) to a pure attribute of essence (as does Ḥillī) must have been influenced by Murtaḍā's position, rooted in the theory of states, that God both does the act of willing and has a state of being willing.

Speech

The question of the relation between the Qurʾān as God's speech and His essence provided theological justification for the inquisition, inasmuch as the caliph al-Maʾmūn insisted that the Qurʾān, being other than God, must be created (*makhlūq*). The caliph's policy is still much debated, with varying emphases on the political motive (his concern with consolidating the caliph's authority), intellectual considerations (his inclination towards rationalism as opposed to traditionalism) and communal affiliation (his preference for pro-ᶜAlid Shiᶜi rhetoric).[135] This episode was so critical in Islamic history that it has been argued that the subsequent decline of the Muᶜtazilis was a consequence of their being blamed for it.[136] On the level of theology, responses to the claim of the Qurᵓān's createdness ranged from refusal to issue a judgement to the counterclaim that the Qurᵓān is pre-eternal. Either way, the core of the problem lies in deciding whether God's speech is to be taken as an essential attribute or an attribute of act, a decision that, in turn, is based on understanding the nature of speech (*kalām*).

For Murtaḍā, speech is an accident that must subsist in a body,[137] that is, a sound inhering in the substrate of air. Therefore, a speaking being is in reality one who does speech (*ḥaqīqat al-mutakallim man faᶜala al-kalām*).[138] Based on the premise that the only method to affirm God's attributes is to examine His acts, it may be said that no act can prove His being speaking through evidence, in contrast to His being knowing, able and living. The most that can be evidenced from His acts is His power to speak – speaking being a possible act – but not the actual occurrence of His speech. Therefore, the only manner to affirm His being speaking is revelation.[139]

This rationale makes it clear that God's being speaking can only be an attribute of act. This conclusion leads to the judgement that the Qurᵓān, which is an instance of this divine act, cannot be pre-eternal. Nevertheless, faithful to the Imami tradition, Murtaḍā avoids the term *makhlūq*, since it has connotations related to fabrications and falsehood, preferring instead to use the term 'originated' (*muḥdath*).[140] This terminological difference is the only point of disagreement between Murtaḍā – and the Imami position in general – and mainstream Muᶜtazilis on this question.[141] It is also one of the rare instances in which Murtaḍā invokes authority, that of the Imams, to defend a theological position while admitting that this position is conjectural and uncertain. This acknowledged laxity is significant since it reveals Murtaḍā's keenness to emphasise his Imami identity despite the intensely Muᶜtazili character of his theology. His investment in stressing Imami identity is reflected in his abandonment of the usual self-proclaimed standard of certitude in order to preserve the established Imami position, though it was not exclusively Imami and is likely to have been informed more by the Imamis' need to distance themselves from Muᶜtazilis than by serious theological considerations.[142]

Theoretical model

Murtaḍā's approach to the question of divine essence and attributes represents a sketch of God's image that merges Basran Muᶜtazili influence and the Imami tradition into one conceptual framework. This sketch has great potential to contribute further insights into Murtaḍā's views, especially in light of the troubled methodological history of the *kalām* tradition. With this consideration in mind, it is useful to attempt a more accurate sketch of Murtaḍā's positions, based on two major questions that set the limits of possibility for his view of God's attributes. The first is the prescribed method that must be followed in investigating the divine essence and attributes; the second is Murtaḍā's view of language, which defines the limits of propriety in speaking of God. Focusing on these two questions allows us to construct a better understanding of Murtaḍā's overall theory by limiting the range of possibilities within the methodological requirements expressed in the course of addressing these questions.

Given the reasoning that God is known only through His acts, Murtaḍā rules categorically that the first attribute to be evidenced is God's being able. His being knowing may come immediately after, or it may be preceded by His existence, pre-eternality and life. Evidencing to His being perceiving must in any case be preceded by the knowledge of His being living, since the latter is its prerequisite. Evidence of the Attribute of Essence may be produced only after at least one of the essential attributes has been established, together with its mode of existence. As for the knowledge of God's will and aversion, they must follow the evidence of His being knowing. This is because they are based either on His commanding and forbidding (which can be trusted only following belief in His being knowing, since only one who knows the vileness of falsehood would refrain from lying) or on His being willing to perform certain acts (whose wisdom can be construed from His being knowing).[143] The only prerequisite for the validity of revelation as an argument in the context of divine attributes is the impossibility of God's committing a vile act, which is a result of His being able and knowing. Once established, this precludes the possibility that an impostor be allowed to produce miracles and thus guarantees the veracity of prophets, which is necessary for the transmission of revelation to be reliable.[144]

Just as revelation is auxiliary as a method of knowing God, it is also marginalised as a source of legitimacy for the manner of speaking about Him. If human reason draws the road map to be followed in order to arrive at the knowledge of God, it is equally human language that is used to refer to Him: unless prohibited, a term consistent with the proper theological positions derived by rational arguments is predicable of God.[145] This position is informed by the view that the origin of language is not divine inspiration but human convention, which renders it a human prerogative to decide on the use of language – even in divine matters.[146] Although this view on language opens up enormous possibilities, Murtaḍā's sparse ontology resurfaces in the guise of language usage that limits these possibilities: for him, all acceptable predicates can be lumped under the five categories of attributes described earlier, including attributes of acts, the essential attributes and those grounded in entities. Therefore, each of these predicates denotes a particular case of one of the categories. Predicates that have to do with sovereignty are all discussed within the context of His being able; those related to wisdom are subsumed under His being knowing; and His creation, reward and punishment are all acts that form the basis for calling Him the Creator, the Rewarder and the Punisher.[147]

In this, Murtaḍā is in agreement with the Basran Mu'tazilis against Mufīd, given the latter's greater admission of scriptural control into his theological apparatus. Mufīd states explicitly that the only source of legitimate names for God is the Qur'ān and the traditions of the Prophet and the Imams. To support his position, he appeals to the convergence of traditions on this matter, also reporting that this was the view of the majority of Imamis, the Baghdadi Mu^{c}tazilis, the majority of non-Shi^{c}is and many Zaydis.[148] Here, too, Ṭūsī's position agrees with Murtaḍā's.[149]

Conclusion

Content

On the level of basic assumptions, Murtaḍā's epistemology depends to a large extent on the assumption that language is sufficient to cover the conceptual world. This assumption explains why he deems it valid to reject propositions based on their divergence from the standards of Arabic. The Method of Negation is a key feature of Murtaḍā's system. Its cornerstone is the assumption that there are limited ways for humans to understand the world, and this limitedness finds expression in the impossibility of anything being proven or understood that cannot be covered by these ways. On the level of argument, evidencing from the known to the unknown, a very common technique in classical *kalām*, is ubiquitous in his works. This technique harks back to the two previous assumptions: whereas language bounds human comprehension, which in turn limits the conceptual world, evidencing from the known to the unknown serves to show that human understanding needs no radical change to grasp the divine.

The theory of states in understanding the essence and attributes of God represents Murtaḍā's struggle to reconcile certain of his positions with each other. Specifically, its purpose is to reconcile his belief in the sufficiency of language and in the similarity between the world and what relates to God, on the one hand, with the attempt to speak of God in a manner that seems to have no clear equivalent in the known world, nor can it be easily expressed in common language.

Context

In his entire theological corpus, it is in the discussion of the nature of the divine and the world that Murtaḍā comes closest to the Basran Mu^{c}tazilis and departs most from Mufīd. This constitutes the climax of his concurrence with Mu^{c}tazili thought, since his works on this topic do not show any divergence that would set him outside the pale of Mu^{c}tazilism.

Many points of disagreement between him and Mufīd can be counted. In speculating about the divine essence and attributes, most of the differences between the two are due to Murtaḍā's belief in the theory of states, categorically rejected by Mufīd. From this disagreement follow their divergent views on divine will, perception and the Attribute of Essence. These conceptual disagreements lead to terminological discrepancies, particularly regarding the legitimate attribution of divine names. On all of these points, Ṭūsī usually agrees with Murtaḍā.

This assessment provides an appropriate angle from which to assess Murtaḍā's influence in context: Mufīd's frequent references to the consensus of the Imamis and his remarks about recent dissident voices, coupled with Ṭūsī's almost wholesale support of those of Murtaḍā's views that diverge from those of Mufīd, show that Murtaḍā must have been instrumental in bringing about a new phase in Imami theology.

Notes

1. 'Religious experience' is used throughout this book in reference to the awareness of God's presence and activity; see Düzgün, 'Contextualizing', 497.
2. As put by Melchert, 'Adversaries', 234–5, the problem was not with the Muᶜtazila but with the whole rationalist tendency, be it in theology or even in law. For a description of the theologians' fear of the traditionalists, see Hurvitz, 'Miḥna', 99–101.
3. See the imaginary debate between the two parties in Shahrastānī, *Nihāya*, 180–202; see also Jurjānī, *Sharḥ*, 8:44; for the opposite view, see Jishumī, *Risāla*, 31–2.
4. See Abrahamov, *Anthropomorphism*, 1–8; van Ess, 'Tas͟hbīh wa-tanzīh'; a vivid depiction in Jishumī, *Risāla*, 32–45.
5. ᶜAbd al-Jabbār, 'Faḍl', 214 (ᶜAlī, Ḥasan and Ḥusayn), 226 (Zayn al-ᶜĀbidīn and Bāqir).
6. *Amālī*, 1:162–6; he cites traditions from ᶜAlī, Bāqir (whom the editor erroneously takes for Jawād), Ṣādiq (d. 765), Kāẓim and Riḍā to support this claim.
7. *Dhakhīra*, 154. The translation of *sukūn al-nafs* depends on whether one is to prioritise the subjective or the objective, and whether the Muᶜtazili view is judged from within or without; see, for example, Vasalou, 'Subject', 289, who uses 'restfulness'.
8. *Dhakhīra*, 157–8; the examples are identical to those provided by ᶜAbd al-Jabbār, *Mughnī*, 12:36–7. See Zīna, *al-ᶜAql*, 74–85, for a detailed study of ᶜAbd al-Jabbār's treatment of the problem.
9. *Dhakhīra*, 155; Murtaḍā is expressing doubt about the status of knowledge accruing from reports since he probably considers it a form of knowledge that must occur following its determinant and not due to norm.
10. *Dhakhīra*, 161.
11. *Dhakhīra*, 156; *Mulakhkhaṣ*, 146–8. The many translations of *qabīḥ* differ inasmuch as they emphasise the aesthetic, the affective or the moral in the more classical sense; see, for example, Ormsby, *Theodicy*, 21, and El-Rouayheb, 'Must God', 421 ('repugnant'), as well as the discussion of other possibilities by Heemskerk, *Suffering*, 113n5, who eventually chooses 'bad'. Nevertheless, 'vile' seems most suitable as it covers the various different connotations of the term.
12. *Dhakhīra*, 158–60.
13. *Dhakhīra*, 160–1.
14. *Dhakhīra*, 161.
15. *Dhakhīra*, 157. To effect (*aḥdatha*), do (*faᶜala*) and bring into existence (*awjada*) are interchangeable according to Murtaḍā; *Mulakhkhaṣ*, 456–7.
16. *Dhakhīra*, 163.
17. ᶜAbd al-Jabbār, *Mughnī*, 12: 59–60.

18. *Rasāʾil*, 2:138–9; Naysābūrī, *Masāʾil*, 330–2; ᶜAbd al-Jabbār, *Mughnī*, 12:60–2; Mufīd, *Awāʾil*, 61, 89; McDermott, *Theology*, 66–9.
19. Ṭūsī, *Iqtiṣād*, 92–8; cf. Murtaḍā's wording in *Dhakhīra*, 154–67.
20. *Dhakhīra*, 121–2; *Mulakhkhaṣ*, 453, 333.
21. *Mawsūᶜa*, 5:523.
22. Mufīd, *Awāʾil*, 44; see the conflicting readings of his position by McDermott (*Theology*, 60–2) and the editor of Murtaḍā's *Sharḥ Jumal*, 125n3.
23. ᶜAbd al-Jabbār, *Mughnī*, 12:166ff; cf. Zīna, *al-ᶜAql*, 120–7, and ᶜUthmān, *Naẓariyya*, 65–89.
24. Ṭūsī, *Iqtiṣād*, 5–20.
25. On the meanings of *dalīl* and *dīlāla* in dialectical theology, see van Ess, 'Logical structure', 26–30; van Ess, *Flowering*, 177–8. Although translating *dalīl* as evidence causes some stylistic difficulty, it comes closest to what the term signified in the works of theologians; see for example, Jāḥiẓ, *Ḥayawān*, 1:33–4, 2:135, 3:215, 431; Jāḥiẓ, 'Ḥujaj al-nubbawa', 226; Jāḥiẓ, 'al-Maᶜāsh wa-l-maᶜād, 121; Jāḥiẓ, 'al-Jidd wa-l-hazl', 240.
26. Translations of *ḥukm* depend on the context, as the term's function varies. In the epistemological context it is translated as 'judgement', ontologically and morally, as 'characterisation' (Frank, *Beings*, 190, though in Frank, 'Moral obligation', 207, he prefers 'ethical valuation' for the latter); see also Reinhart, *Before Revelation*, 16, who opts for 'assessment'.
27. *Mulakhkhaṣ*, 130.
28. *Dharīᶜa*, 555–6; *Rasāʾil*, 2:102.
29. *Rasāʾil*, 2:102.
30. *Mulakhkhaṣ*, 160, 380–1, 422; *Sharḥ Jumal*, 62–3.
31. Van Ess, 'Logical structure', 23–5.
32. There have been many translations of this Arabic phrase, as it is ubiquitous in theological works, especially pre-Avicennan ones. My translation is based on Murtaḍā's definition of *shāhid* as known (*maᶜlūm*) and *ghāʾib* as unknown (*ghayr maᶜlūm*) in the context of elaborating on the concept; see *Mulakhkhaṣ*, 135, where he declares that the main aspect of the *shāhid* is not being present or observed. However, translating the expression as 'based on the evidence of phenomena' is also an apt choice. On this demonstrative device, particularly its Stoic roots, see van Ess, 'Logical structure', 34–6.
33. *Mulakhkhaṣ*, 136, 170.
34. An exemplary case is that of the tradition narrated by Kulaynī (d. 941) (*Kāfī*, 1:79), in which Ṣādiq is faced by the challenge whether God can squeeze the world into an egg without either of the two changing in size, and the Imam answers in the affirmative. Murtaḍā vehemently rejects this tradition on the basis that the question is fallacious, blaming Kulaynī and other traditionalists for their indiscriminate collection of traditions; *Rasāʾil*, 1:408–11.
35. *Rasāʾil*, 3:156.
36. *Mulakhkhaṣ*, 135–6.
37. *Mulakhkhaṣ*, 136–7, 172–3.
38. *Mawsūᶜa*, 1:212, reading *narjiᶜ* for *yarjiᶜ*.

39. Abrahamov, 'Necessary knowledge', 30; see the case of ruling out the possibility of God lying in El-Rouayheb, 'Must God', 427.
40. Dhanani, *Physical Theory*, 17–20.
41. Murtaḍā does not provide a formal definition of essence, but conclusions can be drawn from his work, see for example *Mulakhkhaṣ*, 209, 403. For atoms and accidents, see *Mulakhkhaṣ*, 207, 213; *Rasāʾil*, 3:333. For bodies, see *Mulakhkhaṣ*, 219. See Frank, *Beings*, 37–8, 111–12, and Dhanani, *Physical Theory*, 145–8, for the general understanding of these terms among Basran Muʿtazilis.
42. *Mulakhkhaṣ*, 306; *Amālī*, 2:255–7.
43. The translation of *maʿnā* has proved problematic due to its multivalence in theology and its conceptual ambiguity, even within each discourse; see, for example, Wolfson, *Philosophy*, 114–20, 147–66, and Frank, *Beings*, 12–13, for the various translations used in different contexts.
44. Van Ess, *Flowering*, 93.
45. Van Ess, *Theologie und Gesellschaft*, 2:482.
46. *Rasāʾil*, 4:305–17, where the terms *ʿaraḍ* and *maʿnā* are used interchangeably.
47. Compare Wolfson, *Philosophy*, 468–9, who opts for a theological justification and Dhanani, *Physical Theory*, 187–8, who deems all physical theories equally plausible from a theological viewpoint. Ultimately, each argument is premised on the respective author's assessment of the significance of theology for intellectual activity in Muslim contexts.
48. *Dhakhīra*, 79, where the text – despite obvious gaps – betrays his belief that one part of motion can take place in one part of space during one part of time; McDermott, *Theology*, 202–11; Dhanani, *Physical Theory*, 190–91; and Dhanani, 'Atomism'.
49. Mufīd, *Awāʾil*, 96, 98; McDermott, *Theology*, 200–2.
50. Ṭūsī, *Rasāʾil*, 63–79.
51. Dhanani, 'Atomism'.
52. *Mulakhkhaṣ*, 42; *Rasāʾil*, 3:150–1, 4:23.
53. For a survey of the Basran Muʿtazili views on the question, see Frank, 'al-Maʿdūm', 205–9; Wisnovsky, *Avicenna's Metaphysics*, 145–54. See also Ṭūsī, *Rasāʾil*, 66, 80.
54. Mufīd, *Awāʾil*, 98.
55. Alternatively, pre-eternality and existence might also be rendered 'meta-attributes', in the sense that they describe the other attributes; see Wisnovsky, *Avicenna's Metaphysics*, 230–1.
56. On the difficulties surrounding the understanding of the theory, see Frank, 'Abū Hāshim's theory', 85–100, particularly 94–5. Recently, Frank pointed out the recurrent problems with translating *ḥāl* as state; Frank, 'Yā Kalām', 9. For a survey of the various definitions of states according to different theologians, see Shahrastānī, *Nihāya*, 131–49, and Wolfson, *Philosophy*, 205–34.
57. *Mulakhkhaṣ*, 406–7.
58. See, for example, *Mulakhkhaṣ*, 349, and more generally *Rasāʾil*, 4:27; also the sudden switch to the term 'states' following a lengthy discussion in which the term 'attributes'

was used; *Mulakhkhaṣ*, 132, 133. The terminological discrepancy has been noted by Frank, *Beings*, 23–6, 72. The same stylistic considerations underlie my choice to translate *qudra* as power and *qādir* as able.

59. See Vasalou, 'Subject', 276.
60. Compare, for example, the opposite views of Sabra, 'Simple ontology', 77, and Frank, 'Science', 36–7.
61. *Mulakhkhaṣ*, 208–9.
62. *Mawsūʿa*, 2:4.
63. Wolfson, *Philosophy*, 518–44; Frank, 'Science', 36 argues otherwise.
64. *Mulakhkhaṣ*, 54, 121, 310–11; *Rasāʾil*, 1:395–8. On the ambiguity arising from confusing this sense of *ʿilla*, shared by the theologians, and the ontological sense adopted by philosophers, see van Ess, 'Logical structure', 36–42.
65. On the difference between the two types of causes see *Dharīʿa*, 461–2, 476, 480–1.
66. *Dhakhīra*, 83–4.
67. On the nature of the determinant model of causality and its difference from the cause model, see Frank, *Beings*, 112, and Vasalou, *Moral Agents*, 95–102.
68. *Amālī*, 1:404 (medications); *Rasāʾil*, 1:422 (magnets); *Mulakhkhaṣ*, 296 and *Rasāʾil*, 1:422 (impregnation); and *Mulakhkhaṣ*, 198 (nourishment).
69. *Mulakhkhaṣ*, 240; *Mawsūʿa*, 1:398. I have rendered *wājibāt* as 'inevitable' to avoid confusing it with *ḍarūrāt*, for which 'necessary' is the standard translation.
70. *Mawsūʿa*, 1:213, 397.
71. See below on the classical cosmological argument.
72. *Amālī*, 1:363, 2:173–6. See Stearns, *Infectious Ideas*, 25–37, for the various interpretations of these traditions.
73. Thus, dreams are an act of the sleeping person because foods have no effect whatsoever in themselves; it cannot be said that God is the effecter either, because dreams contain false illusions (*takhayyulāt bāṭila*), which cannot be ascribed to God (*Amālī*, 2:327; *Rasāʾil*, 2:12).
74. *Awāʾil*, 101, 129–31; Naysābūrī, *Masāʾil*, 132–49; McDermott, *Theology*, 211–12, 215–16; Frank, 'Attribute', 260, 276.
75. Shihadeh, 'Existence', 197–9, 206.
76. *Mulakhkhaṣ*, 44, 181; *Sharḥ Jumal*, 39–42.
77. *Mulakhkhaṣ*, 68–70; *Sharḥ Jumal*, 45.
78. Shihadeh, 'Existence', 207–8.
79. *Mulakhkhaṣ*, 101–6; *Sharḥ Jumal*, 49–50.
80. Shihadeh, 'Existence', 205.
81. *Mulakhkhaṣ*, 55–7.
82. Ibn Mattawayh, *Majmūʿ*, 1:58–9; Mānkdīm, *Sharḥ*, 114–15.
83. For a survey of different views on the question and their reception in various milieus, see Ajhar, *Ibn Taymiyya*, 169–226; for Ibn Sīnā's case, see the extensive treatment in Mayer, 'Ibn Sīnā', 25–35.
84. *Rasāʾil*, 1:106, 395.
85. *Mulakhkhaṣ* 61–2; cf. Ibn Mattawayh, *Majmūʿ*, 1:61.

86. *Mulakhkhaṣ*, 60–1; in passing in *Rasāʾil*, 1:105. The subject has been elaborately discussed in the lost 'al-Kalām fī-mā yatanāhā wa-lā yatanāhā'.
87. *Mulakhkhaṣ*, 69–71; *Sharḥ Jumal*, 45.
88. *Mawsūʿa*, 2:5.
89. Madelung, 'Abū l-Ḥusayn al-Baṣrī', 275–7.
90. Ṣadūq, *Tawḥīd*, 300–4.
91. McDermott, *Theology*, 327.
92. Ṭūsī, *Iqtiṣād*, 20–7.
93. See the exposé by ʿAyyād, *Kalām*, 97–145, who is less inclined to accept influence as such; see also Keating, 'Reflections', 26–7. Compare with the different position of Wolfson, *Philosophy*, 58–70, from whose work the terms 'Attributist' and 'anti-Attributist' are borrowed as they are less polemical and more accurate representations of each side's views than are other possible renderings; see also Aradi, 'Origins', 165.
94. Gilliot, 'Attributes'.
95. Jāḥiẓ, 'Khalq', 300; Jāḥiẓ, 'al-Radd ʿalā al-Naṣārā', 351; Jāḥiẓ, 'Risāla fī al-nābita', 2:18; Ashʿarī, *Maqālāt*, 34–6; Baghdādī, *Farq*, 224, 228, 230; Ibn Ḥazm, *Fiṣal*, 4:182; Shahrastānī, *Milal*, 1:189–91; Ibn Taymiyya, *Minhāj*, 1:71–2.
96. For non-Imami literature on him, see Khayyāṭ, *Intiṣār*, 108–23; Ashʿarī, *Maqālāt*, 31–3. For Imami responses to these reports, see *Shāfī*, 1:81–3; Mufīd, *Awāʾil*, 38, 55; Mufīd, *Ḥikāyāt*, 77–81, 85. For modern scholarship, see van Ess, *Theologie und Gesellschaft*, 1:358–64, where these reported views are treated as relatively credible, but with more in-depth analysis of their possible connotations; Modarressi, *Tradition*, 1:259–69. See also Jaʿfarī, 'Kalām', 171–99, particularly 192–5, for a more recent reproduction of the defensive attitude of classical Imami theologians.
97. Gilliot, 'Attributes'; Wolfson, *Philosophy*, 175–82, 211–17.
98. El-Bizri, 'God', 137–8.
99. Mufīd, *Ḥikāyāt*, 49–56.
100. *Rasāʾil*, 1:371–81.
101. *Mulakhkhaṣ*, 174–9; *Sharḥ Jumal*, 67–8.
102. *Mulakhkhaṣ*, 172–4.
103. *Mulakhkhaṣ*, 380–1.
104. *Mulakhkhaṣ*, 160–72.
105. *Mulakhkhaṣ*, 132–5.
106. On the significance of these seven, see El-Bizri, 'God', 128–9.
107. Mankdīm, *Sharḥ*, 182–96; cf. ʿAbd al-Jabbār, *Mughnī*, 5:233, and Ibn Mattawayh, *Majmūʿ*, 1:152, 160 (see below on God's pre-eternality).
108. Mufīd, *Awāʾil*, 54.
109. Mufīd, *Awāʾil*, 52, 56; see also McDermott, *Theology*, 134–42.
110. Ṭūsī, *Rasāʾil*, 78, 81.
111. Ansari and Schmidtke, 'al-Shaykh al-Ṭūsī', 489.
112. *Mulakhkhaṣ*, 158–9, 174–83; *Sharḥ Jumal*, 68–9.
113. Wisnovsky, *Avicenna's Metaphysics*, 234–41.
114. Frank, *Beings*, 68, concerning a passage in ʿAbd al-Jabbār, *Mughnī*, 11:432.

115. ᶜAbd al-Jabbār, *Mughnī*, 5:233, 11:433; cf. *Mulakhkhaṣ*, 206, 434.
116. Ibn Mattawayh, *Majmūᶜ*, 1:160.
117. *Mulakhkhaṣ*, 41, 165.
118. *Mulakhkhaṣ*, 133–5, 163.
119. *Mulakhkhaṣ*, 172–4.
120. *Mulakhkhaṣ*, 171.
121. *Mulakhkhaṣ*, 130–1, 171; on the methodological concern dictating the rejection of such a proposition in general, see pp. 454, 460 and 470; *Sharḥ Jumal*, 61–2; cf. Ibn Mattawayh, *Majmūᶜ*, 1:154–5.
122. Ṭūsī, *Rasāʾil*, 79–83.
123. *Mulakhkhaṣ*, 367–70; *Dhakhīra*, 600; cf. the similar wording in ᶜAbd al-Jabbār, *Mughnī*, 6{2}:53–4 (what it means to say '*uḥibbu Zaydan*', particularly Abū Hāshim's position). See Frank, 'Autonomy', 332, for a discussion on translating *irāda* as will.
124. *Mulakhkhaṣ*, 355–6; *Rasāʾil*, 1:372–3.
125. *Dhakhīra*, 600. On how being willing is not synonymous with effecting the act of will but rather denotes a state of the willing agent, see ᶜAbd al-Jabbār, *Mughnī*, 6{2}:3, 22, 47–51.
126. *Mulakhkhaṣ*, 371–2; *Sharḥ Jumal*, 56–7.
127. *Mulakhkhaṣ*, 356, 383–4; *Sharḥ Jumal*, 60; cf. ᶜAbd al-Jabbār, *Mughnī*, 6{2}:104–75.
128. Mufīd, *Awāʾil*, 52; Mufīd, *Taṣḥīḥ*, 40–2, and *Masʾala fī al-irāda*, 12–14.
129. *Dhakhīra*, 600.
130. *Sharḥ Jumal*, 56.
131. Mufīd, *Awāʾil*, 53.
132. Ṭūsī, *Rasāʾil*, 80–2.
133. Ṣadūq, *Tawḥīd*, 336n3. Ṭabāṭabāʾī bases his view on the distinction between *irāda* and *mashīʾa*, which is a later development in the tradition; Ṭabāṭabāʾī, *Mīzān*, 14:363–4; see his other remarks in Kulaynī, *Kāfī*, 1:150n1.
134. Schmidtke, *Theology*, 202–7.
135. For a survey of these views, see Nawas, 'Reexamination', whose author supports the first explanation; see also Jadᶜān, *Miḥna*.
136. See, for instance, Akoğlu, 'Major breaks', 205.
137. *Mulakhkhaṣ*, 397–9; *Amālī*, 2:178; cf. ᶜAbd al-Jabbār, *Mughnī*, 7:6–7, where he gives the same example of an indiscriminate sound, the squeaking of the door (*ṣarīr al-bāb*). Compare also *Mulakhkhaṣ*, 405, and *Mughnī*, 7:34–5, where both Murtaḍā and ᶜAbd al-Jabbār give the same example of the relation between the sound and movement of objects in the air, namely, stopping the motion of a metal urn (*taskīn ṭanīn al-ṭast*).
138. *Mulakhkhaṣ*, 409–13, 441; *Sharḥ Jumal*, 90–1; *Rasāʾil*, 4:27.
139. *Mulakhkhaṣ*, 413–14; *Sharḥ Jumal*, 89.
140. *Mulakhkhaṣ*, 442–5; *Sharḥ Jumal*, 91–2; *Rasāʾil*, 1:153, 301.
141. ᶜAbd al-Jabbār, *Mughnī*, 7:208–24; for a survey of the question, see Madelung, 'Origins'; Hinds, 'Miḥna'; and Heemskerk, 'Speech'.
142. The terminological distinction was not unique to Imamis; see van Ess, *Theologie und Gesellschaft*, 2:741–2; also, Wolfson, *Philosophy*, 291–303, provides a survey of the

many who held this view but fails to mention Imamis among them. See also Sayyid, *Jamāᶜa*, 261–2, who detects the political benefits of the Imami position but ignores its theological content.

143. *Mulakhkhaṣ*, 132–3.
144. *Mulakhkhaṣ*, 200, 252, 285, 372; *Amālī*, 2:142–5, 187.
145. *Dhakhīra*, 571–4.
146. *Dhakhīra*, 509, 570; *Rasāʾil*, 1:69, 3:326.
147. *Dhakhīra*, 574–604.
148. Mufīd, *Awāʾil*, 53–4; McDermott, *Theology*, 151–2.
149. Ṭūsī, *Tibyān*, 5:39–40.

CHAPTER

3

MORAL THEORY AND DIVINE JUSTICE

The significance of the controversy surrounding divine justice in the development of Islamic theology cannot be overestimated. It split the community of theologians into two rival camps, with the Muᶜtazilis being the most outspoken representatives of the first and the Ashᶜaris of the second.[1] The paramount theological importance of the split is manifest in the fact that the groups of the first camp, including the Imamis and the Zaydis, although also agreeing with each other on other theological matters pertaining to divine essence and attributes, often styled themselves collectively as the 'upholders of justice' (*ahl al-ᶜadl, al-ᶜadliyya*), not without a hint of pride.[2] The importance of the issue may also be gauged by the relatively abundant space that discussion of this precept occupies in their theological works;[3] the claim that the study of all five precepts of Muᶜtazili doctrine may be called 'the sciences of justice' (*ᶜulūm al-ᶜadl*);[4] and the tendency to reduce these precepts to only unicity and justice, with the first including the discussion on divine attributes and the remaining precepts going under justice.[5]

Both camps agreed that God is just, but they diverged over the definition of justice, which led to a debate over the definition of the morality of acts and their consequences. Thus, at the core of the discussion lie the respective moral theories adopted by the two camps. The first camp, that containing the Muᶜtazilis, believed in rationally comprehensible moral values, postulating the existence of objectively good and vile acts whose nature is independent of their agent and which necessitate clearly defined consequences. The other camp defended the thesis that acts are good or vile only as a consequence of divine command; they are morally neutral in themselves.[6] But despite the fact that this sharp polarisation was centred on the disputed status of objectivist morality,[7] it is also important to note that vehement disputes were taking place within each of these main camps. This fact is attested by the relatively meagre attention that the Basran Muᶜtazilis gave to traditionalists and Ashᶜaris compared to the elaborateness of their arguments against the views of Baghdadi Muᶜtazilis.[8]

While the theological bounds of Muᶜtazili moral theory are in line with the larger Muᶜtazili project, stressing them risks underestimating the project's worldly concerns, which relate to the social aspect of moral theory.[9] Although the theological is strongly present in the Muᶜtazilis' moral discussions, we are left to wonder why this obsession with God's morality, so to speak, showed itself in this particular discourse of theology. Also, their unwillingness to surrender their position despite all the trouble, both theoretical and practical, resulting from sticking to this understanding of His morality can hardly be explained by grounding it in the realm of pure theology. At best, relegating the worldly dimension of their moral system to a secondary position in comparison to theology begs the question of causality or merely changes its perceived order; it relies on theology to justify a moral theory that is not necessitated by any theology unless the latter is already undergirded by certain moral presumptions. The picture, therefore, must be more complex. Given the Muᶜtazilis' pre-modern framework, it would be a long shot to propose that theirs was strictly a worldly perspective; but it is still unlikely that they were driven by detached speculation about metaphysics, as the following examination of their moral theory reveals. The two factors must have interacted, but the respective weights and assigned functions of each in the theory remain to be established.

This chapter studies the main areas of Murtaḍā's moral theory. It starts by focusing on the classification of acts before proceeding to analyse the grounds of moral value, with special emphasis on the moral value of will. A discussion on the intricate question of desert follows, focusing first on its causal power. The question of divine assistance and corruption is then analysed inasmuch as it provides the assumptions needed to explain the exact nature of each of the deserved treatments that are studied later, that is, compensation, praise and reward, blame and punishment, and thanksgiving. The chapter closes with a discussion of the relationship between rational and revelational morality.[10] As in the discussion on divine essence and attributes, Murtaḍā largely concurs with ᶜAbd al-Jabbār's circle on these issues. The question of pardon, which constitutes his main disagreement with them, is treated in detail given its crucial significance in highlighting his distinct Imami identity in the context of moral thinking.

Moral theory

Classification of acts

The general agreement of Murtaḍā's moral theory with that of contemporary Muᶜtazilis, particularly as reflected in ᶜAbd al-Jabbār's work, is instrumental for understanding the former. On the one hand, Murtaḍā is immensely influenced by the Muᶜtazilis' prevalent discourse on moral theory, but on the other, his moral theory is much more teleologically governed by theological considerations than theirs is, or at least its presentation shows more sensitivity to these considerations. Although it proposes a distinction between the moral value of acts and the desert (*istiḥqāq*) of the agents, the concern with the moral value of acts is restricted to their effect on the agent's desert. This is clearly reflected in Murtaḍā's taxonomy of acts on two levels. First, any acts whose moral value has no bearing on desert are omitted; second, in some cases the only distinction between categories of acts lies in their eventual otherworldly consequences for the agent's desert.

In his taxonomy, the first basic distinction Murtaḍā makes is based on the assumption that good and vile acts are not contradictories but contraries. This definition allows for a third category, namely, that of morally irrelevant acts. In the absence of both intent (*qaṣd*) and consequence, as in the case of speech uttered by sleeping persons, acts cannot have any moral value.[11] They are pure ontological essences, and their only attribute is their origination (*ḥudūth*).[12] Since purposelessness assumes an agent's intention, these acts cannot even be labelled purposeless – and thus vile. Their agent is, a fortiori, neither praise- nor blameworthy. Once both intent and consequence are present but the agent is compelled (*mulja*ʾ) to act, he is still neither praise- nor blameworthy (*yakhruju min bāb mā yustaḥaqqu bihi al-madḥ aw al-dhamm*).[13] Compulsion is the state of an individual who has a single plausible option; there are no conflicting considerations to weigh in making the decision to choose an act. This can be due either to the implausibility of alternatives (for example, if a potential assassin knows that an assassination plot cannot be carried out single-handedly, he is compelled to refrain from undertaking it because of this knowledge, regardless of the strength of his motives) or to the irresistibility of the motive to take a particular course of action (for example, a person confronted by a lion will run away even if offered a great reward to stay).[14] The greater emphasis that Murtaḍā places on the intentionality of the act is seen in the different weights given to compulsion and coercion (*ikrāh*) in assessing the moral desert of the agent. A compelled agent is less subject to moral accountability than a coerced one is,[15] doubtless due to the former's lack of judgement, whereas the latter retains his judgement. But in practice, coercion and compulsion are not mutually exclusive: the compelled person has less 'internal' freedom of choice given his psychological state, while the coerced has less 'external' freedom because of a present danger, which might lead to compulsion. However, Murtaḍā's clarity concerning the desert of the agent in these cases is not matched by his position on the moral value of the act. Rather, he remains conspicuously silent on whether these kinds of acts are to be judged as vile or good. His definition and exhaustive classification of types of acts lends itself easily to affirming the moral value of compelled acts, since he holds that their value is independent of their agent,[16] in agreement with the view common in ʿAbd al-Jabbār's circle.[17] Therefore, the reason for Murtaḍā's failure to address their moral value explicitly must have been their lack of relevance for the larger theological framework. For what ultimately matters is not the act's moral value but its effect on the agent's desert, which is eventually translated into its otherworldly equivalent. The same applies to acts that are, though committed unaware, consequential (harmful or beneficial) to others, like a sleeping person's slapping or tickling someone. Such acts do have attributes beyond their mere origination and do affect others, but their agent's lack of awareness makes him neither blame- nor praiseworthy. The moral value of such acts, contrary to acts such as issuing orders or prohibitions, does not depend on the agent's intent, implying that the absence of such intent is inconsequential for our judgement of the act.[18] Here, too, Murtaḍā is in agreement with ᶜAbd al-Jabbār,[19] as is Ṭūsī, who seems, however, to have held a different position earlier.[20] Pushed to its logical conclusion, this position leaves us with acts of tangible consequences in the form of harm or benefit. Therefore, it would be consistent with Murtaḍā's own classification to place these acts in the same category as compelled acts, despite his own omission of them. Like the agents of compelled acts, the agents of such unintended though consequential acts are neither blame- nor praiseworthy, but these acts are not morally irrelevant.

It is only when the agent is unrestrained (*mukhallā*) and aware of the nature of his acts that he is considered blame- and praiseworthy.[21] Therefore, the two necessary and sufficient conditions for blame- and praiseworthiness are unrestraint and awareness; not meeting the former condition does not deprive the act of its moral value, but it does spare the agent desert. The absence of the latter condition produces a more complex situation, in which the nature of the act itself comes into play. If the moral value of the act is dependent on the agent's belief, then it cannot be judged due to the absence of this necessary element. Otherwise, it may be judged based on its effect on others.[22] But Murtaḍā's looming theological considerations are evident in his relatively dismissive attitude towards such acts: although they might be extremely consequential, they do not merit a detailed discussion, since they lack a matching entry under deserts that reflects the eventual status of the agent.

Translating the moral categories into legal ones provides an opportunity for Murtaḍā to further tailor these details to fit theological considerations. The category of vile acts is monolithic, and it is subsumed in its entirety under the legally prohibited (*maḥẓūr*). Good acts, however, are much more diversified. They are broadly divided into acts that are licit (*mubāḥ*), recommended (*nadb*) and obligatory (*wājib*). Although this division agrees with the general approach in Murtaḍā's time, it diverges from it in two ways that are important for later theological elaborations of agents' deserts. First, Murtaḍā avoids defining a licit act as one that can be equally done and forgone, that is, as the exact equivalent of a plain-good act (*ḥasan*). Instead, he restricts himself to the condition that the agent of such an act is neither blame- nor praiseworthy. The value of this uncanny approach for theological considerations will become clear in the later discussion of God's treatment of sinners. Second, Murtaḍā devises a subcategory of recommended acts and separates it from other licit acts. The agent of a recommended act whose benefit extends to others, described as initiated benevolence and bounty (*in^c^ām*), merits not just praise but also gratitude expressed in thanksgiving. This distinction is premised on the different deserts of these subcategories, but it will also prove consequential in the justification of religious experience from a moral standpoint.[23]

The method of the *mutakallimūn*, largely reliant on evidencing from the known to the unknown, must have made it necessary that such abstract categories of moral acts be grounded in tangible reality. In addition, the strong nexus between law and theology would also have pushed in this direction. It is no surprise, therefore, that Murtaḍā stipulates that for each class of acts, a model must be (*lā budda*) proposed as the necessarily known archetype (*aṣl*) of the corresponding moral value:[24] injustice serves this role for vile acts; fairness (*inṣāf*) and gratitude for obligatory acts; and intransitive self-benefit for plain-good acts.[25] Given that the aspect of vileness is the only one whose effect on the moral value of acts is unconditional, the fact that Murtaḍā finds injustice to be the necessarily known archetype of vileness supports the observation that 'injustice might be identified as the master category of [Muᶜtazili] ethics'.[26] It may also be added that benevolence is its good counterpart, though subject to the conditions that govern good acts.

Vile acts

Vile acts are a sharply defined category of moral acts, since they all translate into the category of the prohibited. In addition, they constitute an urgent requirement in establishing moral theory for theological purposes, since Murtaḍā's overwhelming concern is with injustice as a morally negative value that cannot characterise God's treatment of His creation.

Again, the cornerstone of Murtaḍā's position is the concept of necessary knowledge. Despite its strongly subjective undertones, it is used to anchor many positions in a manner that protects them from rigorous questioning. Therefore, according to Murtaḍā, the category of injustice is necessarily known to be vile, and so is every unjust act once it is recognised as an instance of injustice. Even when he is willing to consider the possibility of such knowledge being acquired, he remains resistant. In cases such as encountering a person murdering another, the mental effort needed to investigate the situation before arriving at a moral judgement affects the necessity of our knowledge, but it does not suffice to move the judgement from the category of necessary knowledge to that of evidenced (*mustadall ᶜalayhi*) knowledge. At most, it might 'downgrade' such knowledge from necessary to acquired, and Murtaḍā continues to insist that the process involved in reaching the moral judgement is one of consideration (*bi-iᶜtibār wa-iktisāb*).[27] He proposes this unmediated form of acquired knowledge mainly to keep the function of evidencing from affecting the workings of moral theory at this basic level. The underlying reason may well be the fact that allowing evidence any role in discussing the 'master category' could undermine the pillars upon which the theological edifice stands. For if it relies heavily on moving from the known to the unknown, and the known is no longer the site of necessary knowledge, then the level of certainty – 'authentic confidence', to use the Muᶜtazilis' terminology – concerning God's acts will drop drastically. This line of reasoning explains why a similar insistence characterises Murtaḍā's discussion of ingratitude (*kufr al-niᶜma*), given its very crucial role in the justification of religious experience.

Nevertheless, Murtaḍā does not entirely dispense with evidencing in establishing the moral categories. It makes its most frequent occurrences in his discussion of the moral value of lying (*kadhib*). But even within this limited scope, evidencing does not reign supreme. Necessary knowledge gives rise to Murtaḍā's foundational assumption regarding lying, namely, that inconsequential lies, intended neither to deflect harm nor to incur benefit, are vile. The matter gets complicated in situations in which a lie may lead to good consequences. Here evidence is needed to extrapolate from the known to the unknown. If inconsequential lies are vile not because of their lack of consequences but because they are lies, then all lies must be vile.[28] Therefore, evidencing ends up being a mere instrument to protect the foundational assumption of necessary knowledge, not a way to develop new categories. This conclusion leaves no doubt about the nature of the deepest layers of Murtaḍā's moral theory: they are first and foremost based on necessary knowledge, whose function is, ultimately, to answer any objection by begging the question, leading to circular arguments. In short, if the universal concept itself requires some analysis to be judged vile, then the corresponding particular act will require more analysis to be characterised as such. This is the only role left for evidencing. If, however, the vileness of the universal concept is necessary knowledge, then the ease of judging the particular act will depend on the ease with which it can be matched with the relevant concept. Such connections may be confined to necessary knowledge or may constitute an unmediated form of acquired knowledge.

Grounding moral judgement in necessary knowledge, however, does not fully spare us the challenge of justifying such judgement; it remains at least to investigate whether our knowledge is undergirded by an ontological cause. Similar acts can be moral opposites, in the way that physical violence, for example, can range from deserved punishment to aggression, prompting a need to explain the reasons behind these opposite attributes (*ṣifāt*) of otherwise identical occurrences that belong to the same class (*jins*). The question, therefore, is what gives rise to these attributes, and this question takes us back to the ontological discussion.

The attribute of vileness must be entailed by something (*muqtaḍī*) that makes the vile act be judged differently from its good counterpart. The alternative models of causality, that is, the determinant and cause models, suggest themselves as natural candidates to explain the situation. However, the determinant model is not helpful for a number of reasons. First, it is conditional, whereas the vileness of vile acts cannot be altered by or be contingent on any other consideration. Second, it is not instantaneous and therefore does not apply in this case, because the moral judgement on the act is not temporally separate from its occurrence. And third, it is physical, which gives rise to a host of uncanny propositions, including that the determinant exists independently of the act itself or the other way around; it also involves proposing an explanation of the nature of the special connection between the act and this presumed determinant from within the array of possible relations in natural philosophy. The cause model is also problematic, although to a lesser extent. Since it is taken to be an entity (*maʿnā*) that allows an essence to be qualified by a state, the cause model's explanatory power is curtailed by the fact that the possible entities are restricted to a list that mostly includes perceived and cognitive elements, but not judgements as such. But the cause model is very helpful otherwise: it is unconditional and instantaneous, and its effect is not physical. Thus, in proposing why vile acts are such (*al-wujūh allatī lahā taqbuḥu al-qabāʾiḥ*), Murtaḍā avoids both models of causality. Instead, he relies on what he terms 'aspects' (*wujūh*) that seem to function like causes (*yajrī majrā al-ʿilla*),[29] but without the unnecessary burden of having to populate the physical world with new entities. The unconditional effects of these aspects are the desert of certain treatment by the moral agent.

But if these 'aspects' are not to be located among the furniture of the physical world, what exactly are they? Indeed, the aspects shift the focus away from the object of moral perception to its subject, adding much flexibility to Muʿtazili moral theory, while also increasing its vagueness.[30] But again, necessary knowledge – now in the guise of identity – provides the crucial justification for Murtaḍā's position. What makes each of these vile acts acquire such an attribute is its identity with the corresponding moral category. So the aspects turn out to be a list of self-identities: the aspect of vileness in injustice is its being injustice (*kawn al-ẓulm ẓulm*[an]), the aspect of vileness in lying is its being lying (*kawn al-kadhib kadhib*[an]), and so on. According to Murtaḍā, any rational being would judge an act as vile simply upon knowing it to be an instance of, say, injustice. The fact that the mere existence of injustice is enough to cause a judgement of vileness proves that it explains the act's vileness.[31] But this emphasis on the sufficiency of knowing the aspect of vileness or goodness of the act can hardly be maintained, despite Murtaḍā's apparent investment in it, as acts are rarely separated from their concrete consequences. The moment other factors come into play, such as the act's having good consequences, the judgement of vileness is no longer certain. It is against this background that Murtaḍā, in discussing God's motives for actions, states that it can only be assumed that He acts based on the intrinsic value of the act, as He cannot enjoy any benefits.[32] In addition to implicitly affirming that consequences determine moral value for humans, this statement indicates that the reason Murtaḍā argues otherwise lies in his need to bind God and humans by the same moral code to preserve his more theologically sensitive position on human agency and responsibility.

The requirement that an agent know the exact aspect of vileness is aptly met this way, but it is useful only with vile acts that are known by reason, that is, without the word of revelation (*samʿ*). In the case of those acts that cannot be judged by reason, the requirement becomes a burden. Murtaḍā's way out of this conundrum reflects the general spirit of like-minded theologians. For when it comes to vile acts that cannot be judged by reason, it is assumed that revelation prohibits them because of a hidden connection between them and rationally known aspects of vileness: reason unveils the cause of vileness while revelation merely indicates the connection to such a cause.[33]

Given the centrality of necessary knowledge in establishing this position, it is unsurprising that the main challenge to it consists of questioning the claim that rational beings necessarily know acts such as injustice to be vile. Murtaḍā's defence, beyond ad hominem arguments that cast doubt on the integrity of his adversaries, is preoccupied with defending the claims of necessary knowledge by pushing the debate to a different corner. The problem, he repeatedly states, lies not in whether people consider such acts to be vile – since they do, as he volunteers to assert – but rather in the misconception of believing an act's moral value to be contingent on the station of its agent – a claim whose correctness can only be known from evidence.[34] Similarly, he covers the remaining opposing positions by exhaustive division and elimination (*al-sabr wa-l-taqsīm*) and using the Method of Negation.[35] The precarious efficacy of evidencing is most eloquently expressed in the fact that Murtaḍā is willing to invoke it only in the context of explaining a mistaken viewpoint.

Good acts

Murtaḍā's discussion on the way of knowing the goodness of acts – whether such knowledge is necessary or acquired and how it relates to reason and revelation – is identical to that on vile acts.[36] The main difference between good and vile acts relates to the causal explanation of their respective moral values, for the problem of justifying the goodness of acts is thornier than that of justifying their vileness. We saw earlier that for Murtaḍā, aspects of vileness function unconditionally, making any proposed aspect of goodness in an act sterile once it conflicts with an aspect of vileness. Thus, the problem lies in justifying how an aspect, whose causal power is considered to resemble that of necessitating causes, can lose this power for external reasons. This paradox is what made many Muᶜtazilis reject the position adopted by the two Jubbāʾīs. Later generations seem to have taken a detour: they defined good acts by elimination, namely, as acts that have no aspect of vileness, and they stipulated, in addition, that these acts still have a moral value, that is, that they serve an end (to pre-empt the challenge of irrelevant acts).[37]

Murtaḍā treads a middle path: he proposes the existence of aspects of goodness, but he nonetheless stresses that these can effect goodness only in the absence of any aspects of vileness (*bi-sharṭ intifāʾ wujūh al-qubḥ*). This way, he retains a positive definition of goodness that does not work solely by elimination, while still dodging the challenge of conflicting aspects at work. The reason elimination is insufficient is that an aspect must have a special correlation (*yakhuṣṣuhu*) with the act in order to qualify it; the absence of aspects, being mere negation, cannot bring about any moral value since it lacks such a special correlation with the act. On the other hand, proposing absence as a condition is not problematic since it does not work against the causal connection but against its actualisation, just as it is said that a perceiving being (*mudrik*) can perceive only given the absence of obstacles (*bi-sharṭ intifāʾ al-mawāniᶜ*). Murtaḍā can thus speak of the imposition of moral obligation as an act whose conditions of goodness have been perfected and met (*takāmalat shurūṭ ḥusnihi*) and that becomes vile once any of these conditions is missing, as if what matters more is the conditions and not, as with vile acts, the aspects.[38] This approach also underlies his justification of the goodness of bringing unbelievers under moral obligation, despite God's foreknowledge of their failure to meet its requirements: Murtaḍā establishes the goodness of imposing moral obligation and then proceeds to eliminate the possible aspects of vileness in this act.[39] But this is not to say that such justification need be grand: the slightest purpose (*adnā gharaḍ*) suffices; it can be as simple as entertaining one's friends.[40] This position speaks to a significant jurisprudential discussion on whether it is possible for God to delay the clarification of His commands until individuals actually need to apply them. Contrary to ᶜAbd al-Jabbār, Murtaḍā accepts this possibility, arguing that in addition to the absence of aspects of vileness in such a case, there exists an aspect of goodness: individuals are able to resolve to obey orders once they are clarified. This ability provides the aspect of goodness needed to meet the requirement of the act's serving an end, as opposed to it being a purposeless, and thus vile, act.[41]

The act of punishment exacted by God posed a peculiar challenge to moral classification, at least for those who upheld the position that reason does not rule it vile of God to pardon transgressors, whether sinners or unbelievers. If divine punishment is neither obligatory nor recommended nor vile, the only option left is that it is plain-good, a category of licit acts whose doing and forgoing are morally identical. However, God deserves praise for forgoing punishment. Based on the connotations of the term 'licit', it may be argued that licitness cannot apply to God; for an act becomes licit once the agent is informed of its permissibility.[42] Thus punishment goes under the category of plain-good in terms of meaning (*lahu maᶜnā al-mubāḥ*), but without application of the term since it does not apply to God.[43] This mitigates the terminological difficulty, already noted by ᶜAbd al-Jabbār,[44] but leaves the act of divine punishment itself immune to conceptual classification within the scheme. A classical solution adopted by the Basran Muᶜtazilis was pragmatic: since pardoning will not take place, such a counterfactual scenario is not one of concern, and God's act of punishment may still be subsumed under plain-good acts.[45] In addition to its effective evasion of the problem, this answer served only those who deemed pardoning counterfactual. Those who believed in the possibility of pardon, like Murtaḍā, had to carve out another solution. Just like the Muᶜtazili solution did little more than explain away the conceptual difficulty, his answer is rather pre-emptive. He escapes the problem by providing a definition of plain-good acts that is less restrictive in the first place, since divine pardon will still meet the conditions of plain-good acts without being burdened by some of the undesirable consequences of this designation. It should be recalled that Murtaḍā was silent on the desert of blame and praise for someone who forgoes a plain-good act, clearly pointing out the problems arising from discussing such a person's status. A creditor who accepts a debtor's repayment is doing a plain-good act; however, if he forgives him, he is praiseworthy. So symmetry is not a condition in plain-good acts. A turn of the argument would have taken the discussion in a different direction. If pardoning were considered an act and punishment its forgoing, then pardoning would have been easily classified as a recommended act in the sense that performing it is praiseworthy and forgoing it neutral. The problem, however, arises in the larger scheme of desert, since punishment is the normal counterpart of blame, which itself is deserved by vile acts. Pardon cannot be justified as a more advanced consequence of another act because the only conceivable counterpart of blame here would be repentance, but repentance – regardless of the contentious issue of its necessitating power and the fact that it is to be performed by the agent himself and not by others – can only be a resultant of prior vile acts, thus reintroducing the same loop. Therefore, even though forgoing it earns the agent praise, the act of pardoning still falls under the category of plain-good.[46] The theologian in Murtaḍā overrides the jurist, for his grappling with the definition of licit is inconsequential in jurisprudence. This is probably the reason the more juristically inclined Ṭūsī still defines a plain-good act as one whose doing and forgoing are neither praise- nor blameworthy.[47]

Will: moral aspects

Will, being an independent act,[48] is subject to the same logic in that it is judged as good or vile. Nonetheless, its relationship to the act that follows it and to the thing willed (*murād*) merits a more nuanced analysis of its moral value. Just as aspects of vileness are unconditional once they are found in an act, they can be equally efficient in affecting the will to do the act: willing a vile act is vile will. The analysis of aspects of goodness in acts and their conditional effect can also be extrapolated to good will: if the willed act is good, then the will itself is good as long as it is clear of any aspect of vileness. One reason for this condition is the gap separating the conceptual world of will from the physical world of action. For example, willing a good act from someone who cannot do it is an instance of the vile obligation to do the impossible.[49]

The above concerns the static context, in which the will and the willed act are not interacting but rather are locked in a relationship that allows a fixed judgement on the moral value of each. The more complex discussion, however, has to do with the dynamic context, that is, situations in which the will affects (*tuʾaththiru fī*) the moral value of the willed act. The hallmark of this category of acts is that they are defined by the will, as opposed to acts that are immune to its effect. An example of the former is paying one's debt: what the creditor receives depends on the debtor's will; it may be the payment of a debt as well as a gift or a bribe. An example of the latter is returning a deposit regardless of one's will in returning it: the act can only be a returning of a deposit by virtue of its mere occurrence, which depends only on the earlier act of placing a deposit.[50]

As a reminder of the centrality of the theory of states in his worldview, beyond theology proper, Murtaḍā notes that despite the reference to the will in this whole discussion, what really (*ᶜalā al-taḥqīq*) affects an act's value is not the agent's will but his being willing (*kawnuhu murīd*[an]). This state affects the act's moral value indirectly: it has no bearing on the act's origination but rather on the aspects that may or may not characterise it upon its occurrence. These aspects, in turn, are what cause its moral value. Thus, a statement is a report only when the reporter wills it to be one as opposed to another form of speech. The moral value of the statement is due to the aspect of goodness (truthfulness) or vileness (falsehood) that characterises the report.[51] However, the effect of the will on the moral value of the act is not a one-way street: just as willing that which is vile is vile, a vile will makes the following act vile, too. Therefore, if someone gives charity to earn good reputation, his vile will deprives his charity of its aspect of goodness and makes it a vile act of pretense (*riyāʾ*), so the agent ends up with two vile acts.[52] It follows that if he refrains from giving charity for reasons other than moral ones, he is accountable only for his vile will.

Desert

The problem of desert and its functioning in the Muᶜtazili moral system has been studied in light of the relation between necessitating causes (*ᶜilal*) and deserved treatments. Muᶜtazilis, despite their insistence on developing a nomological model, did not allow necessary causation to be part of the theory. This inconsistency has been explained in terms of the threat that causality would pose to the doctrine of mutual cancellation (*taḥābuṭ*): the proposition that deserved treatments are necessary effects of these causes cannot be reconciled with the belief that such treatments do not materialise immediately – let alone that they may be cancelled by the agent's later acts. The Muᶜtazili solution to this dilemma is a complex matrix of causality: aspects of the act's moral value necessarily give rise to desert, thus satisfying the nomological demands of the system; desert, however, brings about deserved treatments only conditionally. In other words, such treatments are contingent upon the agent's subsequent behaviour.[53] Thus, the problem is centred on the relation between desert and deserved treatments.

But even if this explanation of the Muᶜtazili discomfort with necessary causation is granted, it still falls short of explaining why someone who rejects mutual cancellation (like Murtaḍā) would not endorse necessary causation. In fact, his system makes no exceptions when it comes to the necessitating power of desert: once a treatment – be it reward or punishment – has been deserved, there is no rational cause that could waive its delivery, regardless of the religious status of the agent. Exceptions are made only in the case of punishment, whose desert and waiver alike are established by word of revelation; they lack any necessitating power, and the latter is understood as mere initiated benevolence. Were it not for revelation, unbelievers would deserve both reward for their good acts and punishment for their vile ones, unbelief included.[54] Thus, there is no real necessary causation (*ᶜilal ḥaqīqiyya*) in Murtaḍā's system.

The system's incompatibility with necessary causation lies elsewhere. The problem appears in a different light when we take Murtaḍā's definition of real necessary causes into account. For him, a cause is an essence that causes another essence to be in a state, so aspects of moral value fail to meet the definition on both grounds: they are neither essences nor do they cause states in other essences. Their only effect is a characterisation (*ḥukm*) of the act. The distinction is shown perfectly in Murtaḍā's own words: 'Whenever we say about something that neither is an essence nor necessitates a state but rather entails a characterisation that it is a cause, we do so by way of alerting' (*wa-idhā qulnā fī-mā laysa bi-dhāt annahu ᶜilla aw [fī-mā] lā yūjibu ḥāl*^{an} *wa-innamā yaqtaḍī ḥukm*^{an} *fa-ᶜalā ṭarīq al-tanbīh*).[55] This definition may have been formulated to pre-empt theological challenges, working with the assumption that ontology (and epistemology) was subservient to theology. However, a proper theological explanation, independent from the belief in mutual cancellation, is also possible. If moral obligation is the *raison d'être* of the system, then its preservation is an indispensable need; this, however, necessitates that reward and moral obligation be separated by a veritable time gap. If no such gap exists, both moral obligation and reward lose their meaning. On the one hand, reward, being pure pleasure, cannot be mixed with moral obligation, which is always accompanied by effort and hardship.[56] On the other hand, moral obligation in the absence of such effort would cease to be carried out by voluntary choice; it would become an instance of compulsion, since the individual would reap the pleasant fruits of his acts as he is doing them, and his irresistible motive for obedience would no longer be the goodness of the ordained acts. As a result, he would be deprived of the desert of reward, which was the reason he was brought under moral obligation in the first place.[57] Taken to its logical conclusion, therefore, real necessary causation between desert and deserved treatments would annul moral obligation. Even though reasons that relate to the doctrine of mutual cancellation can help to explain the Muᶜtazili reluctance to accept the workings of necessary causation within their scheme of desert, it is the graver threat that this causal model poses at a more fundamental level that explains its rejection by theologians who were not preoccupied with this doctrine.

God as moral agent

Divine assistance and corruption

The significance of belief in divine assistance was noted by theologians who pointed out the internal complications that arise from this position in the form of inconsistencies as well as the theological problems that it causes in connection with God's absolute freedom of action.[58] For the Muᶜtazilis, divine assistance is a form of divine intervention that prepares the optimal physical and psychological conditions for individuals to meet their moral obligations. As such, it must not be confused with the more obvious requirement of divine justice, that is, that individuals be enabled (*tamkīn*) to meet their obligations.[59] The absence of divine assistance would not make an individual unable to fulfil his obligations, even if it would weaken his motives and eventually cause him to decide unwisely. The twin concept of divine assistance is corruption (*mafsada, istifsād*), that is, the existence of optimal conditions for the individual to violate his moral obligations.[60]

Theologians who believed in the obligatoriness of divine assistance struggled with providing a clear explanation of its function in religious experience, beyond the abstract concepts. The precise nature of divine assistance is visible in the context of moral theory that classifies acts into ones whose moral value is known by reason and ones whose value is known by revelation. Only the former are essentially good or vile acts, constituting the dictates of rational moral obligation (*al-taklīf al-ᶜaqlī*); the remaining acts, even if obligatory, are seen as means to increase one's chances of obeying the rationally based dictates. Therefore, ritual obligations such as prayers and fasting, whose moral value is decided merely by word of revelation, are good inasmuch as they serve this purpose. Divine assistance, therefore, consists of strengthening the individual's incentives to fulfil his moral obligations in every conceivable manner, within the limits of freedom of choice. In addition, the Muᶜtazilis view divine assistance in light of the position that the power to act must precede the action itself, a position premised on both natural philosophy and the belief in human responsibility. As such, it comes as no surprise that Murtaḍā argues that divine assistance must precede the act towards which it is supposed to motivate the agent,[61] and that it must be compatible (*munāsib*) with the act in order to take effect. Given the ambiguity of this requirement, it is not imperative that the exact nature of the compatibility be known; similarly, an ill person takes medications and observes a diet that help him overcome his pain and illness without requiring him to know the exact dynamic at work.[62] Therefore, most of the examples of this compatibility are expressions of the need for a receptive psychological state, as in the affirmation that the individual, upon frequently performing ritual obligations, becomes more aware of the divine presence, which in turn facilitates the observance of rational obligations, since both are acts of obedience to God.[63]

Such are the general contours of the concept. Nevertheless, disagreements were vehement even among those who accepted the necessity of divine assistance. Most salient is the debate about its locus, usually termed the question of best interest. In agreement with ᶜAbd al-Jabbār, Murtaḍā points out the terminological aspect of the debate: that it largely – though not solely – depends on the meaning of the terms *ṣalāḥ* and *wājib*.[64] The central point of contention is whether God's assistance is meant to provide individuals with optimal conditions only for attaining the best possible treatment in the hereafter, or whether His assistance must also cater to their worldly best interest.[65] Views on this question have been proverbially divided between the Baghdadi and Basran schools of Muᶜtazilism: the former are said to have believed that God is required to look also after people's best worldly interest, while the latter restricted the goal of divine assistance to the otherworldly realm.[66]

The limits set by these theologians on God's assistance reflect the extent of His commitment to human affairs within their respective systems. But if the cornerstone of human religious experience is the concept of moral obligation, and the telos of moral obligation the attainment of eternal reward, one can see why the view ascribed to the Basrans became the more prominent position. Murtaḍā repeatedly defends this understanding of God's assistance, pointing, in addition to this theoretical consideration, to the practical advantages that must have also helped its spread. He notes that the evidencing from the known to the unknown is usually based on experiencing this world, and this experience does not support the assumption that God is doing His best to maximise every individual's worldly lot, for it is always possible for the fortunate to ask for more and for the wretched to plead for less. The assumption would thus compromise either God's benevolence or His omnipotence.[67] In such contexts, the advantage of emphasising the exclusively otherworldly purpose of God's assistance is evident, for in this world only a limited number of obligations can be ordained because of physical constraints, whereas such constraints do not affect moral obligations that have to do with mental acts (*afʿāl al-qulūb*).[68] As for the shortcomings of this world (the greatest challenge to the Baghdadi view), they can be rectified in the hereafter by various forms of reward and compensation. This debate provided an opportunity for the perennial practice of showing the grave consequences of any theological disagreement: Jubbāʾī ruled that the Baghdadi position is not unbelief in itself, but it leads to unbelief in many ways.[69] But although this discussion bred internal disagreement in some Muʿtazili circles, it proved of much utility for Murtaḍā's theology in light of his Imami convictions. For Murtaḍā, God's concern for people functions as a justification for the existence of a divinely designated Imam whose authority is the concrete representation of divine assistance within the Muslim community since it provides the optimal conditions for the community's members to meet their moral obligations.[70]

Another pertinent debate concerns the justification of God's assistance. Although both our proverbial groups believed that it is incumbent upon God to provide assistance, the Baghdadi view was that this is a consequence of God's generosity (*jūd*), whereas the Basrans saw it as a consequence of His justice. To a great extent, the debate is a matter of emphasis, in addition to depending on the definitions used for key terms, as noted earlier. Both groups differentiate between enablement and assistance: even if divine assistance were withheld, the individual would still be able to observe his obligations. This is why the Baghdadis did not consider the provision of assistance an act of divine justice. The Basrans looked at the situation from a different angle, more mindful of the evidencing from the known to the unknown. In Murtaḍā's analogy, it would be vile of someone who has invited people to dinner to refrain from smiling to them if he knew that they would eat his food only once he had done the effortless act of smiling; in fact, it would be as vile as preventing them from reaching the banquet by locking them out. In God's omnipotence, all acts are effortless, and it would thus be vile of Him not to provide the necessary motives for His servants to access His rewards. Therefore, the provision of divine assistance is obligatory and cannot, by definition, be an act of generosity; rather, it is an act of justice.[71]

The importance of divine assistance in Murtaḍā's theology shows in the fact that its only limit is the freedom of the individual to make his own moral choices. Divine assistance is a requirement on God and a right of the individual, who continues to enjoy it as long as it does not reach a level that renders him a mere instrument of divine will. Short of this extreme, divine assistance overrides even the jewel in the crown of Muʿtazili theology, that is, moral obligation itself. Thus, if the divine assistance meant for one individual may involve the creation of a context that would corrupt another individual and would therefore be detrimental to the latter's otherworldly interest, the solution that Murtaḍā expects God to use is not to withhold divine assistance from the first individual but to annul his moral obligation altogether.[72] Similarly, if the divine assistance of one individual depends on another individual's actions, God can impose moral obligation on the first individual only if the second carries out the desired actions; otherwise, the moral obligation of the first individual is void.[73] Another case is that of an individual who has a chance of meeting his moral obligations without the aid of divine assistance by enduring hardship and consequently attaining higher rewards. Despite the temptation to sanction the higher risk strategy, Murtaḍā argues that it is incumbent on God to provide this individual with divine assistance, even if it leads to less reward due to the absence of hardship.[74] The implicit reasoning is obvious: divine assistance is a right that cannot be sacrificed for an unnecessary increase in reward; such an exchange would be an act of injustice. On the other hand, in the case of an obligation that can be met in either of two ways, God is not required to prescribe the easier way as long as He has provided the necessary divine assistance; the individual carrying out the obligation will be compensated for any unnecessary hardship in the hereafter.[75] The most striking example appears in the context of his discussion of the limits of moral obligation on sinners. In rejecting the possibility of God's sending a prophet who would not communicate the divine message, Murtaḍā argues that such a scenario is impossible because it would obstruct the delivery of divine assistance to its putative recipients.[76] It seems that the infallibility of the prophet, as necessary as it is in Murtaḍā's theology, is subservient to the delivery of divine assistance; it is stipulated primarily to ensure that the prophet infallibly fulfils his function of providing his subjects with their respective lots of divine assistance.

So much for divine assistance. But what about the function of corruption? Murtaḍā's main discussion of this topic concerns the misguidance that takes place in this world due to the work of the Devil and through impostors, since such misguidance can be depicted as acts of God intended to lead people astray before punishing them in the hereafter. Murtaḍā's scheme has to handle a double problem here: on the one hand, he needs to dissociate God from this misguidance; on the other, his theory of divine assistance necessitates that God actually prevent it in cases in which people would err only on its account. These assumptions undergird his denial that the oracles (*kuhhān*) of pre-Islamic times foretold the future, since such predictions would have been an instance of corruption that God would have prevented.[77] Murtaḍā argues that no corruption is involved when the Devil leads people to sin, since the Devil's enticement is either a temptation intended to provide reward when resisted, or inconsequential because everyone who acquiesces would have sinned anyway.[78] Even the acts of impostors, usually the example par excellence of causing people to stray from the right path, can be explained away by blaming those who fail to investigate properly in order to distinguish miracles from sorcery, as in the story of the Samaritan and the golden calf.[79] The interplay of the moral forces of divine assistance and corruption is eloquently expressed in the case in which one person's assistance would constitute another's corruption; as noted in this situation, Murtaḍā asserts, it would be vile to impose moral obligation on either of them, since it would inevitably cause one of the two to fall short in his duty.[80] In short, the discourse on divine assistance is a powerful expression of Murtaḍā's commitment to the Basran Muᶜtazili moral theory of divine justice. The insistence on presenting divine assistance as a right of the individual and not as an instance of divine generosity betrays the Basran Muᶜtazili attitude that placed less stress than did the Baghdadi one on humans' dependence on divine initiative for their salvation.

Pain

Of the many objections against the evidence of God's existence, it is the presence of evil that enjoyed most acceptance as a moral argument challenging God's omnipotence and/or benevolence. Theodicy, the branch of theology aiming to vindicate divine goodness, gains greater significance against the background of a rationally defined morality that does not allow the mere possibility of capricious behaviour on God's part. Within the context of early Islamic theology, a recurrent locus of this issue is the discussions of pain (*alam*) and suffering, broadly perceived as a form of harm (*ḍarar*, *ḍarr*) affecting all of God's sentient creatures and ranging from the concrete effect of physical violence to all forms of psychological distress.[81] In Murtaḍā's theology, divine assistance is instrumental in addressing the problem of the moral value of pain in a manner that serves the purposes of theodicy. This, however, is not to say that he invokes divine assistance as the blanket response to this challenge. In fact, he keeps it as the last recourse to handle instances of pain that cannot be justified based on the dictates of moral theory within the limits of reason – specifically, pain that is an act of God. Pain that humans inflict on each other does not pose a theological problem when it can be blamed on its accountable agents. But since the evidencing from the known to the unknown is the guiding principle in Murtaḍā's moral theory, he expends considerable effort to circumscribe the realm of vile pain in human interactions in order to bring it to a minimum whose divine counterpart is then the only category of pain that needs justification. Accordingly, Murtaḍā expands the category of just pain to include all pain that is deserved, done by way of self-defence (*ᶜalā sabīl al-mudāfaᶜa*) or outweighed by consequences such as the incurrence of great benefit or avoidance of even graver harm.[82] In agreement with ᶜAbd al-Jabbār,[83] Murtaḍā displays an evidently consequentialist tone: undeserved pain is considered harm only in view of its eventual consequences, even if these are based on mere conjecture, and good consequences can disqualify pain from being a form of harm.[84] The consequentialist approach justifies many instances of undeserved pain in human transactions, allowing the agent much freedom to inflict pain on himself or others for the sake of favourable consequences, especially when his actions affect minors under his custody. The main condition restricting the infliction of pain in these cases is the lack of means to achieve the desired consequence in a painless manner.[85]

This discussion provides a moral context for pain in the known realm of this world, whereas evidencing to the unknown leads us to pain inflicted by God. Given His omniscience, God does not inflict pain based on conjecture; given His omnipotence, He does not inflict pain to deflect greater harm.[86] This same reasoning does not smoothly apply when dealing with God's justice, since not all the pain He inflicts is deserved. Traditionally, the pain suffered by children provided an obvious basis for many Muslim theologians to argue that God's acts can lead to undeserved pain;[87] alternatively, some groups, such as the Bakriyya, went as far as claiming that children do not feel pain.[88] Murtaḍā, for his part, invokes divine assistance. It is easy to argue that pain is inflicted only for desert in the hereafter or on deserving individuals in this world.[89] But the conspicuous presence of pain affecting many undeserving parties – oftentimes ones who are not even subject to moral obligation – calls for a different explanation. Even the most elaborate works of Muᶜtazili theology seem not to offer much clarification beyond the general reassurance that there must be divine assistance latent in these instances of pain.[90] The ubiquitous theological recourse to the mysterious ways of the Lord finds expression in Murtaḍā's argument that God acts for a certain consideration (*iᶜtibār*). But given the relevant conditions governing the goodness of inflicting pain, this consideration cannot be anything but the best interest of humans in the hereafter, attested in Murtaḍā's usage of the term 'interest' (*maṣlaḥa*) in the proverbial context for discussing theodicy, that is, the story of Job.[91] This interpretation is further supported by Murtaḍā's suggestion that the divine consideration in such cases may also be a divine trial (*imtiḥān*).[92] The circle of justice, nevertheless, cannot be perfected unless the victim is compensated for the undeserved pain. Thus, while God's hidden consideration pre-empts the vileness of purposelessness, the promise of otherworldly compensation neutralises the vileness of injustice. The otherworldly nature of this consideration is what makes it qualify as an instance of divine assistance.[93]

A few awkward consequences follow from Murtaḍā's insistence that undeserved pain inflicted by God must be taken exclusively as a form of assistance in otherworldly matters.[94] A classic case is when God inflicts pain on Zayd to protect him from an injustice that ᶜAmr would certainly have done unless Zayd were in pain. Initially, this scenario was proposed to counter the original claim that God does not inflict harm to deflect graver harm. But in light of the reasoning outlined above, Murtaḍā argues that the deflection of harm is not the reason God inflicts pain on Zayd. Rather, the pain inflicted on Zayd is an instance of divine assistance for ᶜAmr, as it spares the latter of the vile act he is about to commit. As befitting divine assistance, it does not affect his power to commit the vile act but only his motive to do so.[95] According to this logic, then, the slightest otherworldly harm is worth deflecting from the person bent on incurring it, even if the deflection requires inflicting immense worldly pain on his presumed victim or any other creature, as long as it makes the person disinclined, or less inclined, to commit the vile act. Compensation in the hereafter will take care of the resulting worldly inconveniences to others.[96] Another consequence, more related to divine omnipotence, results from the assumption that God is required to provide divine assistance to humanity. Thus, in this situation God could not have provided His assistance except by inflicting pain on an undeserving individual and relying on the infinite otherworldly assets to correct this wrong; He had no other option to meet His moral requirement. This restrictive view of divine omnipotence is still more accommodating than that of the Baghdadi Muᶜtazilis, espoused by Mufīd, who went as far as to argue that it is unbecoming of God's generosity to inflict pain – even on animals – for purposes that He could have attained without it.[97]

Consequences as deserved treatments

Despite the elaborate hierarchy of deserved treatments, they serve a single purpose: they are the currency by which Murtaḍā tries to maintain a form of equilibrium in his moral universe. In the following discussion, categories of treatment are discussed inasmuch as they are effective currencies; thus, compensation and thanksgiving are studied separately, whereas praise is grouped with blame and reward with punishment.

Compensation

Although Murtaḍā uses divine assistance to justify the existence of undeserved pain, it does not suffice to vindicate the world of its negative mark. In a sense, the moral equilibrium of the world cannot be restored as long as the outcome is unjustly detrimental to some agents. This lack of equilibrium is pervasive: its scope extends beyond the pale of believers to include unbelievers, children, animals and insane individuals. In short, every sentient being able to feel pain can be party to this disequilibrium, unless the situation is corrected by addressing grievances. It is here that compensation proves most effective. As a category of deserved treatments, its sole function is to address grievances without having to commit to other problematic theological consequences, especially when dealing with subjects that are not to be rewarded in the hereafter. Thus, the definition of compensation: benefit that is both deserved and free of reverence. It differs from initiated benevolence by being deserved and from reward by being free of reverence.[98] The assumption, therefore, is that the world needs to be kept at a deeper equilibrium than that established by moral obligation. Even within the domain of morally obligated agents, punishment or reward is an act of God that is independent of the consequences – even unintended ones – of actions that might leave others in pain. Compensation is a more basic category; its purpose is to establish fairness in various transactions before agents are presented with their other deserved treatments, if any. The world is thus far from being the most perfect world, and in fact some of its imperfections must wait till the day of judgement to be fixed.

The master moral agent is God, responsible for correcting situations in which His provision of divine assistance causes undeserved pain. The most common such cases derive from His status as the source of divine assistance in the form of revelational moral obligation.[99] For example, killing harmless animals is vile, but God has allowed people to use certain animals for various purposes. This divine licence causes pain to animals, and it is God's responsibility to compensate them for it; humans are left with the responsibility for compensating animals they abuse against the word of revelation.[100] But when it comes to slavery, Murtaḍā is more careful: he refrains from explicitly designating it as a vile act. He proceeds, however, to argue that God must compensate slaves for their hardship because revelation, not reason, is what makes slavery lawful.[101] This care shows that his awareness of the problem goes beyond the merely legal aspect and is deeply grounded in the moral dimension inspired by theology.

But even when all such cases are corrected, the world is still full of harms: humans wronging each other, children dying of negligence, animals devouring other animals, and so on. The moral equilibrium of the world thus needs much more calibration. In addition to providing compensation for His own acts, God is presented in Murtaḍā's work as the 'master bookkeeper'[102] whose function is to check what agents owe each other and then establish fairness by transferring credit from the wrongdoers to the victims. But different agents have different accounts: believers have credit in their reward and compensation accounts; the remaining sentient beings have credit only in their compensation account. To make transfers meaningful and still allow non-rational agents to be party to them, rewards and punishments are excluded from their scope, in contrast to compensation accounts, which are replenished merely by the agent's endurance of undeserved pain and are thus shared by all agents.[103]

The unsavoury consequences of sticking to this approach go well beyond the development of an almost impossibly convoluted theological corpus to justify the world's endless train of pains and accidents. Two examples suffice to illustrate the conceptual drawbacks involved and the unlikely strategies that they force theologians to resort to. The first is Murtaḍā's admission that he and likeminded theologians were mocked for asserting that animals might be required to provide compensation to each other or to humans. Despite this being a relatively secondary issue, it is one of the rare instances on which Murtaḍā invokes the authority of Prophetic traditions to support a theological viewpoint, which shows his unmistakably defensive position.[104] This view was not new, since early Qadarī theologians had adopted a similar position.[105] Murtaḍā's investment in elaborating his theological system led him further afield than Mufīd; for despite the latter's more frequent resort to traditions, he is silent on whether animals owe anyone anything, merely stating that God will provide compensation for animals out of His generosity, not His justice.[106] The other example is a more recurrent one. It concerns the case of a tyrant whose compensation account cannot possibly cover all the harms he has caused. This particular question perplexed generations of Muᶜtazili theologians, probably more inspired by the behaviour of contemporary politicians than by the pure theological dilemma, in a manner similar to the developments in Islamic law concerning the role of doubt, which was expanded substantially by jurists to check the criminal excesses of political authorities in applying capital punishment.[107] As Murtaḍā is quick to note, it is untenable to hold that the tyrant's account will eventually be filled by God to secure sufficient credit for subsequent transfer to his victims. Nor is it acceptable to assume that God will allow him to carry out his vile acts because He knows that the tyrant will live long enough to secure sufficient credit. In both cases, the tyrant would be governing God's actions, necessitating that He give him either extra credit or a fixed lifespan. This is one of the few instances in which Murtaḍā disagrees with ᶜAbd al-Jabbār, although his proposed solution seems to save theological appearances at the expense of the world of political experience. In his attempt to protect God's omnipotence from the inconveniences of past solutions to the dilemma, Murtaḍā proposes that God permits the tyrant to do injustice only when he has already accumulated enough credit to make up for it. Thus, a tyrant will have undergone or will be undergoing great pains, regardless of their origin, while wronging others. Given the gravity of his crimes, it can only be God who is inflicting such pain on him; in return, He is obligated to compensate him, and this compensation will later be given to his victims.[108] This argument pays little respect to the evidencing from the known to the unknown, given the glaring lack of distress in most tyrants. More significantly for theological considerations, it contains the implicit assumption that the alleged distress is undeserved – hence God's obligation to compensate the tyrant for it. The need to defend God's justice, it must be recalled, was the main driver for the whole discourse on morality in Muᶜtazili circles; but pushed to its logical end, it leads to situations in which God's treatment of individual humans is tailored to fit the theological discourse on justice and provides no grounds for objecting to political injustice.

The rigid stance on the need to restore the world's moral equilibrium extends to the respective agents' rights to waive compensation and to the duration of the compensation. Because the hereafter is the abode of pure accountability in which God takes care of the records, agents are not entitled to waive their rights; they are rather like minor orphans who own money but are not authorised to use it except with the permission of their custodian.[109] As for the duration, it must be transient (*munqaṭiᶜ*), since unbelievers are also entitled to compensation. Their compensation, then, must be provided in this world; otherwise, they must receive whatever compensation is left in the hereafter before being punished.[110] The Basran insistence on justice also leads Murtaḍā to disagree with Mufīd, who, laying more emphasis on the unbelievers' total loss of standing before God, argues that God is not required to provide compensation to them: the pain they suffer is part of the punishment they deserve.[111] Furthermore, the moral equilibrium of the world decides who will be resurrected in the hereafter. Unbelievers, animals and children who have not been fully compensated will be brought back to life in the hereafter. The sole purpose of this resurrection is to restore their rights through delivering compensation, after which they may be returned to dust except if they are awaiting other deserved treatments, as in the case of unbelievers waiting for their punishment afterwards.[112]

For Murtaḍā, a major point of divergence from the positions of ᶜAbd al-Jabbār concerns the question of compensation for hypothetical harm. The latter endorses Abū Hāshim's position to the effect that compensation is due for causing the loss of hypothetical benefits. The classic example is usurped property: upholders of this position believe that the owner of such property must be compensated not only for the value of his property but also for the revenues that it would have generated since it was usurped.[113] A more otherworldly example is compensation due to the murdered from the murderer, regarding which ᶜAbd al-Jabbār and Abū Hāshim argued for the need to compensate the victim for the benefits that he would have enjoyed had he been left to live.[114] Murtaḍā's position categorically denies the legitimacy of compensation for such hypothetical losses, for the infinite possibilities of the world prevent any reliable prediction of hypothetical developments. In addition, such hypothetical considerations might be used to argue that the victim would have suffered the loss anyway, which would absolve the perpetrator of actual – let alone hypothetical – harm.[115]

These limits of compensation as a moral parameter are drawn by Murtaḍā's uncompromising attitude on the inevitability and duration of compensation and his unconditional refusal to countenance compensation for hypothetical losses. His position is dictated by a minimalist stance: compensation, as a category, seems to have been invented in the first place to avoid the many problematic situations that arise from uncorrected injustices that cannot be addressed by the more charged categories of reward and punishment. Once these injustices are corrected, Murtaḍā is unwilling to go a single step further to elaborate the workings of compensation in his moral universe. His admission of compensation in the hereafter is prompted by the impossibility of meeting all its demands in this world: animals cannot take care of their accounts; some human harms can be properly assessed only by God; for others it may be beyond the agent's capacity to appease the victim in a just manner; and oftentimes the victim dies, ruling out the possibility of worldly compensation. Even the sacred law, intended to preserve the dictates of rational moral obligation in Murtaḍā's view, cannot help in certain cases. For example, since compensation must be provided to the victim, blood money, payable to the victim's next of kin, is not considered compensation. Rather, it is rather a mere act of obedience to the law (*taᶜabbud*), with compensation being deferred to the hereafter.[116]

Praise and blame

Necessary knowledge, repeatedly invoked as a means of developing moral judgements on various acts, also underlies the scheme of deserved treatments that will be meted out to moral agents. Thus, praise and blame, together with the more consequential reward and punishment, can be deserved only when the agent is motivated by his knowledge of the aspects of goodness and vileness in acts and chooses to act accordingly.[117] Vile acts that are caused by the agent's negligence are not excusable, as they also reflect his failure to heed the obligation to learn about these aspects.[118]

Praise and blame are two social categories par excellence, in the sense that they are predicated on the judgement of rational beings concerning the desert of the agents. Although the theologians of Murtaḍā's time, regardless of their sectarian affiliations, discuss these rational beings as if they constitute an abstract category of individuals, it is in fact the conventions of the theologians' social context that dictate the boundaries of these rational beings' judgements. Aside from polemics, much of the disagreement among theologians concerns divergent evaluations of what the imaginary group of rational beings would say about a given situation. Going back to praise and blame, the assumption is that these rational beings would agree that the agent deserves praise or blame. Therefore, the 'right' to praise or blame is a public one; each member of the imaginary group is equally entitled to practise it.[119] The publicity, in turn, comes at a price: the theologians concur that both praise and blame are immaterial (*lā yuḥfalu bi-mithlihi*),[120] in the sense that neither suffices as a motive for action. The hierarchy of deserved treatments is well captured in a passing comment by Murtaḍā. In analysing why a blameworthy person should fear the consequences of his acts, he says that the desert of blame indicates the desert of punishment and vice versa (*aḥad al-istiḥqāqayn amāra li-l-istiḥqāq al-ākhar*).[121] Naturally, a person undergoing unbearable punishment is unlikely to be concerned about whether he is also worthy of blame; it is the blameworthy agent who should be worried about whether the blame, which he knows is deserved, indicates more dire consequences lying in store for him.

Reward and punishment

The more critical discussion concerns the deserts of reward and punishment, for the eventual outcome of religious experience in the theologians' view consists of being destined to paradise or to hell, beyond sectarian affiliations or particular interpretations of what constitutes these destinations. Moreover, already early on belief in 'the promise and the threat' (*al-waʿd wa-l-waʿīd*) became a Muʿtazili doctrine that was subsequently elaborated by generations of theologians. The promise and the threat were, of course, not conceived as matters of verbal articulation and social position, but rather as divine expressions of what lies in the hereafter for moral agents. In fact, Murtaḍā's definitions of reward and punishment – in agreement with many Muʿtazili positions – are tailored to avoid overlap with their worldly counterparts, that is, praise and blame. Thus, in addition to the conditions for deserving praise and blame, an agent deserves reward only if he has to endure hardship to meet his moral obligations, and he deserves punishment only if his failure to meet his obligations also causes him to lose benefits.[122] A straightforward implication is that God's self-sufficiency makes both definitions inapplicable to Him. But less expected results also emerge from these tailored definitions. In the *ḥadīth* corpus, reward is promised for acts that do not meet the requirement of involving hardship or unpleasant experiences. Most theologians usually gave little attention to such instances, as the authority of traditions never weighed heavily in their considerations. But Murtaḍā's writings provide a bizarre case in which he decides to address a tradition that promises rewards for a Muslim who has sex with his wife. Without much explanation of why this tradition should deserve to be treated independently instead of being dismissed like countless others, Murtaḍā proceeds to argue that the reward here is not promised for the pleasure of intercourse but for the hardship of restricting oneself to lawful sexual activity.[123]

Nevertheless, the difference between these categories of deserved treatments goes well beyond definitions. Even if every rational being is entitled to express praise or blame, the same cannot be the case with reward and punishment. On the practical level, it is not feasible to allow everyone to dispense rewards and punishments.[124] Otherworldly considerations also weigh heavily against this possibility. Worldly transactions are premised on agents' responding to each other in a manner that brings about deserved treatments based on the moral value of the acts that shape these transactions, such as compensating for harms or providing benefits. In none of these contexts do humans, let alone irrational agents, define the moral value of the acts in question. For the many obligations introduced by God, it is His prerogative to mete out the deserved treatments to their agents.[125] However, this means different things in the cases of reward and punishment. Murtaḍā's position here concurs with the Basran Muᶜtazili position that once the individual's desert of reward is established, it is to be seen as a right of his that cannot be waived.[126] God's prerogative is, therefore, to provide reward but not to waive it, for the latter would be unjust. The question of punishment, however, is much more complex.

Most of the time, the debate about 'the promise and the threat' lacked symmetry; it tended to be centred on the threat, as the promise was much less controversial. This is hardly surprising, for the original debate concerned the status of grave sinners, not devout believers. Even within the ranks of the theologians who shared the Muᶜtazili view on the rational basis of morality, the issue of punishment was a key bone of contention. This issue relates to many problematic questions about, inter alia, the exact way to establish the agent's desert of punishment, the expectations about its eventual delivery and the moral value of pardoning deserving agents. The Muᶜtazili formulation of the position, at least in the case of ᶜAbd al-Jabbār and his circle, emphasises that reason can establish the agent's desert of both reward and punishment. In fact, the two are inseparable: it cannot be rationally established that an agent deserves reward for good deeds unless it is assumed that he deserves punishment for behaving otherwise. If no punishment is threatened, an agent who decides not to pursue the promised hefty reward can at best be blamed by rational beings, but he does not deserve punishment by God.[127] Ultimately, the controversy is not about the desert of punishment but about its inevitability, that is, the possibility of divine pardon. Consequently, it should not be problematic for someone who allows this possibility to accept nonetheless that the desert of punishment is established by reason, as long as it may be waived later by God, whose prerogative it is to punish. Therefore, it is not clear why Murtaḍā objects to this formulation, especially since he had originally accepted it.[128] His articulation of his view draws heavily on conceiving the aspects of morality in acts as self-sufficient motives for the agent to take that action that makes him deserve the proper treatment. These aspects also justify God's decision to bring the individual under specific moral obligations. Praise is deserved upon the performance of these acts, and reward makes up for the hardship suffered by the agent in the process.[129] In avoiding the term 'compensation' and using 'in return' (*bi-izāʾ*), Murtaḍā pays lip service to the oft-repeated position that compensation credit cannot be exchanged for either reward or punishment. But the underlying rationale shows that his theory involves a form of compensation that becomes reward after being combined with praise. He uses the same rationale to argue that the trials and tribulations (*balāʾ*) of believers in this world might contribute towards the mitigation of their punishment in the hereafter. These trials, Murtaḍā insists, do not amount to punishment;[130] they are thus not deserved and they accordingly replenish the sufferer's compensation account. Once more, the exchangeability of compensation and punishment is implicitly admitted, this time under the label of purging one's sins (*tamḥīṣ min al-dhunūb*).[131] Compensation, even if disguised behind other labels and presented in a different argumentative context, is the basic category of deserved treatments that gives rise to the more theologically significant ones.

To justify a desert of reward, there is, then, no need for punishment as a necessary incentive: the rational being, when informed by revelation about the obligatoriness of an act, knows that it must contain an aspect of goodness that suffices to motivate him to observe the obligation. This way, Murtaḍā severs the conceptual connection between the deserts of reward and punishment, making punishment much more dispensable in his theological system. It is, in a sense, demoted from a dictate of rational morality to a matter of consensus and the usually less celebrated revelational morality.[132] Murtaḍā's position is explicitly noted and addressed in the works of Muᶜtazili theologians who insist on the insufficiency of aspects of goodness and vileness to justify the imposition of moral obligation on individuals. These Muᶜtazilis propose a more sophisticated scheme that does not restrict itself to the agent and the act but extends its concern to the party that would bring the agent under the obligation to do the act (*ījāb*). For example, in the case of an individual who is bullied by a politician to give up his wealth, the fact that it would be good of him to do so is separate from the fact that it is vile of the politician to force it on him. Therefore, one should not only consider the aspect of goodness in the act itself but also account for any aspects of goodness in the imposition of the act. Succinctly put, the distinction is between the aspect of obligatoriness (*wajh al-wujūb*) and the aspect of obligating (*wajh al-ījāb*). The Muᶜtazilis in question consider Murtaḍā's argument insufficient because it is concerned only with the former. To address the latter, they argue that obeying God's imposition of moral obligation must be the only way to avoid deserved harm, that is, punishment.[133] Murtaḍā's departure from the Muᶜtazili position betrays a less consequentialist disposition on his part, although not a purely deontological one. His belief in the sufficiency of knowing the moral aspects makes him less keen to designate the avoidance of harm as the individual's sole purpose in every specific act. This reluctance is in line with his earlier stipulation that the agent be motivated by his knowledge of the moral value of the act and not by the need to avoid harm. But this is not to say that such knowledge per se is the justification of moral value, whether on the level of praise and blame or that of reward and punishment. Despite the apparent tension between consequentialist and deontological approaches, the consequentialist position still looms large in Murtaḍā's assumption that it is God's word – with the implicit threat of dire consequences – that conveys the moral knowledge to the individuals in these cases.

Pardon

The desert of punishment, however, is no guarantee that punishment will inevitably take place. It is God's prerogative to pardon, as long as this does not lead to injustice, just like it is the creditor's right to forgive a debtor.[134] It is here that one encounters the theological relevance of the definition of licit acts mentioned earlier: although meting out punishment is not blameworthy, it is praiseworthy to refrain from it. This position leads to the debate about the inevitability of punishment of sinners, which constitutes Murtaḍā's major disagreement with the Muᶜtazili position in its doctrinal formulation. Unlike their Baghdadi fellows, the Basran Muᶜtazilis do not go so far as to argue that reason necessitates that God punish sinners and unbelievers. For them, reason stops at the desert of punishment. Beyond that point, revelation needs to be consulted, and their reading of scripture leads them to conclude that God will punish both sinners and unbelievers in order to preserve the credibility of His threat to do so.[135] Again, Murtaḍā goes the extra mile. Just like he demoted the desert of punishment from rational to revelational morality, he demotes the delivery of punishment from an inevitable occurrence supported by categorical scriptural declarations to a possible scenario challenged by other Qurʾānic statements. His argument leaves the door open to divine pardon for sinners, although the consensus of the community prevents the same position on unbelievers.[136] Thus punishment, unlike reward, may be waived by God in the hereafter, for this would not constitute injustice.

The Basran Muᶜtazilis, as early as Abū Hāshim, argued that only punishment can counterbalance the appeal of vile acts in a way that effectively deters humans from giving in to temptation.[137] But this claim seems to miss a significant fact about human nature, namely, the efficacy of fear in dictating a particular course of behaviour, even if such fear is a mere prospect, especially given the scale of the threat. It is exactly this investment in fear that allows Murtaḍā to argue that there is no need for the individual to know that he deserves punishment for a given act or, even if he knows it, to believe that it will be delivered without fail: his belief in the mere possibility of being punished incites enough fear to deter him from committing the act.[138] The Basran Muᶜtazilis were aware of this challenge, and their answer to it betrays reserved willingness on their part to account for the efficacy of fear. ᶜAbd al-Jabbār argues that although belief in the possibility of punishment suffices to deter the individual from falling into vile temptation, the belief is efficacious only if the individual knows he would deserve punishment. He thus accepts justified fear – that is, fear of the possibility of deserved punishment – but not delusional fear – that is, the fear of an individual who is not sure whether he deserves to be punished in the first place.[139] The context of this discussion is the question whether the desert of punishment is known by reason or by revelation. Therefore, the Basran Muᶜtazili view on the fear of deserved punishment is not challenged by later Ashᶜari positions that contend that mere belief in the possibility of punishment provides a sufficient motive to meet one's moral obligations. The Ashᶜari arguments forgo the whole question of desert, insisting instead on the efficacy of the fear of punishment regardless of whether God will in fact deliver His threat.[140] Murtaḍā's position falls between the two. Although he rejects the position that the desert of punishment may be established rationally, he agrees with the Basran Muᶜtazilis that revelation does establish the desert of punishment. Nevertheless, his strong investment in the efficacy of fear brings him closer to the later Ashᶜari view.

The belief in mutual cancellation – that is, that the agent's reward and punishment cancel each other out – had become a Muᶜtazili doctrine long before Murtaḍā's time, whereas the Imami doctrine necessitated the rejection of this view.[141] As usual in cases of conflict, Murtaḍā adheres unequivocally to the Imami position.[142] But the problem that arises from the rejection of mutual cancellation, as previously noted, is how conflicting deserts affect the respective treatments of the agent. In the case of an unbeliever who joins the community of faith, no problematic situation arises; revelation promises such a person a fresh start, and he is left only with the desert of reward caused by his new status as a believer.[143] The acute situation is that of an apostate, subject to two conflicting positions: on the one hand, deserved reward cannot be waived; but on the other, unbelievers are not entitled to reward. Even worse, this same individual may eventually deserve both everlasting reward and everlasting punishment. To pre-empt this conundrum, Murtaḍā denies that unbelievers can do any act of obedience, mental or bodily, for which they might deserve reward.[144] But this claim exacerbates the problem and pushes his position to an even more extreme point, this time capitalising on knowledge as a motive required for the agent to be rewarded. Given that we are not privy to the motives of unbelievers, we must rely on our sure knowledge of their desert of punishment to judge their acts of charity and worship as mere appearances for which no reward is deserved.[145] This course of argument eventually finds its expression in Murtaḍā's version of the doctrine of perseverance (*muwāfāt*) regarding one's final state of belief upon one's death. According to this doctrine, once a believer, always a believer – but not vice versa; if a person seems to become an unbeliever later in life, this means he has never been a believer in the first place.[146]

Repentance and intercession

In addition to mutual cancellation and the desert of punishment, Murtaḍā develops a different view from that of Basran Muᶜtazilis on two other questions that pertain to the necessitating power of desert; these are the questions of repentance (*tawba*) and intercession (*shafāᶜa*). ᶜAbd al-Jabbār, following Abū Hāshim, maintains a characteristic assertive position concerning the causal power of desert, minimising the margin of change left for other factors, including the word of revelation. Thus, when it comes to repentance, the Basran Muᶜtazilis, appealing to the judgement of the imaginary group of rational beings, claim that one is obliged to accept the apology of wrongdoers and to forgive past wrongs. This applies also to God, who does not have the freedom to turn down repentant sinners, given the necessitating power of desert.[147] The same rationale applies with even greater force to intercession, since acceptance of the possibility of intercession would conflict with the Muᶜtazili doctrine of the threat. If the unrepentant sinner's desert of punishment were to be waived through the intervention of an intermediary, then the latter would be overriding one of the fundamentals of the Muᶜtazili moral universe.[148] In Imami circles, repentance and intercession had been addressed by previous generations of scholars, though apparently in a manner that relied heavily on scripture and traditions.[149] While adhering to these reported Imami positions, Murtaḍā appeals to the imaginary group of rational beings, this time to have them reject the earlier Muᶜtazili appeal: one is not, in fact, obliged to forgive a wrongdoer. Theologically, this stance translates to a more reserved position on the limits of reason: the repentant sinner is pardoned not because he deserves it but because God has promised it, out of His benevolence. Murtaḍā thus dismisses the elaborate discussion on the limits and definition of repentance, portraying it as inspired by the Muᶜtazili belief in the causal power of repentance.[150] In a telling formulation that echoes the underlying view on causality, he states that punishment is annulled upon (*ᶜind*) repentance, not that repentance annuls (*tusqiṭu*) punishment.[151] The narrower margin of reason is also reflected in Murtaḍā's treatment of intercession, since he relies on the consensus of the community and the word of revelation to argue that sinners may be pardoned thanks to the intercession of the Prophet and the Imams.[152] Mufīd mentions that pious believers will intercede for their believing sinful friends,[153] but it is not clear whether this claim is a matter of disagreement between the two scholars, as Murtaḍā is silent on the question. Whether on repentance or intercession, the implicit background of Murtaḍā's argument, beyond the Imami position, is formed by his fundamental rejection of the Basran Muᶜtazili understanding of the desert of punishment. In rejecting the rational argument for this desert and confining it to the domain of divine decision, Murtaḍā is able to use the same logic to waive it. This approach spares him the risk of proposing further restrictions on God's actions, a position to which the Basran Muᶜtazilis are lured by their insistence on maximising the power of desert.

These are the limits of reason in Murtaḍā's scheme of otherworldly deserts. After establishing the inevitability of reward and the possibility of pardon, he appeals solely to revelation to answer questions about the hereafter. Only revelation conveys the information that reward and punishment are everlasting (*dāʾim*), that the transient (*munqaṭiᶜ*) punishment of believers will take place before they receive their reward and that reward must not be adulterated with any unpleasant experience, physical or psychological.[154]

The Muᶜtazilis, in insisting on the deontological vileness of lies in contrast to other, consequentialist justifications of vileness, were motivated by a consequentialist concern, namely, protecting the reliability of the transmission of the divine message against falsehood, for they saw this as the only way God could be trusted to refrain from approving an impostor's message or worse, sending one.[155] Nevertheless, the belief that God can do evil for a greater moral purpose leaves the problem unsolved for practical purposes;[156] one can only imagine the Muᶜtazilis resorting, once more triumphantly, to necessary knowledge and affirming that God's omnipotence and benevolence preclude the need for such a scenario. Thus, the price to pay was to disallow His pardoning of grave sinners lest His word of threat be falsified, a reasonable price considering that it took place at the expense of those already outside the pale of concern.[157] Although the same logic applies to Murtaḍā's thought system, the price he has to pay is even smaller than that required of his Muᶜtazili fellows. By arguing that revelation does not even necessitate the punishment of sinners, Murtaḍā is left with unbelievers as the only scapegoat in his deontological position: protecting God's word against the accusation of falsehood prevents any possibility of God pardoning unbelievers.[158] The coherence of the system is maintained at a minimum price that is paid only in light of the system's need to guard against falsehood, which is seen as a source of logical inconsistency, not as a moral consideration.

Thanksgiving

Thanksgiving is the odd one out in the Muᶜtazili scheme of deserved treatments. It reveals the tension caused by the Muᶜtazilis' attempt to grant reason a paramount role in establishing moral theory, while still arguing for the possibility of justifying the particular human obligations toward God within the boundaries defined by revelation. Thanksgiving consequently emerges as an extremely complex deserved treatment in terms of three aspects: its scope, that is, the range of people who are eligible to receive or provide thanksgiving; its relationship to human agency vis-à-vis divine agency; and its relationship to the more concrete treatments, that is, reward and punishment.

First, the definition of thanksgiving obviously places it very close to praise: both reflect approval of the agent's actions by rational beings.[159] What distinguishes thanksgiving from both praise and blame is its 'private' character: whereas every rational being is entitled to praise and blame respective deserving agents, thanksgiving must be done only by the party that benefitted from the agent's benevolence. Rational beings can approve of this benevolence, but their approval can only take the form of praise. Thus, despite the similarity in the acts of praise and thanksgiving as general categories, their major distinction lies in their scope: praise is always public, thanksgiving private. Even if every individual in a given community benefits from a particular agent's benevolence, the resultant desert is a collective of private expressions of thanksgiving, with everyone doing his individual obligation rather than exercising a public right. Therefore, thanksgiving can be construed as a form of praise highly conditioned by the scope of the benefit distributed by the benevolent agent. This is corroborated by the suggestion that in its specific form of thanking the benefactor (*shukr al-munᶜim*), it was intimately related to the archaic cultural context of Arab tribal humanism, in which thanksgiving was considered a central value in social interactions that depended on the generosity of the chieftain. On the other hand, the negative Ashᶜari valuation of this position may well echo the more sophisticated context of a majoritarian Muslim community less dependent on the particular cultural values of any ethnic group and less interested in proving its intellectual mettle before other traditions.[160]

This observation leads to the second aspect of the complexity of thanksgiving as a moral category. In contrast to praise and reward, which are seen as rights of individuals, and to reward and punishment, which depend on God for their delivery, thanksgiving is exclusively human.[161] God does not exercise it, for no one could possibly benefit Him. It is an obligation that humans have towards God because every individual is a recipient of His benevolence. It is, therefore, the only universally particular moral obligation: it is shared by all, but for individual reasons.[162] Praise, the only possible human action before God, is too banal to qualify human obligations. To make it more fitting for divine–human interaction, it must be upgraded to result not just in another case of praiseworthiness, but in a more demanding moral claim by God on humans. Thanksgiving fits the bill perfectly in this regard.

Third, praise and blame, despite their importance as detectors of moral value in society, are mere preludes to the theologically more consequential reward and punishment. It is not possible to provide a parallel case when it comes to thanksgiving, since there is nothing more that humans can provide to God. Thanksgiving must therefore be reinforced in a manner that stresses its intrinsic value without reference to subsequent treatments. This is probably what underlies the stipulation of numerous conditions required to make an agent entitled to thanksgiving, which have the effect of limiting this prerogative to very few agents. The concept also helps with the argument for the moral foundation of worship in Muᶜtazili theology: it is the ultimate form of thanksgiving to God for His omnibenevolence that cannot be shared by any other.[163]

The special nature of thanksgiving as a moral category is the price paid by Murtaḍā and like-minded theologians to preserve the position of reason in their moral universe. The task would have been much easier if a new category of moral obligation, expressed in worship, had been proposed to justify human obligation before God. But the problem of sustaining the rational basis of morality would remain if such a category could not be classified under the available options. What Murtaḍā and his fellows eventually did was to single out a specific case from among the available ones, impose enough restrictions on it as to make it almost inapplicable to human interaction and, for good measure, make sure that its occurrence in human contexts will always be deficient. Thus, even if a human being shows the greatest benevolence towards another, he will never be able to claim that he gave him life or similar good gifts. This restrictive definition reserves for God the status of the ultimate benevolent agent towards every individual, and the form of thanksgiving He deserves for His benevolence is worship. Murtaḍā's mathematical tone in arguing that worship is indivisible (*lā yajūzu fīhi al-inqisām wa-l-tabᶜīḍ*)[164] must be read in the context of an all-or-nothing scenario, in which no fraction of worship is deserved by any other party: God deserves all of it, and no one else deserves any of it. Nevertheless, it remains to justify the revealed law that defines acts of worship within the restrictions of Murtaḍā's moral theory.

Rational and revelational morality

Acts whose moral value can be grasped by reason are referred to as rational moral obligations. Given the Muʿtazilis' commitment to the position that all moral obligations can theoretically be accounted for by reason, they face the stumbling block of explaining moral obligations that cannot be justified by reason alone, that is, the prescriptions of the sacred law collectively referred to as revelational moral obligations. Within the particular discussion of prescribed acts, revelational moral obligations are used interchangeably with legal moral obligation(s) (*al-taklīf al-sharʿī*; *al-takālīf al-sharʿiyya*).[165] In fact, objections to religion, usually ascribed to the Barāhima – the proverbial deniers of prophethood in Islamic tradition – seem to have focused on questioning the latter, based on their belief in the self-sufficiency of human reason.[166] The preferred objects of their mockery were the bodily postures in the ritual prayers and the details of the pilgrimage to Mecca.[167] It is safe to assume that our imaginary group of rational beings would be closer to the Barāhima than to the Muʿtazilis in these matters. Paradoxically, it must have been not only the Barāhima who felt comfortable with this attack; upholders of divine command ethics among Muslim theologians must have also savoured the moment.[168] Therefore, the attempts by proponents of objectivist moral theory to answer these objections are doubly apologetic. In addition to bearing the burden of defending the criticised ritual practices, they have to argue – pursuant to their own acclaimed rationality – that such practices can be justified by recourse to reason. The proposed solution, on which Murtaḍā is in full agreement with the Basran Muʿtazilis, sought to bestow meaning on these revelational obligations by invoking divine assistance and appealing to God's omniscience while still maintaining that the moral value of acts cannot be established based on divine command.

To begin with, an implicit hierarchy pervades Murtaḍā's theology with regard to his scheme of moral obligation. The dictates of reason are always granted pride of place, in terms of both their universality and their finality. All rational beings are subject to rational moral obligation, and no rationally established moral value can be transmuted – not even by God's explicit command. The starkest example of this can be seen in the long list of conditions required for His commanding an act to be good, a list concluded by the bold verdict, 'Even if He obligates us to be ungrateful for His assistance, it does not become obligatory'.[169] The dictates of revelational moral obligation, therefore, must be made to fit within this scheme. On a more practical level, the conflict mostly concerns those prescriptions of sacred law that can be construed as instances of self-harm, injustice or purposelessness. Thus, prayers and fasting might be considered harmful for the individual, slaughtering animals and owning slaves unjust, and refraining from alcohol and adultery purposeless.[170] Since it would be impossible, within the limits of Murtaḍā's moral theory, to approve of such acts while conceding the negative moral judgement, the mystery of the Lord's ways proves an invaluable lifeline.

The answer works on two levels, although Murtaḍā does not admit its complexity. First, there is the generic level: the revealed prescriptions, at the end of the day, are all details of a larger body of ordained beliefs and practices required by God. Thanksgiving is deserved for great benefits, and worship is the ultimate form of thanksgiving following ultimate benefits.[171] Thus a bird's-eye view of the question would show the bigger picture and convey the overall meaning of this body of prescriptions. The more challenging problem lies in the second level, that is, the rational justification of detailed prescriptions. Ultimately, the most contentious aspect is the form (*ṣūra*) of acts: even if the interlocutor concedes the need to thank the Creator, why would the expression of gratitude be restricted to a particular form that is not, so to speak, the most elegant? What benefit is there in starving oneself, or in suppressing a harmless desire? Aware of the distinction between the act's form and its aspect of moral value, Murtaḍā stresses the importance of taking the form into consideration in judging the moral value of the act, while still admitting that the aspect of the moral value is the more important consideration.[172] The only way out of this dilemma would be to assign particular meanings to each of these actions within the bounds of rational morality. But the range of rationally defined moral values, no matter how far one is willing to stretch it, is not infinite; it can accommodate only a well-defined set of good and vile values and subsume particular instances under their respective categories. With the prescriptions of sacred law, such sorting is not a straightforward task, for a number of reasons. Not only is it difficult to pinpoint the prescriptions' latent moral value; they are also not always universal – for example, not every rational being is obligated to pray all the time. Here divine assistance and omniscience prove most useful. The prescriptions of revealed law are assigned a derivative value; that is, their moral value comes from their serving as means for the observant individual to better meet the dictates of rational moral obligations. As such, they are merely instances of divine assistance, intended – like assistance is – to maximise the individual's chances of attaining reward in the hereafter.[173]

The benefits of this formulation, within Murtaḍā's framework, cannot be overstated. First, since God's assistance is specific to each individual and given the diversity of people's needs, it is not required that divine assistance be uniform.[174] One person's divine assistance can be another person's corruption. Therefore, the challenge posed by discrimination in the dictates of revelational moral obligation is turned into an opportunity. In a broader context, this natural variation also helps to justify the abrogation of the sacred laws of earlier religions, according to the mainstream Muslim understanding of the relationship between Islamic and previous revealed laws.[175] The changes in divine laws are explained by the changing interests of individuals and their respective lots of divine assistance. Second, Murtaḍā is able to pre-empt the problem of pinpointing the moral value of divinely prescribed acts:

the finality of rational moral obligation is invoked to bestow meaning on the prescriptions of the sacred law, even if their moral value is seen as merely instrumental. No need, then, to identify new aspects of goodness or vileness; it suffices to refer the seeker to the already known moral aspects, trusting that God would not have prescribed the details of the sacred law were they not helpful for people in acting in accordance with these aspects.[176] Third, his formulation allows Murtaḍā to avoid another problematic situation, one that is in fact the most detrimental to his theological system: accepting that these acts acquire moral value by being divinely prescribed. Thus, he repeatedly states that divine injunctions only distinguish (*tabyīn*), disclose (*tamyīz*), order (*tartīb*) or elaborate (*tafṣīl*) the rational moral value that reason failed to grasp because of the inaccessibility of information,[177] and that informing individuals of their obligation must not be confused with bringing them under this obligation.[178] Revelation, therefore, does not establish the moral value of acts; rather, it aids reason in fulfilling what properly belongs to its sphere of activity.

Thus, going back to the challenges of the Barāhima, prayer would have indeed been a vile instance of self-harm were it to be judged only by unaided reason. The word of revelation does not change this rational judgement by altering the givens and promising a good consequence for the act; rather, it corrects it by indicating the true moral value of prayer.[179] The promise of reward, therefore, must not be seen as a step intended to change the act's moral value, but as something that was there in the first place but could not be detected by unaided reason. Thus, although the hidden connection between the dictates of rational and revelational moral obligation is known only to God, this connection is not a random matching of two types of injunctions, but is governed by the consideration of maximising humans' otherworldly interests. This rationale is what underlies Murtaḍā's attempts to locate these connections, while conceding the inadequacy of unaided reason to do so.[180] In either case, whether the individual is observing rational or revelational moral obligation, he is effectively obeying God's judgement (*ḥukm allāh*).[181] The main difference between the two types of obligation is the more flexible range of possibilities in revelational moral obligation. Thus, when Murtaḍā emphasises the possibility that no sacred law had been revealed,[182] the implicit implication is that there would not be any dictates of revelational moral obligation either – an impossible scenario with respect to rational moral obligation. The reason for this flexibility is itself the reason for the varying obligations of individuals, namely, the different needs of different people. In the hypothetical scenario of no revealed law, people may need no other means to fulfil their moral obligations, and they may not need prescribed actions for this purpose. In any case, the limits of reason, especially its moral knowledge, are fixed – even when measured against the limits of divine power.

Conclusion

Content

The gap between the moral value of acts and the desert of their agents is wide in Murtaḍā's system; this is reflected in the considerable variety of acts that are morally significant but whose agents cannot be judged. The agent's sanity and psychological state are what sustains this gap, which opens the door for developing a concept of responsibility as a function not only of action but also of awareness. Although reason is ostensibly the main definer of the moral value, it is the imaginary group of rational beings, believed to be universal but in fact a reflection of Murtaḍā's context, that is charged with this role.

The yardstick of the value of acts is their consequences; the system can safely be characterised as consequentialist. The only judgement that, at first glance, seems to be deontological (namely, the vileness of lying) is in fact an instance of higher-order consequentialism: its main function is to keep the transgressors of moral dictates under the sway of future punishment. But even in this case, the vileness of lying can be manipulated for the greater otherworldly benefit of the individuals concerned, and therefore consequentialism still rules.[183]

Upholding the objective moral value of acts naturally leads to compromising God's omnipotence. In Murtaḍā's system, however, this compromise is weakened by his refusal to venture into the realm of hypothetical cases with the certainty exhibited by both Basran and Baghdadi Muᶜtazilis. Murtaḍā rejects the theses that God is required to take a person's life or keep it, obligate him to a particular act, accept his repentance, refrain from inflicting harm on him in the presence of harmless alternatives, exact punishment from him or attend to his worldly interest. The wholesale rejection of all these propositions preserves God's omnipotence to a greater extent than is achieved in Mufīd's and the Muᶜtazilis' systems. Murtaḍā's reserved attitude extends to denial of the results of speculation on the nature of deserved treatments, such as their duration and purity. Since much of Murtaḍā's argument is dedicated to undermining the claim that reason can decide on situations of the invisible realm, it might be said that the role of reason in his moral discourse is largely confined to abstract discussions.

Context

Rejecting the doctrine of the promise and the threat is Murtaḍā's main departure from Basran Muᶜtazilism on moral theory and divine agency. In addition to maintaining the mainstream Imami position, Murtaḍā's view embodies an equilibrium that allows it to avoid many practical communal problems. In addressing the issue of sinning believers, of whom there was never a dearth, adhering to the doctrine of the divine threat would create unnecessary tension in the community, with some of its members judging others on behalf of God, whereas allowing the possibility of pardon precludes such judgement.

In most of the points on which Mufīd and Murtaḍā disagree, the disagreement is due to the fact that the former concurs with the view of the Baghdadi Muᶜtazilis whereas Murtaḍā prefers the Basran Muᶜtazili position. Examples of such points are the questions of worldly best interest, compensation for unbelievers and animals, and the nature of repentance. Ṭūsī sides with Murtaḍā on most of these issues. Often, he simply copies Murtaḍā's position verbatim, adding his own comments or modifications thereafter.

Notes

1. Vasalou, *Moral Agents*, 4–8; Gimaret, 'Muᶜtazila'.
2. The full version of this self-proclaimed epithet is 'upholders of justice and unicity' (*ahl al-ᶜadl wa-l-ṭawḥīḍ*). That the brief form retains only the aspect of justice confirms the significance they placed on this precept; Gimaret, 'Muᶜtazila'.
3. For example, volumes 6–14 of the *Mughnī* are dedicated to this discussion and its direct ramifications; prophethood, although also pertaining to justice, is discussed in separate volumes since it has to do with divine threat and not with the rationally comprehended moral obligation; ᶜAbd al-Jabbār, *Mughnī*, 14:461. In Murtaḍā's two full theological works, the *Mulakhkhaṣ* (together with the *Dhakhīra*) and *Sharḥ Jumal al-ᶜilm wa-l-ᶜamal*, the discussion on justice takes up 427 out of about 970 pages and eighty-four out of about 210 pages, respectively.
4. ᶜAbd al-Jabbār, *Mughnī*, 6{1}:51.
5. *Rasāʾil*, 1:165–6.
6. The criticality of the moral value of acts is evident, for example, in the work of Juwaynī (d. 1085). He repeatedly states that rejecting objectivist moral theory suffices to refute the Muᶜtazili position on pain, compensation, divine assistance, worldly best interest, moral obligation, punishment and reward. Still unsatisfied, he further asserts that upholding the moral value of acts is the cornerstone of the rejection of prophethood by the Barāhima (on whom see below); Juwaynī, *Irshād*, 279, 281, 286, 295, 296, 303. A succinct survey of the development of this debate from an Imami perspective is found in Subḥānī, *Risāla*, 3–139. The author, a contemporary scholar, argues that eleven key Imami doctrines have their roots in the position taken on the moral value of acts, among them the eternal validity of religious law, in addition to the points mentioned by Juwaynī; Subḥānī, *Risāla*, 86–98.
7. The controversy to which the term refers is more concerned with the theory of ethical knowledge than with the ontology of value; for the distinction, see Hourani, 'Origins', 84.
8. As noted in Reinhart, *Before Revelation*, 145, 218n2.
9. As in Vasalou, *Moral Agents*, 22–6.
10. The study of human agency, which usually develops into a discussion of free will, is often lumped under the broader topic of justice. But this can be justified only after establishing a moral-theoretical position that considers freedom of choice a prerequisite for judging an agent's act and holding him justly accountable. Human agency is thus addressed in the following chapter on human religious experience.

11. The other example provided in *Mulakhkhaṣ*, 308 is that of the sleeping person's moving his limbs as long as it does not affect others. This last caveat is better read as an example of an irrelevant act, not as a necessary and sufficient condition for such an act. For a sleeping person harming himself would still be committing a vile act according to Murtaḍā. The gist of this example is, thus, the act's status as inconsequential and not the identity of whoever would have suffered its consequences otherwise.
12. *Mulakhkhaṣ*, 306, 308; *Dharīᶜa*, 391, 393; see the very similar wording in ᶜAbd al-Jabbār, *Mughnī*, 6{1}:5–6.
13. *Mulakhkhaṣ*, 306; *Dharīᶜa*, 392; *Shāfī*, 1:164; *Rasāʾil*, 2:233, 4:332–3; a slightly different formulation in *Dharīᶜa*, 143.
14. *Dhakhīra*, 124–5.
15. *Dhakhīra*, 561–2.
16. *Mulakhkhaṣ*, 318–19.
17. ᶜAbd al-Jabbār, *Mughnī*, 6{1}:13.
18. *Mulakhkhaṣ*, 308–9.
19. ᶜAbd al-Jabbār, *Mughnī*, 6{1}:11–12, 82–4, 87–8.
20. Ṭūsī, *Rasāʾil*, 85; the opposite can be construed from his *ᶜUdda*, 1:25, which was written earlier in his career, as suggested by the editor (pp. 75–7).
21. *Mulakhkhaṣ*, 306, 309; *Dharīᶜa*, 392.
22. *Mulakhkhaṣ*, 475.
23. *Mulakhkhaṣ*, 307; *Dharīᶜa*, 392–3, 544; *Dhakhīra*, 112, 278–9, 286, 295. The relevant section in the *Mulakhkhaṣ* manuscript begins by dividing good acts into five subcategories, but the text omits the fourth one without indicating a lacuna through empty space or a marginal note, although it does skip a number in the sequence. The editor has sought to fill the logical gap by inserting an introductory phrase for the fourth subcategory even though its content is blank, causing some confusion; compare with the manuscript, 82a. The view that there are only four categories of good acts is also supported by referring to Ṭūsī, *Rasāʾil*, 85–7; idem, *ᶜUdda*, 1:25–6. ᶜAbd al-Jabbār, *Mughnī*, 6{1}:7–8, apparently subsumes Murtaḍā's third category under his second as a particular case of it, while at the same time failing to mention thanksgiving among the deserts of this particular case even when it is explicitly mentioned, as in Ṭūsī's *Rasāʾil*.
24. *Dhakhīra*, 130.
25. *Dharīᶜa*, 546.
26. Vasalou, *Moral Agents*, 59.
27. *Mulakhkhaṣ*, 309–10.
28. *Mulakhkhaṣ*, 310.
29. *Mulakhkhaṣ*, 310–11; the printed text is corrupt; see MS, 83.
30. Reinhart, *Before Revelation*, 150–1.
31. *Mulakhkhaṣ*, 311.
32. *Dhakhīra*, 135, similarly 142.
33. *Mulakhkhaṣ*, 311–12.
34. *Mulakhkhaṣ*, 313–14.
35. *Mulakhkhaṣ*, 317–22.

36. *Mulakhkhaṣ*, 322–4; briefly in *Dharīᶜa*, 547.
37. ᶜAbd al-Jabbār, *Mughnī*, 6{1}:70–4, 11:84–5, 17:247; Vasalou, *Moral Agents*, 87–9.
38. *Dhakhīra*, 290–1; on the difference between conditions and causes and their relations, see *Dharīᶜa*, 105–6; *Rasāʾil*, 1:145.
39. *Dhakhīra*, 127–31.
40. *Dhakhīra*, 132.
41. *Dharīᶜa*, 279–82. That the argument is against ᶜAbd al-Jabbār's position is attested by the abovementioned examples; cf. ᶜAbd al-Jabbār, *Mughnī*, 17:52–3. Compare *Dhakhīra*, 230, and ᶜAbd al-Jabbār, *Mughnī*, 13:395, where the same example of purposelessness is used: hiring someone to carry water from one river to another or from one side of the sea to another.
42. *Mulakhkhaṣ*, 307.
43. *Dhakhīra*, 208; *Dharīᶜa*, 544.
44. That ᶜAbd al-Jabbār is mindful of the problems related to the application of the term 'licit' is clear when he states that God's punishment is to Him what licit is to us (*bi-manzilat al-mubāḥ minnā*), or even more explicitly when he insists that what God does is similar to licit (*mithl al-mubāḥ*); ᶜAbd al-Jabbār, *Mughnī*, 11:68, 429, 14:71, 17:247.
45. Vasalou, *Moral Agents*, 89–91.
46. *Dhakhīra*, 208; *Dharīᶜa*, 544–5.
47. Ṭūsī, *Rasāʾil*, 85–7.
48. *Mulakhkhaṣ*, 68.
49. *Mulakhkhaṣ*, 347; *Sharḥ Jumal*, 88.
50. *Mulakhkhaṣ*, 348, 373.
51. *Mulakhkhaṣ*, 348.
52. *Mulakhkhaṣ*, 348–9.
53. Vasalou, *Moral Agents*, 95–102.
54. *Rasāʾil*, 2:375–6.
55. *Rasāʾil*, 1:396–7; see also *Mulakhkhaṣ*, 310–11.
56. *Dhakhīra*, 142–3; *Sharḥ Jumal*, 104.
57. *Dhakhīra*, 142–3; cf. ᶜAbd al-Jabbār, *Mughnī*, 11:520–9.
58. See, for example, Juwaynī, *Irshād*, 300–1.
59. *Dhakhīra*, 186; *Sharḥ Jumal*, 107; also the commentary on Q3:8 in *Amālī*, 2:25–6.
60. *Dhakhīra*, 133, 186.
61. *Dhakhīra*, 187.
62. *Dhakhīra*, 187; *Rasāʾil*, 4:344–5.
63. *Rasāʾil*, 4:343–5.
64. *Dhakhīra*, 199–200; cf. ᶜAbd al-Jabbār, *Mughnī*, 14:35–7, 45–56, where the phrasing is very similar.
65. McDermott, *Theology*, 75, offers a problematic understanding of the concept of other-worldly best interest based on a certain reading of a passage in ᶜAbd al-Jabbār's *Mughnī*, 13:212. Instead of reading it to mean 'When God imposes moral obligation, He must do that to which nothing is superior in [helping the individual] choose what He has obligated him to do', McDermott reads it to mean 'When God morally imposes the doing

of a certain act, nothing more advantageous than that can be chosen'. An implication of this reading is that McDermott sees ᶜAbd al-Jabbār's position as explaining away a Muᶜtazili thesis full of difficulties. However, the alternative reading is more faithful to ᶜAbd al-Jabbār's theology.

66. The discussion in ᶜAbd al-Jabbār, *Mughnī*, 14:55–110, is primarily addressed to Balkhī, who is presented as the representative of the Baghdadi viewpoint; Ibn Mattawayh, *Majmūᶜ*, 3:130–3; cf. Juwaynī, *Irshād*, 287–8.
67. *Dhakhīra*, 201–2; *Sharḥ Jumal*, 109–11; cf. ᶜAbd al-Jabbār, *Mughnī*, 14:56–61; Ibn Mattawayh, *Majmūᶜ*, 3:134–52.
68. *Dhakhīra*, 206.
69. ᶜAbd al-Jabbār, *Mughnī*, 14:140–1.
70. See Chapter 5 for a full discussion on the necessity of the Imama.
71. *Dhakhīra*, 190–2; *Sharḥ Jumal*, 107–8. See Balkhī, *ᶜUyūn*, 123–9, for the Baghdadi construal of this as an act of generosity.
72. *Dhakhīra*, 195–6.
73. *Sharḥ Jumal*, 107–8.
74. *Dhakhīra*, 197–8.
75. *Dhakhīra*, 197–8.
76. *Dhakhīra*, 136.
77. *Rasāʾil*, 1:415–18.
78. *Dhakhīra*, 190.
79. *Rasāʾil*, 1:420–2.
80. *Dhakhīra*, 195–6.
81. Ormsby, *Theodicy*, 16–30.
82. *Dhakhīra*, 215–17; cf. Heemskerk, *Suffering*, 126–41 for a discussion of justified pain in ᶜAbd al-Jabbār's theology.
83. ᶜAbd al-Jabbār, *Mughnī*, 13:293–8. Compare *Dhakhīra*, 218–20, and ᶜAbd al-Jabbār, *Mughnī*, 13:228–9, for the parallel hesitation in reporting Abū Hāshim's position on why pain is *qabīḥ*.
84. *Dhakhīra*, 218–20; *Rasāʾil*, 4:349–50; *Tanzīh*, 147–8.
85. *Dhakhīra*, 221–8; cf. Heemskerk, *Suffering*, 155–6.
86. *Dhakhīra*, 226; *Sharḥ Jumal*, 116–18.
87. Ormsby, *Theodicy*, 244–6.
88. *Dhakhīra*, 232–3; on the Bakriyya, see van Ess, *Theologie und Gesellschaft*, 2:108–18.
89. *Dhakhīra*, 226; *Sharḥ Jumal*, 111–13.
90. For example, Heemskerk, *Suffering*, 151, reports that ᶜAbd al-Jabbār is not clear on how pain would motivate the individual, and she therefore provides possible explanations of his position.
91. *Tanzīh*, 135. There is some confusion surrounding the translation of *iᶜtibār*. McDermott, *Theology*, 184, opts for 'lesson', and Heemskerk, *Suffering*, 159, translates it as 'giving a warning'. But *iᶜtibār* is used in a broader sense, usually to signify some hidden wisdom. This meaning is best illustrated by Ṭūsī's substitution of it for *gharaḍ ḥikmī*, 'purpose of wisdom'; Ṭūsī, *Iqtiṣād*, 86.

92. *Amālī*, 1:29, 2:45–6; *Tanzīh*, 111. See also Bray, 'Practical Muᶜtazilism', 125–6, for Tanūkhī's (d. 994) observations of such cases in real life, which concur with Murtaḍā's theoretical analysis.
93. *Dhakhīra*, 229–30. Murtaḍā thus admits that his earlier statement (on p. 226) that God inflicts pain for benefit, which is compensation, should not be taken literally; see also *Sharḥ Jumal*, 111–12.
94. *Dhakhīra*, 229–30; *Sharḥ Jumal*, 113–15.
95. *Dhakhīra*, 227–8; cf. the very similar example in ᶜAbd al-Jabbār, *Mughnī*, 13:370.
96. *Dhakhīra*, 228–30; cf. ᶜAbd al-Jabbār, *Mughnī*, 13:370, who agrees with Murtaḍā.
97. Mufīd, *Awāʾil*, 108–9.
98. *Dhakhīra*, 239; *Sharḥ Jumal*, 118, 134; a briefer form in *Amālī*, 1:72.
99. *Dhakhīra*, 242–3; *Sharḥ Jumal*, 119–21.
100. *Dhakhīra*, 239–40; *Sharḥ Jumal*, 119–20; *Rasāʾil*, 2:372–3.
101. *Dhakhīra*, 241–2.
102. I borrow this apt term from Vasalou, *Moral Agents*, 81, who qualified an earlier rendering by Heemskerk, *Suffering*, 178.
103. *Dhakhīra*, 250–2; cf. ᶜAbd al-Jabbār, *Mughnī*, 13:545–6.
104. *Dhakhīra*, 247–8; the tradition, labelled a famous report (*khabar mashhūr*) by Murtaḍā's brother Raḍī, appears in the latter's *Majāzāt*, 98–9. Compare with ᶜAbd al-Jabbār, *Mughnī*, 13: 503–4, for the very similar wording of the opponents' attacks, following the same example of how an animal might be required to provide compensation. See Heemskerk, *Suffering*, 187–9, for the views of ᶜAbd al-Jabbār and his circle.
105. See van Ess, *Theologie und Gesellschaft*, 2:53.
106. Mufīd, *Awāʾil*, 110.
107. Rabb, 'Reasonable doubt', 79–82.
108. *Dhakhīra*, 243–5, 249; *Sharḥ Jumal*, 121–3; *Amālī*, 1:37–8; ᶜAbd al-Jabbār, *Mughnī*, 13:472, 540–4.
109. *Dhakhīra*, 253–4.
110. *Dhakhīra*, 250–2; *Rasāʾil*, 2:376.
111. Mufīd, *Awāʾil*, 109–10; McDermott, *Theology*, 184–5.
112. *Dhakhīra*, 151–2; *Amālī*, 1:68, 108–14, 2:240–1; *Rasāʾil*, 1:423–31, 4:34.
113. ᶜAbd al-Jabbār, *Mughnī*, 13:555–68.
114. ᶜAbd al-Jabbār, *Mughnī*, 13:547–55.
115. *Dhakhīra*, 256–61.
116. *Dhakhīra*, 245–7.
117. *Dhakhīra*, 278, 286; *Sharḥ Jumal*, 134; cf. ᶜAbd al-Jabbār, *Mughnī*, 11:506.
118. *Dhakhīra*, 286; *Sharḥ Jumal*, 136–7.
119. *Dhakhīra*, 297.
120. *Dhakhīra*, 297; cf. Ibn Mattawayh, *Majmūᶜ*, 3:343; Mānkdīm, *Sharḥ*, 619.
121. *Dhakhīra*, 176.
122. *Dhakhīra*, 295–7; *Sharḥ Jumal*, 135–7; see also Ibn Mattawayh, *Majmūᶜ*, 3:341.
123. *Dhakhīra*, 279.
124. *Dhakhīra*, 299.

125. *Dhakhīra*, 280; *Sharḥ Jumal*, 139; *Amālī*, 1:73.
126. *Dhakhīra*, 302–3; *Sharḥ Jumal*, 145–6.
127. Ibn Mattawayh, *Majmūᶜ*, 3:341–2; Mānkdīm, *Sharḥ*, 619–20.
128. *Sharḥ Jumal*, 140–1, where he admits the change in his opinion; see also *Rasāʾil*, 1:148.
129. *Dhakhīra*, 296; *Tanzīh*, 90–1; *Sharḥ Jumal*, 140–1.
130. *Dhakhīra*, 237.
131. *Rasāʾil*, 1:131; *Amālī*, 2:78–9.
132. *Dhakhīra*, 298.
133. Ibn Mattawayh, *Majmūᶜ*, 3:342–3; Mānkdīm, *Sharḥ*, 620–1, where Murtaḍā is mentioned for his rejection of rational justification of the desert of punishment and his insistence on revelation instead.
134. *Dhakhīra*, 313–14; *Sharḥ Jumal*, 145–6.
135. Ibn Mattawayh, *Majmūᶜ*, 3:412–13; Mānkdīm, *Sharḥ*, 651–63.
136. *Dhakhīra*, 509–21; *Sharḥ Jumal*, 150–4.
137. Ibn Mattawayh, *Majmūᶜ*, 3:343; Mānkdīm, *Sharḥ*, 620–1.
138. *Dhakhīra*, 296–7; *Sharḥ Jumal*, 134–5. There is a similar statement concerning the influence of fear in *Amālī*, 1:497, commenting on Q8:24.
139. Ibn Mattawayh, *Majmūᶜ*, 3:343; Mānkdīm, *Sharḥ*, 619–21.
140. Vasalou, *Moral Agents*, 82, provides an interesting reading of an argument proposed by the Ashᶜari theologian al-Ījī (d. 1355): 'But if the main concern was with motivation, the only necessity that one could deduce from this argument [...] was that human beings should *believe* in the occurrence of punishment. Once motives are past being affected –once the utilitarian value of deterrence has lapsed – what reason remained for the actual event of punishment to take place?' This reading of Ījī's argument questions the utility of punishment at the time of its delivery – in line with Vasalou's main thesis on desert as a non-consequentialist ground of moral value. Elsewhere (*Moral Agents*, 217n40), Vasalou states that Mānkdīm's answer to this challenge is not persuasive. It must be noted, however, that Mānkdīm's answer addresses a different question from the problem posed by Ījī, as the former is discussing the desert of punishment and not belief in its inevitable delivery.
141. For the earlier tradition, see Kulaynī, *Kāfī*, 2:276–8. See also Mufīd, *Awāʾil*, 82, for the theological tradition of Murtaḍā's time; Mufīd singles out the Banū Nawbakht as the Imamis who accept mutual cancellation.
142. *Dhakhīra*, 302–6; *Sharḥ Jumal*, 146–7; *Amālī*, 2:304; *Tanzīh*, 35–6; *Rasāʾil*, 1:149.
143. *Dhakhīra*, 521; *Sharḥ Jumal*, 158.
144. *Dhakhīra*, 521–4; *Sharḥ Jumal*, 158–60.
145. *Rasāʾil*, 1:162–3.
146. *Dhakhīra*, 521–2; *Sharḥ Jumal*, 158–60. I am aware of the Christian connotations in translating *muwāfāt* as 'perseverance', but the two terms both boil down to 'enduring to the end' in faith; on the term's varied connotations in Christian theology, see Marquardt, 'Perseverance'. Murtaḍā does not reject the possibility that unbelievers know God, as long as they do not know Him in a manner that entails reward; *Rasāʾil*, 2:329–30. Earlier, he states explicitly that his rejection of the possibility of unbelievers' arriving

at knowledge of God is driven by their unworthiness of reward, from which he reasons backwards to preclude that such knowledge could have existed; *Rasāʾil*, 1:163–4. This is elaborated further in Ṭūsī, *Tibyān*, 1:192–3, 314–15, 346, 2:15, 551. The problem is not epistemic, then, as Kohlberg – following McDermott – proposes, but rather rooted in the theological arithmetic of the consequences of moral acts; cf. Kohlberg, 'Muwāfāt', 54; McDermott, *Theology*, 241.

147. ᶜAbd al-Jabbār, *Mughnī*, 14:337–43; Ibn Mattawayh, *Majmūᶜ*, 3:392–3; Mānkdīm, *Sharḥ*, 643–4.
148. Mānkdīm, *Sharḥ*, 687–9.
149. Mufīd, *Awāʾil*, 79–80, 85–8; in addition to stating the positions of the majority of the Imamis, Mufīd admits that the views he reports are those of Imami legal scholars (*fuqahāʾ*) and traditionalists, since he could not find any statements on the question by Imami theologians.
150. *Dhakhīra*, 316–21; *Sharḥ Jumal*, 148–9; *Tanzīh*, 47–8; see Vasalou, *Moral Agents*, 39–56, for a general outline of the discussion and its legal undertones. McDermott, *Theology*, 265, ascribes to Mufīd the claim that all Muᶜtazilis believe in the necessitating power of repentance, which McDermott rightly judges inaccurate given ᶜAbd al-Jabbār's and Mānkdīm's assertion (*Sharḥ*, 790) that the Baghdadi Muᶜtazilis held that punishment would be waived upon repentance by way of initiated benevolence. But it is unlikely that Mufīd makes such a mistake in presenting the teachings of the theological school with which he was most acquainted, especially given the absence of any motive on his part to deviate from them on this point. Apparently, the Baghdadis did believe in the necessitating power of repentance, but they did so out of their belief in worldly best interest, which necessitates that God is required to do something out of His benevolence. For them, and also for Mufīd, benevolence is a valid ground of obligatoriness (*wujūb*), whereas the Basrans held obligatoriness and benevolence to be contradictory.
151. *Tanzīh*, 141–2.
152. *Rasāʾil*, 1:131; *Dīwān*, 1:217, 489, 503, 2:155, 168–9.
153. Mufīd, *Awāʾil*, 79–80.
154. *Dhakhīra*, 280–2, 299–300, 307; *Rasāʾil*, 1:150; *Sharḥ Jumal*, 142–3, 149–50.
155. Compare this with the way in which a later Ashᶜari uses the same principle to discredit Muᶜtazili trust in prophethood. Fakhr al-Dīn al-Rāzī (d. 1209) argues that if using equivocal speech is good, then God may be doing the same thing to us, without lying; Reinhart, *Before Revelation*, 163. In a different context, an early Muᶜtazili author addresses a similar question, arguing that the purpose of the Qurʾān's ambiguous verses is to provoke people's thought; cf. Adang, Madelung and Schmidtke, *Baṣran Muᶜtazilite Theology*, 240.
156. El-Rouayheb, 'Must God', 412.
157. Vasalou, *Moral Agents*, 85–6.
158. *Tanzīh*, 90–1.
159. See their definitions in *Dhakhīra*, 276–7.
160. See Reinhart, *Before Revelation*, 108–20, for the particular social and cultural contexts, in addition to the problems of translating the term; see also Hourani, 'Origins', 87. A

classic Ashʿari response to the Muʿtazili justification of the moral value of gratitude is presented in van den Bergh, 'Ghazali', 81–3.

161. See Zilio-Grandi, 'Gratitude', 60, for an insightful analysis of the exclusivity of thanksgiving as a human virtue.
162. *Amālī*, 1:49.
163. *Sharḥ Jumal*, 136.
164. *Dhakhīra*, 108; cf. the very similar phrasing in ʿAbd al-Jabbār, *Mughnī*, 11:418.
165. *Intiṣār*, 355; *Rasāʾil*, 1:81, 83, 2:317, 319; *Amālī*, 1:305.
166. The identity of the Barāhima is still much disputed, and with time, they became a topos as people who denied prophethood, abrogation or the authority of divinely guided humans; Stroumsa, *Freethinkers*, 145–62.
167. Bāqillānī, *Tamhīd*, 137; Ibn Mattawayh, *Majmūʿ*, 3:447–8; Mānkdīm, *Sharḥ*, 563–5; cf. Ījī's text in Jurjānī, *Sharḥ*, 8:266–7.
168. Juwaynī, *Irshād*, 262–3.
169. *Dharīʿa*, 144.
170. *Dharīʿa*, 78; *Dhakhīra*, 239–40; *Sharḥ*, 119–20; *Mulakhkhaṣ*, 320–1.
171. *Dhakhīra*, 170–1.
172. *Dharīʿa*, 398–9.
173. *Dharīʿa*, 412; *Rasāʾil*, 2:335, 4:344.
174. *Dharīʿa*, 397–8.
175. For abrogation, see Chapter 6.
176. *Dhakhīra*, 108–12.
177. *Rasāʾil*, 1:136–8.
178. *Mulakhkhaṣ*, 311–12; *Rasāʾil*, 1:81.
179. *Dharīʿa*, 316–17.
180. *Rasāʾil*, 4:345.
181. *Dharīʿa*, 409; *Rasāʾil*, 1:318.
182. *Shāfī*, 2:8, 20; *Rasāʾil*, 1:81.
183. This is reminiscent of the distinction between 'intrinsic values' and 'consequences' as presented – and rejected as unimportant – by Anscombe, 'Modern moral philosophy', 9.

CHAPTER

4

HUMANS AND THE ORIGINS OF RELIGIOUS EXPERIENCE

The question of divine justice, studied in the previous chapter, involves attempts to understand God's work in a manner that fits with human morality – some theologians would say morality *simpliciter*. The general framework of moral theory, in addition to elements specific to divine agency such as assistance and corruption, serves as a prelude to the ultimate concern of theologians: the creatures' destiny in their interaction with the Creator.

This chapter investigates how Murtaḍā's theology makes sense of religious experience. It first covers his definition of the human being and touches on the history of this sensitive debate in the Imami context, and then proceeds to his view on human agency inasmuch as it affects human responsibility before God. The next section analyses God's general act of creation in light of the considerations that govern moral theory, given that this act must be understood before the more specific question of human experience can be addressed. This discussion is followed by an examination of Murtaḍā's view on the relationship between humans and God in the form of moral obligation, covering the roots, duration and scope of moral obligation and how it materialises in real life.

These were controversial topics in Islamic theology. Like the debate on divine essence and attributes, the debate on human agency became a question of dogmatism and group identity. The origins of the controversy need not be foreign to the concerns of the Muslim community, although the avowed positions coincide neatly with the then available views of major religions and intellectual movements.[1] Despite some attempts to propose less polarising solutions, the major fault line dividing believers in human agency, on the one hand, and those who ascribed human actions to God's work, on the other, was not overcome, as attested by the name calling practised by the two camps: the former would refer to their adversaries as 'determinists' (*mujbira*; *mujabbira*; *jabriyya*), whereas the latter would dub the former 'deniers of God's decree' (*qadariyya*) – although this term has a more complex history in that both groups tried to apply it polemically, but the latter group was more successful.[2] The nature of moral obligation, particularly the obligation to do the impossible (*al-taklīf bi-mā lā yuṭāq*), also prompted such name calling, with accusations ranging from questioning God's justice to denying His omnipotence, to use the polemical phrasing.[3] In this discussion, Murtaḍā's views are closest to those of ᶜAbd al-Jabbār's circle, and his wording is exceedingly similar to that of the *Mughnī*. Like them, Murtaḍā does not evade the difficulties but engages with complications related to the relationship between the agent's psychological states and his actions,[4] although whether they were successful in this regard remains an open question. His main disagreement with ᶜAbd al-Jabbār, reflecting the priority of his Imami identity, concerns the importance of the presence of authority figures for moral obligation to be fulfilled.

The human being

Definition

The essence or definition of the human being (*māhiyyat insān*),[5] though seemingly a question of subtle theology, is in fact intimately related to the main premise of grand theology, that is, moral obligation, because the concern of theologians is to identify the subject of moral obligation in every human being. They refer to this subject as the living and/or active subject (*al-ḥayy al-faᶜᶜāl*; *al-dhāt al-faᶜᶜāla*).[6] Their concern, therefore, is not an epistemic one centred on the classification of beings, but a theological one aimed at detecting the moral agent eligible for reward and punishment. Moreover, theologians' discussions of the question display a plethora of relevant terms issuing from revelation: *insān*, *rūḥ*, *nafs*, *ḥayāt*, and – less commonly because it is not Qurᵓānic – *ᶜaql*.[7] Thus, any attempt to address the question had to reckon with the meanings of these terms and their relationship to the essence of the human being.

The disagreement between Mufīd and Murtaḍā concerning the essence of the human being merits close analysis. The reason for this is twofold. First, a comparison of their respective positions reveals a change of approach in expressing Imami theological positions; specifically, their disagreement can be situated in the context of the increasing marginalisation of traditions. Although both represent the rationalist tendency within Imamism, the extent to which each is willing to sideline traditions is rarely depicted as clearly as in this discussion. Second, the debate illustrates a change related to the tension between the esoteric and exoteric dimensions of Imami Shiᶜism; or, more accurately, between gnostic[8] and non-gnostic elements, though this approach comes with its own problems.[9] For the purposes of this discussion, gnosticism denotes an emphasis on inner experiences, as opposed to the primary preoccupation with the ritual and legal aspects of religion.[10] The present discussion shows that Mufīd's and Murtaḍā's positions illustrate the movement away from gnosticism that the two scholars spearheaded. Despite McDermott's excellent presentation (consulted here) of Mufīd's view on the nature of man,[11] it is necessary to give additional attention to the internal development of Mufīd's thought in order to place it in its Imami context, particularly in relationship to Murtaḍā's views.

A common feature of Mufīd's discussion of the human being is his invocation of traditions, even when he also employs rational arguments.[12] This shows that despite his investment in theologising Imami doctrine along rational lines, Mufīd is still careful to adduce evidence from the tradition in a manner that highlights the continuity between his positions and those transmitted by traditionists, even when he disagrees with the traditionalist interpretation of these traditions. This concern for continuity is also evident when he states that his position is that of the rationalist Imami theologians of the Banū Nawbakht and also – though his tone is hesitant here – of Hishām b. al-Ḥakam.[13] The early Muᶜtazili theologian Muᶜammar b. ᶜAbbād al-Sulamī (d. 830) supported the same view.[14] Thus in his commentary on Ṣadūq's *Iᶜtiqādāt*, Mufīd objects to the latter's statement that *rūḥ* and *nafs* are synonymous, listing the different meanings of each term as they appear in revelation and customary Arab usage. With some indecision, he concludes that the subject of moral obligation is the *rūḥ*, which is what philosophers call simple substance (*jawhar basīṭ*).[15] This statement does not, however, match his more systematic theological terminology: elsewhere, he defines the *rūḥ* as a transient accident (*ᶜaraḍ lā baqāᵓ lahu*), equating it with *ḥayāt*.[16] Mufīd's positions are to be seen in light of his answers to specific questions that dictate his approach: whenever he is discussing the question from a technical standpoint as a theologian, his position is that the *rūḥ* is a transient accident. The only occasions on which he is willing to take it to refer to the subject of moral obligation or – more explicitly – to identify it with the human being are when he has to engage with traditions.[17] Only then does he take *rūḥ* to refer to the human being, since the theological definition is not compatible with how the *rūḥ* is described in the traditions; but even then he hints that this usage is not literal. It must also be noted that in his works he shows a gradual acceptance of the term *jawhar basīṭ* used by philosophers. His earlier caution appears to disappear over time, as he uses the term freely in his later works. The acceptance probably reflects simple convenience, since his definition of the human being lacked a technical term in the taxonomy of theologians: 'the originated thing, which is self-subsisting and cannot be characterised by the qualities of atoms and accidents' (*al-shayᵓ al-muḥdath al-qāᵓim bi-nafsihi al-khārij ᶜan ṣifāt al-jawāhir wa-l-aᶜrāḍ*).[18] In addition to the length and awkwardness of such a reference, its lack of technicality, most evident in the use of the word 'thing' (*shayᵓ*),[19] explains the appeal of *jawhar basīṭ*. For Mufīd, then, the human being is indeed immaterial, whereas the *rūḥ* is an accident created after the creation of the human body to inhere therein.[20] Despite Mufīd's reliance on traditions, this position already differs from the gnostic understanding of *rūḥ* presented in earlier collections; for him, although the human being is not the human body, nothing of the human being, let alone a primordial world, exists prior to the creation of the human body. Nevertheless, there is also an unmistakable affinity between the two views of the human being as essentially not belonging to the world of matter, whether the human being is believed to originate in a primordial event or to control the human body without being identified with it.[21]

Murtaḍā's treatment of the question departs from Mufīd's in its total disavowal of traditions. Nowhere in his discussion does he quote traditions, and the only time he addresses their relevance is when he dismisses a tradition as fabricated.[22] Otherwise, Murtaḍā is unequivocal in defining *rūḥ* as a body made of air wavering in the apertures of the living being (*al-hawāʾ al-mutaraddid fī makhāriq al-ḥayy*),[23] almost akin to breath. *Ḥayāt*, on the other hand, is the entitative accident inhering in the body[24] and causing this substrate to become a living being. Therefore, the *rūḥ* is not a living being, nor is there equivalence between *rūḥ* and *ḥayāt*, nor between *rūḥ* and the human being.[25] It should be recalled that in Mufīd's case, the equivalence between *rūḥ* and the human being was mostly driven by his need to interpret traditions, a need that does not arise in Murtaḍā's case given his approach. The human being, for Murtaḍā, is therefore the observed totality (*al-jumla allatī nushāhiduhā*; *al-jumla al-mushāhada*)[26] even when the person is dead;[27] whoever proposes any other definition, he claims, is breaking the rules of Arabic.[28] Murtaḍā's engagement with the terminology of philosophers is different from that of Mufīd, showing a more reserved attitude but still stopping short of outright rejection. He does not mention, let alone endorse, the term *jawhar basīṭ* in his discussion, but his remark on the philosophers' usage of the term *nafs* is far from negative; it shows that his reservation might be due to the term's different meanings in customary Arab usage. Thus, Murtaḍā seems content to affirm that in the jargon of the philosophers, the term *nafs* refers to the active living being (*al-ḥayy al-faᶜᶜāl*), which is the subject of moral obligation.[29] But despite Murtaḍā's detailed arguments against other definitions of the human being proposed by theologians, it is Mufīd's position that he treats most extensively – though without mentioning his name. Murtaḍā's argument against this position is based on his thoroughly materialist ontology and the method of exhaustive division and elimination: if the human being is not identical to the human body, nor is he related to it by inherence or other relations that bind atoms and accidents, then there can be no reasonable way of proposing any relation between a particular human being and his body. He uses the same logic to argue that the human being cannot be restricted to any part of this totality, as perception, which presents itself to the whole human being, depends on the coordination of the different organs and capacities rather than on any single one of them.[30] This view is the common one among the Basran Muᶜtazilis.[31] It is compatible with their reserved attitude towards belief in realms unknowable to the world of senses and reason but accessible through other faculties of the human being.[32] It is true that one can read in it a rejection of the duality of the body and the soul; but grounding this position in the Basran Muᶜtazili refusal to allow the inherence of divine power in human bodies is problematic.[33] Such reading reflects a strong emphasis on concerns that might not have been paramount in Muᶜtazili discourse – at least in these exact terms. The tension is probably not between the divine and the human, but between an approach that leaves room for the mysterious and one that looks at the world from the vantage point of moral obligation and that needs everything to be clear for religious experience to make sense. The materialist drive towards this specific understanding of the human being reflects a quest to do away with concepts that might be analytically useless and harmful to the doctrine of moral obligation, as the responsible agent appears always to function only through his body.

Contrary to Mufīd's view, Murtaḍā's view on the human being is not known to have been supported by any early Imami authorities,[34] and Murtaḍā does not claim support for it in the collections of traditions either. The rationalist-led change in Imami doctrine can be seen here on two fronts. First, Murtaḍā's dismissal of traditions constitutes a maximal departure from his predecessors. And second, if Mufīd's view of the human being still preserved some affinity with earlier gnostic positions, Murtaḍā's view no longer allows for it. His view of the human being is completely materialist; there is nothing about the human being that does not belong in the world of matter. Murtaḍā's position is a further step in the direction inaugurated by Mufīd, who had already rejected the pre-existence of human souls. If Mufīd provided a more worldly view of the human being than was available in the works of many earlier Imamis, Murtaḍā's contribution can be seen as a more earthly view of Mufīd's worldly definition of the human being. Therefore, in his discussion of transmutation (*maskh*), Murtaḍā is keen to stress that when a person is transmuted to an ape, he can no longer be considered a human being. The change in form, that is, in the observed and perceived totality, is not a mere change in appearance; the new creature is not a human being in the image of an ape but rather an actual ape. The continuity between what was formerly a human and what is currently an ape lies in that the living being (*al-ḥayy*) is one and the same.[35] The continuity of identity must therefore be associated with the continuity of life, as no other aspect of the creature seems to endure through transmutation. Ṭūsī's position is the same as that of Murtaḍā, using the latter's arguments verbatim.[36]

Agency

The question of human agency is among the earliest controversies in Islamic theology in general. Differences among Imami positions concerning this question existed from early times, but the rationalist tendency had clearly – though to varying extents – avoided association with determinism. By Murtaḍā's time, the rejection of determinism had more or less become the mainstream Imami position with Mufīd's explicit elaboration of a position that affirms human agency: God enables humans to act and alerts them to prohibited and lawful actions, but it is they who decide on and carry out their actions.[37] Murtaḍā's position is no different, and he emphasises the concurrence between the Imamis and all the other groups that support the belief in human agency (*jamīʿ ṭawāʾif ahl al-ʿadl*).[38] In a lengthy tirade, he elaborates the many consequences that would logically follow from the position that God wills or effects all human acts, reproducing a classical list of accusations intended to point out unpalatable and morally reprehensible situations. For example, the determinist position is portrayed as implying that God does not assist unbelievers in any way, because He effected in them unbelief, which leads to eternal hellfire, regardless of the transient benefits He may bestow on them in this world. Even worse, even believers cannot be said to be recipients of God's assistance, since it is not possible to establish that any good done by God is done for good ends.[39] These accusations are produced against the background of objectivist morality. For all the outrage expressed by Muᶜtazilis, their opponents were far from embarrassed; as Juwaynī (d. 1085) put it, 'That which they find outrageous is the literal statement of our view' (*hādhā alladhī istankarūhu naṣṣ madhhabinā*).[40]

Murtaḍā's handling of traditions that fall in the middle between the determinists and their opponents is similar to Mufīd's: he interprets these traditions in a manner that commits them to the anti-determinist camp. For example, commenting on the two famous traditions according to which 'the acts of humans are created by way of designing and not of making' (*afᶜāl al-ᶜibād makhlūqa khalq taqdīr lā khalq takwīn*) and '[the truth on the question of human agency] is neither determinism nor delegation but something in between' (*lā jabr wa-lā tafwīḍ bal amrᵘⁿ bayn amrayn*),[41] Murtaḍā argues that the traditions convey that God's influence on human acts does not affect their creation (*khalq*). Rather, the traditions refer only to His guidance concerning their moral value.[42] However, he is characteristically unwilling to abide by the terminological restrictions inferred from scriptural usage. Therefore, in addition to arguing that human acts are solely effected and originated by humans themselves (*lā fāᶜil lahā wa-lā muḥdith siwāhum*),[43] he approves of 'creation' (*khalq*) as a proper characterisation of the relationship between human agents and their acts.[44] This is contrary to Mufīd, who claims that all Muslims except the Basran Muᶜtazilis reject the application of this term to human acts.[45] Thus, Murtaḍā was probably among the first to diverge from the Imami consensus as reported by Mufīd, and this position is one more instance of his incorporation of Basran Muᶜtazili views into the developing rationalist tendency in Imami theology, if only on the level of terminology. The divergence does not appear to have been widely accepted, as it broke with the textual tradition; this is probably why Ṭūsī avoids the discussion and refrains from characterising human agency as an act of creation, despite his extensive usage of related terms.[46] Nevertheless, Murtaḍā's detailed arguments for his position shed light on the question of human agency within the broader framework of classical theology from two perspectives.

First, they further reveal the versatility, even indispensability, of the concept of necessary knowledge, as well as Murtaḍā's willingness to fully exploit its potential. Recall that he makes frequent appeal to necessary knowledge in the context of establishing certain epistemic and moral positions, both of which are crucial to the development of Murtaḍā's theological system, as in defending his definition of the human being. The core of the debate on human agency is the question of dependency (*taᶜalluq*), that is, whether and how acts depend on their apparent agents. Once this dependency is established, Murtaḍā proceeds to argue that acts depend on their agents inasmuch as they are originated by them, and that it is not possible to conceive of the dependency in any other way. Throughout this discussion, Murtaḍā repeatedly makes the claim that the dependency of acts on their human agents is a matter of necessary knowledge: we are all aware that our actions follow our motives and occur according to our power.[47] Put differently, our intentional acts are conditioned by antecedent motives.[48] To argue otherwise is simply to be in denial (*mukābara*); it is to put on a pretence of ignorance (*tajāhul*) in order to escape undesired theological consequences.[49] Murtaḍā also turns to the considerations of moral theory to support his argument: because these apparent agents are necessarily known to be blame- or praiseworthy, acts must depend on them. It suffices to have a general knowledge (*ᶜalā ṭarīq al-jumla*) of this proposition, since any objection to it is known by necessity to be incoherent; there is no need to get into the details of this dependency, as such details do not lie within the domain of necessary knowledge but rather are acquired through investigation.[50] Similarly, the moral position against the possibility of obligation to do the impossible is the cornerstone of the argument that an agent's state of being able must precede his actual act, lest he be required to meet his moral obligations while unable to do so.[51] Therefore, the real argument in Murtaḍā's case for the dependency of acts on agents in fact boils down to a reliance on phenomena[52] in the guise of necessary knowledge, whether when invoking self-reflection or when appealing to the way in which rational beings advance their moral judgements.

Second, Murtaḍā's handling of the discussion on human agency indicates the primacy of early positions over later developments in theology, even when continued adherence to the former comes at a great cost to other important aspects of the system. This is visible in the relation between the debate on human agency and the classical theologians' arguments for the existence of God. The classical cosmological argument rests on the premise that every originated being needs an originator, thereby heavily relying on dependency as the relationship that binds acts to their agents. The argument poses a challenge for theologians who are unwilling to accept this premise because of its intimate connection to the anti-determinist position. As important as proving the existence of God is, these theologians are prepared to develop another argument for it to avoid having to accept the extremely sensitive premise concerning the dependency of acts on their agents. This order of priorities can be seen in early and contemporary Ashᶜari works.[53] Both Murtaḍā's insistence on the cosmological argument as the only argument for God's existence[54] and the early Ashᶜari theologians' attempts to provide a different argument could be interpreted in light of each party's investment in early positions concerning human agency. Another indicator is Murtaḍā's conclusive verdict at the end of his rebuttal of acquisitionism (*al-qawl bi-l-kasb*), which itself betrays an interest in accepting some form of dependency, for it served as 'a metaphor for responsibility'.[55] Despite his formal critique of the position as incomprehensible (*ghayr maᶜqūl*), conceptually incoherent and terminologically inaccurate,[56] he closes his exposition with a reading of his adversaries' intentions. He insists that acquisitionism, even setting aside all critique of it, does not in fact help one to escape the challenge of determinism that was the purpose (*gharaḍ*) for which acquisition was proposed in the first place.[57] The effort he expends to argue against this position, therefore, is better seen as an act of scholastic debate necessitated by the requirements of standardised polemics; in reality, he views the position from the standpoint of a partisan guarding his dearly held slogans. This is reminiscent of ᶜAbd al-Jabbār's statement that acquisitionism was developed merely to avoid Muᶜtazili arguments against blunt determinism.[58]

The Imami position, which decisively rejected determinism, seems to have also moved away from the chiliastic aspirations of some members of the early Imami community, which was more tolerant of determinist beliefs. Political activism, therefore, did not go hand in hand with theological speculation, although it is a common theme to argue that the rejection of determinism coincided with the disavowal of quietism. The historical records of many theologians, especially of the earliest periods, seem to support the assumption that they belonged to opposition movements. Nevertheless, while early positions gelled into unshakeable formulas in the metaphysical realm, social reality had a different playbook, as a theologian-politician such as Murtaḍā must have noticed.[59]

Creation and moral obligation

Creation

The universality and finality of Murtaḍā's moral theory, particularly regarding the dictates of rational morality, extend beyond the realm of the created; they are also expected to govern God's actions, as in divine reward and punishment. Even God's original act of creation, usually the locus of ontological debates, is subjected to the same moral treatment. It is therefore not a matter of concern in Murtaḍā's system whether God's relationship to the world is defined as an act of creation *ex nihilo* or some variant of emanation; consistent with his habitual dismissal of philosophers, he seems to take it for granted that God created the universe *ex nihilo* at a certain point in time.[60] Expressing his view in unequivocal terms that reflect the primacy of the moral over the ontological in his theology, Murtaḍā states that God's act of creation cannot have been an obligatory act, since that would mean that He would have fallen short of His obligation before doing the act of creation.[61] Since the act of creation cannot have been purposeless, the discussion is bound to become a quest for God's purpose in creation. This purpose, in turn, provides the backdrop for analysing the question of moral obligation, crucial in much of the theological literature of the time. This approach gives the impression that Murtaḍā's concern was not with God's freedom to act in the ontological sense, as was customary in the classical discussion between theologians and philosophers.[62]

In addition to the scarcity of moral categories in Murtaḍā's system, some of them are, by definition, inapplicable to God, such as acts that concern self-benefit and self-harm. Murtaḍā thus readily invokes exhaustive elimination as the main method for identifying the divine purpose behind creation. Whereas benefit (*nafᶜ*) is accepted as the inevitable wisdom (*ḥikma*) of creation, the rest of the debate concerns identifying the party for whose benefit it was done. Just like Murtaḍā's discussion of divine assistance sought to maximise such assistance within the limits of moral obligation, his approach to the wisdom of creation reflects an effort to highlight God's maximal goodness by arguing that the act of creation is characterised by two aspects of goodness (*wajhān*). Thus, God's act of creation is intended for the benefit of the created being itself, but also for other creatures who might benefit from this created being. The maximalist position also motivates Murtaḍā's enumeration of the potential benefits made available by this act: it is an instance of initiated benevolence (*tafaḍḍul*) by God, as it grants all the enjoyment of an advantageous environment, rational beings access to reward and, in case of pain, both rational and irrational beings a right to compensation.[63] Therefore, the benefits of initiated benevolence, reward and compensation complement each other (*tatakāmalu*), making the act of creation one of supreme goodness in terms of the diversity of its benefits and the scope of its beneficiaries. Murtaḍā is in agreement with ^c^Abd al-Jabbār on this issue;[64] Ṭūsī follows Murtaḍā's suit almost verbatim.[65]

Given the all-too-confident assertions of Murtaḍā's theory, his interest in the wisdom of creation quickly develops into a detailed manual intended to prescribe the order of creation that God must have followed for this act to fit the requirements of morality. It is thus that Murtaḍā argues, in agreement with Abū Hāshim and ^c^Abd al-Jabbār,[66] that God's first creation could not have been inanimate (*jamād*), for this would have been a purposeless act since inanimate beings cannot be benefitted nor can they benefit themselves.[67] Consequently, he argues, God's first creation must have been a desiring animate being, which was created together with its object of desire, although the desired object may have been none other than the desiring being itself. Purposelessness is therefore avoided, for life is a requisite for receiving benefit, and the pleasure of satisfying its desire is the benefit that this being would enjoy. Murtaḍā's view agrees with that of ^c^Abd al-Jabbār[68] but contradicts that of Mufīd, who, though restricting God's creative activity to what benefits His creatures, did not require a particular order for such activity to be wise.[69] Ṭūsī, whose view agrees with Mufīd's, implies that Murtaḍā shared his position that God may have first created inanimate beings since He knew that He would subsequently create animate beings whose otherworldly benefit would lie in making use of the first, inanimate created being.[70] If, as is likely the case, Murtaḍā changed his view to argue that God must have first created an animate desiring being, this indicates a move towards an increasingly restrictive understanding of God's freedom to act within the limits of moral theory in a fashion typical of Basran Mu^c^tazili theology.[71] Even the position reported by Ṭūsī, though still restrictive, is not satisfactory, since it leaves an interval of time in which God's creation would be judged purposeless. Given the absence of beneficiaries in this interval and God's power to do things differently, such a scenario represents an unnecessary waste of divine power that cannot fit into Murtaḍā's tight moral universe. If philosophers have been accused by theologians of denying God's freedom in the act of creation, Murtaḍā's system does not seem to fully escape this accusation. God's ontological freedom, in the sense of creating *ex nihilo* at any point He chooses, is preserved; but the restrictions on God's moral freedom are obvious.

The stage is now set to introduce the major relationship that binds all these elements in a universal interaction intended to explain the religious experience and to demarcate the expectations of both the creator and the created. It is to this relationship, that of moral obligation (*taklīf*), that we now turn.

Moral obligation

Moral obligation is a major common theme in classical theological literature,[72] and its particular significance in the worldview of the Muʿtazilis cannot be overestimated.[73] In the bulk of Murtaḍā's discussion of the question he engages with the various positions of the Muʿtazilis, most often singling out the two Jubbāʾīs and the Baghdadi Muʿtazilis, with sporadic mention of other names and groups.[74]

Two key assumptions intersect to give rise to Murtaḍā's discourse on moral obligation, which agrees with that of ʿAbd al-Jabbār. The first is the purposefulness of divine action, already expressed in the grand narrative of creation. The second is a bare admission of the fact that humans, more often than not, desire to do vile things. It is hard to reconcile these two assumptions without introducing a bridging concept to dovetail belief in God's wisdom with His responsibility for our innate disposition to behave in a morally flawed manner. Again, Murtaḍā turns the threat into an opportunity by banking on the consequentialist undertones of his moral theory. Nevertheless, it is important to note that he avoids common answers that assert that God created people in order to test them (*ikhtibār, ibtilāʾ, imtiḥān*), or that they may worship Him, or in order to show His power and lordship,[75] since such views would not fit into God's wisdom as defined in his moral theory – what purpose could there be in such a test? Instead, Murtaḍā's answer is restricted to the bright side of things, with their not-so-bright side treated as a mere by-product: the wisdom of creating humans with innate vile desires is to give them access to reward (*al-taʿrīḍ li-l-thawāb*).[76] Since reward, by definition, entails both material benefits and – more importantly in this context – reverence (*taʿẓīm*) for the deserving agent, it can be earned only through suffering the hardship of resisting one's vile desires, for such reward cannot be deserved without hardship (*lan yaṣiḥḥa istiḥqāq al-thawāb illā bi-mā ʿalā al-mukallaf fī fiʿlihi aw tarkihi mashaqqa*).[77] Punishment, on the other hand, is just the unfortunate consequence of a differently intended scenario. Once more, the imaginary group of rational beings is assumed to judge this context in a society – like Murtaḍā's – in which forms of interaction and mobility are calibrated through an elaborate complex of hierarchical interactions and expressions of respect are not offered for free.[78] It is, therefore, not surprising that Murtaḍā draws on these norms in his assessment of the value of acts in the currency of both material benefits and social status.

On a more theoretical level, Murtaḍā's main interpretative investment is in the liaison of desirability and vileness: through desire, God has created in humans the need (*aḥwaj*) for vile acts. Unless He did that purposelessly or out of sheer malice, it must be that such vile desires are intended to benefit their owners.[79] Although pleasure is the typical benefit in Murtaḍā's scheme, the immutability of rationally defined moral values precludes any positive judgement on the pleasure of satisfying these desires. Thus moral obligation is basically defined in a way that reflects the inconvenience of suppressing these desires, together with God's active role in imposing the obligation: moral obligation arises when one party wills from another something that involves hardship and effort (*irādat al-murīd min ghayrihi mā fīhi kulfa wa-mashaqqa*).[80] The criticality of stressing the significance of divine will should be seen against the background of the rejection of the ethics of divine command in Murtaḍā's moral theory. Therefore, despite Murtaḍā's dispensation with God's word in judging rationally defined moral values, it seems that the consequentialist nature of the theory makes it difficult to require the suppression of desires out of a pure intellectual conviction concerning their vileness. Although it is God who creates in individuals the necessary knowledge through which they grasp the value of acts, it is God's active intervention, through an act of the will, that is needed to justify the inconvenience of human commitment to moral obligation. This rationale underlies Murtaḍā's rejection of the equivalence between moral obligation and knowledge of the value of acts, leading him instead to insist that moral obligation boils down to will (*al-marjiʿ bihi ilā al-irāda*),[81] which alone distinguishes God's imposition of moral obligation on individuals from any other possible intention of His.[82] Therefore, while Murtaḍā still vehemently rejects the ethics of divine command, he invokes God's action as a necessary element in legitimising human commitment to moral activity. This view agrees with that of ʿAbd al-Jabbār[83] but not with that of Ibn Mattawayh and Mānkdīm, who argued that moral obligation is in fact defined as God's informing (*iʿlām*) humans of the beneficial and harmful consequences of specific actions.[84] The divergence of the latter scholars from ʿAbd al-Jabbār's view might be due to the influence of Abū al-Ḥusayn al-Baṣrī's understanding of divine will and knowledge. Contrary to ʿAbd al-Jabbār, who considered divine knowledge – but not divine will – an essential attribute, Abū al-Ḥusayn al-Baṣrī subsumed divine will under divine knowledge, while still considering the latter an essential attribute.[85]

The contractual nature of moral obligation is most evident in the list of conditions required of both the obligator (*mukallif*) and the obligated (*mukallaf*). The list is a faithful reproduction of the conditions of moral acts, specifying the expectations on the respective parties: both must be aware of the exact act required and be able to deliver their respective parts, be it the performance of the obligation or the provision of the deserved treatment.[86] Nevertheless, the unique character of moral obligation is exemplified in two conditions that are divided between the obligator and the obligated in a manner that reflects their specific roles in the contract. First, since reward can be deserved only through the hardship suffered in abiding by the dictates of moral obligation, the obligated must experience pleasure and pain. The interplay of forbidden pleasure and agonising pain is supposed to produce the hardship for which the individual is to be rewarded.[87] As stated boldly by Ibn Mattawayh, had it not been for the prospect of reward, it would not have been possible for God to create the sun in a manner that makes us disturbed by its heat (one cannot but think of the climate in which the text was written at the time and global warming today).[88] Second, the dictates of rational moral obligation do not need justification since the individual knows he is obligated to observe them. But the dictates of revelational moral obligation pose a radical challenge, for they are carried out as acts of worship (*ᶜalā jihat al-ᶜibāda*).[89] It must be recalled that as a category of deserved treatment, thanksgiving is defined by Murtaḍā in a way that satisfies the requirements of his theoretical model while still providing a justification for classifying worship under it. The restrictions imposed by this definition on the desert of worship are transferred into conditions on the bounty bestowed by the obligator. These conditions are all met only in the case of God's care for humans, for His bounty is qualitatively and quantitatively ultimate (*al-ghāya al-ᶜuẓmā fī al-manzila wa-l-kathra*),[90] so much so that Murtaḍā expresses this theological point in poetry.[91]

However, despite Murtaḍā's insistence on the potential of reward as the wisdom of bringing humans under moral obligation, the limits of divine freedom in doing so remain a thorny question. Within the parameters of his moral theory, it is definitely more reasonable to portray God as a supreme benefactor whose bounty may sometimes be received with ingratitude than to present Him as a spiteful examiner bent on demonstrating what He already knows. But the question persists why He instated moral obligation in the first place that would lead many of His creation to unbearable suffering – even if as a by-product of the intended outcome. Murtaḍā's answer reveals the paradox of divine freedom and rational morality, for he asserts repeatedly that the imposition of moral obligation by God is both obligatory and initiated benevolence.[92] This paradox is presented in light of God's options before creation and His lack of options following it. Thus, moral obligation as initiated benevolence reflects the fact that God could have created humans without vile desires, in which case they would also be deprived of the opportunity to attain great reward.[93] But once God created humans with such desires, it is incumbent upon Him to bring them under moral obligation lest they be left to pursue their vile desires freely. The imposition of moral obligation thus admits of no middle ground; it must be either vile or obligatory (*lā wāsiṭa lahu bayna ḥālatay al-wujūb wa-l-qubḥ*),[94] depending on whether its conditions are met, but it is never a plain-good act that can be equally done or neglected. God is never fully free to act once He has created humans the way He has. This position, rather than his oft-repeated argument that each person's destiny is caused by his own actions, may constitute the deeper justification for Murtaḍā's claim that it is equally good to bring believers and unbelievers under moral obligation.[95] He justifies his position by appealing to divine assistance: it is incumbent on God, by way of justice, to enhance the individual's motive to meet his moral obligation by providing assistance towards that purpose.[96] God, within these limits, is much less free to act than are His creatures, who nonetheless need to live with the dire consequences of their unchosen freedom. Despite the continuous resort to reason and responsibility, there is not much room for individual choice in Murtaḍā's theory: it is almost impossible for God to withhold His assistance, even when it leads to the eternal damnation of the assisted. In a turn of the argument that reveals the sobering outcome of excessive investment in an intellectualist understanding of morality, Murtaḍā callously dismisses the conclusion that his position makes God much less merciful than a father who refrains from assisting his son with money once he realises that it might get his son into trouble. This father is not acting morally in Murtaḍā's reckoning but is merely driven by a selfish dread of the grief that would afflict him if his son were hurt.[97]

The preceding discussion concerns the theoretical underpinnings of moral obligation as the relationship that binds God and human beings. It remains to examine how this theoretical construct materialises in concrete situations; that is, how the terms of the grand moral contract apply in each individual's personal history. Although either of the two parties, the obligator or the obligated, may take the initiative to inaugurate moral obligation, both end up using the same trigger towards this purpose. This trigger is the human fear of potential harm in both worldly and otherworldly matters.[98] Within Murtaḍā's consequentialist model, this drive translates into a moral obligation to expend all effort to avoid harm, as long as one does not run into greater harm thereby. The social context proves an extremely apt venue for inducing fear, since a person who grows up among religious people will inevitably be reminded of the eternal punishment that follows negligence of one's obligations.[99] Even in the case of individuals who appear not to experience such fear, Murtaḍā is unwilling to allow for the possibility of a non-religious social context; instead, he prefers to argue that such people have in fact committed a mistake in reasoning that makes them ignore their fear, or they are distracted by other concerns.[100] The only possibility aside from social context that Murtaḍā addresses is a Ḥayy b. Yaqẓān scenario,[101] which he describes as the hypothetical case of a solitary individual (*wa-innamā nafriḍu al-kalām fī munfarid ᶜan al-nās*). If outward signs or putting his reason to proper use do not induce fear in this individual, it is then incumbent upon God to intervene and to provide the individual with an alert (*khāṭir*) in the form of private speech that only he can hear.[102] Reflection on the exact nature of God's intervention – be it a form of written discourse, a special sign or a timely idea that must occur to the individual in question – is a consequence of understanding moral obligation in terms of divine assistance that must be provided to everyone. This preoccupation with the universal delivery of divine assistance proved a liability for the Muᶜtazilis, inviting harsh criticism that ranged from portrayals of this position as belief in private revelation[103] to accusations of manipulating religion (*talāᶜub bi-l-dīn*) for the purpose of protecting their initial claim about divine assistance.[104]

Following the experience of fear, the individual's first moral obligation is investigation in order to obtain knowledge of God (*al-naẓar fī ṭarīq maᶜrifat allāh*). In the most basic chronological sense, an individual comes under moral obligation upon reaching maturity of intellect. Although this criterion shares the Stoic ideal of the primacy of the intellect in human experience of the divine,[105] in Murtaḍā's theology its function is both more modest and more concrete: it marks the moment of realising the fear of potential harm that prompts one to think about God. This scenario applies even to an individual who has no other moral obligation, that is, one who is not in debt nor entrusted with any deposit nor a beneficiary of anyone's favour – situations in which he would be obligated to act accordingly.[106] Therefore, whether socially imparted or privately experienced, the fear of punishment is the moral justification of religious experience. Paradoxically, this is the exact opposite of Murtaḍā's initial justification of moral obligation. Whereas he argues at the abstract level that the potential provision of reward is what legitimises the imposition of moral obligation, when his discussion moves to the concrete level of individual cases, the bright side of things is dimmed, and Murtaḍā invokes fear as the true motive behind human religious experience. This paradox of the theoretical and the practical is engendered by the intersection of divine omnipotence and human helplessness: for maximum efficacy, the best intentions of the strong must be met by the direst needs of the weak, despite their common moral categories. The liaison of desirability and vileness, again, poses the fundamental challenge in a way that leaves no doubt about the consequentialist calculations involved: despite knowledge of the vileness of certain desired acts, a person refrains from them only upon considering the possibility of a creator who might punish him for them.[107] God's presence adds nothing to human moral knowledge on the level of rational moral obligations, but it does change the rules of the game: instead of blameworthiness, which is immaterial, one has to consider the scary prospect of punishment. Therefore, seeking knowledge of God is a form of assistance only inasmuch as it confirms the deserts of punishment and reward, and the whole roadmap leading up to this confirmation is a mere necessary prelude.[108] Although the proper use of one's reason should ideally lead to knowledge about God's existence, His attributes and divine justice, what ultimately matters is the establishment of firm knowledge of the desert of punishment; having secured this, one is given sufficient time to put the newly acquired knowledge to practice. The impracticality of this approach is most evidently manifested in the thorny question of the length of the period needed by each individual to acquire knowledge of God and to apply it in the minimum measure required to justify the desert of reward or punishment. Murtaḍā's discussion of the problem is lacking in clarity, as he contents himself with generic claims about what a person should do while avoiding the more intricate problem of developing a definite temporal demarcation of this period.[109] But the ambiguity regarding the inception of moral obligation is not repeated when it comes to its termination. The need to provide the deserved treatment necessitates that the moral obligation of each individual come to an end – whether by death or by other means. In both cases – the inception and the termination of moral obligation – the particular character of each individual is stressed to the maximum: reward and punishment are individual just like fear, and there is no need for them to be meted out simultaneously for all. The simultaneity of the end of the moral obligation of all individuals on the Day of Judgement is learnt only from revelation.[110]

It is in this particular sense that Murtaḍā argues that moral obligation is established by reason only. At a later point, revelation complements what reason is unable to fully grasp because of a lack of available data, not because of any intrinsic weakness. Knowing God, within the limits needed to justify moral obligation, is totally possible without any resort to revelation. Even the dictates of revelation are brought under the scrutiny of reason, for humans must be equipped with the means required to verify the veracity of the transmitters of revelation in order to enable every individual to arrive at the right conclusions and to endorse the proper creed.[111] It seems that this question was a matter of controversy among Imamis. Some of them apparently held that the basic knowledge of God depends on the Imam's guidance, a claim that Murtaḍā rejects in no uncertain terms.[112] For his part, Mufīd also avoided blunt dependency on the Imam's guidance. In a succinct passage, he makes three points: first, that reason needs revelation to allow the individual to acquire knowledge; second, that reason is inseparable (*lā yanfakku*) from revelation, which alerts rational beings to the way of evidencing (*yunabbihu al-ᶜāqil ᶜalā kayfiyyat al-istidlāl*); and third, that there must be a prophet at the inception of moral obligation (*fī awwal al-taklīf*).[113] This statement caused disagreement among subsequent scholars regarding Mufīd's actual position. Some took the passage to indicate that he believed moral obligation to need revelation to take effect,[114] whereas others argued that he upheld the sufficiency of reason towards this end.[115] Part of the problem seems to be due to the conflation, in Mufīd's terse passage, of two distinct discussions concerning moral obligation: the respective roles of reason and revelation, on the one hand, and the necessity of prophethood, on the other. Either way, Mufīd is unwilling to allow a total disconnect between reason and revelation. While still ascribing considerable agency to reason, his wording leaves no doubt about the hierarchy involved. The inevitable presence of prophets in his scheme may be explained in light of his argument for the necessity of the Imama, which relies on human inability to learn the details of moral obligation through reason only. Murtaḍā, on the other hand, arrives at the same conclusion through a different route: even if humans knew all they need to know, their inclination to ignore this knowledge would necessitate the presence of an authority figure whose function would be to confirm the knowledge and make them less inclined to ignore it. The agreement between the views of ᶜAbd al-Jabbār and Murtaḍā concerning the primacy of reason is thus restricted to the theoretical level of discussion;[116] their readings of the concrete workings of reason and revelation in personal histories diverge, for Murtaḍā is unwilling to allow even the hypothetical possibility of the absence of prophethood.[117] Murtaḍā's position assigns more power to reason in establishing moral obligation than does Mufīd's position, but both scholars ultimately work with the assumption that the presence of an authority figure is inevitable, in contrast to ᶜAbd al-Jabbār. For his part, Ṭūsī provides a lengthy discussion on the question of what a person can be expected to know prior to revelation, ruling that it suffices to know God and to affirm prophethood and thereby siding by Murtaḍā.[118]

His contractual approach to moral obligation leads Murtaḍā to reject the literal understanding of certain traditions that had gained currency in the Imami milieu. One such tradition states that an illegitimate child (*walad al-zinā*) cannot be a believer and will eventually perish in hellfire. This statement constitutes a blatant contradiction of Murtaḍā's claim that the reward of moral obligation is within the reach of any rational being, in addition to contradicting the fact that the individual in this case would be held accountable for a mistake committed by someone else. Murtaḍā questions the tradition's authenticity, but he also attempts an interpretation that would avoid its unmistakably deterministic undertone: whoever seems to be both an illegitimate child and a believer must in fact be either a crypto-unbeliever or a legitimate child.[119] Thus, the apparent social stigma is no longer a cause for unjust eternal punishment; rather, it is an indication of the individual's true conviction or of society's erroneous perception. A similar, though more common, challenge arises from traditions on the primordial existence of humans (*dharr*) and the imposition of moral obligation at that time. For moral obligation to have taken effect then, humans must have been rational beings; but since no one remembers being in such a condition, these reports should be either completely rejected or interpreted to signify God's creating in individuals the power to reason to knowledge of Him.[120] This is also the way in which Murtaḍā understands the famous 'covenant verse' (Q7:172).[121] Mufīd seems more reluctant to dismiss entirely the traditions on the primordial existence of humans. Although he agrees with Murtaḍā's interpretation of the verse, he still allows room for accepting traditions about humans in the primordial condition as long as they do not include moral obligation or betray a belief in the transmigration of souls.[122] Ṭūsī maintains a more lenient attitude towards traditions and includes such reports in his works.[123] Therefore, just as Murtaḍā's view on the nature of human beings represents a clearer departure than does Mufīd's from the earlier gnostic strands within Imami Shiᶜism, the two scholars' divergence on understanding these traditions is yet another example of Murtaḍā's further push in this direction, which was not fully retained by Ṭūsī.

Conclusion

Content

According to Murtaḍā, the human being is matter in both body and spirit, for the latter is just the air breathed by the living person. He allows no otherworldly connections as part of the human being and easily dispenses with such assumptions – usually from traditions – on two counts. First, their epistemological basis is insufficient; and second, they are functionally unnecessary, since they do not help to explain human conduct as that of a morally obligated agent.

Underneath the layers of moral and theological speculation about gratitude and the existence of a creator lies the nucleus of Murtaḍā's reading of religious experience. It is in fact psychological, anchored in fear as the deepest human motive that pushes people into taking all possible precautions to avoid a probable just desert of eternal punishment. Thus, observing the dictates of religion is, for Murtaḍā, first and foremost an act of prudence, not a manifestation of love or justice. The first moral obligation is that of investigation in order to arrive at knowledge of God, whence follow the remaining religious teachings.

In its human dimension, the world is not the best possible world, but rather one that is the outcome of free choices made by human agents. As such, we live among probabilities and in anticipation of events of which we are mostly the makers. Humans are solely responsible for their acts because they are absolutely free to do them. Even God is required to create the world in a way that suits the schema of moral obligation. Except for miracles, the extent of divine intervention is limited; it does not go beyond governing the world through God's norms or explaining what is required of the individual. Any further intervention would infringe on the goodness of moral obligation and thus alter the model of reward and punishment.

Context

Murtaḍā's view of the human being and of human agency is in full agreement with Basran Muᶜtazilism. His disagreement with Mufīd is strongest in the discussion of the human being, for the latter maintains a more lenient attitude towards earlier Imami traditions that include certain gnostic elements. The two scholars are in basic agreement concerning the primacy of reason in establishing moral obligation, but Mufīd's position seems more accommodating of authority, even at the inception of religious experience, which reveals less confidence on his part in the sufficiency of reason. Although Ṭūsī agrees with Murtaḍā on human agency, his view on the human being falls somewhere between those of his two teachers.

Notes

1. Hourani, 'Origins', 76–80, discounts the influence of Greek philosophy but is much more open to the possibility of Christian influence in the case of the Muᶜtazilis; as for determinists, he seems to rule that they appeared 'more purely Islamic' to Muslims (p. 85).
2. On the name and its ambivalent connotations, see van Ess, 'Ḳadariyya'. As an example, both ᶜAbd al-Jabbār and the Ashᶜari al-Juwaynī denounce the Qadariyya in their theological works; Juwaynī, *Irshād*, 255–7; cf. ᶜAbd al-Jabbār, *Mughnī*, 8:326–32; Ibn Mattawayh, *Majmūᶜ*, 1:442–4; Jishumī, *Risāla*, 24, 26, 59–62.
3. On this question, see Gimaret, 'Taklīf'.
4. On the Muᶜtazilis, see Frank, 'Autonomy', 324.
5. The problems with establishing what these theologians meant by *mā huwa al-insān* are noted in Vasalou, 'Subject', 271–2.
6. *Dhakhīra*, 113–14; *Rasāʾil*, 4:30–1; Mufīd, *al-Masāʾil al-Sarawiyya*, 55; Mufīd, *Taṣḥīḥ*, 82.
7. I have chosen to keep these terms in Arabic because any translation at this point would obscure the fact that the various theologians' divergent positions on these concepts require different respective English translations for each term.
8. This is the choice of Halm and is aptly suggested by Amir-Moezzi, 'Spirituality', 109.

Though Hodgson, 'Bāṭiniyya', translates *bāṭin* as 'esoteric' to reflect its relation to hidden meaning, he notes that some of its aspects can be matched among the Gnostics. Crone, *Nativist Prophets*, 215–19, argues for qualifying Shīʿī Extremists as Gnostics. Daftary, *Short History*, 52–9, surveys the esoteric dimensions of Ismāʿīlism; following an examination of their doctrinal system, he concludes that the Ismāʿīlīs founded an 'Islamic gnostic tradition'. While still rejecting the term 'Islamic Gnosis', Asatryan and Burns, 'Ghulāt religion', 85–6, argue that the *ghulāt* did share much gnostic material.

9. Gnosticism has been rejected as a polemical construct intended to define normative Christianity against heterodoxy; King, *What Is Gnosticism*, 218. But there are common features that can still be perceived as belonging to similar phenomena. I use gnosticism as opposed to Gnosticism, since the former term refers not to a specific religious movement but to the features generally shared by these phenomena.
10. Amir-Moezzi, *Divine Guide*, 13–14, presents a succinct summary of the tension between esotericism and exotericism. Although his concern is more with the rationalist/non-rationalist dichotomy given his treatment of *ʿaql* as dialectical reasoning, he accepts that the non-rationalist Akhbārīs were not always esotericist nor were their adversaries always exotericist.
11. McDermott, *Theology*, 222–9.
12. See, for example, Mufīd, *al-Masāʾil al-Sarawiyya*, 58; Mufīd, *Taṣḥīḥ*, 79–83.
13. Mufīd, *al-Masāʾil al-Sarawiyya*, 58. As McDermott, *Theology*, 225, notes, the doctrine ascribed to Hishām by Ashʿarī, *Maqālāt*, 331, seems in harmony with Mufīd's definition. But it does not seem to be identical to it, since Hishām's doctrine – if Ashʿarī's wording is to be trusted – indicates that the *rūḥ*, which is not bodily, is a light that perceives acts and senses, which is also the position ascribed to Hishām in ʿAbd al-Jabbār, *Mughnī*, 11:310. Interestingly, Murtaḍā does not attribute this view to Hishām but only to the Banū Nawbakht, omitting any reference to Mufīd; *Dhakhīra*, 114. Throughout his discussion of this position, he refers to it as Muʿammar's doctrine. Ṭūsī, on the other hand, does mention Mufīd as an upholder of this position; Tūsī, *Iqtiṣād*, 66. See van Ess, *Theologie und Gesellschaft*, 1:368–9.
14. See van Ess, *Theologie und Gesellschaft*, 3:83–8, for Muʿammar's view on the question.
15. Mufīd, *Taṣḥīḥ*, 91; see Atiyeh, 'Al-Kindī's concept', 313–14, and Adamson, *Al-Kindi*, 107–11, for the particular philosophical tradition that Mufīd probably referenced; see Wisnovsky, 'Avicenna', 96–105, for a detailed exploration of the formulation of the later tradition; and see Ivry, 'Psychology', for a brief overview of the general philosophical approach.
16. Mufīd, *al-Masāʾil al-Sarawiyya*, 55.
17. As in Mufīd, *Taṣḥīḥ*, 91; Mufīd, *al-Masāʾil al-Sarawiyya*, 60–1, 65.
18. Mufīd, *Awāʾil*, 77; Mufīd, *al-Masāʾil al-Sarawiyya*, 58.
19. For the theological connotations of *shayʾ* in Muʿtazilism, see Wisnovsky, 'Avicenna', 104.
20. Mufīd, *al-Masāʾil al-Sarawiyya*, 52–3.
21. See Amir-Moezzi, *Divine Guide*, 38–44, for an elaborate description of the esoteric position.

22. *Rasāʾil*, 4:30.
23. *Rasāʾil*, 1:130, 4:30.
24. *Rasāʾil*, 4:30.
25. *Mawsūʿa*, 1:35.
26. *Dhakhīra*, 114, 117–18; *Sharḥ Jumal*, 104–5; *Rasāʾil*, 4:30.
27. *Mawsūʿa*, 1:397.
28. *Mawsūʿa*, 1:396.
29. *Dhakhīra*, 114; see the survey of the meanings of *nafs* in *Tanzīh*, 211–14; the same text also in *Amālī*, 1:317–20.
30. *Dhakhīra*, 114–19.
31. Heemskerk, 'ʿAbd al-Jabbār', 129–36; cf. ʿAbd al-Jabbār, *Mughnī*, 11:310–11; Ibn Mattawayh, *Majmūʿ*, 2:241–58.
32. Vasalou, 'Subject', 290–2.
33. As in Elkaisy-Friemuth, *God*, 53–4.
34. In fact, Mufīd's teacher, Abū al-Jaysh al-Khurāsānī (d. 978), seems to have argued against the Basran Muʿtazili view that Murtaḍā later adopted, as the title of a lost book of his suggests; Najāshī, *Rijāl*, 422.
35. *Rasāʾil*, 1:353–4. The published text is incomplete; it suggests that Murtaḍā approves of the discontinuity between the former and later states of the transmuted person. See Naẓarī, 'Nigarishī (3)', 40, for the full text.
36. Ṭūsī, *Iqtiṣād*, 66–8.
37. Mufīd, *Taṣḥīḥ*, 47.
38. *Mulakhkhaṣ*, 449; his wording is almost verbatim that of ʿAbd al-Jabbār, *Mughnī*, 8:3–4; compare how the view of Ṣāliḥ Qubba is presented.
39. *Mulakhkhaṣ*, 477–8; cf. ʿAbd al-Jabbār, *Mughnī*, 8:199–203.
40. Juwaynī, *Irshād*, 364–5.
41. See Kulaynī, *Kāfī*, 1:160; Ṣadūq, *Tawḥīd*, 206, 216, 362, 407, 416; Ṣadūq, *ʿUyūn*, 1:114, 2:132; cf. Mufīd, *Taṣḥīḥ*, 46–7.
42. *Rasāʾil*, 1:135–9; briefly in *Amālī*, 2:206.
43. *Mulakhkhaṣ*, 63–4, 449; *Sharḥ Jumal*, 93.
44. *Rasāʾil*, 1:136–9.
45. Mufīd, *Awāʾil*, 58–9. McDermott, *Theology*, 162, states that ʿAbd al-Jabbār seems to have also restricted the usage of 'to create' to God, although for reasons different than those of Mufīd. In this, he bases himself on a passage in Mānkdīm, *Sharḥ*, 380–1. However, this is Mānkdīm's position and not ʿAbd al-Jabbār's, since the latter elsewhere states unequivocally that 'to create' is predicable of humans; ʿAbd al-Jabbār, *Mughnī*, 8:162–3; cf. Adang, Madelung and Schmidtke, *Baṣran Muʿtazilite Theology*, 243–52, where the author also uses the term, though cautiously. It must be noted, however, that the text has many layers that are almost impossible to separate (editors' introduction, 7) and that mix the contributions of Zaydi and non-Zaydi Muʿtazilis, which might have prompted this caution.
46. Ṭūsī, *Iqtiṣād*, 55–8.
47. *Mulakhkhaṣ*, 63, 451–2, 466–8; *Sharḥ Jumal*, 95.

48. That is, acts are not caused by motives, despite this dependency; see Frank, 'Dogmatic works', 42; Frank, 'Autonomy', 341–4.
49. *Mulakhkhaṣ*, 63, 451–2, 466–8; cf. ᶜAbd al-Jabbār's view as presented in Frank, 'Autonomy', 325–6. It is significant that Murtaḍā's claim here follows ᶜAbd al-Jabbār in terms of both the principal argument and the objections to previous arguments for the same position advanced earlier by Ibn Khallād; Adang, Madelung and Schmidtke, *Baṣran Muᶜtazilite Theology*, 243. This overlap sheds light on the extent to which Murtaḍā's views were associated with ᶜAbd al-Jabbār's brand of Basran Muᶜtazilism – even assuming that the former relied on earlier works.
50. *Mulakhkhaṣ*, 453; *Mawsūᶜa*, 1:211.
51. *Dhakhīra*, 88–95; *Sharḥ Jumal*, 98–9.
52. On the meaning of the Muᶜtazilī reliance on phenomena, see Vasalou, 'Subject', 274–5.
53. Compare with Ashᶜarī, *Risāla*, 141–57, where he argues that bodies are originated but omits any reference to their need for an originator because of their being originated; rather, he makes reference to the fine design of the world. In *Lumaᶜ*, 17–19, Ashᶜarī also touches on the fine design of the world, but he starts from observing our inability to perform certain acts – a point of departure exactly opposite to that required by the argument from dependency. See also Bāqillānī (d. 1013), *Tamhīd*, 42–3, and *Inṣāf*, 17–18, who focuses on the fine design of the world to argue that it must have a maker. Bāqillānī's mention of dependency is cautious in that he avoids any hint of origination and rather looks at it as a matter of mutual association, almost based on language usage. Later, more philosophically oriented Ashᶜaris were more concerned with necessity and contingency than with origination and pre-eternality. This focus allowed them to diverge from the traditional demonstrative device of evidencing from the known to the unknown; Juwaynī, *Irshād*, 28–30. Arguments of particularisation thus still needed Juwaynī's abovementioned supplement to provide them with stringency; Madelung, 'Al-Baṣrī's proof', 279–80.
54. *Mulakhkhaṣ*, 65, 450–1.
55. Van Ess, *Flowering*, 179.
56. *Mulakhkhaṣ*, 67, 462, 468, 474; *Sharḥ Jumal*, 44, 96.
57. *Mulakhkhaṣ*, 477.
58. ᶜAbd al-Jabbār, *Mughnī*, 8:83–4.
59. This theme is suggested by van Ess in several of his works; for a succinct early presentation, see van Ess, 'Early development', 187. For a different viewpoint, see Murad, 'Jabr', passim.
60. *Mawsūᶜa*, 2:5.
61. *Rasāʾil*, 1:129.
62. Wisnovsky, 'Avicenna', 130–1.
63. *Dhakhīra*, 111.
64. ᶜAbd al-Jabbār, *Mughnī*, 11:127–34.
65. Ṭūsī, *Iqtiṣād*, 62–3.
66. ᶜAbd al-Jabbār, *Mughnī*, 11:69–70. That this position was also Abū Hāshim's can be gleaned from his argument as reported in Ṭūsī, *Tibyān*, 5:452.
67. *Dhakhīra*, 111–12.

68. ᶜAbd al-Jabbār, *Mughnī*, 11:69–78.
69. Mufīd, *Awāʾil*, 107–8.
70. Ṭūsī, *Iqtiṣād*, 63. In Ṭūsī, *Tibyān*, 5:451, in discussing Q11:7 concerning the location of God's throne having been on water before the creation of the heavens and the earth, Ṭūsī explains that this must have been the case because the otherworldly benefit of certain obligated parties lies in knowing that the throne has been created before them; he then comments that this was Murtaḍā's position. This rationale is consistent with Murtaḍā's theological system, but the *Dhakhīra*, in which the contrary opinion appears, was written at a later point in Murtaḍā's career. One clue that supports the conclusion that the position presented in the main text was Murtaḍā's final one is that Ṭūsī states that his view was what Rummānī opted for. Given Rummānī's death relatively early in Murtaḍā's life and bearing in mind that he was Murtaḍā's teacher, it is very unlikely that Murtaḍā came to know of this view after Ṭūsī. In fact, Ṭūsī may have learned about it from Murtaḍā. So, unless Murtaḍā gained a new appreciation for his teacher's opinion after he wrote the *Dhakhīra*, it is probably the case that he changed his mind from the position Ṭūsī relates.
71. Frank, 'Moral obligation', 207.
72. See Frank, 'Moral obligation', for a general treatment of the topic in Basran Muᶜtazili and Ashᶜari theology, with emphasis on the latter.
73. For example, the most elaborate study of ᶜAbd al-Jabbār's theology in Arabic is titled 'The theory of moral obligation'; ᶜUthmān, *Naẓariyyat al-taklīf.*
74. *Dhakhīra*, 114, 132, 138, 140–1, 166, 177; *Sharḥ Jumal*, 105; *Rasāʾil*, 1:136–7.
75. See for example Kulaynī, *Kāfī*, 1:105, 402, 2:8–9; Ṣadūq, *ᶜIlal*, 1:9–14.
76. *Dhakhīra*, 108–9; cf. ᶜAbd al-Jabbār, *Mughnī*, 11:134–6.
77. *Dhakhīra*, 123 (reading *aw* for *law*); similarly *Dhakhīra*, 110, 131; *Sharḥ Jumal*, 100; cf. ᶜAbd al-Jabbār, *Mughnī*, 11:165–6; Ibn Mattawayh, *Majmūᶜ*, 2:191, where it is also ascribed to Abū Hāshim; Adang, Madelung and Schmidtke, *Baṣran Muᶜtazilite Theology*, 235.
78. Mottahedeh, *Loyalty*, 104–8, 121–3.
79. *Dhakhīra*, 110–11.
80. *Dhakhīra*, 105; Murtaḍā uses only the obligator *(mukallif)* in reference to God, although he concedes that it is technically – but rather unconventionally – applicable to other parties; *Dhakhīra*, 107; cf. ᶜAbd al-Jabbār, *Mughnī*, 11:293–4, who also ascribes this definition to Abū Hāshim.
81. *Dhakhīra*, 105.
82. *Dhakhīra*, 109.
83. ᶜAbd al-Jabbār, *Mughnī*, 11:178: 'God is obligating only by [His] will' (*annahu taᶜāla innamā yakūnu mukallif^an^ bi-l-irāda*). See also 11:294–300, where he expounds on the position that will and moral obligation are inseparable.
84. See the discussion in Heemskerk, *Suffering*, 142–5.
85. Schmidtke, *Theology*, 202–7.
86. *Dhakhīra*, 107–8 (obligator), 121–6 (obligated); *Sharḥ Jumal*, 100–2, 104–6. Compare with the lengthy discussion in ᶜAbd al-Jabbār, *Mughnī*, 11:367–405 (obligated) and 406–26 (obligator).

87. *Dhakhīra*, 123–4; briefly in *Sharḥ Jumal*, 100.
88. Ibn Mattawayh, *Majmūᶜ*, 2:184.
89. *Dhakhīra*, 107; contrast this with the Ashᶜari position according to which all obligations are uniformly carried out by way of obedience; Frank, 'Moral obligation', 215.
90. *Dhakhīra*, 107–8; see the interesting Stoic parallel in van den Bergh, 'Ghazali', 80.
91. *Dīwān*, 2:295–6, 542.
92. *Dhakhīra*, 140, 191; cf. ᶜAbd al-Jabbār, *Mughnī*, 11: 1401–1, 12:507; Ibn Mattawayh, *Majmūᶜ*, 2:192, 3:170–2, 175.
93. ᶜAbd al-Jabbār, *Mughnī*, 11:151–2, discusses how God could have created humans in a way as to avoid the inconveniences of moral obligation by denying them the power to do vile acts. While rejecting this scenario on physical grounds, he ignores the possibility of the absence of motives to commit such acts, for this is not part of the physical world, unlike abilities that apply indiscriminately to good and vile acts; cf. 11:492, where he argues that God may alter the motives of certain individuals, thus removing their desire to commit vile acts.
94. *Dhakhīra*, 110; cf. ᶜAbd al-Jabbār, *Mughnī*, 11:481, to which it seems Murtaḍā is referring; Ibn Mattawayh, *Majmūᶜ*, 2:185.
95. *Dhakhīra*, 129.
96. *Dhakhīra*, 112; cf. ᶜAbd al-Jabbār's tripartite division of divine assistance pertinent to meeting one's moral obligation in *Mughnī*, 11:431.
97. *Dhakhīra*, 131; a slightly different argument on pp. 134–5; cf. ᶜAbd al-Jabbār, *Mughnī*, 11:251–2; Ibn Mattawayh, *Majmūᶜ*, 2:196–7, 209–10.
98. *Dhakhīra*, 167.
99. *Dhakhīra*, 171.
100. *Dhakhīra*, 168–9.
101. The reference is not intended to suggest that Murtaḍā had access to the story of Ḥayy b. Yaqẓān authored by Ibn Sīnā, let alone to that of Ibn Ṭufayl (d. 1185); it merely highlights the similarity in the most basic theme of humans exploring their existential prospects. For a broad outline of the work, see Goichon, 'Ḥayy b. Yaḳẓān'.
102. *Dhakhīra*, 171–5, where Murtaḍā provides a lengthy rebuttal of other possibilities concerning the forms of divine intervention. In a later text, Murtaḍā's tone is more decisive in relying on the social context to induce fear in the individual while still allowing other possibilities; *Rasāʾil*, 1:128.
103. In *Dhakhīra*, 175, Murtaḍā apologetically makes a distinction between the belief in private speech and the case of God speaking to Moses. ᶜAbd al-Jabbār's tone is extremely defensive as well, regarding both belief in the alert and its exact form; Ibn Mattawayh, *Majmūᶜ*, 3:247–8. Reinhart, *Before Revelation*, 156–7, discusses the alert as a form of private revelation, without much regard to the Muᶜtazilis' repeated assertion that this is a hypothetical scenario; see also Reinhart, *Before Revelation*, 223n91, for a brief bibliography of discussions of the alert.
104. See Juwaynī, *Irshād*, 270–1.
105. Van den Bergh, 'Ghazali', 77–8, points out the parallels between Stoic thinking and

some Islamic theological views. The fact that he is concerned with non-Muᶜtazili positions does not infringe on the general observation.

106. *Dhakhīra*, 169–70; cf. Ibn Mattawayh, *Majmūᶜ*, 2:244–6.
107. *Dhakhīra*, 176–7.
108. *Dhakhīra*, 179–80.
109. See Abdulsater, 'Reason', for a general discussion of the question in Muᶜtazili theology, particularly pp. 246–9 on the problem of specifying the length of the time period.
110. *Dhakhīra*, 140–3; *Sharḥ Jumal*, 104.
111. *Dhakhīra*, 167–70; *Mulakhkhaṣ*, 478–9; cf. ᶜAbd al-Jabbār, *Mughnī*, 12:237–40.
112. *Rasāʾil*, 1:127–8.
113. Mufīd, *Awāʾil*, 44. Mufīd's phrasing is almost identical to the phrasing of the position that ᶜAbd al-Jabbār discusses in Ibn Mattawayh, *Majmūᶜ*, 3:247–8, which corroborates the assumption that this is the view of the Baghdadi Muᶜtazilis.
114. See McDermott, *Theology*, 60–2, who takes Mufīd's words to mean that investigation of religious questions cannot be brought to conclusion without revelation, even by a rational being of mature intellect; therefore, there is no moral obligation in the absence of revelation. Based on his reading of Mufīd's position, particularly the latter's claim that the Baghdadi Muᶜtazilis agree with the Imamis on this position, McDermott rules that Mufīd reports the view of the Baghdadi Muᶜtazilis inaccurately.
115. See the editor's note in Murtaḍā's *Sharḥ Jumal*, 125, where the editor understands Mufīd's position as concerned not with the obligatoriness of reasoning to knowledge of God, but with the necessity of prophethood. The editor claims this to be the view of the Imamis; this claim, however, rests on the position of later Imami authorities, starting from Murtaḍā himself.
116. See ᶜAbd al-Jabbār, *Mughnī*, 12:273–5, 515. At 12:166–70, he explains what it means in relation to unaided reason when the Qurʾān says that God perfected (*akmala*) religion; the first paragraphs of his explanation, although directed against those who deny investigation in matters of religion, may also work in the context of arguing against a position like Mufīd's, which states that reason needs revelation for proper use of evidence. See also Ibn Mattawayh, *Majmūᶜ*, 1:6–8, 3:247–53.
117. *Dhakhīra*, 323–6.
118. Ṭūsī, *Iqtiṣād*, 17–20.
119. *Rasāʾil*, 1:398–401, where he claims that this belief was almost unanimously held by the Imamis (*kaʾannahum muttafiqūna ᶜalayhi*), and 3:131–2, where his tone is less decisive.
120. *Mawsūᶜa*, 1:33–5.
121. *Rasāʾil*, 1:113–15; *Amālī*, 1:54–6; cf. Amir-Moezzi, *Divine Guide*, 29–37, for the reception of the traditions on humans' primordial existence in the gnostic context.
122. Mufīd, *al-Masāʾil al-Sarawiyya*, 37–54; *Taṣḥīḥ*, 83–6. On the covenant, see Böwering, 'Covenant'.
123. See, for example, Ṭūsī, *Ghayba*, 420.

CHAPTER

5

THE IMAMA AND THE NEED FOR MORAL LEADERSHIP

In the many schools of thought that defined Imami Shiᶜism throughout its history of development and transformation, the question of the Imama represented a doctrinally solid distinction that, in addition to other legal points and social arrangements, placed the Imami community apart from other groups. But the Imama debate is primarily a response to historical circumstances, with theology being used to justify, interpret and filter recorded accounts.

The interaction between historical narrative and religious dicta has long been noted by scholars of Islamic history.[1] Whether one decides to read early reports as unverifiable products of the sectarian milieu or as containing a kernel of historical fact,[2] these reports seem to have become a matter of consensus by the time they were included in the classical works of Islamic historiography.[3] Disagreement was more about certain elements within them or about their interpretation; for a parabolic reading of the material proved useful for both Shiᶜi and Sunni narratives.[4] Therefore, it can be said that these classical works are similar in their formal and teleological framework: they are both 'sectarian' and 'non-sectarian' inasmuch as readers are willing to exploit their latent potential to promote a particular agenda. This complexity underlies the assumption that 'multiple orthodoxies' are represented in Islamic historiography.[5]

The intense historical component in the Imama theological debate reflects the above observation. Nevertheless, it also allows us to consider the various theological structures, superimposed on the body of acceptable reports, as a prism that analyses the historiographical material into as many colours as the theologian needs in order to present his narrative. This chapter and the following one, therefore, do not seek to add a 'dome' of historical thought besides others (*ḥadīth*, *adab*, *ḥikma* and *siyāsa*);[6] rather, they attempt to demonstrate how the handling of material originating from various domes can prove a much more efficient strategy in the hands of theologians who are unwilling to break with the supernarratives set down in the plethora of acceptable reports. Instead of investing in a critical appraisal of the credibility of eyewitnesses, transmitters or historians, theologians can appeal to the 'quintessential literary achievement of pre-modern Arabic prose'; that is, they rely on the contradictory, complementary and concurring accounts to produce the desired chain of associations in the reader's mind.[7] Murtaḍā, as will be seen, argues for an elaborate theological narrative of Islamic history, immersed in Shiᶜi – specifically Imami – doctrinal assumptions, while relying exclusively on the standard histories that a non-Shiᶜi theologian – in this case his interlocutor ᶜAbd al-Jabbār – would use.

Moreover, crafting such a narrative also betrays Murtaḍā's involvement with the primary themes that occupied the Muslim tradition (prophecy, community, hegemony and leadership) and their various functions (preparatory, inception and boundary),[8] though in a much more explicit tone than one encounters in classical historiographies. The reason is that consensus on these themes had already developed by his time; a theologian would concern himself with the interpretative level only in order to construct his narrative. Of these functions, the function of boundary is one distinctly premised on interpretation. The boundaries are those of Muslim sectarian communities and those of the Muslim community as a whole. Thus, the themes of *fitna* and *sīrat al-khulafā*ᵓ – both under leadership – constitute the two dominant questions in the debate about the historical actualisation of Imama theological theory treated in the second half of this chapter, whereas the themes of *nubuwwa* and Qurᵓān-related narratives dominate the corresponding section in the discussion of prophethood in the next chapter.

Shiᶜi efforts were dedicated to investigating historical accounts in order to prove the Shiᶜi view of the succession to the Prophet. This was done by relying on a host of argumentative techniques including quoting sources, analysing their context and discrediting inconvenient versions of events. Such strategies would usually, especially after the elaboration of a theological system, be joined with a methodic attempt to fit these certified accounts into a doctrinal structure that suited the generic theory of Imama. The presence of historical accounts is less acutely felt as one draws further from the crisis of Muḥammad's death; with later Imams, relatively few reports are left to be analysed, and theology becomes almost the sole tool for reading events.[9] It can thus be proposed that 'sacred' history, which goes hand in hand with what might – for the purpose of distinction – be called 'ordinary' history[10] in interpreting recorded events, becomes the more prevalent component of the Imami narrative over time, reaching its peak in the discussion of occultation. Here, sacred history refers to an understanding of history that is aware of divine intervention in the course of events, frequently inserting into them theological or moral problems pertinent to the time of the writer.[11] This approach to the function of the Imama in history is exemplified in the works of some modern scholars of Shiᶜism. Building on the rich material of Imami accounts that emphasise the ontological precedence of the Imams, this scholarly tradition provides a view of the Imams as makers of history for whom real history is not the sociopolitical course of events but the spiritual, esoteric developments of a transcendent realm. As such, it endorses a historical narrative that disavows historicist readings and allows phenomenological ones, to varying extents.[12]

The availability of an elaborate theological system, namely Muᶜtazilism, provided the Imami efforts with a precious resource to carry out the task of refining their narrative into a multilayered approach that envisaged the requirements of both history and theology. The main assumptions of Muᶜtazili theology, particularly in relation to the interplay between divine assistance and human responsibility, furnished the Imami approach with a fresh perspective. It allowed the Imamis to capitalise on the Muᶜtazili concern with moral rectitude to argue both for the importance of the Imama and for the charismatic nature of the Imam.[13]

The main thesis of this chapter is that Murtaḍā was greatly responsible for the elaboration of a complex narrative of history woven into a mature theological system. The two core assumptions that undergird his Imama doctrine are the necessity of the Imama as a moral requirement in the community and the meaninglessness of such necessity unless the Imam is infallible. This 'dual core' draws heavily on the Muᶜtazili conceptions of reason and divine assistance, while aiming to stretch them to fit identical – and already established – Imami doctrines. The Imam's charisma, ultimately, is more intimately related to infallibility than to any of his other traits, and the Imami community's charisma is derived from that of the Imam. Murtaḍā's system also reflects an increasing awareness of the views of Islamic political philosophy about the nature of government, which could explain some aspects of his theoretical approach.

Both Murtaḍā's appraisal of his own work and the extant works of Imami literature on the question suggest that his efforts were unprecedented in exhaustiveness.[14] This chapter thus analyses how he was able to produce such a meticulous narrative by investigating his epistemic tools and the possible influence he had on the overarching view of Islamic history from the vantage point of the Imama controversy. The chapter starts by examining the theoretical aspect of his Imama doctrine, linking it to its possible roots in the then existing Imami discourse, and proceeds to address the application of this theory to various relevant episodes in Islamic history, attempting to situate Murtaḍā's views vis-à-vis the various readings of history within the Imami corpus and the later scholarly tradition.

Murtaḍā discusses the doctrine of the Imama and issues related to it in many of his works. Undoubtedly, it is in the *Shāfī* that he makes the most elaborate presentation of his views on the subject. But it is worth noting that he later changed some of the views expressed in the *Shāfī*, which was written before most of his other relevant works. In addition to such modifications, in other works he either offers more succinct versions of his theory on the Imama or dedicates a whole discussion to a particular problem stemming from his overarching position, such as the question of infallibility in his *Tanzīh* or the issue of occultation in *al-Muqniᶜ fī al-ghayba.*

Theoretical model

Although supposedly an abstract framework intended to present the overall 'philosophy' of the Imama doctrine, the Imama theory formulated by Murtaḍā represents a complex intersection and appropriation of several debates. With a career that spanned five decades, Murtaḍā must have been aware of the general discomfort caused by the fragmentation of the Islamic polity, reflected in an almost unanimous[15] acceptance among theologians of the necessity of a leader for the community – the Imam. Whether they argued that the Imama was necessitated by revelation – as did most of them[16] – or whether they held that it followed from the rational requirement of maintaining social order to manage people's worldly affairs – as did the Muᶜtazilis of Baghdad headed by Balkhī[17] – this consensus prepared fertile soil for the next step, which Murtaḍā undertook. Combining previous arguments and incorporating the central Muᶜtazili doctrine of divine assistance as elaborated in the teachings of ᶜAbd al-Jabbār and his circle, he proposed that the Imama is a rational necessity intended for the preservation of humans' otherworldly interests. Similarly, his formulation of the qualifications of the Imam, couched in the language of generic rules, at times amounts to little more than a refinement of the early debates in the community regarding the respective merits of ᶜAlī and Abū Bakr.[18] Murtaḍā's main contribution, however, lies in exploiting these trends maximally, attempting to present his version of the Imama theory as one that satisfies the intellectual penchant for rational justification, the ever-ready Muᶜtazili eagerness to invoke divine assistance and the traditional Shiᶜi concern with reports that support the Shiᶜi view on the Imama.

The definition and necessity of the Imama

In addition to Murtaḍā's introduction of a definition of the Imama as a generic form of leadership, his claim that its necessity can be established by reason and revelation is tailored to meet the expectations of different trends. On the one hand, the appeal to reason allows Murtaḍā to present a heretofore sectarian view in a manner that not only extends beyond the restrictions of the sectarian Imami – or even Shiᶜi – parameters but purports to be universally valid as a position that is independent from any particular religion. On the other hand, the argument from revelation remains faithful to the expectations of Imami traditionalists and earlier theologians and the more common view in the wider Muslim community, given the centrality of sacred law in the functions of the Imam. In this blend of arguments for the necessity of the Imama, Murtaḍā is also echoing the Būyid zeitgeist: endorsing leadership in general is equally accommodating – or not – of Būyid kingship and of the ᶜAbbāsid caliphate.

The Imama, the rational argument goes, concerns the most generic understanding of leadership (*riʾāsa*). Since it is self-evident for the imaginary group of rational beings that the presence of a just leader is immensely helpful in bringing people closer to moral rectitude, this presence constitutes divine assistance,[19] and it is incumbent upon God to install Imams before the imposition of moral obligation,[20] regardless of the number of these Imams or their exact qualifications, as Murtaḍā repeatedly asserts.[21] This broad definition of the Imama includes prophethood, so every prophet must also be an Imam;[22] but if no sacred law is revealed, there may be no prophets but only Imams.[23]

From a realistic standpoint, Murtaḍā argues that no person with sound political judgement, knowledge of history and familiarity with various literatures can conscientiously object to the usefulness of just leadership.[24] Theological objections to his position centre on the question whether the presence of a leader is a form of divine assistance. This debate boils down to whether, as Murtaḍā argues, the presence of strong leaders brings about worldly and otherworldly benefits in the form of material prosperity and moral rectitude[25] without infringing on individual freedom to pursue their opposite.[26] The cornerstone of his approach is capitalising on the complexities of the Muᶜtazili moral system. Since the moral theory admits of no difference between divine and human morality, he exploits this lack of distinction to make it incumbent upon God to provide leadership for humans from among their ranks, as such leadership helps them in meeting their moral obligations. The other concern of Muᶜtazili moral theory, that is, the freedom of agents, is addressed by highlighting the human ability to reject this leadership.

These positions, while appearing to tally well with Muᶜtazili theology, are in fact much needed within Murtaḍā's Imami framework. The failure of the Imams to hold power can now be seen as a concomitant of divine justice, which does not force people to accept their leadership. This failure can also reinforce the classic Imami vision of the Muslim community as one whose actual history, because of its refusal to endorse divinely designated leadership, diverges sharply from its intended one – which is to be substituted with the sacred history of the Imama. Moreover, the theoretical assumption that the Imam – if holding the reins of power – would help people observe their religious obligations and acquire worldly gains is also in harmony with the Imami teleological narrative of sacred history culminating in a future utopia: the Twelfth Imam, upon his return, shall provide both material and spiritual prosperity.[27] The objection that the Imam himself must be in need of an Imam is turned upside down to support the Imami claim; for forms of divine assistance, even in Muᶜtazili theology, are not uniform.[28] Therefore, the Imam's lack of such a need stands as proof of his inherent superiority over others; it emphasises his unique charisma, which in turn is expressed in his infallibility – which he shares with no others.

This approach thus strips the office of the Imam of much of the mystery that usually surrounds the common Imami conception. Simultaneously, it makes the Imama a basic need of human society if the latter is to be led towards its ultimate good in terms of its members' otherworldly states, even if it is assumed that no religion exists. The resemblance to the teachings of Islamic political philosophy in terms of the moral significance of government is not hard to detect,[29] and it is very likely that Murtaḍā, being at the heart of intellectual activity and engaged in polemics with philosophers,[30] was aware of these teachings. His appeal to *adab* and to *ḥikma* literature, citing ancient Arab and non-Arab sages on the need for government, reveals his willingness to employ various approaches to historical thought to corroborate his theoretical structure instead of restricting himself to theology or to the more traditional forms of historical writing such as *ḥadīth* historiography.

The crux of the revelational argument is that for the sacred law to be protected, revealed teachings must be kept in the trust of an arbitrator who enjoys access to exclusive knowledge. It is not clear whether Murtaḍā, in declaring this view distinctly Imami,[31] is aware of the very similar Ismaᶜili view advanced in the works of al-Qāḍī Abū Ḥanīfa al-Nuᶜmān b. Ḥayyūn (d. 974).[32] The argument rests on classifying matters of religious disagreement into two types: rational and revelational. Of the first type, it is possible to attain knowledge without the help of the Imam; his role is auxiliary, since in these matters reason functions as the needed arbitrator, although his authority makes him better suited than anyone else to the role.[33] The second type is, in turn, divided into two categories: revealed questions that have been reported through prevalence (*tawātur*) and those that have not. The Imam is evidently needed for matters of the second category to make up for the weakness in transmission, but he is also needed with respect to the first, because it may happen that some reports lose the quality of prevalence over time due to transmitters' negligence.[34] Since there is no way to establish that the community's consensus is in itself probative,[35] there needs to be an Imam to guard against potential errors – deliberate or otherwise.[36] But even if the probativeness of consensus is granted, such consensus will not materialise in the majority of rulings, leaving people ignorant of their moral obligations unless there is an Imam to instruct them.[37] It is evident, therefore, why these arguments are peculiarly Imami ones: they hinge on the claim that the Imam is infallible. Murtaḍā usually presents the time-honoured Imami argument after the rational one, often ascribing it to fellow Imamis (*aṣḥābunā*). He is, however, unmistakably in favour of the rational argument, as he always gives it precedence and includes it alone in his shorter catechisms and later works.[38]

The preference for preserving the moral authority of the Imam over his superior knowledge is manifest in Murtaḍā's insistence that most people commit mistakes knowingly. This makes fear of authority more needed than instruction,[39] even if no religious laws were revealed for individuals to learn and apply – which is possible.[40] As for Mufīd, he appears to have undergone a change of mind: in early writings he endorses the revelational argument based on safeguarding the law, although his phrasing is ambiguous,[41] but in the concluding chapter of a very late work he presents an argument similar to Murtaḍā's argument from reason.[42] This shift suggests that the teacher may have been influenced by the student on this specific question.

It is opportune to pause here and observe some of the strategic moves that Murtaḍā makes, which show that an intellectual debate, when infused with dogmatism, in fact bears more similarity to a game of chess than to a truth-seeking endeavour. Seemingly paradoxically for an Imami theologian, Murtaḍā dedicates lengthy sections of the *Shāfī* to undermining the arguments for the necessity of the Imama offered by his opponent. He does so in order to make sure that his understanding of this necessity, inseparable from his Imama theory, is the only option left. Hence, the public utility of the Imama does not suffice to make it necessary;[43] the community's consensus on the matter is neither factual nor binding;[44] and the need to apply the sacred law is meaningful only when an Imam is already installed.[45]

Qualifications of the Imam

The qualifications of the Imam may be divided into two main categories. The first includes necessary qualifications known by reason alone, such as infallibility, recognition by designation or miracle, political acumen and superiority in knowledge relevant to leadership; these are unconditional requirements of the Imam. The second category includes qualifications known by revelation but not required by reason, such as being the most knowledgeable in religious matters, having the most religious merit and being the most courageous.[46] Thus, the qualifications dictated by reason are in fact those more germane to authority than to knowledge, further highlighting the significance of the hierarchical power structure in Murtaḍā's understanding of the Muslim community. His concern is with the discontinuity between the Imam and others, since most of these qualifications cannot be gained through the normal progression of an individual but rather are due to superhuman intervention. It is not mysterious, exclusive knowledge that makes the difference; rather, it is an inaccessible trait of personal moral superiority that legitimises the Imam's occupation of his authoritative position. Since Murtaḍā views this authority as a rational component of religion, his exploitation of Muʿtazili teachings reaches a peak at this point, for such components were considered the most unshakable tenets of Muʿtazili theology, which renders ironic their employment to establish the aspect of Murtaḍā's system that is least acceptable for most Muʿtazilis.

The dictates of reason are based on the stipulation of infallibility; other qualifications derive smoothly from the stipulation either to identify the infallible person or to define the scope of this trait, once detected. Murtaḍā's discussion starts with a definition of this crucial concept in his theory of the Imama: infallibility is the form of divine assistance that, when bestowed upon an individual, causes him to choose to avoid vile acts.[47] Therefore, it contains an element of choice, which makes it praiseworthy given its relation to individual responsibility.[48] Murtaḍā is a proponent of total infallibility, the position that Imams never commit any vile acts or mistakes that would repulse (*yunaffiru*) people from following them.[49] This argument regarding the infallibility of the Imam stems directly from the argument for the necessity of the Imama. If the Imama is necessary to bring people closer to good deeds and deter them from vile acts, then anyone who is prone to neglecting his duties or committing vile acts is in need of an Imam. Unless the Imam is exempt from these tendencies, there will be an infinite regression; so all that is needed to interrupt the chain is one infallible Imam.[50] Mufīd, on the other hand, allows that prophets commit minor sins that do not discredit them, as long as they do so only inadvertently and before their prophethood. However, he holds that Muḥammad did not commit any such acts, quoting the Qurʾān to support his position.[51]

The two poles of Murtaḍā's thought seem to be pulling in opposite directions. The pole of Muᶜtazili rationalist discourse, particularly its moral aspect, underlies his keenness to stress that infallibility is a matter of choice, as he wishes to indicate its praiseworthiness to reflect moral value. The other pole – that of the Imami tradition – seems to tug his position in a different direction. The assumption of the Imams' total infallibility can hardly be digested without allowing for a superhuman conception of the Imams, which militates against the affirmation of infallibility as a matter of choice. Moreover, Murtaḍā makes no effort to explain how this qualification – ostensibly based on choice – happens to be granted to a particular line of individuals while they are still minors in some cases.[52] Claiming an extreme form of infallibility, even within the framework of Muᶜtazili argumentation, must have been made easier by the Imam's prolonged absence than it would have been in his presence; this can be inferred from comparing the Imami case with that of the Fāṭimids, whose caliph-Imams came under attack.[53]

The investment in infallibility gives rise to another necessary component of Murtaḍā's theory. The indiscernibility of infallibility makes it impossible for people to recognise the Imam by reason, and it precludes that he be chosen by the community or inherit his position.[54] This leaves only two ways for the Imam to be identified: either through direct designation by the previous Imam or by the performance of a miracle to confirm the veracity of his claim to the Imama.[55] Both ways converge at the same point: a miracle performed by an initial authority.[56] Miracles are thus an instrumental concept needed to recognise not the person of the Imam per se but his infallibility, which serves to further highlight the centrality of this attribute in Murtaḍā's system. The discussion is aimed at denying that it is possible for humans to recognise, unaided, all the requirements of the Imama in one individual.[57] Here, too, Muᶜtazili precepts are conveniently employed to support a distinctly non-Muᶜtazili position: people's inability to detect infallibility in individuals is used to justify the need for divine designation to avoid the injustice of God's obligating people to do something that surpasses their normal capacities, especially if it is required of them often.[58] Once the Imam's infallibility is accepted as a requirement, the remaining doctrinal articles follow suit. The unbridgeable gap between the community and the Imam is, once more, not grounded in superior knowledge of religion on his part, even if he possesses such knowledge.[59] Rather, it is based on authoritative delegation, that is, divine designation; reason can comprehend the justification of such delegation but is never the means of choosing the right delegate.

The remaining qualifications are related to the needs of holding a position of authority, but unlike infallibility, they are not impossible to detect. Since the inaccessibility of the Imam's designation process has been established and the unbridgeable hierarchical gap has been secured, these other requirements represent aspects of the Imam's persona that are – and must be – within the grasp of human reason, as they are unmistakable signs of the divine wisdom in his entitlement to office. These include political acumen (*wujūh al-siyāsa wa-l-tadbīr*)[60] and reason,[61] a pleasant countenance[62] and superiority over all his subjects in anything pertinent to leadership, with religious knowledge included for this reason.[63]

There are a few observations to make about the remaining qualifications, deemed to be dictates of revelation. In significance, Murtaḍā relegates them to a relatively secondary position, since they depend on the actual occurrence of revelation in history, a condition that is not considered necessary by Basran Muᶜtazilis. This relegation reflects Murtaḍā's strong interest in developing an Imami theory of the Imama that is as faithful as possible to the requirements of the rationalist tendency that Murtaḍā advocated, while still reaping all the fruits of classic Imami arguments and teaching. Murtaḍā's theory is, therefore, old wine poured into new wineskins, meant to get the most out of both.

In terms of particular qualifications, it is conspicuous that the list echoes what is arguably the earliest debate on the respective excellence of ᶜAlī and Abū Bakr, though without the traditional polemic.[64] The Imami positions in that debate are extracted and presented not as the outcomes of an ancient controversy, but as the theoretical requirements of an Imam. The abstract, generic clothing should, therefore, not distract us from the roots of the question, which are much more personal and particular. Instead of harking back to what had become an obsolete debate for an already established community, Murtaḍā develops its formed convictions in a manner that matches the new intellectual apparatus.

Religious merit is gauged in terms of otherworldly rewards, knowledge of which is God's prerogative.[65] This position corroborates the view that the Imama is not earned (*mustaḥaqqa*) and stresses its supernatural aspect.[66] The continuity between 'actual' history and sacred history is best seen in this discussion, as the Imama, while admittedly operating within the constraints of history and politics, is portrayed as grounded in an unseen dimension of otherworldly credit. The hierarchy of authority in this world thus reflects the hierarchy of merit in the other, at least at its highest echelons. Superiority in religious knowledge is required only because the community needs to be governed by religious law, not because such knowledge constitutes an inherent component of leadership.[67] Familiarity with other branches of knowledge that are irrelevant to government is not required of the Imam: since the hierarchical authority needed to further community members' rectitude is secured by the Imam's other qualifications, it is superfluous to expect more. This minimal – if strict – theological requirement allows Murtaḍā to dodge certain theological problems that would accrue from excessive requirements on the Imam's knowledge,[68] and it is all that is needed to sustain the grand framework and minimise its potential weaknesses. It pre-empts possible theological interpretations of historical accounts, mostly from the Prophet's time, that do not neatly fit the presumed order of religious knowledge and/or merit, as in the case of the Prophet's appointment of ᶜAmr b. al-ᶜĀṣ and Khālid b. al-Walīd as leaders over Abū Bakr and ᶜUmar.[69] Courage is treated in terms of military command, that is, leading an army in *jihād*. The word of revelation stipulates that the Imam is obligated to carry out this duty, either in person or through intermediary military commanders, since it would be vile to give precedence to the less competent over the more competent in military leadership.[70] Again, what matters most is not whether the community should engage in *jihād* but the supremacy of the

Imam as the leader, since allowing the Imam to be under anyone else's authority would undermine the hierarchical framework and possibly delegitimise *jihād* itself.

Finally, Murtaḍā attributes the belief that there can be only one Imam at a time to revelation and consensus, although he acknowledges that on the basis of reason only it would have been possible for many Imams to exist simultaneously.[71] In addition to being faithful to the theoretical requirement of the need for leadership (which does not lead to its singularity), Murtaḍā is aware of the limits of his opponents' ability to push the position to an extreme: it is very unlikely that a party that rejects infallibility in the first place propose a multitude of infallible authorities. The language in which this expectation is couched, needless to say, is not that of a debater who knows the limits of the game, but of an ostensibly dispassionate theologian: it is the consensus of the community that dictates the singularity of infallible authority.

The test of history

Before analysing how Murtaḍā's theory applies in practice, it is imperative to recognise that the Imama controversy, more than any other sectarian debate, has been shaped by historical circumstances and political considerations more than by pure theology. Therefore, what I term the 'test of history', though purporting to move from the abstract to the concrete, in fact shows how certain historical narratives served as models to which the theories were later tailored. This process evokes Aristotle's famous comment that poetry, in the sense of the imaginative and fictional, is more philosophical than is history, for the former speaks of universals whereas the latter speaks of particulars.[72] In Islamic debates on the Imama, theology serves as the universal model whose particulars are depicted in history. Whether it shares the beauty of poetry is questionable, but it definitely shares its inconsistency: the handling of conflicting reports is subservient to the desired outcome; narrators' reliability is usually unquestioned unless their reports are inconvenient; and the same author may resort to citing opposite accounts to serve his ends, depending on the context. Murtaḍā's case proves no exception.

The Imama of ᶜAlī

The theoretical aspects of the position, whether based on reason or on revelation, are supposed to characterise all Imams. The main challenge, however, is establishing the Imama of the first Imam ᶜAlī b. Abī Ṭālib; once that is secured, it is much easier to establish the remaining particularities of the doctrine. The strategic advantage of the discussion of ᶜAlī's Imama explains its disproportionate size in Murtaḍā's works.[73] It also further shows the significance of history, as the debate centres mostly on historical accounts. The smoothness of the move from establishing ᶜAlī's Imama to affirming that of the remaining Imams sheds light on the intricate connection between ordinary history and sacred history for the Imamis. The transition does not in fact take place within a historical narrative, but from one narrative of ordinary history into another that serves as a threshold to enter a third narrative that is more theological – that is to say, sacred – than historical. The 'proper' history of the community, then, becomes not that of the great events affecting the grand sociopolitical structure but rather that of the developments related to the succession of divinely designated individuals in an unbreakable chain, regardless of the scale of these developments. As such, a particular understanding of history becomes an article of faith, although in Imami Shiᶜism, it is a result of the political failures rather than successes of the Imams.[74]

Murtaḍā's arguments for ᶜAlī's Imama include revelational arguments in the form of evidence from the tradition that shows ᶜAlī's designation by the Prophet. This category of evidence is divided into two types: purely verbal evidence (*qawl*) and composite evidence, that is, consisting of both word and deed (*fiᶜl*).[75] Verbal evidence also comprises two types: explicit (*jalī*) and implicit (*khafī*) designation. Already in Murtaḍā's time, composite evidence had long lost its lustre, since it belonged to the largely outdated genre of merits, and Murtaḍā accordingly ignores it.[76] This section examines the rational arguments in detail, since these represent Murtaḍā's novel contribution to the debate. Revelational arguments per se are treated in only a cursory manner proportional to Murtaḍā's limited originality in handling them. Instead of analysing the arguments, I emphasise their significance in view of the context of the Imami discourse.

In addition to revelational arguments, Murtaḍā offers three arguments for ᶜAlī's succession to the Prophet that he characterises as rational. Nevertheless, the three arguments can be seen as variations of a single argument that starts from the assumption that the Imam must be infallible, whether the assumption is made explicit (as in the first two arguments) or kept implicit (as in the last). Having established this assumption, Murtaḍā affirms ᶜAlī's Imama through the following arguments: (1) elimination leaves ᶜAlī the only candidate whose fallibility is not a matter of consensus and who therefore has the potential to be infallible;[77] (2) the group that stipulates that the Imam must be infallible takes only ᶜAlī to be the Imam;[78] and (3) ᶜAlī, who never made false claims, believed himself to be the rightful successor to the Prophet.[79]

It is the claim that infallibility is a dictate of reason that allows Murtaḍā to classify such arguments as rational. The first two arguments exclude the Zaydis, who uphold the designation of ᶜAlī but do not share the Imami view on infallibility.[80] Murtaḍā's concern is not with amassing support for his position but with making sure that such support does not cost him more in the long run: accepting the Zaydi view of designation would backfire against the necessity of infallibility and even against the probativeness of consensus as he defines it, which is a precious tool for him in various argumentative contexts. In addition to dismissing the Zaydi position, he dismisses that of any descendants of the Prophet who do not share his belief in ᶜAlī's direct succession to Muḥammad: he claims to have never met any such descendant who did not share his view, and the very few amongst them reported to have deviated from this position were either ignoramuses or opportunists whose opinions have no bearing on the consensus.[81] But Murtaḍā's ad hominem attack on these Prophetic descendants can hardly be accepted as genuine, especially given the breadth of his social exposure. Aside from potential personal considerations, his unusually harsh tone may be explained by his belief in the authority of the consensus of the Prophet's family, which means that any dissent within the family's ranks threatens to deprive him of a potent tool. It does, however, reveal an instance in which Murtaḍā's extremely meticulous methodology and handling of written sources fail to meet the easier task of admitting current facts, an inevitable consequence of the fervent argumentation that had moved him to complain about ᶜAbd al-Jabbār's similar approach. The third argument amounts to little more than begging the question; the opponents are supposed to accept the Imami claim about the position of ᶜAlī, who – according to another Imami claim – could not have uttered falsehood. In his historical documentation, Murtaḍā's method is selective both in the choice of sources and in the interpretation of the texts therein, and it still leaves the argument wanting unless ᶜAlī's authority is already conceded. Again, then, it is the pervasive view of the Imam's infallibility that constitutes the core of Murtaḍā's system, even in handling historical sources after the theoretical foundations have been laid down.

In the practical equivalent of his strategy of refuting all arguments for the necessity of the Imama except his own, Murtaḍā produces lengthy responses against legitimisations of ᶜAlī's caliphate that are not based on Prophetic designation.[82] The primacy of maintaining the doctrinal structure, with the Imam's infallibility at its core, shows itself in Murtaḍā's readiness to sacrifice the support of whoever arrives at the same conclusion following a different route, since accepting such alternative routes would make establishing the remaining articles of Imami doctrine more difficult. Murtaḍā's need to prevail in the argument is most manifest in his outright endorsement of contradictory historical accounts – those reporting that some Prophetic Companions were coerced into paying allegiance to ᶜAlī,[83] and those claiming that they did so willingly.[84] With the first account, Murtaḍā's goal is to highlight the irrelevance of the political process, since ᶜAlī was made caliph by Prophetic designation, whereas the second account serves to argue that since the Companions broke the promises they made to ᶜAlī, it is no wonder that they earlier disobeyed the Prophet's will regarding his succession. Such is the price of forcing history into the straitjacket of sectarian narrative, required to satisfy the needs of a theological system under construction.

In contrast to rational arguments, revelational arguments are the equivalent of documents that a claimant produces to argue a case, in this case taking the form of Prophetic traditions; and just like such documents, their value depends on their clarity and authenticity. As for clarity, the explicit traditions are ones whose prima facie (*ẓāhir*) meaning can be immediately grasped by the audience. According to Murtaḍā, this type is almost exclusively transmitted by the Imamis, though some non-Shiᶜi traditionists have inadvertently reported elements of this type given their lack of awareness of their connotations. Implicit traditions, on the other hand, are also comprehended by the audience, but we cannot be sure whether they are self-evident. This type is reported by Shiʿis and non-Shiʿis alike, the dispute being centred on their real meaning.[85] The benefit of this classification of traditions is that it allows Murtaḍā to pre-empt objections to the Imami view, which affirms the immediate significance of these reports for their audience.[86] Murtaḍā's exposé is representative of the typical Imami approach. The extent to which the Imami tradition owes these arguments to him is not clear, however, given the scarcity of information in sources that predate his teachers, but many of the arguments can be traced – in abridged or incomplete formulations – to earlier theologians. Murtaḍā's strategy with regard to revelational arguments rests on two pillars, prevalence and hermeneutics, that treat authenticity and clarity, respectively. However, his focus differs depending on the type of evidence: for explicit evidence, the focus is on prevalence; for implicit evidence, on hermeneutics. Murtaḍā gives two prime examples of explicit traditions: '[ʿAlī] is my successor after me' (*hādhā khalīfatī min baʿdī*) and 'Greet [ʿAlī] as the commander of the faithful' (*sallimū ʿalayhi bi-imrat al-muʾminīn*).[87] (ʿAbd al-Jabbār denounces both as later fabrications.)[88] Murtaḍā's core claim is that only the Imamis have been sufficiently numerous to establish prevalence regarding the designation of their Imam,[89] and that works compiled by early Imami scholars prove that this has been their doctrine from the earliest times.[90]

This debate is significant in that it portrays the gradual theoretical maturation and political ascendancy of the Imami community in Murtaḍā's time as well as the resistivity to both by the established intellectual elite and the broader non-Shiʿi political community, presumably represented by ʿAbd al-Jabbār. Murtaḍā's appeal to sheer numbers, although in the theoretical context of prevalence, represents a marked departure from a rooted Imami ethos, for it shows a growing confidence in the size of a minority that had been forging connections with the Būyid court to the point of being able to see its past in light of a prosperous present; the frequent – even ubiquitous – discourse about the scarcity of believers must have been very inopportune to invoke at this time.[91] Moreover, the dismissal of the Bakriyya[92] and the ʿAbbāsiyya, while not entirely based on their numerical insignificance, finds its strongest support in numbers, which is also emblematic of an emerging different ethos. Finally, ʿAbd al-Jabbār's insistence – though not restricted to him – that the texts were fabricated at a known point in time and Murtaḍā's response affirming both their early provenance and their presence in the relevant old books compiled by the Imamis can be read as a debate about the genuine intellectual tradition of the Imamis against the derision depicting them as a less sophisticated group.[93]

Within the group of implicit traditions, prevalence is much easier to show on the basis of only non-Shiʿi authorities. But since the texts are not explicit, the burden of proof falls on the second pillar of Murtaḍā's strategy, hermeneutics. This group includes more famous traditions; first and foremost, it is here that we find the two key traditions of *Ghadīr Khumm*[94] and of *al-manzila*.[95] Murtaḍā appears to favour these two traditions over all others, implicit and explicit, and dedicates enormous efforts to expounding on every single detail relevant to them. He is, however, hardly original in these efforts, as he simply reiterates previous positions more elaborately.[96] But his preference for these texts, particularly the *Ghadīr Khumm* tradition, reflects a growing Imami tendency, while increasingly infusing the tradition with connotations that were not previously associated with it.[97]

A conspicuous site of conflict between common historical reports and the sectarian narrative needed to support the theoretical theological framework is the question of ᶜAlī's behaviour following the Prophet's death. The opponents of the Imamis emphasised that ᶜAlī refrained from making any claims to succession and participated in the political process. He is also said to have maintained cordial personal relations with the caliphs, in addition to leaving many of their rulings unaltered once he assumed the caliphate, although these rulings contradict his own positions as presented by the Imamis.[98] The importance of these arguments can be seen in the fact that responses to them take up considerable space, even in catechisms. Murtaḍā resorts to his favourite, twofold strategy: he does not concede his opponent's claim but then proceeds to show that even were it to be conceded, it is still inconsequential for the discussion. So he reports several historical accounts, mostly from non-Shiᶜi sources,[99] that contradict the reports cited by his opponents.[100] He is also willing to engage in political analysis, arguing that the atmosphere of oppression did not allow for overt opposition[101] and that flexibility was merely a means to an end – not an admission of the government's legitimacy.[102] In short, his justification of ᶜAlī's behaviour rests on the somewhat paradoxical combination of cautionary prudence (*taqiyya*) and self-sacrifice for the cause of Islam.[103] The paramount concern of his theological project disguises itself in what might be construed as a more realistic reading of history but is in fact simply a more convenient tool for guarding the temple of sectarian narrative and the theology that serves it. In rejecting the Imami view that ᶜAlī's quietism was due to his prior knowledge of future developments imparted to him by the Prophet,[104] Murtaḍā does not contest the theological technicality of foreknowledge or the practical plausibility of the explanation. Since this view has no bearing on his conception of the infallible Imam nor does it affect the ease of defending the sectarian narrative, there is no need for him to burden himself with the vulnerabilities of relying on supernatural elements to explain historical developments. All that is necessary is denying that there has ever been consensus on any of the first four caliphs, which is within the reach of realistic political analysis. Realism, therefore, is a more prominent feature of Murtaḍā's argumentative strategy than it is of his historical investigation.

The Imama of the twelve Imams

Although Murtaḍā claims that prevalent reports exist regarding the explicit designation of every Imam[105] – and even the occultation of the Twelfth[106] – from the Prophet himself[107] or from ᶜAlī,[108] it is infallibility that serves as his ultimate trump card to prove their Imama.[109] All other claimants, he argues, were either fallible (in the cases of the Zaydiyya[110] and Faṭḥiyya[111]) or, when 'legitimate', dead (in the case of the Nāwūsiyya[112] and the Wāqifiyya[113]).

The cornerstone of Murtaḍā's argument is not merely the belief in the Imam's infallibility, but the claim that it is only the Imamis who properly subscribe to this belief. Confronted by those who share this belief but disagree on the identity of the Imam, Murtaḍā swiftly summons history to put the question to rest, not through a theological formulation but by simply affirming the claimant's death. This strategy is deceptively efficient, as the case of the Isma^cilis shows. The Isma^cili claimant ruling the Fāṭimid empire was certainly alive – his presence was felt more than that of the Twelfth Imam. But the arcane nature of infallibility, being undetectable and elusive – features that usually serve Murtaḍā's purposes well – complicated matters further. The infallibility of the Isma^cili Imam, upheld by his followers,[114] was not easily undermined. Even accounts of sacred history, with the names of rightful Imams foretold by their forebears, were shared by the Isma^cilis, who had their own versions of them.[115] This awkward situation is probably what forced Murtaḍā to change his response over time, resorting to ad hominem attacks[116] and eventually settling for a simplistic formula that ignores the nuances of Isma^cili Imama doctrine: Ismā^cīl was fallible and died before his father, which delegitimises all subsequent Isma^cili claimants.[117]

It is here, in Murtaḍā's discussion of an Imama that has lost political power and has gradually become a matter of communal/religious authority, that the tools of political analysis take a back seat. Sacred history overrides ordinary history, and teleological interpretations of developments suddenly prevail. This approach works in two directions: the past can be invoked to interpret the present, and the present to justify the past. In the former case, the disclosure of the Imams' names at the outset of Islamic history must be accepted as a compelling justification of their later legitimacy, even if no other arguments are invoked. In the latter – more curious – case, the unfolding of ordinary history is imbued with a strong justificatory tone: the disappearance of certain groups is framed as proof that they could not have been right.[118] It must be noted that believing in the influence of future events upon preceding events is an unmistakable sign of subscribing to a narrative of sacred history.[119] Despite Murtaḍā's resistance to the claim that the success of a doctrine proves it correctness – much expected in a group that adopts a sacred-historical approach[120] – he accepts the other side of the claim: failure proves incorrectness. However, Murtaḍā's appeal to the power of the course of history, though implicit, has a triumphant tone that is alien to the Imami spirit before the return of the Twelfth Imam.

This is also an apt occasion to examine Murtaḍā's narrative from the perspective of the various readings, historicist and phenomenological, of Islamic history within the Imami tradition. Despite his consistent investment in the political justification of the Imama and his concern to avoid any gnostic claims regarding the Imams' status, Murtaḍā is far from accepting a historicist reading – although his approach might seem particularly amenable to it. The unacceptability of the historicist reading is revealed in Murtaḍā's attempt to answer the challenge of the Imams' failure to seize political power and their frequent persecution, which did not abate in spite of their prayers and protest. He argues that the Imams cannot be makers of history, for they did not cause this persecution to happen or ask for it – a position that distances Murtaḍā from the gnostic reading in its extreme form. Nevertheless, to claim that they were mere subjects of history – powerless individuals whose petitions were ignored by God – would deprive them of all status. Thus, his dismissal of the gnostic in discussing the human being is not matched in an equal measure when it comes to the Imam, who, though fully human, is still involved in the workings of the unseen world. Murtaḍā's suggested solution betrays his typical pattern of questioning the basic claim: the Imams are too dear to God for their prayers to be left unanswered, and too pious for them to ask for any worldly thing – whether the seizure of political power or the cessation of persecution. Thus, they must have not really prayed for either of these things; their ostensible petitions are either mere expressions of humility before God or requests for benefits pertaining to their followers.[121] Such an explanation falls largely within the scope of a phenomenological reading of history inasmuch as it seeks to understand apparent events through recourse to the realm of the unseen. Nevertheless, it is a long way from elaborating a whole narrative of suffering and meaning; in this case, simply proposing that events took the course they did for a concealed divine wisdom suffices to save the face of Murtaḍā's theological edifice. This tension, together with the accompanying solution, supports the observation that the integration of historicist and phenomenological readings is fundamentally problematic, particularly in the case of the Imama.[122]

This observation leads to another aspect of Murtaḍā's theology that seems quite unorthodox for an Imami theologian. Murtaḍā holds that it is possible that even after the Twelfth Imam returns and subsequently dies, people's moral obligation will be still in effect, in which case other Imams will be charged with preserving the religion. This possibility does not invalidate the appellation 'Twelvers' (*ithnā ᶜashariyya*), since all that the title signifies is the belief in the twelve Imams, which would be unaffected.[123] The justification of this daring assertion lies in its insignificance for the theoretical framework of Murtaḍā's Imama doctrine. Although the statement seems to neither assert nor deny such a future scenario, the mere possibility stands in stark contrast to Murtaḍā's usual militant attitude against anything that contradicts his theological premises. It further highlights the fact that sacred history depends on its events meeting the requirements of theology more than on their occurrence, whether in the course of actual developments or in the pronouncements of traditions.

Vindication of the Imams

Since the belief in infallibility is a core of his Imama doctrine, Murtaḍā provides an extremely elaborate defence of the Imams' controversial acts. His extensive stock of such acts draws entirely on historical accounts, as the acts are seen as taking place in contexts in which the Imams were arguably expected to behave differently. The objections apply to certain of the Imams' legal views and many of their political actions that seem contradictory. In general, Murtaḍā's solution to the problem consists of producing explanations to support the Imams' legal positions (in the case of ᶜAlī),[124] analysing their motives to show the efficiency of their moves (for ᶜAlī[125] and Riḍā[126]) and – as the final and most reliable resort – appealing to the need for cautionary prudence (applicable to most of the Imams in view of their quietist attitude).[127] The defence is not particularly difficult, given both the consequentialist moral theory to which Murtaḍā subscribes – which extols the virtues of prudence and avoiding self-harm – and the nature of political and legal disputes, which permit a considerable polemical margin. Even if Murtaḍā's approach is deeply rooted in established conclusions about the Imams' necessarily right decisions, there is little need to explain away inconsistencies by appealing to sacred-historical projections or grand theological arguments – although he does mention the latter perfunctorily.[128]

But the battle of Karbalāʾ can hardly be given the same treatment. In addition to its sensitivity from the Imami theological and communal perspective, it is not easily explainable in terms of cautionary prudence, nor does the tragic outcome allow for a justification based on political expediency. Moreover, the incident does not seem to tally particularly well with the moral requirements of consequentialism. Though flooded with details intended to show Ḥusayn's initial prudence in planning and later eagerness to escape the bloody outcome at almost any cost, Murtaḍā's interpretation places the greatest weight in frequent mention of the battle's consequences. The only possible solution presented to the Imam was one that, in addition to taking his life, would have also taken his dignity. He chose to die in honour instead of getting killed in shame; choosing the lesser evil thus became an obligation on him. His course of action did not contradict the need for self-preservation, let alone political expediency, and it also accords with the requirement of infallibility, since he picked the only right alternative.[129] As long as this requirement is satisfied, the portrayal of the historical events can tolerate phrasing that might have been objectionable to many other Imamis, as, for example, when Murtaḍā describes Ḥusayn and his folks as having been deceived (*yukhdaᶜu*).[130] Mufīd's view is somewhat different: although he does not affirm that Ḥusayn had prior knowledge of his failure, he allows its possibility on the basis that God may have aimed to grant the Imam exceptional honour in the hereafter for dying without resistance, in addition to the great divine assistance given to people because of such a death.[131]

The defence of infallibility, once more, falls on the shoulders of the Muᶜtazili system, without the need to rely on the Imam's prior knowledge of unalterable developments or his willingness to be martyred. So long as the rational theological foundations can be defended by kindred tools, the Imama doctrine need not be burdened by revelational or legal – let alone metaphysical – aspects.

Inconvenient outcomes

The question of the Companions

It has been suggested that accounts of the first civil strife (*fitna*) can be used to examine how historical narrative is shaped within religious rhetoric,[132] and that the *fitna* theme was inaugurated by the Shiᶜis of Iraq.[133] Of all matters related to this episode, the question of the character of the Companions has been one of the thorniest issues in the relations between the Imamis and non-Shiᶜis. The main accusation levelled against the Imamis concerns their belief that with a few exceptions, all of the Companions were hypocrites who either revealed their true colours or apostatised after the Prophet's death. The reason for such a harsh judgement on the part of the Imamis is the Companions' rejection of ᶜAlī's designation as the Prophet's successor. In what might seem like a more nuanced presentation of the Imami position, Murtaḍā relies on the early Imami theologian Ibn Qiba (d. before 931), making the controversial claim that Ibn Qiba's view is the standard Imami belief while using it for a different end than did Ibn Qiba. According to this view, the Companions can be divided into three groups, two minorities and a majority. The first minority comprises those who were aware of the Prophet's designation of ᶜAlī but deliberately ignored it. The second minority consists of those who remained faithful to ᶜAlī and passed the word to their associates. The majority of the Companions, however, had no understanding of the state of affairs at the time and were thus simply misled.[134]

But this nuanced and more sophisticated analysis of the Companions does not indicate milder theological consequences. This is to be expected given that the issue touches on a sensitive theological theme, namely, disobedience to the infallible Imam, as well as a more crucial emotional one related to the traditional Imami view. The strict theological verdict is carefully formulated, in a manner that does not reveal quarrelsome bitterness over a lost battle. Since denying the Imama, whether knowingly or otherwise, is tantamount to disbelief (*kufr*),[135] and given Murtaḍā's definition of perseverance, the first minority and the majority are unbelievers, although on different counts.[136] That Murtaḍā's nuanced categorisation of the Companions' status does not mitigate his theological view is also evident in his acceptance of certain aspects of other Shiᶜi narratives that are far less tolerant and cross the boundary from historical/political analysis to grand conspiracy, for example when he endorses the Shiᶜi narrative about a conspiracy that took place before the death of the Prophet to make sure that ᶜAlī would be prevented from seizing power after him.[137] The need to harmonise the historical accounts with the severe theological judgements becomes more challenging in light of certain legal consequences of such judgements. Again, the potent tools of theology are summoned to patch up an incoherent narrative: belief and disbelief being inner states of a person, the behaviour of these Companions guaranteed them the status of Muslims since people must base their interactions on appearances and not attempt to peek into each other's hearts.[138] In addition, it is noteworthy that ᶜAlī's customs regarding his enemies show that some unbelievers merit treatment different from that deserved by other unbelievers, with differences among, for example, the People of the Book, apostates and infidels.[139] The reliance on distinctions between different forms of disbelief, in addition to invoking the perseverance doctrine, reveals an aspect of the sacred-historical approach, namely, its placement of individual events belonging to ordinary history in a 'definite connection not disclosed by history itself'.[140]

The awkward clash of sacred histories reaches a peak in Murtaḍā's handling of the accounts of ᶜAlī's fight against the leading trio in the battle of the Camel: ᶜĀᵓisha (d. 678), Ṭalḥa (d. 656) and Zubayr (d. 656). The latter two are among the ten who have been promised paradise according to non-Shiᶜi reports, and the first is the Prophet's beloved wife. The preservation of Murtaḍā's sectarian narrative is relatively easy, as all that he needs to do is to challenge reports about the good intentions of ᶜAlī's opponents at any point in the battle using quotations from major mainstream historians.[141] Resting one's head on the pillow of reports – regardless what lies underneath – is always a better alternative than trying to invoke the distant concepts of theology when historical accounts seem inconvenient.

This background of nuanced narrative undergirds the triumphal tone in which Murtaḍā declares ᶜAbd al-Jabbār mistaken when he accuses the Imamis of believing in the Companions' apostasy, hypocrisy and conscious disobedience to the Prophet.[142] Though Murtaḍā does not say it explicitly, ᶜAbd al-Jabbār's mistake lies not in misidentifying the beliefs of his opponents but in failing to grasp the theoretical framework that encompasses their beliefs. Murtaḍā's objection, in the final analysis, seems driven more by protest against a mischaracterisation of the Imami position that makes it seem naïve than by genuine rejection of ᶜAbd al-Jabbār's argument, as the subsequent tradition makes clear: a cursory comparison of Murtaḍā's and Ṭūsī's texts shows the latter to be less ambiguous in wording and attitude.[143]

The occultation of the Imam

Initially, the death of the apparently childless Ḥasan al-ᶜAskarī in 874 had left the Imami community in shock. But the theological problem was restricted to the historical aspect of the Imama: the existence of a hidden heir was enough to solve the difficulty, and appeal to political threats justified his occultation. The office of the Safīr, an intermediary between the community and its hidden leader, was able to address the problem till the end of the Minor Occultation in 941.[144] But the passage of time added new problems, pertinent to different aspects of the Imama doctrine. In terms of political polemics, the Imam's life was no longer in danger, as the Shiᶜi Būyids had assumed power and the Imami community flourished in an unprecedented manner. The challenge now was theological. It concerned two aspects: the Imam's unusually long life and the meaning of the Imama of a hidden person.

The difficulty of the situation lay in its evident incompatibility with a framework that prided itself on an increasingly rationalist discourse compared both to its forebears and to its critics. The argument from elimination – the same line of reasoning used to defend the Imama of the other Imams – was theoretically feasible[145] and had been adopted earlier by Ibn Qiba and Abū Sahl al-Nawbakhtī (d. 924),[146] but it would still have left the Imamis in a precarious position given the combination of a reassuring argument and an unconvincing reality.

Murtaḍā's attempted solution to these problems makes full use of his formidable arsenal of intellectual weaponry. He capitalises on his novel justification for the necessity of the Imama, the unbridgeable gap between charismatic leadership and the community, the requirements of sacred history and the Muᶜtazili moral system's conception of both divine assistance and human responsibility; to these he adds an unusual emphasis on the priority of his smaller community over other Muslims. The outcome is an answer whose originality is announced with unmistakable confidence.

Because the Imam was forced into hiding because of the community's disloyalty, its members' inability to benefit from the divine assistance brought by his presence is their own fault, for which they are blameworthy.[147] Since the Twelfth Imam's mission, which must be carried out by him alone,[148] is to effect change by force,[149] the majority of the community is bound to wait and be deprived of divine assistance until obstacles have been removed – at a time unknown to us.[150] The blameworthiness of the community holds even in the hypothetical case of their failing to observe their obligations due to ignorance of the sacred law, for his inability to emerge from hiding and provide instruction is caused by their shortcomings.[151] The change in Murtaḍā's thinking on the question reflects the increasing primacy of the charismatic leader over the community, for he had initially argued that the Imam is bound to emerge, even if it is not safe for him to do so.[152] The gulf between the Imam and the community and the irreplaceability of the former because of his function in sacred history make him weightier than a community of Muslims who have erred and missed out on their lot of divine assistance. This primacy is also expressed in Mufīd's works, though based on a different justification.[153] Ṭūsī, who notes the change in Murtaḍā's views over time, still adheres to the latter's earlier opinion.[154] But that is not to say that the collective deprivation is universal to all Muslims; for if this were granted, then the natural consequence would be that the Imam's absence would be similar to his inexistence – an admittedly tough challenge frequently raised by opponents.[155] The sectarian worldview, coupled with a definition of the Imama as mostly grounded in otherworldly benefits, is maximally utile here. If the Imam cannot exercise his political functions in occultation, then one might as well restrict these functions to worldly matters: avenging enemies of the Imami community and restoring its rights – both unessential to divine assistance.[156] But the core of Murtaḍā's theory, that is, people's moral rectitude as the *raison d'être* of the necessity of the Imama, can still be salvaged: those who believe in the hidden Imam, by dint of his inscrutability, are more motivated to meet their obligations since they cannot be sure about escaping the scrutiny of his stealthy supervision in any context,[157] even if some of them can recognise him.[158] Murtaḍā's concern with the Imam's occultation in connection with his function, which is primarily otherworldly, betrays a sacred-historical approach given his preoccupation not with the event but with the theological response to the challenge posed by the event.[159] That the community of believers benefits at the expense of the larger community poses no challenge, as it tallies well with Murtaḍā's theological foundations and reflects the Imami community's rising fortunes and its growing sectarian awareness, which had crystallised since the early ninth century[160] although it had already been present in the early eighth century.[161]

The ᶜAlids were always resourceful in explaining their lack of good fortune,[162] and Murtaḍā – or the Imami discourse he represents – is no exception in turning threats into opportunities: the Imam's absence, by an inversion of the opponents' logic, is turned into a pretext for ubiquitous presence; he is more present in his absence than he would have been in his presence. This answer also saves him the trouble of justifying the Imam's hiding: it allows Murtaḍā to invoke the Imam's initial fear for his life[163] – no matter how insignificant it has become – while still maintaining that the function of the Imama has not been impeded by that fear, therefore dodging any attempt to make this dysfunction a compelling cause for his reappearance. Moreover, Murtaḍā sidesteps the question of whether the Būyid dynasty ought to be ranked among the enemies of the Imam, which must have been sensitive and whose avoidance was probably aptly rewarded. His argument must have benefitted from the diminished importance of the office of the caliphate that seems to have accompanied the earlier peak of conversion to Islam.[164] As the community's need for the caliphate decreased, views like Murtadā's became less polarising, though not necessarily more acceptable.

Not surprisingly, the Zaydis were extremely dismayed by Murtaḍā's explanation and considered his position most antagonistic to the surviving ᶜAlids, as it deprives their claims to the Imama of all legitimacy regardless of how competent they may be – a position that even Kharijis would not endorse.[165] Despite mentioning other possible answers, Murtaḍā insists on the novelty of his,[166] which cannot be divorced from the novelty of the Imama being defined as an office whose necessity lies in otherworldly considerations. Once again, Murtaḍā has exploited the Muᶜtazili system, particularly in its moral dimensions, to defend the most non-Muᶜtazili of doctrines, at least in the polemical sense. Mufīd, for his part, offers a different justification: the absence of the Imam is to be seen in light of the Imamis' best interest; because of the greater difficulty involved in believing without seeing him, he is obliged to hide himself so that they may earn more otherworldly rewards.[167] Ṭūsī, on the other hand, relies almost verbatim on Murtaḍā's *Muqniᶜ* in his discussion of occultation; however, he chooses a position other than his teacher's preferred one from the list of possible answers suggested by Murtaḍā.[168]

The unusual longevity of the Imam's life represented another challenge, all the more so since it was used by Imami theologians before Murtaḍā to reject the claims of other groups.[169] Relying on 'subtle theology', the centrepiece of Murtaḍā's defence is the natural possibility of long life. He argues that ageing and death are not necessarily caused by the passing of time but rather by factors created by God, who could also decree otherwise.[170] The appeal to the Qurᵓān and literary anecdotes about the lives of ancient figures serves as a second line of defence,[171] and the portrayal of the Imam's longevity as a miracle – in case the preceding arguments were not compelling – serves as his last.[172] Here, too, he makes an attempt to capitalise on aspects of Muᶜtazili theology, although the other lines of argument are clearer regarding Murtaḍā's underlying strategy: his willingness to resort to miracles signals the real significance of the debate more than his readiness to use theology, since the sensitivity of the question allows for no margin of movement.

Other controversial points

A survey of other miscellaneous points related to Murtaḍā's Imama doctrine reveals the priorities of the theological system under construction. There is a clear disavowal of views that seem to tarnish the desired image of an emerging orthodoxy characterised by a strong rationalist colouring. Murtaḍā's dismissal of these views is immensely helpful for him in his debate with ᶜAbd al-Jabbār, who consistently ascribes them to the Imamis. Such views, which Murtaḍā usually renounces and attributes to extremists who are less discriminating and sophisticated, affirm the ontological significance of the Imams in justifying the creation of the cosmos,[173] deny the Imams' human nature[174] or ascribe to them supernatural powers that serve no clear theological purpose.[175] Other contexts, though exceedingly similar, allow for a metaphorical interpretation and are thus treated more leniently, since such interpretations can neutralise their theologically problematic content – be it regarding the ontological significance of the Imams[176] or their supernatural powers – while still accommodating doubts about their authenticity.[177] But whenever the occasion arises for a discussion that affects the belief in infallibility, Murtaḍā's approach changes drastically, and his belief in the Imam's exceptionalism brings him closer to the gnostic views that he usually disavows. For example, a question that stirred much controversy is the age at which Imams attain intellectual perfection, since some Imams assumed office while still minors.[178] Murtaḍā cannot permit a time lag before the Imam becomes infallible, lest a crack appear in the wall of his theological edifice. Therefore, he argues that a child may have fully developed intellectual capacities, but even if this were not the case, the Imams would be an exception, their capacities constituting a miracle proper to their status.[179]

Conclusion

Content

In arguing that the Imama is a rational necessity as a means of providing divine assistance, Murtaḍā's elaborate theory satisfies the requirements of both the Muᶜtazili theological framework and Imami historical narratives. This hybrid system, nevertheless, is not meant as a reconciliation, but rather as an update of the Imami doctrine. It brings the doctrine of the Imama into the heart of the debate concerned with divine assistance to the community.

Murtaḍā's paramount concern is with infallibility; accordingly, other views on the Imams' supernatural qualifications are often renounced not because they conflict with rational methods – whether this is the case or not – but because they are an unnecessary burden for his project. These qualifications do not have much influence on his framework, which is most occupied with the dual core of the necessity of the Imama and the infallibility of the Imam. This dual core provides the indispensable basis for defining Shiᶜi doctrine in contradistinction to non-Shiᶜi teachings, and it further narrows the scope of debate by leaving only the Imamis and a few other Shiᶜi sects relevant to the discussion.

If the moral necessity of the Imama is the body that provides the doctrine of the Imama with a solid texture, the infallibility of the Imam is the soul that permeates this body. It functions as a frequent resort for Murtaḍā to settle theological debates and to demarcate the Imami community. This explains both Murtaḍā's willingness to concede some aspects of the doctrine that are irrelevant to infallibility and his eagerness to reject arguments that might support his conclusions unless they are based on infallibility.

Context

Murtaḍā's main debate on the theory of the Imama is with the Muᶜtazilis, since he shares with them the theological underpinnings of the theory – namely, the concept of God's justice and its concomitant, divine assistance. With other groups, the discussion is less theoretical and more historical in nature.

Murtaḍā follows much of what earlier generations of Imami theologians had to say on the Imama. However, his contribution is unprecedented in scope, although the main theological formulations of the doctrine had already been proposed by scholars such as Ibn Qiba, the Imami Ṭabarī (d. mid-tenth century) and especially Mufīd. The argument for the necessity of the Imama is Murtaḍā's major addition in this regard, and it seems to have been accepted by Mufīd, too, late in his life. In addition to this argument, another original contribution by Murtaḍā is his justification for the Imam's hiding from his followers: his assertion that the essential function of the Imama is enhanced by occultation. Unlike Mufīd, Murtaḍā strictly denies certain Imami beliefs that require of the Imam knowledge of matters unrelated to religion. Except for the argument on the necessity of the Imama, Murtaḍā's original contributions were not endorsed by Ṭūsī, who reverted to Mufīd's position or adopted a position that Murtaḍā held early on but abandoned later in his life, as in the question of justifying the occultation of the Twelfth Imam.

Notes

1. El-Hibri, *Parable*, 296; see also Cooperson, *Classical Arabic Biography*, 101, in reference to the exemplary case represented by the biography of ᶜAlī al-Riḍā.
2. Donner, *Narratives*, 15–25.
3. Donner, *Narratives*, 125–38 (with particular emphasis on Ṭabarī's work), 287.
4. El-Hibri, *Parable*, 296.
5. Donner, *Narratives*, 286.
6. I borrow the concept of dome from Khalidi, *Arabic Historical Thought*; see 28–30 for *ḥadīth*-based, 124–30 for *adab*-based, 131–7 for *ḥikma*-based and 182–4 for *siyāsa*-based historiography.
7. Cooperson, *Classical Arabic Biography*, 192.

8. These four primary themes, each encompassing many issues, are the ones identified by Donner; other classifications are possible, depending on the perspective. See Donner, *Narratives*, 141–6 (for the functions of these themes), 147–203 (for a detailed study of them).
9. Again, the case of Riḍā 'conveys a clear sense of the collaborative and cumulative nature of the Imami biographical project and thus of the sacred history of Twelver Shiʿism'; Cooperson, *Classical Arabic Biography*, 84.
10. The problems of using the term 'salvation history' in connection to Islam have long been noted, due both to the Christian baggage of the term and to the technical difficulty of applying the concept of salvation to other traditions; Rippin, 'Methodologies', 154–5. 'Sacred history' has therefore been used in the main; nevertheless, the overlaps between the concept of salvation history and a possible Muslim analogue will be noted, without committing to the overarching theoretical framework.
11. Cullmann, *Salvation*, 128.
12. See, for example, Corbin, 'Meaning'; Amir-Moezzi, *Divine Guide*, 99–125.
13. Dakake, *Charismatic Community*, 7–9, provides a survey of how the concept of charisma applies to Shiʿism, while acknowledging that it is an uneasy fit.
14. *Shāfī*, 1:34; see the approval expressed in the works of a recent Imami authority, Mughniyya, *Shīʿa*, 121.
15. Ashʿarī, *Maqālāt*, 460–3; ʿAbd al-Jabbār, *Mughnī*, 20{1}:16, 47–8; Ibn Ḥazm, *Fiṣal*, 4:106; Ibn Abī al-Ḥadīd, *Sharḥ*, 2:307. For an overview of the positions of different Muslim communities see Madelung, 'Imama'.
16. ʿAbd al-Jabbār, *Mughnī*, 20{1}:41–7; Ibn Abī al-Ḥadīd, *Sharḥ*, 2:307; cf. similar statements in Ibn Ḥazm, *Fiṣal*, 4:111–12.
17. Mānkdīm, *Sharḥ*, 758; Ibn Abī al-Ḥadīd, *Sharḥ*, 2:307–8. For a survey of the position of Baghdadi Muʿtazilis on the Imama, see el-Omari, *Theology*, 204–25.
18. Afsaruddin, *Excellence*, 271–2, argues that this genre is not a sectarian Shiʿi reconstruction of earlier debates but rather reflects the nature of the original discussion.
19. *Shāfī*, 1:47, 99; *Dhakhīra*, 410; *Sharḥ Jumal*, 191–2; *Muqniʿ*, 35–6; *Rasāʾil*, 1:309–10, 2:294 (without the word *luṭf*).
20. *Sharḥ Jumal*, 191, 192.
21. *Shāfī*, 1:45, 50, 57, 63, 65, 67, 150.
22. *Shāfī*, 1:40–1.
23. *Amālī*, 2:273–4.
24. *Shāfī*, 1:60–3, 66; *Dhakhīra*, 410–11.
25. *Shāfī*, 1:69, 71, 118–19; *Dhakhīra*, 411; cf. ʿAbd al-Jabbār, *Mughnī*, 20{1}:30.
26. *Shāfī*, 1:164; *Dhakhīra*, 411–12; cf. ʿAbd al-Jabbār, *Mughnī*, 20{1}:30.
27. For example, Ṣadūq, *Kamāl*, 317, 668; Mufīd, *Irshād*, 2:384–8.
28. *Shāfī*, 1:53, 164–5; *Dhakhīra*, 415; cf. ʿAbd al-Jabbār, *Mughnī*, 20{1}:63–4.
29. Cf. Butterworth, 'Philosophy', 277–80; see the contrary view in Gutas, 'Study', 22–3, which could explain Murtaḍā's lack of engagement with 'political' philosophy.
30. See *Rasāʾil*, 2:13, 3:141.
31. *Shāfī*, 1:180.

32. Al-Qāḍī al-Nuᶜmān, *Daᶜāʾim*, 1:36–7, 43.
33. *Shāfī*, 1:102.
34. *Shāfī*, 1:102; *Muqniᶜ*, 59–60; similar, but less articulate, statements in *Shāfī*, 138–9, 154–5, 190; *Rasāʾil*, 1:314–15.
35. *Shāfī*, 1:214–75; *Dhakhīra*, 424–9; *Dharīᶜa*, 421–52.
36. *Shāfī*, 1:179–80; *Dhakhīra*, 424–5; less elaborately in *Shāfī*, 276, 283; also *Amālī*, 2:306.
37. *Shāfī*, 1:76, 302–5, less elaborately at 42–3, 75–6, 137–8, 168–9, 307–8; *Dharīᶜa*, 44–6, 140, 377, 467.
38. *Sharḥ*, 191–2; *Rasāʾil*, 2:294.
39. *Shāfī*, 1:142.
40. *Shāfī*, 1:42–4; *Tanzīh*, 348; dispensing with revelation but not with the Imama in *Shāfī*, 99.
41. Mufīd, *Ifṣāḥ*, 27–8, presents four arguments, the first three of which are rooted in the Qurʾān, the Prophetic tradition and consensus, respectively; McDermott, *Theology*, 120–2, argues that Mufīd's fourth argument for the necessity of the Imama is based on reason. Nevertheless, it must be noted that Mufīd stresses the need to observe the law before arguing that reason necessitates that an Imam supervise the process; thus, he still assumes a revealed law.
42. Mufīd presents this argument in his *Irshād*, 2:342. The book was authored in 1020, two years before Mufīd's death, as stated in *Irshād*, 1:3.
43. *Shāfī*, 1:119; cf. ᶜAbd al-Jabbār, *Mughnī*, 20{1}:47.
44. *Shāfī*, 1:123, 188; cf. ᶜAbd al-Jabbār, *Mughnī*, 20{1}:47–9.
45. *Shāfī*, 1:205–6; cf. ᶜAbd al-Jabbār, *Mughnī*, 20{1}:41–3.
46. *Dhakhīra*, 429–30.
47. *Rasāʾil*, 3:325–6, *Shāfī*, 3:135; *Tanzīh*, 124; *Amālī*, 2:292.
48. *Shāfī*, 3:135.
49. *Masāʾil al-Nāṣiriyyāt*, 442. Comparing his wording in discussing the story of Moses' request to see God in *Amālī*, 2:188–9, and *Tanzīh*, 162–9, indicates that his position has become more defined over time. In the former, he still allows, even as a mere possibility, that Moses committed a minor sin before his prophethood; in the latter, he unconditionally repudiates that view.
50. *Shāfī*, 1:53–4, 55, 166, 289–90; *Dhakhīra*, 410, 415; *Sharḥ Jumal*, 192–4; *Muqniᶜ*, 36–7; *Tanzīh*, 44; *Rasāʾil*, 1:296, 324, 2:294. This is why prophets, who are also infallible Imams, do not need Imams for themselves; *Shāfī*, 1:53–4, 289–90. It is also why other leaders of the community, such as the Imam's deputies and vicegerents, do not have to be infallible as long as he is at the head of the chain of command; *Shāfī*, 1:210–11, 296–7; *Sharḥ Jumal*, 194; *Dhakhīra*, 432; *Rasāʾil*, 1:328; cf. ᶜAbd al-Jabbār, *Mughnī*, 20{1}:75–6.
51. Mufīd, *Awāʾil*, 623; McDermott, *Theology*, 100–1.
52. *Shāfī*, 1:295, 2:30, 36, 38, 4:177; *Dhakhīra*, 431; *Rasāʾil*, 1:331–2, 396; cf. ᶜAbd al-Jabbār, *Mughnī*, 20{1}:98.
53. For example, Ṭūsī points out some practices of the Fāṭimid caliphs that are incongruent with the law; Ṭūsī, *Talkhīṣ*, 4:202–3.

54. *Sharḥ Jumal*, 200; clearly, the rejection of choice is directed at those who upheld the legitimacy of Abū Bakr due to his election, while Murtaḍā's denial of inheritance is targeted at those who believed that the Prophet's uncle, ᶜAbbās, was entitled to succeed him by virtue of inheritance; *Sharḥ Jumal*, 202–3; *Dhakhīra*, 437, 471–2. Murtaḍā probably has also in mind the frequent existence of many claimants to inheritance, which brings us back to the challenge of identifying the real Imam among them.
55. *Shāfī*, 1:184, 276–7, 2:5; *Sharḥ Jumal*, 199; *Dhakhīra*, 429.
56. *Dhakhīra*, 333–7; cf. ᶜAbd al-Jabbār, *Mughnī*, 20{1}:113–14.
57. *Shāfī*, 2:59, 63, 4:5–6.
58. *Shāfī*, 2:5–7, 4:6; *Sharḥ Jumal*, 200–1; *Dhakhīra*, 432, 456–7; cf. ᶜAbd al-Jabbār, *Mughnī*, 20{1}:99–102.
59. *Shāfī*, 2:7–8.
60. The printed text of *Dhakhīra*, 429, reads 'message' (*risāla*); however, 'leadership' (*riʾāsa*) is the more probable reading and is also supported by the appearance of a similar discussion, this time with *riʾāsa*, later in the book; *Dhakhīra*, 436n3.
61. *Dhakhīra*, 436.
62. *Dhakhīra*, 437.
63. *Shāfī*, 2:42, 3:173; *Sharḥ Jumal*, 194–6; *Dhakhīra*, 432–3.
64. Cf. Afsaruddin, *Excellence*, 80–98.
65. *Shāfī*, 2:41–2; *Sharḥ Jumal*, 198; *Dhakhīra*, 430, 434.
66. *Shāfī*, 1:326–7, 3:68; also in *Dhakhīra*, 325, in relation to prophethood.
67. *Shāfī*, 2:14–19, 20–1; *Dhakhīra*, 432–3; cf. ᶜAbd al-Jabbār, *Mughnī*, 20{1}:103–4.
68. *Dhakhīra*, 433–4; *Rasāʾil*, 1:394–5; cf. ᶜAbd al-Jabbār, *Mughnī*, 20{1}:106.
69. *Shāfī*, 2:28–30, 52–3; *Sharḥ Jumal*, 197–8.
70. *Dhakhīra*, 430, 436.
71. *Dhakhīra*, 412–13, 430, 436; this is one point on which ᶜAbd al-Jabbār misunderstood the Imami position, according to Murtaḍā; *Shāfī*, 1:45–6; cf. ᶜAbd al-Jabbār, *Mughnī*, 20{1}:21, 25, 27.
72. Carli, 'Poetry', 303.
73. For example, in the *Dhakhīra* it occupies sixty-six (pp. 437–502) out of ninety-six pages (pp. 409–594).
74. Compare with El-Hibri, *Parable*, vii, who views the centrality of history to faith as a result of the successful political careers of the Prophet and his successors.
75. *Shāfī*, 2:65, 3:82–3.
76. *Dhakhīra*, 490–1.
77. *Shāfī*, 2:207–9; *Dhakhīra*, 437; abridged version in *Shāfī*, 211–12; cf. ᶜAbd al-Jabbār, *Mughnī*, 20{1}:131–2.
78. *Dhakhīra*, 437–8.
79. *Shāfī*, 2:187–9.
80. *Shāfī*, 2:212; see Madelung, 'Zaydiyya'.
81. *Shāfī*, 3:126–7.
82. *Shāfī*, 4:311; cf. ᶜAbd al-Jabbār, *Mughnī*, 20{1}:260–2.
83. *Shāfī*, 2:135–6.

84. *Shāfī*, 4:311–14.
85. *Shāfī*, 2:67–8; less elaborately in *Rasā'il*, 1:338–9. Murtaḍā's position on whether the significance of explicit appointment is necessarily known to its direct audience seems to differ a little in these two sources, with the first making clear his firm affirmative belief and the second – a later text – betraying uncertainty about the question. Nonetheless, at least some Imamis, as Murtaḍā himself acknowledges, did hold this view; *Shāfī*, 1:80.
86. *Shāfī*, 2:93–107; cf. ᶜAbd al-Jabbār, *Mughnī*, 20{1}:113–28, whose lengthy discussion is entirely based on questioning the claim that explicit designation is known to Imamis by necessity. Apparently, ᶜAbd al-Jabbār took this to be Ibn Qiba's position, although without naming him, as Murtaḍā shows by pointing out the venue of the claim in the beginning of Ibn Qiba's *Inṣāf*; *Shāfī*, 2:323–4.
87. *Shāfī*, 2:67; *Dhakhīra*, 463; the wording is slightly different in the two sources. For the sources of these texts, see Mufīd, *Risāla*, 39; Ṭūsī, *Iqtiṣād*, 203.
88. ᶜAbd al-Jabbār, *Mughnī*, 20{1}:128.
89. *Shāfī*, 2:107–25, 144–5; *Dhakhīra*, 467–72; cf. ᶜAbd al-Jabbār, *Mughnī*, 20{1}:118–19, 188.
90. *Shāfī*, 2:119–20; *Dhakhīra*, 464, where Murtaḍā asserts that the works of early Shiᶜis like Ibn Maytham do contain arguments of this type. Murtaḍā almost certainly means ᶜAlī b. Ismāᶜīl b. Shuᶜayb b. Maytham, also known as al-Maythamī (fl. first half of the ninth century), considered by Ṭūsī to have been the first Imami theologian and credited with a book on the Imama entitled *Kāmil* as well as with many debates with the leading Muᶜtazilis of the time, such as Naẓẓām and Abū al-Hudhayl. On him, see Najāshī, *Rijāl*, 251; Ṭūsī, *Fihrist*, 150; Khū'ī, *Muᶜjam*, 12:299–300; for examples of his debates, see Mufīd, *Fuṣūl*, 23, 24, 29, 58, 69, 76, 86. Van Ess, *Theologie und Gesellschaft*, 2:428, considers Maythamī's positions much closer to those of the Muᶜtazilis except when it comes to his view of history.
91. Kulaynī, *Kāfī*, 2:242–4; Ṣadūq, *Kamāl*, 288.
92. The label 'Bakriyya' notwithstanding, Madelung, *Succession*, 54, argues that the belief in Abū Bakr as the Prophet's designated successor is likely to have been the official view during his caliphate. This could possibly explain the early origins of the debate among various parties inasmuch as it assumes designation as a common principle, not as contrast between designation and consultation.
93. The tone of dismissal and sarcasm can easily be detected in the attacks on the Imamis, although they were not alone as targets – traditionalists were usually also mocked; see, for example, Jāḥiẓ, 'Risālat al-ᶜUthmāniyya', 24–5; ᶜAbd al-Jabbār, *Mughnī*, 20{1}:14–15; Tawḥīdī, *Baṣā'ir*, 4:233, 7:225, 247, 8:42, 158–9, 161–2; Tawḥīdī, *Akhlāq*, 395.
94. The tradition and pertinent discussions have been studied exhaustively in the multivolume work *al-Ghadīr* by ᶜAbd al-Ḥusayn al-Amīnī (d. 1970). For the tradition, see, for example, Ibn Ḥanbal, *Musnad*, 4:370; Ṭabarānī, *Muᶜjam*, 3:180, 5:166. Murtaḍā, in his discussion, seems to have taken the tradition to be non-prevalent but a matter of consensus; *Dhakhīra*, 443–4.
95. See the text in Muslim, *Ṣaḥīḥ*, 7:120, 121; Tirmidhī, *Sunan*, 5:304; Ibn Ḥanbal, *Musnad*,

1:177, 182, 184, 185, 3:32, 338, 6:369, 6:438; Ṭabarānī, Muʿjam, 1:148, 2:247, 4:184, 5:203, 24:145, 146.
96. See, for example, the work by the Imami Ṭabarī, Mustarshid, 470–4, 446–9; Mufīd, Irshād, 1:8, 156–8; Mufīd, Ifṣāḥ, 33.
97. Dakake, Charismatic Community, 46–7.
98. Shāfī, 3:260–73; Dhakhīra, 474; Sharḥ Jumal, 214.
99. Murtaḍā usually quotes Ṭabarī (d. 923) (Shāfī, 3:197, 4:206–10) and Balādhurī (d. 892), often pointing out the non-Shiʿi leanings of the latter and his credibility as a historian; Shāfī, 3:197, 240–1, 243, 4:114, 204–5, 210–11; see the editor's notes providing the parallel references in the original works.
100. Shāfī, 2:148–9, 3:220–30; Dhakhīra, 485–6; Sharḥ Jumal, 217.
101. Shāfī, 2:149–54; Dhakhīra, 486–7; Sharḥ Jumal, 215; Tanzīh, 180–6.
102. Shāfī, 2:154–6; Dhakhīra, 476; Sharḥ Jumal, 217; Tanzīh, 187.
103. Shāfī, 3:237–47; Dhakhīra, 476; Sharḥ Jumal, 214; Dhakhīra, 474–8; Rasāʾil, 1:290–1, 340–1, 346, 3:246; cf. ʿAbd al-Jabbār, Mughnī, 20{1}:126.
104. Shāfī, 3:247, 4:13; Sharḥ Jumal, 216; Rasāʾil, 1:346.
105. Shāfī, 1:77, 100, 3:145–6.
106. Dhakhīra, 502–3.
107. Dhakhīra, 502; less explicitly in Sharḥ Jumal, 225.
108. Shāfī, 3:145.
109. Shāfī, 3:146–8; Dhakhīra, 503; Sharḥ Jumal, 219.
110. Dhakhīra, 503; in the later Sharḥ Jumal, 222, Murtaḍā dismisses the claim made by some later Zaydis that Zayd was infallible. The particular Zaydi group meant by Murtaḍā's statement is not clear. The common Zaydi doctrine is that the Imams are not infallible, but some late Zaydis have conceded infallibility to the first three Imams, namely ʿAlī, Ḥasan and Ḥusayn; Madelung 'Zaydiyya'; Madelung 'ʿIṣma'.
111. Sharḥ Jumal, 224; see Modarressi, Crisis, 59–60.
112. Dhakhīra, 503; Sharḥ Jumal, 223; Muqniʿ, 38–9; on the Nāwūsiyya, see Modarressi, Crisis, 54–7, who doubts such a group ever existed.
113. Shāfī, 3:146–8; Dhakhīra, 503; Sharḥ Jumal, 225–6; Muqniʿ, 38–9; see Modarressi, Crisis, 60–1.
114. Daftary, Ismaʿilis, 84, 137; also Madelung, 'Imāma'.
115. Al-Qāḍī al-Nuʿmān, Daʿāʾim, 1:43.
116. Sharḥ Jumal, 225.
117. This argument appears only in his very late work Sharḥ Jumal, 224–5. It is not clear why a discussion on Ismaʿilism is totally absent from the relevant section of Shāfī. In his later Dhakhīra, 503, Murtaḍā takes a more simplistic approach to the question: he lumps Ismaʿilis into the same category as the Wāqifiyya, Kaysāniyya and Nāwūsiyya, arguing that they all uphold the Imama of a dead person; in doing so, Murtaḍā is restricting his attack to the so-called pure Ismaʿilis (al-khāliṣa), who believed Ismāʿīl to have gone into concealment. Among the Ismaʿilis, the Mubārakiyya did not deny Ismāʿīl's death but rather maintained that the Imama was transferred from him to his son Muḥammad – therefore making the claim, in retrospect, that he had been the Imam even when Jaʿfar

was still alive; these Ismaᶜilis represented the more common trend endorsed by the Fāṭimids. The reason for Murtaḍā's adjustment of his argument is not clear; it is improbable that he was unaware of such basic details of Fāṭimid doctrine during the compilation of *Shāfī* and *Dhakhīra*, especially given the fact that the distinction is made by Imami heresiographers such as Nawbakhtī (d. between 912 and 922) and Qummī (d. 914) – sections of the former's material being reported by Murtaḍā himself in Mufīd's *Fuṣūl*, 318ff.; on the schism, see Daftary, *Ismaᶜilis*, 95–8.

118. See the example of the Wāqifiyya in *Dhakhīra*, 503, and *Sharḥ Jumal*, 223, 226; the wording in *Shāfī*, 3:148, and *Muqniᶜ*, 40, is slightly different, as he acknowledges the existence of a few individuals who still upheld this doctrine.
119. Cullmann, *Salvation*, 167.
120. Cullmann, *Salvation*, 23.
121. *Rasāʾil*, 3:217–20.
122. See Refudeen, 'Phenomenology', 71.
123. *Rasāʾil*, 3:145–6; cf. Mufīd, *Irshād*, 2:387, who is inclined to believe that the Mahdī will die forty days before the end of time, and Ṭūsī, *Ghayba*, 127, who stresses that the number of Imams is fixed at twelve.
124. *Tanzīh*, 309–22.
125. *Tanzīh*, 278–9.
126. *Tanzīh*, 342–3.
127. *Tanzīh*, 283–91, 326–32, 341.
128. *Tanzīh*, 266–7.
129. *Tanzīh*, 335–41. The narrative is also found in Murtaḍā's poetry; *Dīwān*, 2:313–14.
130. *Dīwān*, 1:500.
131. Mufīd, *al-Masāʾil al-ᶜUkbariyya*, 70–2. McDermott's reading of Mufīd's position is thus incomplete; McDermott, *Theology*, 109.
132. El-Hibri, *Parable*, 5.
133. Donner, *Narratives*, 187.
134. *Shāfī*, 2:126–30. He also mentions the two minorities in his *Dīwān*, 1:483, and the theme of envy and grudge is recurrent in his poetry; *Dīwān*, 2:514.
135. *Sharḥ Jumal*, 235; *Rasāʾil*, 1:283–4; also in *Dhakhīra*, 495, where Murtaḍā states that erudite and fair members (*al-muḥaṣṣilīn al-munṣifīn*) of the Muslim community agree unanimously that such deniers are transgressors and grave sinners (*fāsiq ṣāḥib kabīra*).
136. *Dhakhīra*, 495, 535–6; *Rasāʾil*, 1:336–43, 2:251.
137. *Shāfī*, 2:173; cf. Kulaynī, *Kāfī*, 8:179–81; Qummī, *Tafsīr*, 2:356; Ṣadūq, *Maᶜānī*, 412.
138. *Shāfī*, 2:139–40, 4:12–13; *Rasāʾil*, 1:336–7; also in the context of justifying the marriage of ᶜAlī's daughter to ᶜUmar in *Rasāʾil*, 1:290–1.
139. *Dhakhīra*, 495–6; *Sharḥ Jumal*, 237–8.
140. Cullmann, *Salvation*, 139–40.
141. *Shāfī*, 4:328–33, 341, 352–8; *Dhakhīra*, 496–500; quoting Balādhurī (*Shāfī*, 4:332–3, 334, 336–7, 357–8; *Dhakhīra*, 497), Ṭabarī (*Shāfī*, 4:335–6, 355; *Dhakhīra*, 499) and Wāqidī (*Shāfī*, 4:329–31, 336, 352–5; *Dhakhīra*, 498); see the editor's notes in which he provides the parallel references in the original works.

142. *Shāfī*, 2:130.
143. Compare Murtaḍā's text (*Shāfī*, 2:28–30, 52–3; *Sharḥ Jumal*, 197–8) with Ṭūsī's (*Talkhīṣ*, 1:235–7); compare also *Shāfī*, 3:198, with *Talkhīṣ*, 3:71, 195, 245–6, 4:34.
144. Abdulsater, 'Dynamics', passim.
145. *Muqniᶜ*, 33–5; *Rasāʾil*, 2:293–4.
146. Modarressi, *Crisis*, 125, 149–51, 188–9.
147. *Muqniᶜ*, 58–9; *Shāfī*, 1:51, 208, 210, 279–80, 3:150; *Sharḥ Jumal*, 226–7, 231; *Dhakhīra*, 416; *Tanzīh*, 345–8; *Rasāʾil*, 2:297–8.
148. *Shāfī*, 1:147; *Sharḥ Jumal*, 228–9.
149. *Muqniᶜ*, 54–5; *Rasāʾil*, 2:296.
150. *Rasāʾil*, 1:283.
151. *Sharḥ Jumal*, 233; *Rasāʾil*, 1:312. However, he still believes that consensus confirms that such a loss of legal knowledge has not taken place; *Rasāʾil*, 1:313.
152. *Muqniᶜ*, 59–60, 65; *Shāfī*, 1:173, 193, 278, 285–6, 307, 4:105; *Sharḥ Jumal*, 232; *Dhakhīra*, 419; *Tanzīh*, 349.
153. McDermott, *Theology*, 128.
154. Ṭūsī, *Talkhīṣ*, 4:211–13; Ṭūsī, *Ghayba*, 96–7.
155. The question is presented in full detail in *Dhakhīra*, 417–19.
156. *Muqniᶜ*, 82–3; *Dhakhīra*, 423. The expectation of the reappearance of the Mahdī can be seen in Murtaḍā's poetry, in which he stresses the concept of revenge; *Dīwān*, 1:182–3, 292–4, 2:24, 120.
157. *Muqniᶜ*, 74–8, 87–9; *Dhakhīra*, 419, 423–4; *Rasāʾil*, 2:297. Arguing that the Imam's absence is not tantamount to non-existence, Mufīd took a different course. For him, the real religious benefit of the Imam's existence is in the otherworldly rewards that believers attain by merely acknowledging his existence, upholding his Imama and awaiting his return; McDermott, *Theology*, 128–9.
158. *Muqniᶜ*, 55–6; *Shāfī*, 1:149; *Sharḥ Jumal*, 230; *Dhakhīra*, 423; *Tanzīh*, 347; *Rasāʾil*, 2:297.
159. Cullmann, *Salvation*, 306–7, in connection to the interval separating the resurrection of Christ and the end of time.
160. Dakake, *Charismatic Community*, 126.
161. Haider, *Origins*, 249.
162. Lassner, *Shaping*, 243.
163. *Muqniᶜ*, 51; *Shāfī*, 1:146; *Sharḥ Jumal*, 226–8; *Dhakhīra*, 421; *Tanzīh*, 344–5; *Rasāʾil*, 2:295.
164. Bulliet, *Conversion*, 129.
165. See a fifth-century Zaydi refutation of Murtaḍā's argument as it appears in the *Muqniᶜ*; Ansari, '(2) Yak raddiy-i'.
166. *Shāfī*, 1:148–9; *Sharḥ Jumal*, 229–30; *Tanzīh*, 349–51. In these works Murtaḍā does not unequivocally adopt any of these arguments; he ascribes them to his coreligionists but still refrains from presenting his preferred one, as he subsequently does in *Muqniᶜ*.
167. Mufīd, *Fuṣūl*, 114; McDermott, *Theology*, 125–7.
168. Ṭūsī, *Ghayba*, 85–7, 104–5.

169. Abū Sahl al-Nawbakhtī, 'Kitāb al-Tanbīh', partly preserved in Ṣadūq, *Kamāl*, 92–3.
170. *Amālī*, 1:272–3.
171. *Amālī*, 1:237–71; *Sharḥ Jumal*, 234.
172. *Sharḥ Jumal*, 234.
173. Thus Murtaḍā categorically denies that any Imami at any point in time held the view, quoted by ᶜAbd al-Jabbār, that 'Had it not been for the Imam, earth and heaven would not have been stable nor would people's deeds have been accepted'; *Shāfī*, 1:42; cf. ᶜAbd al-Jabbār, *Mughnī*, 20{1}:18. But it is worth noting that the view appears in common collections of Imami traditions from before Murtaḍā's time, even in those compiled by traditionalists later considered to be far from extremism; Kulaynī, *Kāfī*, 1:179; ᶜAlī b. Bābawayh, *Imāma*, 30; Ṣadūq, *ᶜUyūn*, 1:246–7; Ṣadūq, *ᶜIlal*, 1:196–9.
174. For example, the view that the Imams are themselves angels, ascribed by ᶜAbd al-Jabbār to Imamis and repudiated by Murtaḍā; *Shāfī*, 4:117–18. Some *ghulāt*-type extremists did consider the Imams prophets – that is, recipients of revelation – or angels; Modarressi, *Crisis*, 25.
175. As in the belief of some Imamis that upon the death of the Imam, the prayer at his funeral must be performed by the next Imam; *Rasāʾil*, 3:155–7.
176. *Rasāʾil*, 1:284–5.
177. *Rasāʾil*, 1:280–1; 3:133–4.
178. On the historical context of this controversy, see Modarressi, *Crisis*, 32–3.
179. *Shāfī*, 2:255–6.

CHAPTER

6

PROPHETHOOD AND THE VALUE OF DIVINE GUIDANCE

When listing the precepts of religion, Murtaḍā mentions three: divine unicity, divine justice and prophethood (*nubuwwa*).[1] But he notes that although prophethood is a precept (*aṣl*) of religion, theologians (namely the Muᶜtazilis) usually do not enumerate it among the five precepts because it is implicitly included in the precept of divine justice. This classification he finds objectionable, saying that by the same token the only precepts that should be explicitly mentioned are divine unicity and justice since the other three Muᶜtazili precepts (the station between the two stations, the promise and the threat, and enjoining the good and forbidding the wrong) may also go under justice; this is not to mention the fact that for Imamis the list should also include the Imama.[2] But despite this appreciation for prophethood, Murtaḍā's writings on it are considerably less extensive than his writings on the Imama. The reason is probably the relative lack of controversy surrounding prophethood, as much of the discussion on it involved Muslim theologians answering the objections of non-Muslim theologians. Since Murtaḍā's project is first and foremost directed at systematising and consolidating Imami Shiᶜi teachings, it is natural that his investment in the question of prophethood is on a different level than his investment in the Imama. After all, most of what he would say agrees with the general contours of other theological schools; the real difference concerns aspects of their doctrine that could contradict Imami beliefs. However, prophets being also Imams according to Murtaḍā,[3] the works on the Imama may also be considered works on prophethood. In this chapter, the focus is on the distinctive features of prophethood; the features in common with the Imama are addressed in the theoretical part of the chapter on the Imama. Some of these common points, however, are most elaborately argued as part of the prophethood doctrine due to considerations such as their Qurʾānic basis (as in the question of comparing prophets and Imams to angels) and their pertinence to prophethood in terms of the primary function of the office (as in one of the two arguments for infallibility). Such points are thus given more attention in this chapter despite not being related exclusively to prophethood.

The conceptual similarity between Murtaḍā's view of the Imama and his view of prophethood must not mask some critical differences. Most important is the overwhelming character of the relationship between history and theology in each of the two. His discussion of the Imama is heavily historiographical, building mostly on themes and functions characteristic of Islamic historical writing. Prophethood, on the other hand, is much less entangled in the web of history. There is not much historiographical material to sift for the proper reports. This is because non-Muslims' narratives about their prophets are of little significance for Murtaḍā's framework, since he does not consider them reliable in terms of transmission. The only way to establish knowledge about these prophets is through Muḥammad's revelation concerning previous prophets. This immediately moves the discussion beyond the grip of historiography; or, differently put, there is no 'ordinary' history but only sacred history in the discussion of prophethood before Muḥammad. The Prophet of Islam, however, provides ample material for historical thinking, although most of the debate is centred on establishing the miraculous aspects of his message rather than on investigating particular episodes. This approach, focused as it is on Muḥammad and on making the legitimacy of other prophets dependent on his, reflects the Muslims' high confidence in the course of history running in their favour. In the case of Murtaḍā as an Imami, the approach mirrors the attitude revealed in his discussion of the Imama, in which he plainly appeals to numbers and continuous scholarly tradition to overcome the objections made by smaller or less powerful communities; it thus also represents the political ascendancy of the Imami community. In Murtaḍā's model of sacred history, the meaning of the course of time is bestowed backwards: it is the story of Muḥammad that, by dint of its exclusivity as a reliable source of knowledge, gives meaning to previous history through Abraham until Adam.[4]

Theoretical model

The definition and necessity of prophethood

Murtaḍā provides no clear definition of prophethood in his works; however, it has been noted that the Imama is the more general category under which he subsumes prophethood. Therefore, I take the definition of the Imama as part of the definition of prophethood, using the points of distinction between the two as differentiae to arrive at a better understanding of the latter. For Murtaḍā, the distinctive feature of prophets is that they convey God's message, having received it from Him either directly or indirectly through a non-human intermediary, that is, an angel.[5] It follows that the Imams do not receive such revelation; therefore, they must rely on prophets, who function as human intermediaries, to acquire divine knowledge. Despite Murtaḍā's claim that his view of the relationship between the Imama and prophethood is a known belief of the Imamis (*maʿrūf^un^ min madhhabihim*) and that prophets are superior to Imams,[6] both were divisive questions in the Imami community. The context of Murtaḍā's statement is apologetic, its goal being to escape the accusation made by ᶜAbd al-Jabbār that Imamis elevate the Imams over prophets and probably the related Muᶜtazili argument aimed at embarrassing the Imamis (*ilzām*) by cornering them into admitting that the Imams are also prophets.[7] Nevertheless, other Imami authorities at the time do not confirm Murtaḍā's claims. On this question, Murtaḍā thus departs from both Mufīd and Ṭūsī, who accept that the Imams receive divine inspiration from a non-human source while awake, with Mufīd accusing the Imamis who believed otherwise of having no knowledge of traditions – an accusation suggestive of Murtaḍā's regular dismissal of traditions in most of his theological corpus.[8] Mufīd's position leans towards considering the Imams superior to all other humans except Muḥammad on account of traditions. He also rules that the only reason the Imams are not referred to as prophets is the prohibition against such usage, not any conceptual difference.[9] Ṭūsī apparently follows Mufīd's suit in upholding the superiority of the Imams over prophets, probably also because of his more lenient attitude towards traditions, as he uncritically narrates traditions – many on Mufīd's authority – reminiscent of this view.[10] On the question of the nature of the difference between the offices of the Imama and prophethood, Ṭūsī's position seems to have developed in a more complicated manner than those of his two teachers. Its general thrust, however, is closer to Mufīd's position.[11]

Prophethood, then, is most intimately related to the private experience of the prophet; by itself, it is not necessarily connected to authority in society, for the societal responsibility of prophets derives from their simultaneous status as Imams.[12] But the inseparability of the two functions is what prevents the strongest form of divine guidance, that is, revelation, from lapsing into the absurdity of a mere private experience. The special vertical connection between God and an individual is always given meaning through the horizontal connection between the individual and the community. The sacred-historical outlook, felt most in Murtaḍā's Imama discussion, governs his view of prophethood as well, even in a more rigid manner; the community's prefigured arrangement is founded not on divine assistance furtively present in an infallible individual, but on unequivocal divine intervention meant to establish social hierarchy. The need to braid prophethood and social responsibility together must be the underlying reason for the argument that prophethood cannot be earned but is rather a mission whose bearer is chosen by God. Such a view pre-empts the hypothetical scenario of an individual attaining prophethood without being commissioned with any social duty to help the members of the community fulfil their moral obligations.[13]

Murtaḍā's theology seems indifferent concerning the distinction between the two terms 'prophet' (*nabiyy*, *nabīʾ*) and 'messenger' (*rasūl*), though he still points out the lexical distinction in that they both refer to a human individual chosen by God to bear His message.[14] His position on this distinction is thus close in eventual outcome to that of ᶜAbd al-Jabbār and his circle, who likewise deny it, although he does not follow in their line of thought leading to that position. For them, 'messengership' refers to the individual's burden, while 'prophethood' refers to the divine reward honouring him for bearing that burden; therefore, the two concepts are inseparable in any individual, as are the terms.[15] Once more, Murtaḍā's position on non-prevalent traditions makes his views contrast with those of Mufīd who, basing himself on traditions common in the Imami compendia, ruled that the difference between prophets and messengers lies in the respective ways in which these individuals receive revelation, eventually proposing that every messenger is a prophet but not vice versa.[16] Ṭūsī's view effectively agrees with Murtaḍā's.[17]

Within the framework of fitting God's acts into a presumed set of moral restrictions, the argument for the necessity of prophethood must present itself in a language of moral justification other than that provided for the Imama. This requirement, evidently needed to avoid a situation in which prophethood may become dispensable, also calls for a justification centred on the distinctive feature of prophethood as opposed to the Imama. The latter is founded on people's fear of authority, believed to be a positive drive in the case of a just sovereign, not to mention that of an infallible Imam. This formulation, though applicable to prophets in their capacity as Imams, does not suffice to explain why an individual's reception of revelation is necessary for the community to move in the right moral direction. What is needed is a formulation that dovetails the necessity of proper morality with the contingency of revelation. Murtaḍā locates such a formulation in proposing that fear alone, issuing from the putative function of the Imama office, does not provide individuals with the necessary knowledge to carry out their moral obligations. The absence of such knowledge makes unjust all acts of divine punishment and reward; in addition, God's assistance, presumably incumbent on Him to provide, is consequently lacking. But if reason is believed to be sufficient in developing moral judgement, in accordance with Murtaḍā's view, the problem is complicated further. Any attempt to question the autonomous moral powers of reason could well undermine the theological foundations of divine justice, moral obligation and – in this particular case – the justification of the Imama. As noted earlier, the classic solution to the problem, which Murtaḍā adopts, lies in proposing the existence of hidden connections between two types of acts, those whose moral value is rationally recognisable and those whose moral value is not rationally recognisable. Acts of the second type can, nevertheless, influence an individual's readiness to meet his moral obligations, represented by acts of the first type. Murtaḍā thus depicts God's assistance as consisting of informing people about the acts of the second type, guiding them in the direction that furthers the performance of their obligations. Human reason is not privy to the hidden connections, which makes it incumbent upon God to reveal sacred laws. If this knowledge is to be imparted to humans without infringing on their ability to choose for themselves, it can be done only through sending prophets to deliver its details. Thus, according to Murtaḍā, the commissioning of prophets by God is incumbent upon Him as long as it is possible that certain acts can promote people's inclination to meet their moral obligations. This divine requirement does not depend on whether the people respond favourably to the call of the prophets; it is also unrelated to the exact nature of the prophets' teachings, which may be a mere affirmation of rational moral judgement.[18] The relation between reason and revelation is also seen in light of the hypothesis that revelation only exposes the details of rational judgement. Prophets are sent to relate these details to us, but never to contradict reason. Murtaḍā states this in response to the Barāhima's classical objection that if prophets are sent to affirm reason, then there is no need for them; if to contradict it, then their teachings are vile.[19] The insufficiency of reason, therefore, is the theological justification of prophethood. This insufficiency can be due to some individuals' lack of rational power or to the intrinsic inadequacy of rational proofs because of missing data. The role of prophets, as they impart the word of revelation, is either to complement reason or to support it.

This position, though intended to justify the necessity of prophethood, fails to conceal the veritable advantage enjoyed by the Imama in Murtaḍā's theology. The rationale of both offices is predicated on the assumption that it is a divine requirement to maximise people's opportunities to attain otherworldly reward. Moreover, both, given the paramount importance of divine assistance, are derivative of a morality inspired by the Muʿtazili understanding of divine assistance. Nevertheless, the Imama is always necessary, as it is grounded in human nature; prophethood, on the other hand, is contingent, for it may well be the case the God restrict moral obligation only to the dictates of reason without requiring individuals to perform other acts. In such circumstances, fear, the deep moral root of the Imama, would still be active, but not so ignorance, the counterpart of fear for prophethood. This is why it is morally conceivable that there be no prophets, whereas there must always be an Imam.[20] A clear expression of this prioritisation is found in Murtaḍā's emphasis on the possibility of God sending a prophet who is not commissioned with delivering a sacred law, since he would still have the mission of affirming the dictates of reason and calling people to follow them.[21] Murtaḍā's efforts to justify prophethood by relying on the significance of revelatory knowledge comes to look more like an attempt to reckon with the discrepancy in the historical functions of prophets and Imams, not like a response to the broader contours of Murtaḍā's theology. Thus, hypothetically, what remains of the prophetic office is the dimension grounded in the Imama. Though compatible with the justification for the necessity of prophethood in the teachings of ʿAbd al-Jabbār and his circle, Murtaḍā's position, as on many other occasions, reflects the need to balance the imports of Muʿtazili theology with the dictates of the Imami tradition. Thus, the distinction between prophethood and the Imama serves to satisfy two needs, namely, the need to carve a niche for revelational knowledge without compromising the elevated status of reason within the framework of Muʿtazili theology, and the need to preserve the indispensable place of the Imama in the traditional Imami worldview.

Qualifications of the prophets

As with the questions of the office's definition and necessity, the inclusion of prophethood within the Imama underpins the assumption that all qualifications of Imams are shared by prophets. It must, nevertheless, be noted that the supreme standards of the Imama in Murtaḍā's thought – first and foremost, total infallibility – make it difficult for him to propose new qualifications for prophets that would set them apart from Imams. Consequently, his discussion on the qualifications of prophets is almost a repetition of his parallel discussion on the Imama. His main departure from it consists not of proposing other qualifications but rather of occasionally arguing for the same ones in a different manner; this applies equally to the dictates of reason and to those of revelation. The qualifications pertinent to the hierarchical operation of authority in the desired Muslim community, such as political acumen and moral superiority, are thus assumed of prophets and Imams alike, as are qualifications related to perfect knowledge of the sacred law and superiority in otherworldly merit.

Whether he is discussing prophethood or the Imama, belief in infallibility can be considered the governing principle that drives Murtaḍā's view of God's intervention in guiding the administration of human society.[22] His inclination to ground this principle in a Muᶜtazili framework was probably inspired by the appeal of the rationalist tendency and led to an elaboration of the Imama against the background of a presumed human moral need to be brought under the authority of an infallible sovereign. With prophethood, given its distinctive feature of the direct connection between God and the prophet, infallibility is established on different grounds. The starting point is not the moral shortcomings of the presumed followers of the prophet, but the need to create the optimal conditions for them to respond positively to his call. Thus, the cornerstone of Murtaḍā's argument is the unacceptability of repulsion (*tanfīr*): if the prophet were lacking in any aspect, people would be less inclined to endorse his teachings, which would compromise the requirement of maximising divine assistance. Prophets, being commissioned with calling people to the way of God, should present the most attractive face in bringing people to the straight path. A prophet's audience will not be fully receptive to his call if they consider it possible for him to commit vile acts or to show himself ignorant of his duties.[23] The possibility of a prophet's infidelity in conveying the divine message is a special case; such infidelity would go beyond repulsiveness and amount to defeating the purpose of prophethood, since it would make it impossible to believe him.[24] The inadmissibility of lying is, therefore, more epistemic than moral, as it undermines the credibility of revelation as a source of knowledge. This argument for the infallibility of prophets is probably what ᶜAbd al-Jabbār has in mind when arguing against the Imami justification of the necessary infallibility of the Imams;[25] it is Mufīd's only argument for the infallibility of both prophets and Imams.[26] Since ᶜAbd al-Jabbār's attack is irrelevant to Murtaḍā's position, it may have been directed at the Imami position known to him from the works of Mufīd and his teachers, whereas Murtaḍā's view was fashioned precisely to neutralise these attacks while still casting this development as an established position, thus attaining the dual purpose of escaping the challenge and demonstrating, again, his opponent's lack of acquaintance with the Imami position.

The distinctive feature of prophethood – that is, its connection with the divine source of knowledge – makes the image of the prophet gravitate more towards that of a master than towards that of a sovereign. He is a guide rather than a leader, and the intuitive response to him is to apply his authoritative teachings, not to heed his authoritarian presence. In this, the Imam and the prophet are different; but again, both offices are hybrid. Neither of the two offices is totally devoid of the primary qualifications of the other. Thus, when the Imam is required to act as a source of religious knowledge, the importance of avoiding any form of repulsiveness is highlighted as a requirement of infallibility.[27] In contrast to the case of the Imam, the unbridgeable gap between the prophet and the community is premised more on the epistemic than the moral.

The requirements of veracity

Classical Muslim theologians, regardless of their doctrinal school, seem to have concurred on considering miracles the required proof for the veracity of claims to prophethood. The predominance of this view is to be expected, given the polemical context in which much of Islamic theology developed, especially debates with non-Muslims, whose claims appealed frequently to reports about miracles ascribed to their revered figures.[28] Murtaḍā's thought is no exception to the broader Muslim context, nor is it an exception to the narrower Imami discourse, known for its liberality when it comes to the miracles of the Imams.[29] Nevertheless, Murtaḍā's views merit further study with respect to his philosophical understanding of the nature of miracles, the emphasis he places on them as an absolute proof of prophethood and the scope of the individuals who are expected to produce miracles.

Miracles must be effected by God; they also must break the norm in the eyes of the people addressed by the prophet's call.[30] These two conditions depend on Murtaḍā's view of the ontological structure of the world. While it allows some degree of inevitability in the world in that events in the world may not contradict the necessary principles of human reason, there is nothing that would preclude the occurrence of irregularities in it meant to serve as proofs for the veracity of claimants to prophethood, such as the sun rising from the west, or a person displacing mountains. Murtaḍā's concern is not with affirming the possibility of such things, because his occasionalist view of the world removes this hurdle; rather, his goal is to restrict their significance to the effect of divine intervention. The displacement of a mountain is not the miracle; the miracle is, instead, God's act of equipping the person with sufficient power to carry it out.[31] Moreover, the force of the miracle is further governed by theological needs: since all that is needed is to command the assent of a particular audience, the norm to be broken is only that known to the audience. Though Murtaḍā provides no specific examples, the mere statement that the established norm in a certain country may be considered a breaking of the norm in another[32] suffices to demarcate the horizon of expectations of the miraculous. Thus, any regular act could have been miraculous had God decided that the norm be other than what it is,[33] and a miracle ceases to be one if it takes place so often as to become a new norm.[34]

Murtaḍā's stress, once again, is on the sound judgement of a particular audience, not on the abstract conception of universal reason. The prophetic claimant does not need to come up with unprecedented feats of superhuman magnitude, but only to demonstrate to his putative followers acts that go beyond their familiar abilities, so long as these followers can protect themselves against all-too-human acts of deception and trickery. Therefore, in an act that breaks the norm, the ontologically miraculous aspect of the act is the one closest to God, not the one most apparent to human observers; but the theologically relevant aspect is the opposite, that is, the aspect that the act's human observers perceive. The full meaning of this distinction becomes apparent only in the discussion of Murtaḍā's view of the inimitability of the Qurʾān later in this chapter.

The absolute necessity that each prophet prove himself by producing a miracle is an issue on which Murtaḍā's views reflect the particulars of Imami apologetics. In principle, he rules that the only way to ascertain the veracity of a claimant to prophethood is a miracle; whoever does not produce one is an impostor.[35] Nevertheless, he elsewhere qualifies this statement in light of objections against the Imami belief in Imams whose infallibility cannot be detected by reason and is not confirmed by miracles. His cautious acceptance of reports ascribing miracles to the Imams notwithstanding, the eventual formulation of his position ends up anchoring the entire sequence of successive sacred individuals in a moment of divine intervention in ordinary history. This is seen in his assertion that even if the Imams and prophets did not themselves produce miracles, their designation can always be traced back to someone who initially established his claim to such status through a miracle.[36] The absoluteness of the requirement for miracles as proof of prophethood or of other forms of special divine favour is thus preserved in principle even though it need not be present in every single claim. The primacy of prevalence is encountered once more, since prevalence allows one miracle to suffice to establish proper belief in a line of individuals who would otherwise need enough miracles to match their number. In the absence of prevalent reports, claimants must perform miracles to prove their claims, and miracles can also be done by pious believers.[37] This inclusive view of the scope of miracles reveals Murtaḍā's need to accommodate the needs of defending Imami theology but also his awareness of the richness of the Imami corpus in such material. His main debate is with the Muʿtazilis, who restrict the performance of miracles to prophets; their position, from the perspective of what is relevant from an Imami position, rests on the premise that the Imam is not infallible as a religious authority, nor is he divinely designated.[38] Although Murtaḍā claims the Imamis are in agreement only with the traditionalists (*aṣḥāb al-ḥadīth*) in expanding the scope of the individuals believed to have been granted miraculous powers,[39] it seems that this characterisation is accurate only if one counts the Ashʿaris among the ranks of traditionalists.[40]

Historical disclosure

Despite their almost universal acceptance of miracles as the indisputable proof for the veracity of prophets, Muslim theologians were acutely aware of the difficulty of applying this theoretical consideration to Muḥammad's career. The reason theologians faced this difficulty is related to the epistemic standards of knowledge outlined earlier. For if a historical report is to generate certainty, it must be attested to an extent that is not reached by most reports of miracles ascribed to Muḥammad. Although theologians claimed that many of these reports had attained the standard of prevalence, a survey of the major theological writings of the time makes clear that the Qurʾān usually tops the list of Muḥammad's miracles. Murtaḍā's presentation agrees with this general mood. The Qurʾān is the most solid proof for Muḥammad's prophethood because it is universally attested, in contrast to his other miracles, whose occurrence may be disputed.[41] Moreover, its chronological precedence over the other miracles makes it the primary vehicle through which Muḥammad himself sought to validate his claim.[42] Nevertheless, Murtaḍā accepts many reports about Muḥammad's other miracles, basing his position on prevalence and proceeding to demonstrate that in most of these miracles – including Muḥammad's movement of a tree, the moaning of a trunk and his splitting of the moon – there was no possibility of a trick or a visual illusion.[43] But it is not easy to accept Murtaḍā's claim that these miracles were treated by earlier generations of theologians as valid proofs for Muḥammad's prophethood comparable to the Qurʾān,[44] for the sources are replete with the names of theologians, particularly Muʿtazilis, who denied these miracles.[45] The statement is therefore better taken as an extension of Murtaḍā's polemical attitude than as an accurate representation of the state of theological discussions. The keenness to carve out a protected domain of Muḥammadan miracles appears also in Murtaḍā's rejection of the claim that oracles can foretell the unseen. His rejection does not rest on denying the human capacity to predict the future. Rather, his formulation manifests the primacy of theology: given that Muḥammad invoked discerning the unseen as a miracle, and since miracles must break the norm, then such vision must lie beyond the reach of humans.[46] The other reason Murtaḍā adduces to reject this possibility is representative of another aspect of his epistemological framework, namely, the inclination towards observation, even when he in fact bases his position on scriptural proof texts: the misfortunes of astrologers (*munajjimūn*) and their false predictions serve as empirical evidence of their ignorance of future developments.[47] This statement is also indicative of the popularity of astrologers within the high intellectual and social circles to which Murtaḍā belonged;[48] it influenced even the two Jubbāʾīs, who seem to have laboured to reconcile their theoretical rejection of astrology with a practical conviction in its benefits.[49] Jubbāʾī's work, though, seems to not have been well received by some thelogians of the time who thought his refutation of astrology was wrong-headed.[50]

The Qurʾān

The evidentiary value of the Qurʾān in Murtaḍā's theological thought merits a separate discussion. For although the status of the Qurʾān as the major miracle of Muḥammad is commonly affirmed by Muslim theologians, Murtaḍā's elaboration of this position provides valuable insights into the debates about the Qurʾān on three levels: the question of the integrity of the Qurʾān in Imami literature, the various theories of Qurʾānic inimitability current in Murtaḍā's time and the detailed explanation of Murtaḍā's theory of divine intervention intended to deter Arabs from successfully answering the Qurʾānic challenge, that is, the theory of *ṣarfa*.

Doubts concerning the integrity of the Qurʾān have long been associated with Imami thought in an almost exclusive manner, based on a specific appraisal of pre-Būyid sources.[51] Murtaḍā's presentation of his position changes over time. In earlier works, he does allow the hypothetical possibility that the Qurʾān has been transmitted inaccurately because of the believers' weakness at the inception of the call to faith; but he quickly adds that we know that this did not happen because in every age God designates an authority to preserve the right faith. Murtaḍā thus relies on the infallibility of the Imam to protect the Qurʾān's integrity.[52] However, in the late *Dhakhīra*, Murtaḍā uses another argument to deny categorically any alteration of the Qurʾānic text. Being the foundation of the religion, the Qurʾān has an advantage over all other things that have been carefully reported; in addition, the meticulous work of scholars, paying attention even to the most insignificant details of the text, makes it impossible that the text be incomplete or altered.[53] Already during the lifetime of the Prophet, the text was compiled, its order was fixed and the Companions used to verify their memorisation of it with the Prophet.[54] After his death, the Qurʾān became so prevalent that it was no longer possible to alter its word.[55] The views of some Imamis and superficial traditionalists (*ḥashwiyya*) who argue otherwise are inconsequential, argues Murtaḍā, since they are based on weak traditions.[56]

In his later formulation, reliance on the authority of an infallible individual is still the cornerstone of Murtaḍā's defence of the integrity of the Qurʾān, though it is chronologically followed by prevalence as a flawless guarantee of sound transmission. The combination of infallible authority and prevalence fortifies the Qurʾān against both inadvertent and deliberate alterations. This way, Murtaḍā no longer needs to rely on the community to safeguard the Qurʾān's integrity, nor does he give ᶜUthmān any credit for compiling the codex. Rather, he circumvents the whole controversy by basing his position on Prophetic authority and then on prevalence, the latter not as a theological proposition but as an epistemic one, regardless of the theological status of the individuals who constitute the chain of transmission. On the level of doctrine, the sectarian advantage of this formulation is evident.

Murtaḍā's curt dismissal of different Imami positions on the question may not reflect the true extent of the debate within the community. His position has been considered by many non-Shiᶜis the strongest Imami view in support of the Qurʾān's integrity,[57] probably due to their lack of familiarity with Imami literature but also due to his exceptionally categorical wording. Mufīd's position on the question developed differently, although he arrived at the same conclusion. Apparently, he initially held that the ᶜUthmānic codex suffers from certain omissions, basing himself on numerous reports in the tradition. Later, he modified his understanding of those traditions, taking them to mean that the authentic interpretation of these verses, not their text, has been lost. As for additions, the most that reason allows is the addition of a couple of letters to words, no more.[58] Although Ṭūsī adopts Murtaḍā's position on the question, his wording is in fact closer to Mufīd's: he categorically denies any additions, but his statements on potential omissions – although still unequivocal in rejecting them – are less categorical.[59]

Inimitability

Beyond the diverse details of theologians' explanations of the inimitability of the Qurʾān, the core of these explanations lies in the claim that the Qurʾān was actually presented as a challenge that Muḥammad's adversaries failed to meet. This claim is the basic assumption that underpins the various theories of inimitability, which are otherwise highly discordant. To establish the Qurʾān as a miracle, it is enough for Murtaḍā to show that Muḥammad challenged the Arabs to imitate it, that they could not despite their eagerness to do so and that the nature of this inability contradicted the norm (*wajh khāriq li-l-ʿāda*).[60] Murtaḍā subsequently exploits this minimal position to support doctrinal positions pertaining to other theological discussions. Although Murtaḍā categorically upholds the integrity of the Qurʾān, the apologetic need to defend Imami Shiʿism against the ubiquitous accusation of believing otherwise must be the drive behind his insistence on separating the integrity of the Qurʾān from its inimitability; the inability of the Arabs to meet Muḥammad's challenge suffices to demonstrate his veracity, even if we did not have access to the actual text with which he challenged them.[61] The argumentative value of this qualification presents itself when Murtaḍā counters the anti-Imami polemic according to which one cannot accept Muḥammad's prophethood without affirming the integrity of the Qurʾān. Murtaḍā's position also tallies well with his strong inclination to rely on history to corroborate doctrinal positions, since it contextualises the miraculous nature of the Qurʾān in Muḥammad's challenge and does not view the text's current availability as a valid proof. For later generations, the miracle of the Qurʾān is no longer accessible, although the text is; only reports about the miracle are transmitted, thus putting it on a par with other miracles worked by Muḥammad and previous prophets that are known only through historical transmission. In addition, grounding the miracle in the moment of confrontation between the Prophet and his adversaries is more compatible with the view that the Qurʾān is originated in time, for upholding the text's pre-eternality would elevate it above the flow of history and necessitate that its miraculous nature be entrenched in its metaphysical superiority, not in the course of a contextual challenge. However, although the Qurʾān is not fixed in eternity, it is not fully subject to history; the very fact that its revelation inaugurates the moment of faith suffices to show that it functions as a powerful transformer of ordinary into sacred history. Initially, Murtaḍā argued – in harmony with this minimal position – that this feature of the Qurʾān holds regardless of the particularities of the Qurʾān's miraculous nature, even if the text survives intact.[62] In later works, however, he expresses a different view, stating that the doctrine of *ṣarfa* is the only sound way to establish the Qurʾān as a miracle and that it is not enough to know only that the Qurʾān has not been imitated.[63]

The easier part of establishing the claim is affirming that Muḥammad challenged the Arabs with the Qurʾān: it is necessary knowledge – that is, beyond prevalence – to know that Muḥammad claimed that God has revealed the Qurʾān to him through the angel Gabriel as a distinctive sign of prophethood.[64] The contents of the Qurʾān confirm this claim, as the book is replete with verses calling on the Arabs to imitate it or even to match any of its *sūra*s.[65] The problem of showing that the Qurʾān has indeed not been imitated in response to that challenge (*muʿāraḍa*) is much more complicated, as it inevitably involves relying on some form of *ex silentio* argument. This is probably why this approach resembles an attempt to exhaust all possibilities in order to eliminate them, as if to make sure that one's opponent will run out of objections. Although the starting point of Murtaḍā's argument is the claim that the absence of any response to Muḥammad's challenge stands as proof that no such thing ever existed, the argument soon evolves into an enquiry into why it is impossible for such a response not to have been transmitted if it ever existed.[66] But even if a response did not in fact exist, it remains to show that the Arabs were fully motivated to answer the challenge; that is, their failure was not due to their negligence of the Prophet's threat to their established lifestyle, misunderstanding of what exactly his challenge required of them, preference for warfare as a means to manage the situation, erroneously believing their existing literature to be a match for the Qurʾān, or any other consideration that could have made them refrain from answering Muḥammad's challenge.[67]

Nevertheless, it is clear that the core of Murtaḍā's argument is a position on prevalence that endows it with tremendous epistemic power. He uses the same argument for the integrity of the Qurʾānic text – that is, the great care of consecutive transmitters – also to argue for the absence of a response by the Arabs. Whatever caused the Qurʾān to be carefully transmitted must also apply to the hypothetical response if it existed; even more so, in fact, since the response would constitute a cogent argument against the Qurʾān, which would thereby be invalidated.[68] The fact that Murtaḍā uses the same argument for both crucial theological claims is a clear indicator of the importance of sound transmission in his theology, which also explains his extremely strict standards for the reliability of reports. Although this argument reflects the limits of the theologians' epistemological framework as presented in the Method of Negation, it simultaneously serves as the bridge that links various aspects of Murtaḍā's system, ontological and theological.

Murtaḍā follows the same approach of eliminating possible objections also in his attempt to show that the absence of a response constitutes a miracle. Most of his arguments for this point repeat those he discusses in analysing the lack of possible motives to answer the challenge of the Qurʾān on the part of the Arabs.[69] However, in the context of defending the miracle of the Qurʾān, Murtaḍā expresses a view that betrays the character of his investment in prophethood as a component of his theology. Responding to the possible objection that the Arabs' failure could simply be due to Muḥammad being the most eloquent among them, he stresses that the Prophet was not the most eloquent of the Arabs; his words, as showcased in the *ḥadīth* corpus, do not attest to superior eloquence, even when he tried his best.[70] Given the tendency, since early times, in many Imami circles to emphasise the perfection of infallible individuals on all possible levels[71] and the importance of eloquence as a praiseworthy trait, this assertion is not insignificant. It strongly reflects the precedence of Murtaḍā's dual core, that is, the necessity of the Imama and the infallibility of the Imam, over other considerations that define the image of the perfect individual in Imami theology. If the ultimate purpose of prophets, being also Imams, is to assume communal leadership, it becomes much easier to abandon any beliefs that might not support this conception of prophetic purpose, especially if it helps protect a more important doctrine, that is, the inimitability of the Qur^ʾān.

Belief in the inimitability of the Qurʾān was widespread to the point that Murtaḍā claims it a matter of consensus.[72] The earliest extant literature on the question, representing a variety of theories intended to explain and defend this belief, dates from the period in which Murtaḍā lived; it includes works by Rummānī, Baqillānī, Khaṭṭābī (d. 998) and ʿAbd al-Jabbār.[73] Murtaḍā probably had direct contact with some of them through the scholarly circles and court life of Baghdad. Given this circumstantial advantage and Murtaḍā's immense interest in literature and rhetoric – in addition to his capacity as theologian – it is natural that his discussion of the inimitability to the Qurʾān is quite elaborate, dealing at length with the various theories before offering his own. Nevertheless, it is perplexing that with the exception of ʿAbd al-Jabbār, none of the abovementioned names appears in Murtaḍā's discussions, although his answers are evidently directed against their positions. His standard practice is to refer to earlier authorities who had proposed these theories, such as Naẓẓām and the two Jubbāʾīs, but it is hard to believe he was not aware of later contributions. The most likely explanation is that he did not feel a need to tackle positions that he might have seen as mere refinements of earlier, untenable positions. Before proceeding to elaborate on his chosen theory, Murtaḍā surveys different views on the exact nature of the inimitability of the Qurʾān. These views include the arguments that the Qurʾān's eloquence is intrinsically miraculous and unattainable by humans, even the most eloquent of them; that its linguistic arrangement is distinct from all known styles – that is, stylistically Other; that it foretells the unseen; that it is pre-eternal; and that it is unusually consistent. Although the present study is concerned with the elaboration of his theory of *ṣarfa*, it is nevertheless worthwhile to touch on his rejection of other theories as this can shed light on the varied reception of the Qurʾān at the time.

The most common of these views is the one based on the Qurʾān's superhuman eloquence, which apparently still commands the largest following in the present day.[74] Although the eloquence of the Qurʾān does not seem to have been questioned, the contention was centred on whether this eloquence is superior to the high literature of classical Arabic. Some proponents of this view indeed dedicated copious discussions to comparing the Qurʾān with excellent poetry, hoping to prove its superiority.[75] But a literary critic such as Murtaḍā is not content with this comparison; he resorts to his mastery of literature to rule – in an authoritative tone – that no difference can be discerned between the most eloquent words and poems of the

Arabs and some short *sūra*s of the Qurʾān.[76] Also common is the view that bases the Qurʾān's inimitability on its foretelling the unseen, ascribed to many theologians, most notably Naẓẓām.[77] While accepting that the Qurʾān does foretell future events (which is itself a miracle), Murtaḍā argues that the debate must be situated in the context of investigating the evidentiary value of the Qurʾān as a miracle meant to establish Muḥammad's prophethood since the inception of his call. As such, this miraculous aspect of the Qurʾān does not satisfy the requirement on two levels: first, only very few verses contain such predictions, although the whole text was produced as a challenge; and second, even these verses can be considered miraculous only after their predictions have materialised, which leaves Muḥammad's adversaries justified in rejecting his claim during the interlude following their revelation.[78]

The remaining three views are less common than these two; sometimes there is no mention of any of their presumed proponents. The view arguing that the Qurʾān's inimitability lies in its pre-eternality echoes the heated dispute over divine speech and memories of the inquisition; argumentatively, it is hardly useful in the context of proving Muḥammad's prophethood and is probably better situated in the context of intra-Islamic sectarian polemics, since its function amounts to equating the denial of the Qurʾān's pre-eternality with the failure to defend belief in Islam. As such, Murtaḍā's dismissal of it in his writings stems from his position on divine attributes.[79] The judgement that the Qurʾān is miraculous on account of its unusual consistency probably reflects a strong scripturalist inclination, since it probably relies on a literal reading of Q4:82 (*What, do they not ponder the Qurʾān? If it had been from other than God, surely they would have found in it much inconsistency*). Nevertheless, Murtaḍā's rejection is based on his belief that consistency – though a virtue of the Qurʾān – is plausible in any long text if the author is duly attentive and careful, an additional consequence of rejecting claims concerning the Qurʾān's metaphysical superiority.[80] The last view, namely, that the arrangement of the Qurʾān is inimitable or stylistically Other, seems to have been unclear, even in Murtaḍā's time. He ascribes it to Balkhī and a group of Muʿtazilis. There has been some ambiguity regarding Balkhī's position, as he seems to have presented it in equivocal terms. Murtaḍā points out this difficulty, arguing that Balkhī probably meant something else but expressed himself badly (*asāʾa al-ʿibāra*). But in any case, he concludes, it is not possible to ground the inimitability of the Qurʾān in its ontological structure, for it is made of letters whereas composition is only predicable of atoms (*taʾlīf al-jawāhir*).[81]

The theory of ṣarfa

A careful survey of the various theories on the inimitability of the Qurʾān makes it clear that a few authors combined two or more of them. But even scholars who subscribed to one theory did not deem the views contradictory. Nevertheless, one particular theory is often rejected uncompromisingly, sometimes being considered a form of insolence in judging God's word. This is the theory of *ṣarfa*, that is, divine deterrence of Muḥammad's adversaries and their Arab contemporaries from answering the challenge of the Qurʾān. Although several explanations of this theory were proposed, they all share the assumption that these Arabs would have answered the challenge had it not been for this divine intervention; that is to say, it was not the text itself that made them unable to respond but rather some external force, which altered the setting of the putative challenge against their favour. The poignant reaction against this theory was probably caused by its inevitable implication concerning the Qurʾānic text; namely, that it is not miraculous in itself.

The theory of *ṣarfa* is Murtaḍā's choice for explaining the miracle of the Qurʾān,[82] although he is keenly aware of the stigma that accompanies this belief and attempts to respond to it.[83] Although not the most common theory on the question, it did enjoy the support of some prominent theologians from various theological schools throughout Islamic history. Of those, the earliest mentioned is Naẓẓām; however, the particularities of his theory are unclear and seem to have been lost as early as Murtaḍā's time. The Muᶜtazili grammarian and theologian Rummānī is also reputed to have supported this view, although his extant writings also reveal an inclination towards other views, particularly the Qurʾān's superhuman eloquence. The famous Ẓāhirī theologian and Murtaḍā's younger contemporary Ibn Ḥazm (d. 1064) also adopted the belief in *ṣarfa*.[84] But Murtaḍā's lengthy polemic on the question, the *Mūḍiḥ*, is the most comprehensive extant work in support of the doctrine.[85]

I plan to discuss the probable reasons behind the rise of the theory of *ṣarfa* in a separate study. Here it suffices to say that adherence to the theory was occasioned by the concurrence of two positions: believing in the inimitability of the Qurʾān and admitting that its eloquence is not superior to that of many classical texts. Naẓẓām's position can serve as an indicator of how the discussion developed. He seems to have argued that the Qurʾān was not imitated because of divine intervention;[86] nevertheless, the proof (*ḥujja*) for Muḥammad's prophethood lies in the Qurʾān's foretelling of the future.[87] This position could well have developed into the theory of *ṣarfa* as the two distinct – though related – concepts of inimitability and proof coalesced into one, especially in light of the terminological kinship between the terms *iᶜjāz* and *muᶜjiza*, with the latter coming to mean a miracle, which, in turn, was made into the sole proof for prophethood.

Since the *ṣarfa* theory did not gain wide acceptance, later references to it are mostly made by its opponents. These references often present it in three different formulations: God intervened to remove the Arabs' motives to answer the challenge, or to remove their power to meet it, or to remove the knowledge they needed to produce an answer.[88] Murtaḍā's presentation, nevertheless, seems to address only the last formulation, which raises the question of whether the first two enjoyed any actual currency; in addition to their absence from Murtaḍā's lengthy discussion, they contradict the theoretical frameworks of theologians said to have subscribed to them. For to argue that divine intervention affected the motives of Muḥammad's adversaries amounts to a negation of the challenge itself; it portrays the Qurʾān as a text that merely managed to escape the attention of its presumed audience. The problem with proposing divine intervention that removed the adversaries' power to imitate the Qurʾān lies in its deterministic undertones in a theology of human agency: if God prevented people from meeting the challenge, this could be perceived as a vile act inasmuch as it nullified these individuals' power to act while still holding them accountable.

The remaining formulation – divine intervention to remove the adversaries' knowledge – survives such objections thanks to the view that knowledge is not located within human power but rather is created in humans through God's normative action. Given this view, the inimitability of the Qurʾān can be proven through four propositions: first, that the Arabs were challenged to imitate it in both eloquence and linguistic arrangement;[89] second, that the composition of metrical poetry would not have constituted an adequate response to the challenge; third, that the Qurʾān possesses a particular linguistic arrangement unlike any of theirs; and fourth, that the Arabs would have produced a proper response had they not been deterred by God.[90] These propositions are attested in the Arab tradition, for a literary challenge concerned both eloquence and linguistic arrangement: a poet who was challenged was expected to produce a more eloquent poem of the same metre and rhyme. Since many of the Qurʾānic passages are not more eloquent than certain Arab sayings, the fact that the Arabs did not invoke the latter demonstrates that they were mindful of the relevance of the Qurʾān's linguistic arrangement to the challenge.[91] Now, the thinking runs, anyone who is able to produce words following a certain linguistic arrangement can do the same with any other linguistic arrangement; a poet can write verse in any metre as long as he can do so in one.[92] Both eloquence and linguistic arrangement were thus within the adversaries' reach, yet they could not produce a proper response. This phenomenon is to be explained by divine intervention only with respect to their attempt to imitate the Qurʾān, not in any other literary endeavour.[93] Their inability to imitate the Qurʾān must have its roots in a lack of the knowledge needed for that act; God broke the norm by removing this knowledge, which otherwise remained available to them.[94] This, for Murtaḍā, is the meaning of the Qurʾān's miraculous nature as a norm-breaking phenomenon.

Murtaḍā's theory of *ṣarfa* betrays many aspects of his understanding of the Qurʾān, both as a miracle and as the authoritative text of Islam. Since a miracle must break the norm of the world, defining the Qurʾān as a miracle inevitably raises the question of which norm this miracle breaks. Murtaḍā is clearly aware of the problem caused by this situation: the claim that the eloquence of the Qurʾān is norm-breaking is controversial and will always be open to disputation, as eloquence is a highly subjective quality of any speech/text. The need for objectivity drives Murtaḍā to base his argument on a less controversial claim, namely, the absence of any proper response to the Qurʾān. But the Arabs' inability to produce such a response is in no way norm-breaking, as it does not have to be justified by any intrinsic quality of the Qurʾān, and this again opens the door for subjectivity. A breaking of the norm is best demonstrated by postulating that the Arabs did not lack the power to produce a response, yet they failed to do so. This underlying logic holds together Murtaḍā's theory of the *ṣarfa*, whereas other theories suffer from either the subjectivity of their central claims (as in the Qurʾān's superhuman eloquence) or the absence of the norm-breaking aspect (as in the Arabs' inability to produce a response). His willingness to preserve the belief in the inimitability of the Qurʾān without sacrificing major theological assumptions leads Murtaḍā to downplay any claims about the superiority of the Qurʾān that serve no purpose in establishing Muḥammad's prophethood. These considerations underlie the fact that he interprets a non-prevalent tradition from Riḍā in accordance with his view on the *ṣarfa* while still adhering to the position that such traditions are not binding.[95] Moreover, he rejects all miraculous interpretations of the Prophetic tradition that states, 'If the Qurʾān were on an untanned hide and were then thrown into a fire, it would not burn', opting instead to take the tradition as a figure of speech meant to show the Qurʾān's excellence.[96] Just like Murtaḍā's understanding of the Imam's occultation is based on a sacred-historical approach, his approach to the inimitability to the Qurʾān is sacred-historical since it is not concerned with actual events but rather with the theological response to the challenge posed by the events.[97] The important event here is not one in history but one that takes place outside historical time, analogously to the historical occurrence:[98] it is not the Arabs' failure to meet the challenge that matters but the unseen divine intervention that causes it, whose result can be detected by the audience of the prophetic message. Once more, Murtaḍā's use of history centres on sacred-historical readings that help craft a theological narrative.

The theory of *ṣarfa* has a variegated trajectory in Imami intellectual history. It is a question on which Ṭūsī departs from Murtaḍā, and possibly from Mufīd as well. At some point, Mufīd did support the *ṣarfa* theory, although his extant works do not contain an elaborate presentation of this view.[99] But he also advances an alternative theory, namely the belief in the Qurʾān's superhuman eloquence, in some of his works – although in ambiguous language.[100] It is hard, however, to establish which one was his final position. Nevertheless, judging by Ṭūsī's language in his later discussions, it is more likely that Mufīd eventually abandoned the theory of the *ṣarfa*, since Ṭūsī ascribes it to Murtaḍā only. Ṭūsī himself seems to have changed his opinion on the question over time, or at least refrains from presenting his true position out of respect for Murtaḍā;[101] in later writings, he expressly adopts the position that the Qurʾān's inimitability lies in both its (superhuman) eloquence and its linguistic arrangement (*al-naẓm wa-l-uslūb maʿ al-faṣāḥa*). Ṭūsī answers Murtaḍā's main objections to the theory of the Qurʾān's superhuman eloquence, but he nonetheless follows him faithfully in his arguments against other theories.[102] Murtaḍā's student Abū al-Ṣalāḥ al-Ḥalabī also followed his teacher on the issue of *ṣarfa*.[103]

Vindication of the prophets

Murtaḍā's stringent view of the infallibility of prophets leads to a situation similar to that encountered in his discussion of the Imama: the emergence of a host of problematic questions concerning the applicability of this view to relevant material. The main difference between the two situations lies in the nature of the material, which in turn engenders different approaches. In the case of the Imams, most of the objections were based on historical reports and the Muslim legal corpus. By contrast, the material about prophets derives from other sources, primarily exegetical lore. Given Murtaḍā's strict standards of transmission and his drive to avoid much of the problematic episodes related in extra-Qurʾānic literature, it is natural for him to dismiss episodes originating from this literature on account of its weak attestation, without the need to engage with them further. However, Qurʾānic passages on the same topic pose a challenge of a different nature, since Murtaḍā cannot resort to questioning their authenticity. Therefore, he dedicates the bulk of his relevant work to dealing with those Qurʾānic passages. It can thus be said that whereas the historian in Murtaḍā takes charge of vindicating the Imams, it is the exegete in him that does the same for prophets.

Most of the discussion is carried out in *Tanzīh al-anbiyāʾ wa-l-aʾimma*, in which Murtaḍā addresses problematic questions pertaining to thirteen prophets: Adam, Noah, Abraham, Jacob, Joseph, Job, Shuʿayb, Moses, David, Solomon, Jonah, Jesus and Muḥammad.[104] A standard method, comprising four techniques, governs his approach to each problematic passage. His aim is to protect the theological position on infallibility without sacrificing larger epistemic assumptions about language and prevalence. Thus, for any word or phrase that might be read to signify a violation of divine law by a prophet, he provides examples from the Arabic literary tradition to show the same word or phrase being used in a different sense.[105] When this approach is not applicable, he invokes syntax and grammar to offer an understanding other than the problematic one.[106] These two techniques are usually given precedence; nevertheless, some passages do not lend themselves easily to either reading. In such cases, other techniques need to be used, although they are less consistent with Murtaḍā's position and can, therefore, be seen as instances in which the greater good of defending infallibility trumps certain methodological concerns – though only selectively. A good example is his incorporation of extra-Qurʾānic details in order to give problematic passages a context more in line with his theological framework.[107] Finally, on occasion Murtaḍā cites variant readings of a verse to support his desired reading of it.[108] In addition to this primarily exegetical exercise, he gives the same treatment to certain traditions from the Prophet, especially when their authenticity is not easily disputable.[109]

Inconvenient outcomes

The question of abrogation

At the crossroads of ordinary and sacred history lies the question of abrogation (*naskh*), that is, the question of how the law of Islam came to replace the laws of previous religions, particularly Judaism,[110] and consequently how certain later rulings override earlier rulings within Islamic law itself. The discussion of abrogation, common among various circles of Muslim theologians,[111] is intimately related to sacred history, since it seeks to examine the procession of God's work in the course of time through the explanation of discrepancies between different religious laws. Nevertheless, the fact that this procession is received in a sequence of events that constitute the trajectory of human experience makes abrogation equally entangled in ordinary history – at least to the extent that it justifies divergent divine laws in light of worldly developments. These general considerations made the need to devise a proper justification for abrogation ubiquitous in Islamic theology, regardless of sectarian affiliation. The doctrinal relevance of this debate for the discussion on prophethood stems from the assumption that Muḥammad cannot be accepted as a prophet unless abrogation is shown to be theologically legitimate. The inconvenience of upholding abrogation as a theological position extends to encompass the theoretical framework that defends belief in God's omniscience as well as and the test of history that seems not to conform easily to such a position – even if its theoretical underpinnings are granted.

On the theoretical level, allowing for different religious laws is suggestive of contradiction in the Lawmaker's judgement, which itself reveals a lack of knowledge on His part. As much of Murtaḍā's discussion concerns legal matters, his analysis turns into an attempt to dissect the multifarious aspects of rulings in order to locate dissimilarities between cases that justify the difference in their respective rulings. Such dissimilarities include the different timeframes and identities of the subjects of the law.[112] Although this argument is intended to differentiate Muslim and Jewish law by distinguishing their historical contexts, its consequences – even if unexploited – are enormous for a worldview based on the finality of the divine word. For grounding law itself in ordinary history elevates the latter into a position of precedence: not only is the divine word to be seen as inextricably bound to human transient existence, it is this existence that defines the contours of validity for it. When the human subjects of the law cease to be, the law itself is suspended; its later applicability depends not on the previous ordainment but on a reinstatement identical to the original formulation of the law. Laws follow goods/interests (*al-sharāʾiʿ tābiʿa li-l-maṣāliḥ*);[113] what is good in a particular time period might be vile in another. The power of this position is fully perceivable in Murtaḍā's likening the change of the law to the turn of individual fortunes in life: for him, abrogation is on a par with the normal experience of illness and health in the same individual.[114] A change in the individual's health does not indicate ignorance on the part of God who established the norm of the world; rather, it must be seen as a new state born out of a different set of conditions.

Nevertheless, this discussion does not suffice to establish that Muḥammad's message, in its legal dimensions, replaces previous ones. The theoretical possibility of abrogation is far from its actual realisation; the former is a question of theology, the latter of history. This point brings Murtaḍā's discussion of abrogation very close to that of the Imama, since moving from establishing the office's necessity to arguing for the Imama of particular individuals transformed the discussion into an exercise in historical polemic in which epistemic positions on the validity of transmission concurred with theological assumptions about the teleological course of history and continuous divine assistance. In a similar vein, the argument for Islam's abrogating previous laws needs to reckon with the claim, typically ascribed to Jewish polemicists, that the law of Moses was made irreplaceable by divine decree. Here, too, the construction of sacred history relies on short-circuiting the opponents' claims by appealing to the foundational epistemic assumption that discredits non-prevalent reports while still employing the tools of ordinary historical analysis. Thus, the unceasing persecution of the Jews makes it impossible for their reports to meet the conditions of prevalence necessary for certain knowledge, particularly in terms of continuous transmission since the time of Moses. This problem is reversed to become a trump card for Murtaḍā's arguments that favour sacred history in the guise of heeding the requirements of reliable reporting: the Qur'ān is the only proof text that can inform us about times as ancient as that of Moses, which makes belief in his prophethood – as well as in that of other prophets – contingent on accepting the word of the Qur'ān.[115] The view of history then becomes compounded by a division of labour: ordinary history takes care of the recent leg separating Muḥammad from later times, while sacred history is entrusted with engendering knowledge about the older leg.

Although usually associated with discussions of the Imama, the controversial belief in a change in the divine decision (*badā'*) is handled by Murtaḍā in the course of his discussion on prophethood. This choice is not a simple outcome of formal considerations governing the presentation of his work; rather, it is part of his overall project of distancing Imami theology from inconvenient positions prone to stigmatisation. Typically, belief in *badā'* is one of the criticisms levelled against the Imamis by their opponents, although it was originally a Kaysānī view adopted by some Imamis. The first significant instance in Imami doctrine on which the apparent change of divine decision was invoked occurred upon the death of Ismāʿīl, the son of Ṣādiq who was believed to have been his designated successor. The death caused an apparent change in the identity of the Imam and made resorting to a change in the divine decision a convenient interpretation. A similar problem arose following the death of Muḥammad (d. 866), son of ʿAlī al-Hādī (d. 869).[116]

The Imami theologians of the generation before Murtaḍā had taken a number of different approaches to deflect this critique by redefining the concept or by employing their linguistic skills to present a different semantic reading of the phrase *badā li-*. Murtaḍā, while not rejecting *badā'* outright, questions its provenance in Imami traditions and then tries to interpret it in a manner that makes it equivalent to abrogation as understood by the Muʿtazilis. Eventually, he portrays the difference as a purely semantic-terminological one, caused by the occurrence of the word *badā'* in some traditions, which made use of the term acceptable to the Imamis.[117] This approach is likewise taken by both Mufīd[118] and Ṭūsī, who suggests other possibilities as well.[119] The core of Murtaḍā's theological position on abrogation thus lies in his attempt to protect God's will against change while arguing for Muḥammad's prophethood. The debate, though theological, is heavily anchored in legal language, as the controversial change in divine decision is to be seen in the varying demands of sacred laws. While agreeing in wording and structure with the Muᶜtazili position reflected in the tradition of ᶜAbd al-Jabbār,[120] Murtaḍā's position capitalises on the discussion to utilise it to sideline certain Imami viewpoints and to infuse Imami theology with more common discourses in matters that are not relevant to the Imamis' particular communal identity. The outcome is that the Qur'ān's central position is reinforced; in addition to its being the major proof for Muḥammad's prophethood and the most reliable legal and doctrinal source, Murtaḍā portrays it as the indisputable judge on matters pertinent to the believers' knowledge of past history. In both of its natures, worldly (as a satisfactorily transmitted document) and sacred (as an inimitable divine text), the Qur'ān is the pole around which Murtaḍā's view of Islam as a particular religious experience revolves.

Other controversial points

As in the discussion of the Imama, the needs of the theological system override other considerations related to Murtaḍā's view of prophethood. At times, this leads him to argue for positions that diverge from mainstream Imami views; nevertheless, Murtaḍā's primary concern is with preserving a thoroughly rationalist colouring and the belief in infallibility as the most crucial aspects of his theology of prophethood. Another consideration is relieving the burden of frequent accusations against Imami Shiᶜism that depict it in square opposition to many common views. One controversial point raised in anti-Shiᶜi polemics was the belief of some *ghulāt*-type extremists that several prophets had appeared after Muḥammad; another was the Ismaᶜili view on the scope of the Imams' legal authority. Murtaḍā invokes consensus to reject these views.[121] This choice of argumentative strategy is not simply driven by the needs of polemics; it is also part of his larger project, in which stressing the common ground between Imami and mainstream 'orthodox' views occupies a paramount position.

A significant example is the question of Muḥammad's illiteracy, which for most theologians was growing into an article of faith. The dogmatic position asserting Muḥammad's illiteracy was informed by a particular understanding of the Qur'ān (Q29:48) and furthered by the utility of this position in arguing that the Qur'ān must have been a miracle, since an illiterate man could not have composed such a sophisticated text.[122] Despite this argument, Murtaḍā is not highly invested in taking a position on the question: even when he argues that Muḥammad was illiterate before proclaiming his message, his reasoning is based on historical accounts and not on the word of the Qur'ān, which is not to be considered a proof unless one already believes in Islam. Moreover, as a prophet, Muḥammad did not need to master reading and writing, since they are mere crafts; nor is there compelling evidence that he did, which leaves uncertainty about the whole question the only legitimate position.[123] The insignificance of the debate for Murtaḍā's system, in spite of its currency in Islamic theology, is most evident in his dismissal of the question as irrelevant to the office of prophethood, in a manner similar to his treatment of questions related to the extent of the Imams' non-religious knowledge.

Another controversial issue that serves to clarify the priorities of Murtaḍā's system is the question of dreams as a means of prophetic revelation (*waḥy*). Like the question of Muḥammad's illiteracy, revelatory dreams can be linked to Qur'ānic allusions and Prophetic traditions.[124] Nevertheless, they contradict Murtaḍā's position on the necessary conditions for meaningful speech and action: since sleeping individuals are unaware of their surroundings, they are not rational agents; their beliefs and acts are thus inconsequential and cannot be considered a valid basis for knowledge and moral obligation. The primacy of this epistemological position leads Murtaḍā to a bold assertion: a prophet must be told, in advance and while awake, that his dream will be a form of revelation for it to be legitimately construed as such.[125] This stance is compatible with his uncompromising dismissal of the gnostic; the relative leniency of Mufīd and Ṭūsī towards traditions seems to underlie their more accommodating view of the dreams of prophets and Imams.[126]

In the case of the Imams, Murtaḍā's need to protect the doctrine of infallibility eventually led him to allow that Imams could possess perfect intellectual capacities while still minors. When a similar problem arises in the context of Abraham's reflections on the sun and the moon, which eventually lead him to knowledge of God, Murtaḍā's defence is less dependent on ascribing to him miraculous intellectual powers. In this case, Murtaḍā argues that it suffices for the individual to know his obligation at the time, since he still is in the period of investigation preceding certain knowledge of God. All that need be observed during that period is the rational moral obligations; Abraham's infallibility remains intact and the term 'believer' (*mu'min*) still applies to him, as it would to anyone else in a similar situation.[127] This justification works differently in the case of the Imams because of the restrictions inherent in the Qur'ānic episode being discussed, since it does not leave room for Murtaḍā to dismiss the reports on Abraham's condition, nor does it easily lend itself to claims of miracles as is the case with the Imams. Such an apologetic should, nonetheless, be seen as Murtaḍā's least desired explanation; although it theoretically preserves the belief in infallibility, it brings the analysis to the verge of compromising the prophet's authority at a certain stage of his life, thus risking contradicting a foundational justification for the necessity of prophethood in Murtaḍā's theology.

Conclusion

Content

Prophethood is an office of a primarily epistemic function in Murtaḍā's system. Its *raison d'être* is the same as that of the Imama, namely, the need for an authority to bring people closer to moral perfection in society. The main advantage of the office of prophethood over that of the Imama lies in the way in which some prophets receive their mission – that is, the direct connection with the divine realm. But this connection is fairly demystified in Murtaḍā's theology: it is driven by a need to impart the word of God. The moment this task is fulfilled, the function of the prophet is equivalent to that of the Imam in society.

For Murtaḍā, the miraculous nature of the Qurʾān is restricted to the inability of the Arabs to answer Muḥammad's challenge to replicate it. In addition to denying the Qurʾān any intrinsic supernatural aspect, this position also makes the miracle a function of Muḥammad's time. After the Prophet's death, the Qurʾān was no longer in a position of challenge, since the window in which a response might be produced closed with his death. Given Murtaḍā's view on the Qurʾān's miraculousness and origination, the Qurʾān is for him a text that is revealed in time and whose miraculous aspect is also time-bound. In the broader Muslim context, such a view of the Qurʾānic text falls on the minimalist end of the spectrum of positions regarding the Qurʾān's metaphysical status.

Context

Two points constitute Murtaḍā's main disagreement with the doctrine of prophethood common in Basran Muᶜtazilism. First, Murtaḍā does allow that miracles be performed by other than prophets. Second, his theory of *ṣarfa*, though shared by some Muᶜtazilis, conflicts with the belief in the Qurʾān's superhuman eloquence taught in ᶜAbd al-Jabbār's circle.

Within the Imami context, Murtaḍā's *ṣarfa* theory is the only controversial one of these two. Mufīd's view on the inimitability of the Qurʾān changed over time, but his eventual conviction was probably to believe in the Qurʾān's superhuman eloquence, as did Ṭūsī, who also abandoned belief in *ṣarfa*. Thus, only a few Imami theologians shared Murtaḍā's view on *ṣarfa*.

In Murtaḍā's understanding of the relationship between prophethood, messengership and the Imama, the first two categories are identical and the third is a broader category encompassing both. So prophets and messengers hold all three titles while the Imams hold only one. Both Mufīd and Ṭūsī disagree with Murtaḍā's position, although each of them holds a different view. Nevertheless, they both assert that the Imams are superior to all humans except Muḥammad, whereas Murtaḍā believes that prophets are superior to Imams. Murtaḍā also differs from Ṭūsī and Mufīd in his view that the Imams did not receive divine knowledge without a human intermediary; Mufīd and Ṭūsī claim otherwise. For later generations of Imami theologians, Murtaḍā's treatment of the infallibility of prophets became a standard position, both in content and in method. But on the points of discrepancy between Murtaḍā on the one hand and Ṭūsī and Mufīd on the other, the subsequent Imami tradition usually favoured the latter position.

Notes

1. *Dharīᶜa*, 534–6.
2. *Rasāʾil*, 1:165–6.

3. *Amālī*, 2:273–4.
4. Cf. Cullmann, *Salvation*, 129–31, who sees Abraham in the Biblical context not as an example from scripture but as one whose story leads to the most meaningful development in sacred history.
5. *Shāfī*, 1:39, 2:299.
6. *Shāfī*, 1:41, 3:83.
7. ᶜAbd al-Jabbār, *Mughnī*, 15:218–19, 20{1}:14.
8. Mufīd, *Awāʾil*, 69–70; Ṭūsī, *Amālī*, 407–8.
9. Mufīd, *Awāʾil*, 45; McDermott, *Theology*, 83–4.
10. Mufīd, *Awāʾil*, 70–1; Mufīd, *Fuṣūl*, 61–5 (only ᶜAlī is mentioned here), 103–4; McDermott, *Theology*, 84, 106; Ṭūsī, *Amālī*, 183, 188–9, 294–5, 350, 441–2. Nonetheless, the editor of Mufīd's *Awāʾil* stresses that the consensus of the Imamis is that the Imams are superior to all humans except Muḥammad, referring the reader to Murtaḍā's 'al-Risāla al-bāhira'; Mufīd, *Awāʾil*, 315. I have noted the problem with this text; see Murtaḍā's bibliography, no. 130. But Murtaḍā's unequivocal statements and his line of thought (which he does not seem to have abandoned) here are in harmony with his position in the *Shāfī*, whereas other statements are ambiguous and open to interpretation.
11. On the one hand, Ṭūsī argues at length that the two titles are independent of each other, describing the view that one of the two titles entails the other as 'far from right' (*baᶜīd min al-ṣawāb*) though admitting that it enjoys the support of some Imamis. But on the other hand, he accepts that the term 'Imam' applies partly to prophets in the sense that they ought to be emulated by people, but not in the sense that they constitute authorities over the community in the political sense – the two senses being intrinsic components of the office of the Imama; Ṭūsī, *Rasāʾil*, 111–15. Coupled with the fact that the Imams' word must be unconditionally obeyed as if it came from God, this position leads to the conclusion that the above definition of prophethood applies to the Imams, too, one way or another. Ṭūsī's position in the *Amālī*, 407–8, is thus almost irreconcilable with his statement that the Imams are different from prophets in that the former rely on a human intermediary (that is, the latter) to convey the word of God, unless this statement is qualified further to apply only to a particular form of revelation that is restricted to prophets and by which they convey the divine message; Ṭūsī, *Rasāʾil*, 111. It is more likely, however, that his position in the *Amālī* is the later one given the fact that the material of the book was recorded in meetings held during the last five years of his life; Ṭūsī, *Amālī*, 21–3.
12. *Shāfī*, 3:40.
13. *Dhakhīra*, 325–6.
14. *Dhakhīra*, 322–3; also in *Sharḥ Jumal*, 169, and *Amālī* 1:273–4, he uses the two terms interchangeably, so the term 'prophethood' is used here as a translation of both *nubuwwa* and *risāla* as they appear in Murtaḍā's works.
15. ᶜAbd al-Jabbār, *Mughnī*, 15:14–16, 244–5.
16. Mufīd, *Awāʾil*, 45; see, for example, Kulaynī, *Kāfī*, 1:176–7, for the relevant traditions.
17. Ṭūsī, *Iqtiṣād*, 151–2.
18. *Dhakhīra*, 323–4; *Rasāʾil*, 1:77; more succinctly in *Sharḥ Jumal*, 169–71; *Amālī*, 1:305.

19. *Dhakhīra*, 326–7; *Sharḥ Jumal*, 170–2.
20. *Amālī*, 2:273.
21. *Dhakhīra*, 323–4.
22. *Tanzīh*, 44; *Shāfī*, 1:55.
23. *Tanzīh*, 38–42; *Shāfī*, 2:18, 47–8; *Dhakhīra*, 338–41; *Rasāʾil*, 1:82, 122.
24. *Dhakhīra*, 338; *Rasāʾil*, 1:82, 122.
25. ʿAbd al-Jabbār, *Mughnī*, 20{1}:91–2.
26. McDermott, *Theology*, 107–8.
27. *Shāfī*, 2:17–20; *Rasāʾil*, 1:329–30.
28. Thomas, 'Miracles', 206–10.
29. See, for example, Ḥimyarī, *Qurb*, 331–40; Kulaynī, *Kāfī*, 1:230–56; Ṣadūq, *Iʿtiqādāt*, 94; Mufīd, *Awāʾīl*, 68–9; cf. Ashʿarī, *Maqālāt*, 50–1.
30. *Dhakhīra*, 328.
31. *Dhakhīra*, 328–9; *Sharḥ Jumal*, 173–4.
32. *Dhakhīra*, 329.
33. *Amālī*, 1:272–4; *Rasāʾil*, 4:286
34. *Shāfī*, 1:197–8.
35. *Rasāʾil*, 2:102; *Dharīʿa*, 560.
36. *Dhakhīra*, 335.
37. *Dhakhīra*, 328; *Shāfī*, 1:196; *Sharḥ Jumal*, 199.
38. ʿAbd al-Jabbār, *Mughnī*, 15:218–19, 247–56.
39. *Dhakhīra*, 328.
40. See, for example, Ashʿarī, *Maqālāt*, 296; Bāqillānī, *Kitāb al-bayān*, 48; Juwaynī, *Irshād*, 316–21.
41. *Mūḍiḥ*, 278; *Dhakhīra*, 360–1, 406; this may also be discerned from his position in *Dharīʿa*, 350–1.
42. *Mūḍiḥ*, 279; *Dhakhīra*, 365.
43. *Dhakhīra*, 407–8.
44. *Dhakhīra*, 406–7.
45. As is allegedly the case with Naẓẓām and Balkhī; see Ibn Qutayba, *Taʾwīl*, 70; Ṭūsī, *Tibyān*, 9:443.
46. *Rasāʾil*, 1:418–19.
47. *Rasāʾil*, 2:299–312; *Mawsūʿa*, 1:469–73; *Amālī*, 2:319–25.
48. See Pingree, 'Astrology', 295–9.
49. See the two episodes in Tanūkhī, *Nishwār*, 2:331–2.
50. See Najāshī, *Rijāl*, 63.
51. For a short survey of different views, see the editors' introduction to Sayyārī, *Revelation*, 24–30.
52. *Shāfī*, 1:191–2, 286–7.
53. *Dhakhīra*, 362.
54. *Dhakhīra*, 363.
55. Interestingly, nowhere does he mention reports about ʿAlī being the first to compile a copy of the Qurʾān, despite their apparent convenience for him in establishing the integ-

rity of the Qurʾān based on infallible authority. This omission supports Modarressi's view regarding the non-Shiʿi provenance of these reports; see Modarressi, 'Early debates', 17–22.

56. *Dhakhīra*, 363; in the later *Dharīʿa*, Murtaḍā gives examples of omissions while stressing that they are all non-prevalent; *Dharīʿa*, 312.
57. Modarressi, 'Early debates', 34–5, 37–8. Murtaḍā's similar statements in al-Masāʾil al-Ṭarābulusiyyāt' are also quoted in Ṭabrisī, *Majmaʿ*, 1:42–4. Paradoxically, Murtaḍā's elaborateness and unequivocal statements may have been why Ibn Ḥazm considered him and two of his students the only Imamis to uphold the integrity of the Qurʾān; Ibn Ḥazm, *Fiṣal*, 5:22.
58. Mufīd, *Awāʾil*, 80–2; see the lengthy discussion in McDermott, *Theology*, 92–9.
59. Ṭūsī, *Tibyān*, 1:3.
60. *Dhakhīra*, 360–1.
61. *Dhakhīra*, 364; *Shāfī*, 1:245.
62. *Dhakhīra*, 361, 364; ambiguous, though similar, wording in *Mūḍiḥ*, 45.
63. *Rasāʾil*, 2:324–5 (where he refers the reader to the *Mūḍiḥ* to support this view, but the wording therein is ambiguous and lends itself also to the alternative view described above). This view is his later view, since it is part of 'al-Masāʾil al-Rassiyya', in which he mentions the *Dhakhīra*; *Rasāʾil*, 2:317.
64. *Mūḍiḥ*, 275–6; *Dhakhīra*, 364–5.
65. *Mūḍiḥ*, 280–1; *Dhakhīra*, 366.
66. *Mūḍiḥ*, 288–9, 291–6; *Dhakhīra*, 367, 368–9; *Shāfī*, 1:192–3.
67. *Mūḍiḥ*, 60–3, 287–90, 302–14; *Dhakhīra*, 367–74; briefly in *Sharḥ Jumal*, 178–9; cf. Jāḥiẓ, 'Ḥujaj al-nubuwwa', 273–80.
68. *Dhakhīra*, 366–7; *Sharḥ Jumal*, 176–7; *Mūḍiḥ*, 286; a similar statement in *Mūḍiḥ*, 288.
69. *Mūḍiḥ*, 61–7.
70. *Mūḍiḥ*, 320; *Dhakhīra*, 376–7. The most Murtaḍā is willing to concede is that their inability to answer the challenge made it seem as if the Prophet was more eloquent (*kaʾannahu zād ʿalayhim bi-l-faṣāḥa*); see Naẓarī, 'Nigarishī (3)', 41, for the correct text, which is missing from the published *Rasāʾil*, 1:349.
71. Ṣadūq, *Maʿānī*, 320. An early work also shares Ṣadūq's position, although its ascription to Mufīd is wrong; [Pseudo-]Mufīd, *Ikhtiṣāṣ*, 187. On the ascription, see the editor's introduction (*Ikhtiṣāṣ*, 5); see also McDermott, *Theology*, 27–8; Modarressi, *Crisis*, 48n160.
72. *Dhakhīra*, 364; cf. Baqillānī, *Tamhīd*, 132; ʿAbd al-Jabbār, *Mughnī*, 16:151; Abū Yaʿlā al-Farrāʾ, *Muʿtamad*, 157; Juwaynī, *Irshād*, 345.
73. See the editors' introduction to Rummānī et al., *Thalāth rasāʾil*, 7–12.
74. Martin, 'Inimitability'.
75. See Vasalou, 'Miraculous eloquence', 33–9.
76. *Mūḍiḥ*, 42, 61; *Dhakhīra*, 379–80.
77. For a short survey, see Badawī, *Madhāhib*, 1:213–15.
78. *Mūḍiḥ*, 117–24; *Dhakhīra*, 402–3.

79. *Mūḍiḥ*, 129–32.
80. *Mūḍiḥ*, 124–6; *Dhakhīra*, 403–4.
81. *Mūḍiḥ*, 110–16; *Dhakhīra*, 400–2.
82. *Dhakhīra*, 378–9; Murtaḍā, *Sharḥ Jumal*, 175.
83. *Mūḍiḥ*, 67–78; *Dhakhīra*, 382–3.
84. Martin, 'Inimitability'; Badawī, *Madhāhib*, 1:213–20; Ibn Ḥazm, *Fiṣal*, 3:15–18.
85. *Dhakhīra*, 378; *Mūḍiḥ*, 10–15, 19–23.
86. Ashʿarī, *Maqālāt*, 225.
87. Khayyāṭ, *Intiṣār*, 27–8.
88. See the elaborate discussion of the theory of *ṣarfa* in Maʿrifat, *Tamhīd*, 4:138–91.
89. *Mūḍiḥ*, 39. The above translation is the most generic English rendering of the Arabic term *naẓm*, because it does not lend itself easily to one translation; it could have been also rendered 'structure' or 'construction' in other contexts, especially with ʿAbd al-Qāhir al-Jurjānī's (d. 1078) elaborate theory.
90. *Mūḍiḥ*, 35–6; *Dhakhīra*, 380.
91. *Mūḍiḥ*, 39–40.
92. *Mūḍiḥ*, 42–50.
93. *Dhakhīra*, 380–2.
94. *Mūḍiḥ*, 35, 215; *Dhakhīra*, 380–1.
95. *Rasāʾil*, 1:347–9; see the tradition in Ṣadūq, *ʿIlal*, 1: 121–2.
96. *Amālī*, 1:406–10. On this particular tradition, see Zadeh, 'Fire', passim, esp. 56–60 for Murtaḍā's views.
97. Cullmann, *Salvation*, 306–7.
98. Cullmann, *Salvation*, 141
99. Mufīd, *Awāʾil*, 63; McDermott, *Theology*, 87–8.
100. Mufīd, *al-Masāʾil al-ʿUkbariyya*, 92–3; McDermott, *Theology*, 88. This ambiguity, in addition to the loss of certain works of his, might be the reason behind the doubts expressed by *Mūḍiḥ*'s editor regarding Mufīd's position, although his change of position seems to have been known to some Imami scholars; *Mūḍiḥ*, 19–20.
101. Ṭūsī, *Iqtiṣād*, 173.
102. Ṭūsī, *Iqtiṣād*, 172–81; cf. *Mūḍiḥ*, 169–78; *Dhakhīra*, 389–92.
103. Ḥalabī, *Taqrīb*, 156–9. That Rāwandī (d. 1177–8) also supported this theory, as the editor of the *Mūḍiḥ* states (*Mūḍiḥ*, 21), is uncertain, as his polemic lends itself to different readings; Rāwandī, *Kharāʾij*, 3:981–1004.
104. *Tanzīh*, 45–263; the identification of Shuʿayb with any Biblical figure is problematic; see Tottoli, 'Shuʿayb'.
105. For example, when Murtaḍā surveys and accepts all possible meanings of the verb *hamma* only to exclude premeditation (*ʿazm*) in explaining Joseph's temptation with his master's wife (Q12:24) (*Tanzīh*, 112–15); or when he proposes that the word *ghulām* (in Q18:74) also means 'man' in the story of Moses and the pious servant of God (*Tanzīh*, 177–8); or when he understands the verb *naqdir* as 'to tighten, make narrow, constrict' instead of 'to be able' in the story of Jonah (Q21:87) (*Tanzīh*, 206–7).
106. For example, in the story of Adam (Q7:189–90), Murtaḍā proposes that the dual form

denotes two groups, not two individuals (*Tanzīh*, 52–8); in interpreting Q6:76–7, he argues that an affirmative may in fact be an interrogative (*Tanzīh*, 68–70); and in the context of Q11:74, he allows the past tense to denote the future (*Tanzīh*, 96–7).

107. In the case of Abraham (Q6:76–7), Murtaḍā mentions that Abraham had been hidden in a cave since his birth (*Tanzīh*, 67) and that when Abraham was ill, he gazed at the sky to tell the exact time of his sickness (Q37:88–9) (*Tanzīh*, 74–6). Murtaḍā also couples Abraham's request for God to show him how the dead are resurrected (Q2:260) with a parallel narrative intended to remove any doubt regarding Abraham's faith in God's power (*Tanzīh*, 81–2) and relates Abraham's asking God to forgive his father's sins (Q9:114) to details pertaining to his father's intentions (*Tanzīh*, 88–91). Further, Murtaḍā argues that Joseph was not yet a prophet during his years of slavery to the Pharaoh (*Tanzīh*, 111); that Islamic marriage law justifies Shuᶜayb's marrying off his daughter to Moses (Q28:27) on conditions related to him and not to his daughter (*Tanzīh*, 146); and that Moses asked to have a beatific vision (Q7:143) to show his people how they erred in requesting such a vision (*Tanzīh*, 162–9). The case of Job (Q38:41; Q21:83–4) is an example of an opposite scenario, in which Murtaḍā restricts himself to the Qurᵓān to avoid the extra-Qurᵓānic details that would contradict his position (*Tanzīh*, 185–6).
108. Examples include Abraham's destruction of the idols (Q21:62–3) (*Tanzīh*, 71–3); the story of the poor people whose ship was punctured by the pious servant of God (Q18:79) (*Tanzīh*, 180); and the verse about the Prophet's being astray (Q93:7), on which Murtaḍā quotes a variant reading while admitting it is a weak solution to the issue (*Tanzīh*, 218).
109. As in Muḥammad's response to his uncle ᶜAbbās in making certain legal exceptions (*Tanzīh*, 244–5) and in the tradition to the effect that a deceased person suffers because of his family's wailing (*Tanzīh*, 249–51).
110. *Dharīᶜa*, 308. However, the Barāhima were also interested in this discussion; Stroumsa, *Freethinkers*, 162.
111. Schmidtke and Adang, 'Muᶜtazili discussions', 709.
112. *Dhakhīra*, 357–8; *Dharīᶜa*, 304; slightly different wording in *Rasāᵓil*, 1:116–17.
113. *Sharḥ Jumal*, 185.
114. *Dhakhīra*, 357.
115. *Dhakhīra*, 358–60; *Sharḥ Jumal*, 181–8; *Muqniᶜ*, 48–9; *Rasāᵓil*, 2:251.
116. For an overview, see Madelung, 'Badāᵓ'; see also Hakyemez, 'Bada', 34–5, for a list of various Imami views on the question, although the article relies heavily on confessional non-Imami sources.
117. *Rasāᵓil*, 1:116–19; *Shāfī*, 1:87; contrary to McDermott, *Theology*, 392–3, who argues, based on Murtaḍā's lukewarm acceptance of the term, that he disavows both the idea and the term.
118. McDermott, *Theology*, 329–39.
119. Ṭūsī, *ᶜUdda*, 2:495–501; Madelung, 'Badāᵓ'.
120. See Schmidtke and Adang, 'Muᶜtazili discussions', 713–20, for a comparison of two manuscript traditions based on the discussion of abrogation in Ibn Khallād's *Kitāb al-Uṣūl*; Murtaḍā's text agrees with the tradition preserved in *Ziyādāt Sharḥ al-Uṣūl*.

121. *Shāfī*, 3:127; cf. ᶜAbd al-Jabbār, *Mughnī*, 20{1}:14. For the *ghulāt* views in this regard, see Tucker, *Mahdis*, 59, 78–80; for the Ismaᶜili views, see Daftary, *Ismāᶜīlīs*, 73, 89, 105, 139, 142.
122. Bāqillānī, *Inṣāf*, 60; Bāqillānī, *Tamhīd*, 168–9; ᶜAbd al-Jabbār, *Mughnī*, 16:342, 181; Juwaynī, *Irshād*, 352–3.
123. *Rasāʾil*, 1:104–8; although he does not name any of the Imamis who held the abovementioned position, the flow of argument in Murtaḍā's text is almost congruent with, and meant to refute, Mufīd's arguments as they appear in *Awāʾil*, 135–7.
124. Kinberg, 'Dreams'.
125. *Amālī*, 2:325–8; *Rasāʾil*, 2:12–13.
126. Mufīd, *Awāʾil*, 70; Mufīd, *Fuṣūl*, 128–30; Ṭūsī, *Amālī*, 338.
127. *Tanzīh*, 65–70; *Dhakhīra*, 545.

CONCLUSION

صار هذا المذهبُ مذهبًا بالمرتضى، لأنه صنّف الكتبَ في الأصول والفروع والإمامةِ ونَصَرَه وخلَطَ التوحيدَ والعدلَ به.[1]

الحاكم الجِشُمي

The archetypical rationalist of early Imamism, Hishām b. al-Ḥakam, was reportedly challenged to an argumentative duel by his Muᶜtazili nemesis Abū al-Hudhayl al-ᶜAllāf under the condition that the loser accept the winner's persuasion. 'This is not fair!' Hishām protested; 'Let us debate under the condition that you accept my persuasion if I win, and I turn to my Imam for assistance if I lose'.[2]

The story ends here. Despite – or because of – the fact that the sources do not attempt to hypothesise regarding the events that followed, contemplating this anecdote is a most rewarding exercise. The anecdotal power of the story stems from the room it leaves for readers to imagine what Hishām would have asked the Imam in case of defeat. The abrupt silence that governs the reception of the story conceals the attitudes of various trends within Imami Shiᶜism towards rationalism in general and the Imam's relation to reason in particular. Hypothetically, there are at least three possible scenarios. The first is the absolute *ex cathedra* scenario: Hishām would appeal to the Imam to learn what he should do, and the Imam's authority would override any counterargument merely by virtue of his office. The second scenario is the exact opposite of the first one: Hishām would check whether the Imam could actually rise to the challenge; if he could not, Hishām would revise his commitment to Imamism. The third possibility is a revamped *ex cathedra* scenario: Hishām would solicit the Imam's guidance, being absolutely certain that the latter could answer the challenge and furthermore do so by addressing the argument in question and not simply by invoking his authority.

With time, the second scenario ceased to be a possibility for the Imamis, even hypothetically, although heresiographies preserve accounts of individuals who reneged on their commitment to the Imams because of answers they deemed unsatisfactory.[3] The remaining two scenarios thus dominate the scene. Although it ought to be kept in mind that traditionalism and rationalism were poles on a spectrum that did not admit of a clean break between them, these two scenarios represent traditionalist and rationalist trends within the Imami community since the occultation of the Imam. The first scenario defines the reception of the anecdote by traditionalists, even mild ones such as Ṣadūq. In his *al-I^c^tiqādāt fī dīn al-Imāmiyya*, he includes the anecdote in a section dedicated to discrediting argument and disallowing disputation (*al-nahy ^c^an al-jadal*). The only lawful arguments, he asserts, are those taken from the Imams' teachings.[4] This view also reflects, though potentially on different premises, the emphasis in Imamism on the Imam's esoteric knowledge and 'hierointelligence' still favoured in many contemporary circles of Imami scholarship. The third scenario would be endorsed by rationalist theologians in the Imami community, for it satisfies both the belief in the Imam's infallibility and the belief in the primacy of reason in establishing one's own convictions and in debating with representatives of other communities. Nevertheless, the complexity of this scenario becomes evident when considering how it would unfold for two major representatives of this trend, Mufīd and Murtaḍā.

As Mufīd would have seen it, when Hishām asks the Imam for a decisive argument to silence Abū al-Hudhayl, he shows himself a typical representative of human reason. This view explains Mufīd's failure to comment on the anecdote in the course of his elaborate objections to this section of Ṣadūq's *I^c^tiqādāt* in his critical commentary on the book.[5] Elsewhere, Mufīd states unequivocally that reason needs revelation, which instructs the rational being how to make sense of evidence (*ghayr munfakk ^c^an sam^c^ yunabbihu al-^c^āqil ^c^alā kayfiyyat al-istidlāl*).[6] This statement is consistent with his initial view that the Imama is primarily necessitated by human shortcomings in knowing and applying the law. Murtaḍā repudiates this view of the relation between reason and revelation, for it leads, in his view, to the unacceptable conclusion that people who can reason correctly no longer need the Imam.[7] Given Murtaḍā's confidence in the independent workings of reason, Abū al-Hudhayl's challenge, no matter how strong, must still be within Hishām's ability to answer. Hishām's failure would thus indicate a mistake in reasoning that could have been avoided without resort to the Imam. Therefore, Murtaḍā would suggest a different assessment of the situation: the Imam would still be expected to provide Hishām with an argument by which the latter could defeat his adversary, but such guidance is not what necessitates the Imama in the first place; the necessitating reason is, instead, people's moral rectitude.

The hypothetical disagreements between Mufīd and Murtaḍā regarding this anecdote notwithstanding, their positions and that of Ṣadūq concur on two points: that the Imam is the authority to which an Imami should turn when faced by a tough challenge, and that the Imam's answer would be compelling. However, the three scholars would disagree on the justification for each of these two points: why the Imam is endowed with this authority, and how his answer is compelling. Of course, Mufīd and Murtaḍā are much closer to each other than to Ṣadūq. Seen from the perspective of the earlier distinction between method and content, this divergence serves to show that there is no form without matter, just as there is no formless matter: the difference in method between the three scholars does lead to a difference in content, even if minimal. Nevertheless, it should be noted that they ultimately agree on doctrines, although they disagree on the underlying theology.

Theology, doctrine and influence

It is now possible to read Murtaḍā's contribution in the context of his scholarly interaction with both Imami and Basran Muᶜtazili teachings. For this purpose, one must compare his views and positions with those of Mufīd and of ᶜAbd al-Jabbār's circle and then trace their reception by Ṭūsī, proportionate to the limitations of current knowledge of the latter's theological writings. This approach gives rise to a fourfold classification that elucidates Murtaḍā's position in light of the distinction between theology and doctrine and its significance for the relation between Imamism and Muᶜtazilism.

1. *Points of unanimous concurrence*
   Points on which all of the scholars and groups considered here agree include rejecting Attributist positions and accepting the origination of the Qurʾān, rational morality and free will. These are foundational points, a complex of content and method that governs the remaining aspects of each scholar's theological apparatus. Subscribing to them qualifies an individual for membership among the 'people of unity and justice', since the terms of this epithet refer to anti-Attributist positions (leading to the origination of the Qurʾān) and rational morality (leading to free will), respectively. The strategic advantage of Mufīd's definition of Muᶜtazilism in terms of the belief in the 'station between the two stations' becomes evident here, for within its framework Imamis qualify for this self-congratulatory epithet without being subsumed under the Muᶜtazili umbrella. Therefore, Murtaḍā's concurrence on these points does not indicate any special affiliation with Muᶜtazilism as compared to his teacher.

2. *Points of concurrence between Murtaḍā, Mufīd and Ṭūsī not shared by ᶜAbd al-Jabbār's circle*
   Points on which the three Imami scholars diverge from ᶜAbd al-Jabbār's circle include the propositions that otherworldly intercession for sinners is possible, that the Imama is rationally necessary, that the twelve Imams are infallible and can perform miracles, that the first three caliphs were not legitimate and that *badāʾ* is tantamount to abrogation. Equally significantly, they include refusal to refer to the Qurʾān as 'created' as well as rejection of the doctrines of the threat, the station between the two stations and mutual cancellation. This set of points is significant primarily for Imami communal identity. Murtaḍā conforms to the tradition handed down by Mufīd, and Ṭūsī does not dissent. These are mostly doctrinal points on which the Imamis were frequently attacked; the Imami scholars'

conflict with ᶜAbd al-Jabbār's circle concerns not how these points are argued, but their very content. In addition, the rejected points represent positions by which Muᶜtazilis defined themselves, as if Murtaḍā is stressing Imami identity in contradistinction to Muᶜtazilism. His refusal to call the Qurʾān 'created' and willingness to use *badāʾ* as a synonym of abrogation, both based on traditions from the Imams, reinforce the boundaries of the community defined by charismatic authority.

3. *Points of concurrence between Murtaḍā and ᶜAbd al-Jabbār's circle not shared by Mufīd*
   Points on which Murtaḍā sided with the Basran Muᶜtazilis against his teacher include accepting the theory of states as well as the positions that unaided reason suffices to know God, that divine attributes may be derived independently of revelation, that the essence of the human being is the observed totality, that humans 'create' their acts, that God's assistance is a concomitant of His justice rather than His generosity, that such assistance is targeted only at people's otherworldly interests and that unbelievers are entitled to compensation in the hereafter. Ṭūsī concurs with Murtaḍā on these points, with the exception of humans' 'creation' of their acts. Murtaḍā's disagreement with earlier Imami scholars concerns mostly positions for which these scholars did not invoke the authority of the Imams. The theory of states keeps Murtaḍā firmly in the anti-Attributist camp; but as it is an admittedly late development, its possible conflict with traditions is not difficult to explain away. Similarly, his view on the human being employs the terminology of theologians and not the wording of traditions, just as Mufīd admits in his own case. Murtaḍā's acceptance of the term 'create' for human acts goes against Mufīd's view, but the latter is based not on traditions but pietistic caution. The exception to Murtaḍā's avoidance of overruling traditions is his view on the legitimate source of divine attributes, since Mufīd does invoke the authority of traditions for his opposing position. Most of these discussions are too arcane to substantially change the doctrines in question, although they affect the doctrines' underlying rationale by making them dependent on premises of Basran Muᶜtazili provenance.
4. *Points on which Murtaḍā agrees with neither Mufīd nor Ṭūsī nor ᶜAbd al-Jabbār's circle*
   Points on which Murtaḍā's position stands alone include his theory of *ṣarfa* and the claims that the Imam's occultation makes the function of the Imama more effective, that infallible individuals cannot fall into inadvertence and that the Twelfth Imam may not be the last. This group of points constitutes Murtaḍā's most distinctive contribution; their relevance to Imami doctrines and Muᶜtazili theology varies. Thus, he defends the doctrine of the inimitability of the Qurʾān, a fairly mainstream Islamic view, through the theology of *ṣarfa*, an uncommon theory shared by theologians of various schools. For the key Imami doctrine of the occultation, he offers a novel justification that draws on the understanding of divine assistance taught in Basran Muᶜtazili theology. He does the same for

another sensitive Imami doctrine, the infallibility of the Imams, which he pushes to an extreme. As for the aftermath of the Twelfth Imam's death, his view, though dissenting from Imami doctrine, is an expression of his beliefs concerning future contingencies and not a statement of timeless necessities.

This summary shows that in relation to Imami doctrines, Murtaḍā's work retains to a large extent the terms and ideas of his precursors within the rationalist trend. Nevertheless, he employs these terms and ideas in ways that differ from theirs: God's unicity is now in harmony with states of the divine essence; moral obligation is an expression of human reason free of the authority of revelation; the Imama is an instance of divine justice, not generosity; the necessity of divine assistance lies in the social need for harmony, not a need for the details of the law; and the occultation is a result of divine assistance, not of political fear. Murtaḍā's creative work corresponds to the revisionary ratio *tessera*, in which an author elaborates on a precursor's work as if to save it from being worn out because its argument did not go far enough.[8]

In relation to Muᶜtazili theology, Murtaḍā's work reveals a different kind of influence. He is unwilling to follow Muᶜtazili arguments to the end of the line of reasoning advanced by ᶜAbd al-Jabbār and his circle, for they clearly lead to 'wrong' doctrines: God's justice cannot override His mercy, His originated word cannot be possibly described as fabricated, divine assistance cannot lead to the community installing the Imam, and protecting the finality of Muḥammad's prophethood cannot deprive believers of witnessing miracles. At some point, Murtaḍā has to make a corrective movement, a deviation from previous works in the direction of the 'right' doctrines, to avoid these outcomes. This approach corresponds to the revisionary ratio *clinamen*, in which the author swerves away from his precursors to imply that the precursors should have swerved in exactly the same direction.[9]

Divine assistance as a theology of history

It takes a theologian to transform the literary expression of history into a scholarly theory.[10] This is true of various political theories and models in Islam, but the theological dimension of this transformation rarely reveals itself as manifestly as it does in the case of Shiᶜism in general and Murtaḍā's work in particular, although the latter is far from being the first to theorise Imamism in this way.

At the heart of Muᶜtazilism lies the concept of divine assistance. This concept is the main tool that Murtaḍā uses to forge a theological discourse with profound ramifications for the Imami understanding of the nature, origin and function of the Imama. It should be remembered that for the Baghdadi Muᶜtazilis divine assistance rested on the concept of humans' best interest (*al-aṣlaḥ*), leading to many complications that contradict the evidence of phenomena (*al-shāhid*), for it is hard to see how God's assistance works in this poignantly imperfect world. The Imama, by definition, is an inescapably political endeavour, at least in part. To conceive of it as divine assistance in this sense should not come as a surprise, since the link between political activity and worldly interest is rather obvious. Nevertheless, this conception is problematic given the inconveniences it occasions in its Muᶜtazili context, let alone the difficulties raised by the occultation of the presumptive senior politician in the Imami case. For their part, the Basran Muᶜtazilis restrict divine assistance to the realm of religion; many undeniable worldly imperfections can thus be construed as divine assistance whose meaning will materialise in the hereafter. This Basran formulation of the concept of divine assistance proves remarkably potent when Murtaḍā employs it for establishing a theory of the Imama. To see its full effect, it is worth considering how the Basran Muᶜtazili theological system fundamentally depends on it before proceeding to examine how it unfolds in the context of Murtaḍā's contribution to Imami discourse.

The Basran Muᶜtazilis justify moral obligation, the core of religious experience, as an instance of divine assistance, which in turn is an expression of divine justice. Because justice is immutably good and God is benevolent, divine assistance must be maximally extended to all entitled beings, as long as their free will is not compromised. Thus, the purpose of divine assistance must be to bring people as close as possible to freely observing their moral obligation. These conclusions, for the Basran Muᶜtazilis, were consequences of indubitable rationality. Based on them, they proceeded to argue that the Imam is necessary only because revelation ordained the installation of an Imam for the Muslims; per se, the Imama has no connection to moral obligation. But it is here that Murtaḍā introduces his *clinamen*: if divine assistance must be maximal, and the presence of a just authority brings people closer to meeting their obligations than does his absence, then his presence constitutes divine assistance. It is, therefore, an instance of justice, which makes it rationally necessary. The Imam's infallibility is now argued to be a consequence of the need to maximise divine assistance, since subjects tend to imitate the example of their sovereign. Furthermore, because divine assistance is concerned with religious matters, the Imama's authority need not be confined to political reality for its function to be properly fulfilled, and his occultation thus becomes much less of a challenge. Therefore, morality, the most distinctive domain of Muᶜtazili rationalism,[11] proves extremely useful for the revamped theology of the Imama in Imamism. Murtaḍā would surely forgive the Biblical analogy, for it well describes his work: 'Neither do people pour new wine into old wineskins. If they do, the skins will burst; the wine will run out and the wineskins will be ruined'.[12] Instead, he adopts the much safer approach of pouring old Imami doctrines into new Muᶜtazili theology.

In light of Murtaḍā's conception of the Imama in terms of people's otherworldly best interest, the intimate connection between the Imama and historical narrative leads inevitably to a sacred-historical outlook. The dual core of Murtaḍā's theology – the necessity of the Imama and the infallibility of the Imam – sketches the trajectory of the Muslim community in rigidly hierarchical terms. The Imam, on top, is separated from the community by an unbridgeable, charismatic gap of divine designation; the Imami community, whose otherworldly interest is always secured by the Imam's perceived – though furtive – presence, follows him in the hierarchy; and at the bottom are the remaining members of the Muslim community, who have the option of joining the privileged Imami circle. In the ideal case of the Imam's being in power, the regular operation of a hierarchical political structure ensures the proper reception of divine assistance by as many individuals as possible within the norms of 'ordinary' history. But the absence of the Imam makes the later events of ordinary history insignificant to the religious conscience of the community, unless they are connected to his occultation. This change reintroduces sacred history as the exclusive explanation of the period of occultation, and it also equips Murtaḍā's narrative with a potent interpretative tool to analyse problematic events of earlier periods in retrospect. The case of the Wāqifiyya is particularly interesting, for their theological apparatus was more immune than that of others to theoretical criticism from the perspective of the Imam's lineage and qualifications; in addition, Murtaḍā's family history shows a streak of Wāqifism.[13] Mufīd's earlier refutation of Wāqifi claims based on the death of Kāẓim does not solve the problem, for it seems to beg the question in the eyes of those who believed him to have gone into hiding. Murtaḍā, on the other hand, relies on the concept of divine assistance in his refutation: since the Wāqifiyya are almost extinct – as he asserts in a rather rhetorical manner – their claims being true would mean that divine assistance was about to be withheld from everyone, a possibility that conflicts with divine justice. Appeal to sacred history in the guise of the necessities of rational morality is definitely more reassuring than being captive to the contingencies of historiographical literature. Given the immense benefits of the concept of divine assistance for Murtaḍā's theological system, one wonders whether the concept is not itself an instance of such divine assistance in his eyes.

Murtaḍā's employment of history can be viewed as an attempt to build an edifice of theological historical writing that is distinct from the classical *ḥadīth*, *ḥikma* and *adab* domes of historical writing and at the same time inclusive of these domes. As such, it utilises their methods and findings towards the consolidation of a more comprehensive narrative whose paramount concern is theological. Nevertheless, this concern justifies a highly selective approach to the methods and findings lest they contradict Murtaḍā's sectarian agenda. These restrictions, applied both to the qualifications required of the Imam and the community's obligations towards him, reflect Murtaḍā's involvement with the themes of *sīrat al-khulafāʾ* and *fitna*. They thus betray the intimate connection between historical writing and communal identity.

Such theoretical considerations shaped Murtaḍā's thinking on the Imama. But the more concrete circumstances of his public life and personal experience are equally important. He must have been aware of the flaws in government caused by statesmen and politicians whose shortcomings were more moral than intellectual. Many of them were highly cultured, and some were also Imamis.[14] From Murtaḍā's perspective, this fact might have proved that knowledge of the 'right' doctrines was not sufficient and that the Imams' role was thus primarily concerned with the moral aspect, even if the epistemic aspect was a requisite. On a personal level, as a teenager Murtaḍā witnessed his father's plight at the hands of ᶜAḍud al-Dawla,[15] known for being both cultured and cruel.[16] This experience must also have had an indelible effect on his conviction regarding morality and its primacy in defining the ideal sovereign, the Imam.

* * *

Abū Ḥayyān al-Tawḥīdī, a contemporary of Murtaḍā, had much in common with Jāḥiẓ, whom he considered his idol: encyclopedic outlook, lucid style, court connections (although with much less success, to put it mildly) and negativity towards the Imamis. Added to his intimate association with pro-Imami circles in Būyid palaces, this personal bias makes him well positioned to provide a vivid description of how the Imamis were perceived in the broader Islamic context. The image that emerges is mixed: whereas he habitually mocks the traditions they transmit, he expresses an attitude of disapproving respect towards some of their scholars, whom he knew personally. He applauds Ṣadūq for his vast knowledge[17] and criticises his lack of discrimination;[18] he acknowledges the wit of the theologian Abū al-Jaysh al-Khurāsānī (d. 978)[19] and attacks his views on the integrity of the Qurʾān (though Tawḥīdī does not present these views clearly);[20] and he praises Mufīd's comportment, patience, eloquence and skill in debate, while expressing suspicion about his intentions – also without further explanation.[21]

Though caution is necessary, these comments indicate that the Imami community, in the generation before Murtaḍā's ascent to its leadership, had traditionalists and theologians whose stature in their respective fields vis-à-vis their non-Imami counterparts was recognised. Murtaḍā's career can, therefore, be read in light of his contribution to Imami identity in a context of which the following remarks are emblematic: intellectual calibre (Ṣadūq), provocative opinions (Abū al-Jaysh) and deep mistrust (Mufīd). In its totality, Murtaḍā's corpus seems to address these concerns in the course of presenting his specific formation of Imami identity, which seems to corroborate the general observation that the occultation of the locus of authority forced Imamis to define their tradition more precisely.[22] Given that the problem with identity was, to a large extent, one of boundaries, his activity may be likened to repairing a fence – or the part of it to which he has access. He needed to redefine the contours to make sure only eligible individuals were included, install the fence firmly to prevent incursions that would make these boundaries inadequate, and use a welcoming design that would not block the view from the outside in a manner that would arouse other people's suspicion.

To redefine the contours of Imami identity, Murtaḍā repeatedly lampoons traditionalists, belittles their intellect and disavows their work, going as far as referring to them as 'those who affiliate themselves with our community' (*al-muntamīn ilā aṣḥābinā*),[23] singling out Ṣadūq as the only acceptable Qummi traditionalist.[24] In a previous act of redefining boundaries, the Imamis had renounced the extremists (*ghulāt*) during the period of minor occultation, thus ridding themselves of a perennial problem that had brought upon them political trouble and sectarian vilification. Murtaḍā's insistence on excluding traditionalists represents a similar step, although not necessarily in the same direction: many Qummi traditionalists were in fact theologically further from extremism than were many Baghdadi rationalists whose main difference from the extremists was their avoidance of subversive activism and legal antinomianism.

To install the fence firmly, Murtaḍā stresses characteristic Imami doctrines and practices to reinforce communal identity. He establishes these doctrines on the basis of what he views as a more resilient theological structure than that of his ancestors, that is, by incorporating a more rationalist theology. In addition, he asserts that the probative consensus is in fact that of the Imamis, for it reflects the rulings of the infallible Imam; the consensus of the Imamis thus overrides even the prima facie reading of scripture.[25] This investment in the value of Imami identity as expressed in communal agreement must have inspired confidence in the face of the exclusion associated with accusations of breaking the consensus of the Muslim community.

For a welcoming design, Murtaḍā invests in highlighting the similarities between the Imamis and other theological and legal schools. In addition to blaming traditionalists for doubting the integrity of the Qurʾān,[26] he plays a critical role in defending its integrity within the Imami community, as can be discerned from Ṭūsī's curiously worded remarks that single him out for his cogent argument towards this purpose.[27] Moreover, his theoretical system, greatly resembling that of the Basran Muʿtazilis, must have made Imamism more familiar to the broader audience. In the field of law, where Imamis had been accused of frequent dissent, Murtaḍā dedicated considerable effort to showing that they actually concurred with other groups on many of the controversial issues.

It is true that on the theoretical level, Murtaḍā's longest-surviving contribution to Imami discourse was his theological system. Despite the many modifications it underwent in later generations under the influence of the school of Abū al-Ḥusayn al-Baṣrī, it continued to provide the basic structure of mainstream Imami theology until the Aristotelian turn largely introduced by Naṣīr al-Dīn al-Ṭūsī. But from a different perspective, Murtaḍā's most enduring contribution to Imami identity is exemplified in his ability to utilise the unprecedented and powerful combination of political connections, religious education, material wealth and social status to irreversibly influence Imami historical memory. His network of students and connections must have been part of the powerful social and religious elite within the community that contributed greatly to both the survival of the Būyid state and the vitality of Imami intellectual life. The formation of such elites in various locales of the Muslim world seems to have taken some two centuries following the severance of the connection to the caliphate.[28] In the case of the Imami community of Baghdad, this process appears to have taken less time after the dissolution of ʿAbbāsid power, probably due to the favourable political situation created by the Būyids and the earlier, though sporadic, Imami presence in high social circles. Five centuries later, as Imami scholars inaugurated a new era of intense cooperation with the government under the Safavids that proved much more enduring than their relationship with the Būyids, they became embroiled in heated internal feuds concerning the lawfulness of such an endeavour. To justify his own view on the question, the leading proponent of political involvement, al-Muḥaqqiq al-Karakī (d. 1534), invoked Murtaḍā's precedent as the first in his list of past authorities.[29] This view eventually prevailed.

It is perhaps opportune to return to Jāḥiẓ, whose shadow loomed over Murtaḍā's debate with the Muᶜtazilis, as slyly expressed by Ibn Abī al-Ḥadīd.[30] In another rant, Jāḥiẓ renounces the Rafiḍis on account of their dissident theological views, legal practice, scholarly tradition and communal authority: their teachings regarding the call to prayer (*adhān*), prayer, divorce, manumission, pilgrimage, scholars, Imam, Qurʾānic recitation (*qirāᶜa*), and other practices both lawful and prohibited are, he claims, all unlike 'ours'.[31] Murtaḍā's contribution, roughly two centuries after these attacks, can be situated in the context of generations of Imami scholars whose work attempted to soften this attitude within and beyond the Imami community, in the face of both internal and external resistance. The claim of the Zaydi al-Ḥākim al-Jishumī, quoted in the epigraph to the conclusion, was made within two generations of Murtaḍā's death. The message is curiously ambivalent: while acknowledging Murtaḍā's success in shaping later Imami theology, it doubts his claims about earlier Imami doctrines – therefore agreeing with Jāḥiẓ's earlier accusations and Tawḥīdī's recent suspicions. Whether Murtaḍā's discourse is more an adjustment to dominant discourses or a correction of inaccurate portrayals is a separate question, on which it might be good to consult his words quoted at the beginning of this book.

Notes

1. Jishumī, *al-Risāla fī naṣīḥat al-ᶜāmma*, 59.
2. Ṣadūq, *Iᶜtiqādāt*, 43.
3. Nawbakhtī, *Firaq*, 52–3; Ashᶜarī Qummī, *Kitāb al-Maqālāt*, 75. The account in *Kāfī*, 1:351 is also relevant: ᶜAbdullāh al-Afṭaḥ (d. 765), who failed to answer the challenge, though not considered an Imam in the later tradition, was perceived as such by those who brought the question before him.
4. Ṣadūq, *Iᶜtiqādāt*, 43; according to Modarressi, *Crisis*, 112–13, this remained the dominant position in Imami theology until the middle of the ninth century.
5. Mufīd, *Taṣḥīḥ*, 68–73.
6. Mufīd, *Awāʾil*, 44.
7. *Shāfī*, 1:43.
8. See Bloom, *Anxiety*, 66–8.
9. See Bloom, *Anxiety*, 28–30.
10. Van Ess, 'Political ideas', 155–6, in reference to the concept of the rightly guided caliphs.
11. See Gimaret, 'Muᶜtazila'.
12. Matthew 9:17.
13. See Raḍī, *Khaṣāʾiṣ*, 37–8, who indicates that the majority of Kāẓim's descendants at the time of writing were known to be Wāqifis.
14. See Chapter 1, 'Historical setting'.
15. See the poem expressing relief for his death in Raḍī, *Dīwān*, 1:267. The event is not men-

tioned in Murtaḍā's poetry, which may be due to the fact that unlike his brother, who was primarily a poet, Murtaḍā expressed his reactions in the language of general theological formulae.

16. See, for example, Miskawayh, *Tajārib al-umam*, 7:52–9; Ibn al-Jawzī, *Muntaẓam*, 14:290–7.
17. Tawḥīdī, *Baṣāʾir*, 165–6.
18. Tawḥīdī, *Akhlāq*, 254–5.
19. Little is known about him; see Najāshī, *Rijāl*, 422; Ṭūsī, *Fihrist*, 169.
20. Tawḥīdī, *Akhlāq*, 206–7.
21. Tawḥīdī, *Imtāʿ*, 107.
22. Berkey, 'Islam', 47.
23. *Rasāʾil*, 2:18.
24. *Rasāʾil*, 3:310–11.
25. See, for example, *Intiṣār*, 442–4.
26. *Dhakhīra*, 363.
27. Ṭūsī, *Tibyān*, 1:3.
28. See Bulliet, *Conversion*, 137–8, on how the political and religious dimensions both depended on what Bulliet terms the Muslim establishment.
29. Karakī, *Qāṭiʿa*, 85.
30. Ibn Abī al-Ḥadīd, *Sharḥ*, 16:263–4.
31. Jāḥiẓ, 'Ḥujaj al-nubuwwa,' 233–4.

BIBLIOGRAPHY

Note on citation: Murtaḍā's works are listed and discussed in Chapter 1. They are cited in the notes by title only; for ease of reference, the format '*Rasāʾil*, page number' is used to refer to texts published in the *Rasāʾil*.

ᶜAbd al-Ḥusayn Ḥāʾirī. *Fihrist-i nuskha-hā-yi khaṭṭī-yi kitābkhāna-yi majlis-i shūrā-yi Islāmī*, vol. 19. Tehran: Kitābkhāna-yi Majlis-i Shūrā-yi Islāmī, 2008.

ᶜAbd al-Jabbār, Qāḍī al-Quḍāt. *al-Mughnī fī abwāb al-tawḥīd wa-l-ᶜadl*. Edited by Maḥmūd Muḥammad Khuḍayrī and Ibrāhīm Madkūr et al. Cairo: Wizārat al-Thaqāfa wa-l-Irshād al-Qawmī, 1958–66.

ᶜAbd al-Wāḥid, Aḥmad. *al-Naqd al-adabī fī āthār al-Sharīf al-Murtaḍā*. Jāzān: Nādī Jāzān al-Adabī, 1996.

Abdulsater, Hussein. 'The climax of speculative theology in Būyid Shīᶜism: The contribution of al-Sharīf al-Murtaḍā'. PhD dissertation, Yale University, 2013.

Abdulsater, Hussein. 'Reason, grace and the freedom of conscience: The period of investigation in Muᶜtazilī theology'. *Studia Islamica*, 110, no. 2 (2015), 233–62.

Abdulsater, Hussein. 'Resurgence and spurious ascription: The curious case of *Risālat al-muḥkam wa-l-mutashābih*'. *Al-Abhath*, 60–1 (2012–13), 59–86.

Abdulsater, Hussein. 'To rehabilitate a theological treatise: *Inqādh al-bashar min al-jabr wa-l-qadar*'. *Asiatische Studien*, 68, no. 2 (2014), 519–47.

Abrahamov, Binyamin (ed. and trans.). *Anthropomorphism and Interpretation of the Qurᶜān in the Theology of al-Qāsim ibn Ibrāhīm; Kitāb al-Mustarshid*. Leiden: Brill, 1996.

Abrahamov, Binyamin. 'The attitude of Jaᶜfar al-Ṣādiq and ᶜAlī al-Riḍā toward *kalām* and rational reasoning'. *Jerusalem Studies in Arabic and Islam*, 31 (2006), 196–208.

Abrahamov, Binyamin. *Islamic Theology: Traditionalism and Rationalism*. Edinburgh: Edinburgh University Press, 1998.

Abrahamov, Binyamin. 'Necessary knowledge in Islamic theology'. *British Journal of Middle Eastern Studies*, 20, no. 1 (1993), 20–32.

Abū Yaʿlā Ibn al-Farrāʾ. *al-Muʿtamad fī uṣūl al-dīn*. Edited by Wadīʿ Ḥaddād. Beirut: Dār al-Mashriq, 1974.

Adamson, Peter. *Al-Kindī*. Oxford: Oxford University Press, 2007.

Adang, Camilla, Wilferd Madelung and Sabine Schmidtke (eds). *Baṣran Muʿtazilite Theology: Abū ʿAlī Muḥammad b. Khallād's Kitāb al-uṣūl and Its Reception*. Leiden: Brill, 2011.

Afandī, ʿAbdullāh b. ʿĪsā al-Iṣfahānī. *Riyāḍ al-ʿulamāʾ wa-ḥiyāḍ al-fuḍalāʾ*. Edited by Aḥmad al-Ḥusaynī. Qum: Maktabat Āyatullāh al-ʿUẓmā al-Marʿashī al-Najafī, 1982–95.

Afsaruddin, Asma. *Excellence and Precedence: Medieval Islamic Discourse on Legitimate Leadership*. Leiden: Brill, 2002.

Āghā Buzurg, Muḥammad Muḥsin al-Ṭihrānī. *al-Dharīʿa ilā taṣānīf al-Shīʿa*. Beirut: Dār al-Aḍwāʾ, 1983.

Ajhar, ʿAbd al-Ḥakīm. *Ibn Taymiyya wa-istiʾnāf al-qawl al-falsafī fī al-Islām*. Casablanca: al-Markaz al-Thaqāfī al-ʿArabī, 2004.

Akhtar, Waḥīd. 'An introduction to Imāmiyyah scholars: Al-Sayyid al-Murtaḍā; His life and works'. *al-Tawḥīd*, 4, no. 1 (1986), 125–52.

Akhtar, Waḥīd. 'An introduction to Imāmiyyah scholars: Al-Shaykh al-Ṣadūq; His life and works'. *al-Tawḥīd*, 3, no. 1 (1986), 80–118.

Akhtar, Waḥīd. 'An introduction to Imāmiyyah scholars: Shaykh al-Ṭāʾifah al-Ṭūsī; Life and works'. *al-Tawḥīd*, 4, no. 2 (1987), 126–67.

Akoğlu, Muharrem. 'Major breaks in the history of Mutazilism'. *Islamic Quarterly*, 54, no. 3 (2010), 191–211.

Ali, Aun Hasan. 'Imamite rationalism in the Buyid era'. MA thesis, McGill University, 2007.

ʿAlī Ibn Bābawayh. *al-Imāma wa-l-tabṣira min al-ḥayra*. Qum: Madrasat al-Imam al-Mahdī, 1404 H.

Ālūsī, Abū al-Thanāʾ Maḥmūd Shukrī. *Tafsīr = Rūḥ al-maʿānī*. Beirut: Dār Iḥyāʾ al-Turāth al-ʿArabī, n.d.

ʿĀmilī, Ḥasan b. Zayn al-Dīn. *Maʿālim al-dīn wa-malādh al-mujtahidīn*. Qum: Muʾassasat al-Nashr al-Islāmī, n.d.

Amīn, Aḥmad. *Ḍuḥā al-Islām*. Cairo: Maktabat al-Nahḍa al-Miṣriyya, 1964.

Amīn, Muḥsin. *Aʿyān al-Shīʿa*. Beirut: Dār al-Taʿāruf li-l-Maṭbūʿāt, 1986.

Amīnī, ʿAbd al-Ḥusayn. *al-Ghadīr fī al-kitāb wa-l-sunna wa-l-adab*. Beirut: Dār al-Kitāb al-ʿArabī, 1977.

Amīnī, ʿAbd al-Ḥusayn. *al-Ṣirāʿ bayn al-Islām wa-l-wathaniyya*. Qum: Markaz al-Ghadīr, 1417 H.

Amir-Moezzi, Mohammad Ali. *The Divine Guide in Early Shiʿism: The Sources of Esotericism in Islam*. Albany: State University of New York Press, 1994.

Amir-Moezzi, Mohammad Ali. 'Shiʿite doctrine'. *Encyclopaedia Iranica* [= *EIr*], 2005. http://www.iranicaonline.org/articles/shiite-doctrine.

Amir-Moezzi, Mohammad Ali. 'Al-Ṭūsī, Muḥammad b. al-Ḥasan'. *Encyclopaedia of Islam, 2nd edn* [= *EI²*], 10 (2000), 744.

Ansari, Hassan. 'Āthār-i chapnashuday-i Sharīf-i Murtaḍā (2): Javābāt-i al-Masāʾil al-Sallāriyya va raddiy-i Ibn-i Ṭāvūs bar ān'. *Barrasīhā-yi tārīkhī* (blog), 21 Mihr 1391 SH. http://ansari.kateban.com/post/1935.

Ansari, Hassan. 'Kitāb-i al-Taᶜlīq-i Muqrī-yi Nīsābūrī dar kalām va baḥthī dar bāriy-i al-Mulakhkhaṣ va al-Dhakhīra taᵓlīf-i Sharīf-i Murtaḍā'. *Barrasīhā-yi tārīkhī* (blog), 30 Ādhar 1394 SH. http://ansari.kateban.com/post/2649.

Ansari, Hassan. 'Nuskha-ᵓī kuhansāl az Amāliy-i Sharīf-i Murtaḍā bi-hamrāh-i ijāza-ᵓī arzishmand az adībī shīᶜī'. *Barrasīhā-yi tārīkhī* (blog), 28 Mihr 1394 SH. http://ansari.kateban.com/post/2587.

Ansari, Hassan. 'Taᶜlīq-i sharḥ-i Jumal al-ᶜIlm-i Karājikī'. *Barrasīhā-yi tārīkhī* (blog), 22 Ādhar 1386. http://ansari.kateban.com/entry1249.html.

Ansari, Hassan. '(2) Yak raddiy-i kuhansāl-i zaydī az Nīsābūr-i sadiy-i panjum bar kitāb-i al-Muqniᶜ-i Sharīf-i Murtaḍā dar bāriy-i masᵓaliy-i ghaybat-i imam'. *Barrasīhā-yi tārīkhī* (blog), 28 Urdibihisht 1392. http://ansari.kateban.com/post/1984.

Ansari, Hassan and Sabine Schmidtke. 'The Muᶜtazilī and Zaydī reception of Abū l-Ḥusayn al-Baṣrī's *Kitāb al-Muᶜtamad fī uṣūl al-fiqh*: A bibliographical note'. *Islamic Law and Society*, 20, nos 1–3 (2013), 90–109.

Ansari, Hassan and Sabine Schmidtke. 'Muᶜtazilism after ᶜAbd al-Jabbār: Abū Rashīd al-Nīsābūrī's *Kitāb masāᶜil al-khilāf fī l-uṣūl*'. *Studia Iranica*, 39, no. 2 (2010), 225–76.

Ansari, Hassan and Sabine Schmidtke. 'Al-Shaykh al-Ṭūsī: His writings on theology and their reception'. In *The Study of Shiᶜi Islam: History, Theology and Law*, edited by Farhad Daftary and Gurdofarid Miskinzoda, 475–97. London: I. B. Tauris, 2014.

Anṣārī, Murtaḍā. *al-Makāsib*. Qum: Majmaᶜ al-Fikr al-Islāmī, 1420 H.

Anscombe, G. E. M. 'Modern moral philosophy'. *Philosophy*, 33, no. 124 (1958), 1–19.

Aradi, Naomi. 'The origins of the *kalām* model of discussion on the concept of *tawḥīd*'. *Arabic Sciences and Philosophy*, 23, no. 1 (2013), 135–66.

Asatryan, Mushegh and Dylan Burns. 'Is Ghulat religion Islamic Gnosticism? Religious transmissions in Late Antiquity'. In *L'ésotérisme shi'ite, ses racines et ses prolongements*, edited by Mohammad Ali Amir-Moezzi et al., 55–86. Turnhout: Brepols, 2016.

Ashᶜarī, Abū al-Ḥasan ᶜAlī b. Ismāᶜīl. *al-Lumaᶜ fī al-radd ᶜalā ahl al-zaygh wa-l-bidaᶜ*. Edited by Ḥammūda Ghurāba. Cairo: Maṭbaᶜat Miṣr, 1955.

Ashᶜarī, Abū al-Ḥasan ᶜAlī b. Ismāᶜīl. *Maqālāt al-Islāmiyyīn wa-ikhtilāf al-muṣallīn*. Edited by Hellmut Ritter. Wiesbaden: Franz Steiner, 1980.

Ashᶜarī, Abū al-Ḥasan ᶜAlī b. Ismāᶜīl. *Risālat istiḥsān al-khawḍ fī ᶜilm al-kalām (= al-Ḥathth ᶜalā al-baᶜth)*. Edited by Muḥammad al-Walī al-Ashᶜarī al-Qādirī al-Rifāᶜī. Beirut: Dār al-Mashārīᶜ, 1995.

Ashᶜarī Qummī, Saᶜd b. ᶜAbdullāh. *Kitāb al-Maqālāt wa-l-firaq*. Edited by Muḥammad Jawād Mashkūr. Tehran: ᶜAṭāᵓī, 1963.

Atiyeh, George N. 'Al-Kindi's concept of man'. *Hamdard Islamicus*, 3, no. 2 (1980), 35–46.

ᶜAyyād, al-Ḥabīb. *al-Kalām fī al-tawḥīd*. Beirut: Dār al-Madār al-Islāmī, 2009.

Badawī, ᶜAbd al-Raḥmān. *Madhāhib al-islāmiyyīn*. Beirut: Dār al-ᶜIlm li-l-Malāyīn, 1983.

Baḥr al-ᶜUlūm, Mahdī. *al-Fawāᵓid al-rijāliyya*. Edited by Muḥammad Ṣādiq Baḥr al-ᶜUlūm and Ḥusayn Baḥr al-ᶜUlūm. Tehran: Maktabat al-Ṣādiq, 1363 SH.

Baḥrānī, Yūsuf. *al-Ḥadāᵓiq al-nāḍira fī aḥkām al-ᶜitra al-ṭāhira*. Edited by ᶜAlī Ākhūndī. Qum: Muᵓassasat al-Nashr al-Islāmī, 1363 SH.

Bakrī, Abū ᶜUbayd ᶜAbdullāh b. ᶜAbd al-ᶜAzīz al-Andalusī. *Muᶜjam mā istaᶜjam*. Edited by Muṣṭafā al-Saqqā. Beirut: ᶜĀlam al-Kutub, 1983.

Balkhī, Abū al-Qāsim ᶜAbdullāh b Aḥmad al-Kaᶜbī. *ᶜUyūn al-masāʾil wa-l-jawābāt*. Edited by Rājiḥ Kurdī, Ḥusayn Khānṣū and ᶜAbd al-Ḥamīd Kurdī. Amman: Dār al-Ḥāmid, 2014.

Bāqillānī, Abū Bakr Muḥammad b. al-Ṭayyib. *al-Inṣāf fī mā yajibu iᶜtiqāduhu wa-lā yajūzu al-jahl bihi*. Edited by ᶜImād al-Dīn Aḥmad Ḥaydar. Beirut: ᶜĀlam al-Kutub, 1986.

Bāqillānī, Abū Bakr Muḥammad b. al-Ṭayyib. *Kitāb al-Bayān ᶜan al-farq bayn al-muᶜjizāt wa-l-karāmāt*. Edited by Richard McCarthy. Beirut: al-Maktaba al-Sharqiyya, 1958.

Bāqillānī, Abū Bakr Muḥammad b. al-Ṭayyib. *Tamhīd al-awāʾil wa-talkhīṣ al-dalāʾil*. Edited by ᶜImād al-Dīn Ḥaydar. Beirut: Muʾassasat al-Kutub al-Thaqāfiyya, 1993.

Bar-Asher, Meir M. *Scripture and Exegesis in Early Imāmī Shiism*. Leiden: Brill, 1999.

Baṣrī, Abū al-Ḥusayn Muḥammad b ᶜAlī. *al-Muᶜtamad fī uṣūl al-fiqh*. Edited by Muḥammad Ḥamīdullāh. Damascus: al-Maᶜhad al-ᶜIlmī al-Faransī li-l-Dirāsāt al-ᶜArabiyya, 1964–5.

Bayhom-Daou, Tamima. *Shaykh Mufid*. Oxford: Oneworld, 2005.

Berkey, Jonathan. 'Islam'. In *The New Cambridge History of Islam*, vol. 4, *Islamic Cultures and Societies to the End of the Eighteenth Century*, edited by Robert Irwin, 19–59. Cambridge: Cambridge University Press, 2010.

Bloom, Harold. *The Anxiety of Influence: A Theory of Poetry*. Oxford: Oxford University Press, 1997.

Böwering, Gerhard. 'Covenant'. *Encyclopaedia of the Qurʾān* [= *EQ*]. Brill Online, 2012.

Bray, Julia. 'Practical Muᶜtazilism: The case of al-Tanūkhī'. In *ᶜAbbasid Studies: Occasional Papers of the School of ᶜAbbasid Studies, Cambridge, 2002*, edited by James E. Montgomery, 111–26. Leuven: Peeters, 2004.

Brockelmann, Carl. *Geschichte der arabischen Litteratur, Supplement I*. Leiden: Brill, 1996.

Brockelmann, Carl. 'Al-Sharīf al-Murtaḍā'. *Encyclopaedia of Islam, 2nd edn* [= *EI²*], 7 (1993), 634.

Brown, Jonathan A. C. *Hadith: Muhammad's Legacy in the Medieval and Modern World*. Oxford: Oneworld, 2009.

Bulliet, Richard W. *Conversion to Islam in the Medieval Period: An Essay in Quantitative History*. Cambridge, MA: Harvard University Press, 1979.

Bulliet, Richard W. *The Patricians of Nishapur: A Study in Medieval Islamic Social History*. Cambridge, MA: Harvard University Press, 1972.

Busse, Heribert. *Chalif und Grosskönig: Die Buyiden im Iraq (945–1055)*. Beirut and Wiesbaden: Franz Steiner, 1969.

Butterworth, Charles. 'Ethical and political philosophy'. In *The Cambridge Companion to Arabic Philosophy*, edited by Peter Adamson and Richard C. Taylor, 266–86. Cambridge: Cambridge University Press, 2005.

Cahen, Claude. 'Buwayhids or Būyids'. *Encyclopaedia of Islam, 2nd edn* [= *EI²*], 1 (1979), 1350.

Cahen, Claude. 'Ibn al-ᶜAmīd'. *Encyclopaedia of Islam, 2nd edn* [= *EI²*]. Brill Online, 2016.

Calder, Norman. 'Doubt and prerogative: The emergence of an Imāmī Shīᶜī theory of *ijtihād*'. *Studia Islamica*, 70 (1989), 57–78.

Carli, Silvia. 'Poetry is more philosophical than history: Aristotle on mimêsis and form'. *Review of Metaphysics*, 64, no. 2 (2010), 303–36.

Clarke, Lynda. 'Faith and unfaith in pre-occultation Shīᶜism: A study in theology and social history'. In *Islam and Other Religions, Pathways to Dialogue: Essays in Honour of Mahmoud Mustafa Ayoub*, edited by Irfan A. Omar, 97–112. London: Routledge, 2006.

Cook, Michael. *Commanding Right and Forbidding Wrong in Islamic Thought.* Cambridge: Cambridge University Press, 2010.

Cooperson, Michael. *Classical Arabic Biography: The Heirs of the Prophets in the Age of al-Maᵓmūn.* Cambridge: Cambridge University Press, 2000.

Corbin, Henry. 'The meaning of the Imam for Shiᶜa spirituality'. In *Shiᶜism: Doctrines, Thought, and Spirituality*, edited by Seyyed Hossein Nasr, Hamid Dabashi and Seyyid Vali Reza Nasr, 167–87. Albany: State University of New York Press, 1988.

Crone, Patricia. *The Nativist Prophets of Early Islamic Iran: Rural Revolt and Local Zoroastrianism.* New York: Cambridge University Press, 2012.

Cullmann, Oscar. *Salvation in History.* New York: Harper & Row, 1967.

Daftary, Farhad. *The Ismāᶜīlīs: Their History and Doctrines.* Cambridge: Cambridge University Press, 2007.

Dakake, Maria Massi. *The Charismatic Community: Shiᶜite Identity in Early Islam.* Albany: State University of New York Press, 2007.

de Blois, François C. 'Ṣābiᵓ'. *Encyclopaedia of Islam, 2nd edn* [= *EI*²], 8 (1995), 672.

Dhahabī, Shams al-Dīn Muḥammad b. Aḥmad. *Mīzān al-iᶜtidāl.* Edited by ᶜAlī Muḥammad al-Bajāwī. Beirut: Dār al-Maᶜrifa, 1963.

Dhahabī, Shams al-Dīn Muḥammad b. Aḥmad. *Siyar aᶜlām al-nubalāᵓ.* Edited by Shuᶜayb al-Arnāᵓūṭ. Beirut: Muᵓassasat al-Risāla, 1413 H.

Dhahabī, Shams al-Dīn Muḥammad b. Aḥmad. *Tārīkh al-Islām wa-ṭabaqāt al-mashāhīr wa-l-aᶜlām.* Edited by Muḥammad Maḥmūd Ḥamdān. Beirut: Dār al-Kutub al-Islāmiyya, Dār al-Kitāb al-Lubnānī, 1985–.

Dhanani, Alnoor. 'Atomism'. *Encyclopaedia of Islam, 3rd edn* [= *EI*³]. Brill Online, 2016.

Dhanani, Alnoor. *The Physical Theory of Kalām: Atoms, Space, and Void in Basrian Muᶜtazilī Cosmology.* Leiden: Brill, 1994.

Diaz-Bone, Rainer, Andrea D. Bührmann, Encarnación Gutiérrez Rodríguez, Werner Schneider, Gavin Kendall and Francisco Tirado. 'The field of Foucaultian discourse analysis: Structures, developments and perspectives'. *Historical Social Research / Historische Sozialforschung*, 33, no. 1 (2008), 7–28.

Djebli, Moktar. 'Encore à propos de l'authenticité du *Nahj al-balagha*!'. *Studia Islamica*, 75 (1992), 33–56.

Djebli, Moktar. 'Al-Sharīf al-Raḍī'. *Encyclopaedia of Islam, 2nd edn* [= *EI*²], 9 (1997), 340.

Donner, Fred M. *Narratives of Islamic Origins: The Beginnings of Islamic Historical Writing.* Princeton, NJ: Darwin Press, 1998.

Düzgün, Şaban Ali. 'Contextualizing the term "religious experience" in theological discourse'. *Islam and Christian-Muslim Relations*, 15, no. 4 (2004), 497–514.

El-Bizri, Nader. 'God: Essence and attributes'. In *The Cambridge Companion to Classical Islamic Theology*, edited by Tim Winter, 121–40. Cambridge: Cambridge University Press, 2008.

El-Hibri, Tayeb. *Parable and Politics in Early Islamic History: The Rashidun Caliphs*. New York: Columbia University Press, 2010.

Elkaisy-Friemuth, Maha. *God and Humans in Islamic Thought: ᶜAbd al-Jabbār, Ibn Sīnā and al-Ghazālī*. London: Routledge, 2006.

El-Omari, Racha. 'The theology of Abū l-Qāsim al-Balḫī/al-Kaᶜbī (d. 319/931): A study of its sources and reception'. PhD dissertation, Yale University, 2006.

El-Rouayheb, Khaled. 'Must God tell us the truth? A problem in Ashᶜarī theology'. In *Islamic Cultures, Islamic Contexts: Essays in Honor of Professor Patricia Crone*, edited by Behnam Sadeghi et al., 411–29. Leiden: Brill, 2015.

Erder, Yoram. 'The Karaites and Muᶜtazilism'. In *A History of Jewish–Muslim Relations: From the Origins to the Present Day*, edited by Abdelwahab Meddeb and Benjamin Stora, 778–87. Princeton, NJ: Princeton University Press, 2013.

Flanagan, John. 'Al-Rummānī'. *Encyclopaedia of Islam, 2nd edn* [= *EI*^{2}], 8 (1995), 614.

Frank, Richard M. 'Abu Hashim's theory of "states": Its structure and function'. In *Early Islamic Theology: The Muᶜtazilites and al-Ashᶜarī*, edited by Dimitri Gutas, 85–100. Burlington, VT: Ashgate, 2007.

Frank, Richard M. 'Attribute, attribution, and being: Three Islamic views'. In *Philosophies of Existence, Ancient and Medieval*, edited by Parviz Morewedge, 258–78. New York: Fordham University Press, 1982.

Frank, Richard M. 'The autonomy of the human agent in the teaching of ᶜAbd al-Ğabbar'. *Le Muséon*, 95 (1982), 323–55.

Frank, Richard M. *Beings and Their Attributes: The Teaching of the Basrian School of the Muᶜtazila in the Classical Period*. Albany: State University of New York Press, 1978.

Frank, Richard M. 'Al-maᶜdūm wal-mawjūd: The non-existent, the existent, and the possible in the teaching of Abū Hāshim and his followers'. In *Early Islamic Theology: The Muᶜtazilites and al-Ashᶜarī*, edited by Dimitri Gutas, 185–209. Burlington, VT: Ashgate, 2007.

Frank, Richard M. 'Moral obligation in classical Muslim theology'. *Journal of Religious Ethics*, 11, no. 2 (1983), 204–23.

Frank, Richard M. 'The science of *kalām*'. *Arabic Sciences and Philosophy*, 2 (1992), 7–37.

Frank, Richard M. 'Two short dogmatic works of Abū l-Qāsim al-Qushayrī. First part: Edition and translation of "Lumaᶜ fī l-iᶜtiqād"'. *Mélanges de l'Institut Dominicain d'Études Orientales (MIDEO)*, 15 (1982), 53–74.

Frank, Richard M. 'Yā Kalām'. In *Arabic Theology, Arabic Philosophy*, edited by James E. Montgomery, 5–14. Leuven: Peeters, 2006.

Gardet, Louis. 'Hayūlā'. *Encyclopaedia of Islam, 2nd edn* [= *EI*^{2}]. Brill Online, 2012.

Ghaffār, ᶜAbd al-Rasūl. *al-Kulaynī wa-l-Kāfī*. Qum: Muʾassasat al-Nashr al-Islāmī, 1416 H.

Gilliot, Claude. 'Attributes of God'. *Encyclopaedia of Islam, 3rd edn* [= *EI*³]. Brill Online, 2016.

Gimaret, Daniel. 'Muᶜtazila'. *Encyclopaedia of Islam, 2nd edn* [= *EI*²]. Brill Online, 2012.

Gimaret, Daniel. 'Taklīf'. *Encyclopaedia of Islam, 2nd edn* [= *EI*²]. Brill Online, 2012.

Gleave, Robert. 'Recent research into the history of early Shiᶜism'. *History Compass*, 7, no. 6 (2009), 1593–605.

Goichon, A. M. 'Ḥayy b. Yaḳẓān'. *Encyclopaedia of Islam, 2nd edn* [= *EI*²]. Brill Online, 2016.

Gorji, Abulqasim. 'Shīᶜism in relation to various Islamic sects'. *al-Tawḥīd*, 1, no. 2 (1984), 43–50.

Gulpaygānī, Luṭfullāh al-Ṣāfī. *Risālatān ḥawla al-ᶜiṣma*. Qum: Dār al-Qurʾān al-Karīm, 1983.

Gutas, Dimitri. 'The study of Arabic philosophy in the twentieth century: An essay on the historiography of Arabic philosophy'. *British Journal of Middle Eastern Studies*, 29, no. 1 (2002), 5–25.

Haider, Najam. *The Origins of the Shīᶜa: Identity, Ritual, and Sacred Space in Eighth-Century Kūfa*. Cambridge: Cambridge University Press, 2011.

Ḥājj, Muḥammad Salāma. *al-Shaykh al-Mufīd wa-l-tajdīd al-kalāmī*. Beirut: Dār al-ᶜIlm, 2002.

Haider, Najam. *Shīᶜī Islam: An Introduction*. Cambridge: Cambridge University Press, 2014.

Ḥalabī, Abū al-Ṣalāḥ Taqī al-Dīn b. Najm al-Dīn. *al-Kāfī fī al-fiqh*. Edited by Riḍā Ustādī. Isfahan: Maktabat al-Imām Amīr al-Muʾminīn ᶜAlī al-ᶜĀmma, 1403 H.

Ḥalabī, Abū al-Ṣalāḥ Taqī al-Dīn b. Najm al-Dīn. *Taqrīb al-maᶜārif*. Edited by Fāris Tabrīziyān Ḥassūn. Qum: n.p., 1417 H.

Hakyemez, Cemil. 'Bada and its role in the debates over Shiᶜi doctrine'. *American Journal of Islamic Social Sciences*, 25, no. 1 (2008), 20–39.

Halm, Heinz. *Shiᶜism*. Translated by Janet Watson and Marian Hill. Edinburgh: Edinburgh University Press, 2004.

Ḥasanī, Hāshim Maᶜrūf. *al-Shīᶜa bayn al-Ashāᶜira wa-l-Muᶜtazila*. Beirut: Dār al-Nashr li-l-Jāmiᶜiyyīn, 1964.

Hashas, Mohammed. 'Abdolkarim Soroush: The Neo-Muᶜtazilite that buries classical Islamic political theology in defence of religious democracy and pluralism'. *Studia Islamica*, 109, no. 1 (2014), 147–73.

Havemann, Axel. 'Naḳīb al-As͟hrāf'. *Encyclopaedia of Islam, 2nd edn* [= *EI*²], 7 (1993), 926.

Heemskerk, Margaretha T. 'ᶜAbd al-Jabbār b. Aḥmad al-Hamadhānī'. In *Encyclopaedia of Islam, 3rd edn* [= *EI*³]. Brill Online, 2016.

Heemskerk, Margaretha T. 'Speech'. *Encyclopaedia of the Qurʾān* [= *EQ*]. Brill Online, 2012.

Heemskerk, Margaretha T. *Suffering in the Muᶜtazilite Theology: ᶜAbd al-Jabbār's Teaching on Pain and Divine Justice*. Leiden: Brill, 2000.

Hildebrandt, Thomas. *Neo-Muᶜtazilismus? Intention und Kontext im modernen arabischen Umgang mit dem rationalistischen Erbe des Islam*. Leiden: Brill, 2007.

Ḥillī, al-ᶜAllāma al-Ḥasan b. Yūsuf b. al-Muṭahhar. *Mukhtalaf al-Shīᶜa*. Qum: Muʾassasat al-Nashr al-Islāmī, 1412–20 H.

Ḥimyarī, ᶜAbdullāh b. Jaᶜfar. *Qurb al-isnād*. Qum: Muʾassasat Āl al-Bayt, 1413 H.

Hinds, Martin. 'Miḥna'. *Encyclopaedia of Islam, 2nd edn* [= *EI²*]. Brill Online, 2012.
Holtzman, Livnat. 'Islamic theology'. In *Handbook of Medieval Studies: Terms, Methods, Trends*, edited by Albrecht Classen, 1:56–68. Berlin: De Gruyter, 2010.
Hourani, George F. 'Islamic and non-Islamic origins of Muʿtazilite ethical rationalism'. *International Journal of Middle East Studies*, 7 (1976), 59–87.
Hourani, George F. *Islamic Rationalism: The Ethics of ʿAbd al-Jabbār*. Oxford: Clarendon Press, 1971.
Hurvitz, Nimrod. 'Miḥna as self-defense'. *Studia Islamica*, 92 (2001), 93–111.
Ibn Abī al-Ḥadīd, ʿAbd al-Ḥamīd. *Sharḥ Nahj al-balāgha*. Edited by Muḥammad Abū al-Faḍl Ibrāhīm. Cairo: Dār Iḥyāʾ al-Kutub al-ʿArabiyya, 1959.
Ibn al-Athīr, ʿIzz al-Dīn ʿAlī b. Muḥammad. *al-Kāmil fī al-tārīkh*. Beirut: Dār Ṣādir, 1965–7.
Ibn Ḥajar al-ʿAsqalānī, Aḥmad b. ʿAlī. *Lisān al-mīzān*. Beirut: Muʾassasat al-Aʿlamī, 1971.
Ibn Ḥajar al-ʿAsqalānī, Aḥmad b. ʿAlī. *Tahdhīb al-Tahdhīb*. Beirut: Dār al-Fikr, 1984.
Ibn Ḥanbal, Aḥmad b. Muḥammad. *Musnad Aḥmad b. Ḥanbal*. Beirut: Dār Ṣādir, n.d.
Ibn Ḥazm, ʿAlī b. Aḥmad. *al-Fiṣal fī al-milal wa-l-ahwāʾ wa-l-niḥal*. Cairo: Muḥammad ʿAlī Ṣubayḥ, 1964.
Ibn Ḥimyar, ʿAlī b. Aḥmad al-Sabtī. *Tanzīh al-anbiyāʾ ʿammā nasaba ilayhim ḥuthālat al-aghbiyāʾ*. Edited by Muḥammad al-Dāya. Damascus: Dār al-Fikr, 1990.
Ibn ʿInaba, Aḥmad b. ʿAlī. *ʿUmdat al-ṭālib fī ansāb Āl Abī Ṭālib*. Edited by Muḥammad Ḥasan al-Ṭālaqānī. Najaf: al-Maṭbaʿa al-Ḥaydariyya, 1961.
Ibn al-Jawzī, Abū al-Faraj ʿAbd al-Raḥmān. *al-Muntaẓam fī tārīkh al-mulūk wa-l-umam*. Edited by Muḥammad ʿAbd al-Qādir ʿAṭā and Muṣṭafā ʿAbd al-Qādir ʿAṭā. Beirut: Dār al-Kutub al-ʿIlmiyya, 1992.
Ibn Khallikān, Aḥmad b. Muḥammad. *Wafayāt al-aʿyān*. Edited by Iḥsān ʿAbbās. Beirut: Dār al-Thaqāfa, 1968–72.
Ibn Mattawayh, al-Ḥasan b. Aḥmad. *al-Majmūʿ fī al-Muḥīṭ bi-l-taklīf*. Edited by J. J. Houben, Daniel Gimaret and Jan Peters. Beirut: Dār al-Mashriq, 1965–99.
Ibn al-Murtaḍā, Aḥmad b. Yaḥyā. *Ṭabaqāt al-Muʿtazila*. Edited by Susanna Diwald-Wilzer. Beirut: Dār Maktabat al-Ḥayāh, 1980.
Ibn Qūlawayh, Jaʿfar b. Muḥammad al-Qummī. *Kāmil al-ziyārāt*. Edited by Jawād Qayyūmī Iṣfahānī. Qum: Muʾassasat al-Nashr al-Islāmī, 1417 H.
Ibn Qutayba, ʿAbdullāh b. Muslim. *Gharīb al-ḥadīth*. Edited by Naʿīm Zarzūr. Beirut: Dār al-Kutub al-ʿIlmiyya, 1988.
Ibn Qutayba, ʿAbdullāh b. Muslim. *Taʾwīl mukhtalif al-ḥadīth*. Edited by Muḥammad Muḥyī al-Dīn al-Aṣfar. Beirut: al-Maktab al-Islāmī, 1999.
Ibn Saʿd, Muḥammad. *al-Ṭabaqāt al-kubrā*. Beirut: Dār Ṣādir, 1998.
Ibn Shahrāshūb, Muḥammad b. ʿAlī. *Maʿālim al-ʿulamāʾ*. Edited by Muḥammad Ṣādiq Baḥr al-ʿUlūm. Najaf: al-Maṭbaʿa al-Ḥaydariyya, 1961.
Ibn Ṭāwūs, Raḍī al-Dīn ʿAlī b. Mūsā. *Faraj al-mahmūm fī tārīkh ʿulamāʾ al-nujūm*. Qum: Manshūrāt al-Raḍī, 1363 SH.
Ibn Taymiyya, Aḥmad b. ʿAbd al-Ḥalīm. *Minhāj al-sunna al-nabawiyya fī naqḍ kalām al-Shīʿa wa-l-Qadariyya*. Bulaq: al-Maṭbaʿa al-Kubrā al-Amīriyya, 1321–2 H.

Ibn Zuhra, Ḥamza b. ᶜAlī al-Ḥalabī. *Ghunyat al-nuzūᶜ ilā ᶜilmay al-uṣūl wa-l-furūᶜ*. Edited by Ibrāhīm Bahādirī. Qum: Muᵓassasat al-Imām al-Ṣādiq, 1417–18 H.

Iqbāl, ᶜAbbās. *Āl Nawbakht*. Translated by ᶜAlī al-Asadī. Mashhad: Majmaᶜ al-Buḥūth al-Islāmiyya, 2004.

Iskāfī, Muḥammad b. Hammām. *al-Tamḥīṣ*. Qum: Madrasat al-Imām al-Mahdī, 1404 H.

Ivry, Alfred. 'Arabic and Islamic psychology and philosophy of mind'. In *The Stanford Encyclopedia of Philosophy*, edited by Edward N. Zalta. Summer 2012 edn. http://plato.stanford.edu/archives/sum2012/entries/arabic-islamic-mind.

Jadᶜān, Fahmī. *al-Miḥna: Baḥth fī jadaliyyat al-dīnī wa-l-siyāsī fī al-Islām*. Amman: Dār al-Shurūq, 1989.

Jadᶜānī, Muḥammad b. Ḥāmid. 'al-Ṣila bayn al-tashayyuᶜ wa-l-iᶜtizāl'. MA thesis, Jāmiᶜat Umm al-Qurā, 2000.

Jaᶜfarī, Muḥammad Riḍā. 'al-Kalām ᶜind al-Imāmiyya: Nashᵓatuhu, taṭawwuruhu wa-mawqiᶜ al-Shaykh al-Mufīd minhu'. *Turāthunā*, 30–1 (1992), 143–299.

Jaᶜfariyān, Rasūl (ed.). *Davāzdah risāliy-i fiqhī dar bāriy-i namāz-i Jumᶜa az rūzgār-i Ṣafavī*. Qum: Anṣāriyān, 1381 SH.

Jafri, Husain. *Origins and Early Development of Shiᶜa Islam*. London: Longman, 1978.

Jāḥiẓ, Abū ᶜUthmān ᶜAmr b. Baḥr. *Kitāb al-Ḥayawān*. Edited by ᶜAbd al-Salām Hārūn. Cairo: ᶜĪsā al-Bābī al-Ḥalabī, 1965.

Jāḥiẓ, Abū ᶜUthmān ᶜAmr b. Baḥr. *Kitāb al-Tarbīᶜ wa-l-tadwīir*. Edited by Charles Pellat. Damascus: Institut Français, 1955.

Jāḥiẓ, Abū ᶜUthmān ᶜAmr b. Baḥr. 'Risāla fī al-nābita'. In *Rasāᵓil al-Jāḥiẓ*, edited by ᶜAbd al-Salām Hārūn, 2:7–23. Beirut: Dār al-Jīl, 1991.

Jāḥiẓ, Abū ᶜUthmān ᶜAmr b. Baḥr. 'Risālat ḥujaj al-nubuwwa'. In *Rasāᵓil al-Jāḥiẓ*, edited by ᶜAbd al-Salām Hārūn, 3:221–82. Beirut: Dār al-Jīl, 1991.

Jāḥiẓ, Abū ᶜUthmān ᶜAmr b. Baḥr. 'Risālat al-tarbīᶜ wa-l-tadwīr'. In *Rasāᵓil al-Jāḥiẓ*, edited by ᶜAbd al-Salām Hārūn, 3:53–110. Beirut: Dār al-Jīl, 1991.

Jāḥiẓ, Abū ᶜUthmān ᶜAmr b. Baḥr. 'Risālat al-ᶜUthmāniyya'. In *Rasāᵓil al-Jāḥiẓ*, edited by ᶜAbd al-Salām Hārūn, 4:19–46. Beirut: Dār al-Jīl, 1991.

Jishumī, al-Ḥākim al-Muḥassin b. Karāma. *al-Risāla fī naṣīḥat al-ᶜāmma*. Edited by Jamāl al-Shāmī. Yemen: Markaz Ahl al-Bayt, 2016.

Jishumī, al-Ḥākim al-Muḥassin b. Karāma. *Rasāᵓil al-Shahīd al-Thānī*. Qum: lithograph.

Jishumī, al-Ḥākim al-Muḥassin b. Karāma. *Risālat Iblīs ilā ikhwānihi al-manāḥīs*. Edited by Ḥusayn al-Mudarrisī. Beirut: Dār al-Muntakhab al-ᶜArabī, 1995.

Jishumī, al-Ḥākim al-Muḥassin b. Karāma. 'Sharḥ ᶜUyūn al-masāᵓil'. In *Faḍl al-iᶜtizāl wa-ṭabaqāt al-Muᶜtazila*, edited by Fuᵓād al-Sayyid, 365–93. Tunis: al-Dār al-Tūnisiyya li-l-Nashr, 1393 H.

Jishumī, al-Ḥākim al-Muḥassin b. Karāma. *Tanbīh al-ghāfilīn ᶜan faḍāᵓil al-Ṭālibiyyīn*. Edited by Ibrāhīm al-Darsī. Ṣaᶜda, Yemen: Markaz Ahl al-Bayt, 2000.

Jørgensen, Marianne and Louise J. Phillips. *Discourse Analysis as Theory and Method*. London: Sage, 2002.

Jurjānī, ᶜAlī b. Muḥammad. *Sharḥ al-Mawāqif*. Cairo: Maṭbaᶜat al-Saᶜāda, 1907–9.

Juwaynī, ᶜAbd al-Malik b. ᶜAbdullāh. *al-Irshād ilā qawāṭiᶜ al-adilla fī uṣūl al-iᶜtiqād*. Edited by Muḥammad Yūsuf Mūsā and ᶜAlī ᶜAbd al-Munᶜim ᶜAbd al-Ḥamīd. Cairo: Maktabat al-Khānjī, 1950.

Kalābādhī, Muḥammad b. Isḥāq. *al-Taᶜarruf li-madhhab ahl al-taṣawwuf*. Edited by ᶜAbd al-Ḥalīm Maḥmūd and Ṭāhā ᶜAbd al-Bāqī Surūr. Cairo: Dār Iḥyāʾ al-Kutub al-ᶜArabiyya, 1960.

Karājikī, Abū al-Fatḥ. *Kanz al-fawāʾid*. Qum: Muṣṭafawī, 1369 SH.

Karājikī, Abū al-Fatḥ. *al-Taᶜajjub min aghlāṭ al-ᶜāmma fī masʾalat al-imāma*. Edited by Fāris Ḥassūn Karīm. Qum: Dār al-Ghadīr, 1421 H.

Karakī, al-Muḥaqqiq ᶜAlī b. al-Ḥusayn b. ᶜAbd al-ᶜĀlī. *Qāṭiᶜat al-lajāj fī taḥqīq ḥall al-kharāj*. Qum: Muʾassasat al-Nashr al-Islāmī, 1410 H.

Keating, Sandra Toenies. 'Some reflections on the early discussion concerning the *ṣifāt Allāh*: "Cross-fertilization and cooperation in the Islamic milieu"'. *Islam and Christian-Muslim Relations*, 22, no. 1 (2011), 23–35.

Kenney, Jeff. 'The politics of sects and typologies'. *Nova Religio*, 6, no. 1 (2002), 137–46.

Khalidi, Tarif. *Arabic Historical Thought in the Classical Period*. Cambridge: Cambridge University Press, 1996.

Khamenei, Ali. 'The place of al-Mufīd in the development of Shiᶜi kalam and fiqh'. *al-Tawḥīd*, 10, no. 2–3 (1993), 193–225.

Kharsān, Ṭālib. *Nashʾat al-tashayyuᶜ*. Qum: Manshūrāt al-Sharīf al-Raḍī, 1991.

Khaṭīb Baghdādī, Aḥmad b. ᶜAlī. *Tārīkh Baghdād*. Edited by Muṣṭafā ᶜAṭā. Beirut: Dār al-Kutub al-ᶜIlmiyya, 1997.

Khayyāṭ, Abū al-Ḥusayn ᶜAbd al-Raḥīm b. Muḥammad. *al-Intiṣār wa-l-radd ᶜalā Ibn al-Rāwandī al-mulḥid*. Edited by Henrik S. Nyberg. Cairo: Maṭbaᶜat Dār al-Kutub al-Miṣriyya, 1925.

Khūʾī, Abū al-Qāsim. *Muᶜjam rijāl al-ḥadīth*. Qum: Markaz Nashr Āthār al-Shīᶜa, 1410 H.

Khʷānsārī, Muḥammad Bāqir. *Rawḍāt al-jannāt fī aḥwāl al-ᶜulamāʾ wa-l-sādāt*. Beirut: al-Dār al-Islāmiyya, 1991.

Kinberg, Leah. 'Dreams and sleep'. *Encyclopaedia of the Qurʾān* [= *EQ*]. Brill Online, 2016.

Kohlberg, Etan. 'Introduction' to *Shīᶜism*. Edited by Etan Kohlberg, i–xlix. Burlington, VT: Ashgate, 2003.

Kohlberg, Etan. *A Medieval Muslim Scholar at Work: Ibn Ṭāwūs and His Library*. Leiden: Brill, 1992.

Kohlberg, Etan. 'Muwāfāt doctrines in Muslim theology'. *Studia Islamica*, 57 (1983), 47–66.

Kraemer, Joel L. *Humanism in the Renaissance of Islam: The Cultural Revival during the Buyid Age*. Leiden: Brill, 1986.

Kraus, Paul. 'Ibn al-Rāwandī or al-Rēwendī'. *Encyclopaedia of Islam, 2nd edn* [= *EI*²], 3 (1979), 905.

Kulaynī, Muḥammad b. Yaᶜqūb. *al-Kāfī*. Edited by ᶜAlī Akbar Ghaffārī. Tehran: Dār al-Kutub al-Islāmiyya, 1388 H.

Kulinich, Alena. 'Beyond theology: Muᶜtazilite scholars and their authority in al-Rummānī's *tafsīr*'. *Bulletin of the School of Oriental and African Studies*, 78, no. 1 (2015), 135–48.

Lambton, Ann K. 'Political theory and practice'. In *Expectation of the Millennium: Shiᶜism in History*, edited by Seyyed Hossein Nasr, Hamid Dabashi and Seyyed Vali Reza Nasr, 92–107. Albany: State University of New York Press, 1989.

Lassner, Jacob. *The Shaping of ᶜAbbāsid Rule*. Princeton, NJ: Princeton University Press, 1980.

Lockman, Zachary. *Contending Visions of the Middle East: The History and Politics of Orientalism*. Cambridge: Cambridge University Press, 2010.

Maᶜarrī, Abū al-ᶜAlāᵓ Aḥmad. *Saqṭ al-zand*. Beirut: Dār Ṣādir, 2005.

Madan, ᶜAlī. *Taṭawwur ᶜilm al-kalām al-Imāmī: Dirāsa fī taḥawwulāt al-manhaj ḥattā al-qarn al-sābiᶜ al-hijrī*. Baghdad: Markaz Dirāsāt Falsafat al-Dīn, 2010.

Madelung, Wilferd. 'Abū l-Ḥusayn al-Baṣrī's proof for the existence of God'. In *Arabic Theology, Arabic Philosophy*, edited by James Montgomery, 273–80. Leuven: Peeters, 2006.

Madelung, Wilferd. 'ᶜAlam-al-Hodā'. *Encyclopaedia Iranica* [= *EIr*], 1985. http://www.iranicaonline.org/articles/alam-al-hoda-abul-qasem-ali-b.

Madelung, Wilferd. 'The assumption of the title Shāhānshāh by the Būyids and "the reign of the Daylam (Dawlat al-Daylam)"'. *Journal of Near Eastern Studies*, 28, no. 3 (1969), 168–83.

Madelung, Wilferd. 'Badāᵓ'. *Encyclopaedia Iranica* [= *EIr*], 1988. http://www.iranicaonline.org/articles/bada-theological-term.

Madelung, Wilferd. 'Imāma'. *Encyclopaedia of Islam, 2nd edn* [= *EI²*], 3 (1979), 1163–9.

Madelung, Wilferd. 'Imâmism and Muᶜtazilite theology'. In *Le Shîᶜisme Imâmite*, 13–30. Paris: Presses Universitaires de France, 1970.

Madelung, Wilferd. 'ᶜIṣma'. *Encyclopaedia of Islam, 2nd edn* [= *EI²*], 4 (1978), 182.

Madelung, Wilferd. 'The origins of the controversy concerning the creation of the Koran'. In *Orientalia hispanica sive studia F. M. Pareja octogenario dicata*, vol. 1, *Arabica-Islamica*, edited by J. M. Barral, 504–25. Leiden: Brill, 1974.

Madelung, Wilferd. *The Succession to Muhammad: A Study of the Early Caliphate*. Cambridge: Cambridge University Press, 1997.

Madelung, Wilferd. 'A treatise of the Sharīf al-Murtaḍā on the legality of working for the government (masᵓala fī 'l-ᶜamal maᶜa 'l-sulṭān)'. *Bulletin of the School of Oriental and African Studies*, 43, no. 1 (1980), 18–31.

Madelung, Wilferd. 'Zaydiyya'. *Encyclopaedia of Islam, 2nd edn* [= *EI²*], 11 (2002), 477.

Madelung, Wilferd and Sabine Schmidtke (eds). *Al-Ṣāḥib Ibn ᶜAbbād, Promoter of Rational Theology: Two Muᶜtazilī* Kalām *Texts from the Cairo Geniza*. Leiden: Brill, 2016.

Majlisī, Muḥammad Bāqir. *Biḥār al-anwār*. Beirut: Muᵓassasat al-Wafāᵓ, 1983.

Mānkdīm, Aḥmad b. al-Ḥusayn. *Sharḥ al-Uṣūl al-khamsa*. Edited by ᶜAbd al-Karīm ᶜUthmān. Cairo: Maktabat Wahba, 1965.

Marcinkowski, Muhammad I. 'Twelver Shīᶜite scholarship and Būyid domination: A glance on the life and times of Ibn Bābawayh al-Shaykh al-Ṣadūq (d. 381/991)'. *Islamic Quarterly*, 45, no. 3 (2001), 199–222.

Maᶜrifat, Muḥammad Hādī. *al-Tamhīd fī ᶜulūm al-Qurᵓān*. Qum: Manshūrāt Dhawī al-Qurbā, 1431 H.

Marquardt, Manfred. 'Perseverance'. In *Religion Past and Present*. Brill Online, 2016.

Martin, Richard C. 'Inimitability'. *Encyclopaedia of the Qurʾān* [= *EQ*]. Brill Online, 2012.
Martin, Richard C, Mark R. Woodward and Dwi S. Atmaja. *Defenders of Reason in Islam: Muʿtazilism from Medieval School to Modern Symbol.* Oxford: Oneworld, 1997.
Masʿūdī, ʿAlī b. al-Ḥusayn. *Murūj al-dhahab wa-maʿādin al-jawhar.* Edited by Yūsuf Dāghir. Beirut: Dār al-Andalus, 1965.
Maṭrūdī, Muḥammad Ibrāhīm. *al-Sharīf al-Murtaḍā wa-adabuhu.* Riyadh: M. I. al-Maṭrūdī, 1992.
Maʿtūq, Aḥmad. *al-Sharīf al-Murtaḍā: Ḥayātuhu, thaqāfatuhu, adabuhu wa-naqduhu.* Beirut: al-Muʾassasa al-ʿArabiyya li-l-Dirāsāt wa-l-Nashr, 2008.
Māwardī, ʿAlī b. Muḥammad. *al-Aḥkām al-sulṭāniyya wa-l-wilāyāt al-dīniyya.* Cairo: Muṣṭafā al-Bābī al-Ḥalabī, 1966.
Mayer, Toby. 'Ibn Sīnā's "Burhān al-ṣiddīqīn"'. *Journal of Islamic Studies*, 12, no. 1 (2001), 18–39.
Māzandarānī, Muḥammad Ṣāliḥ b. Aḥmad. *Sharḥ Uṣūl al-Kāfī.* Edited by ʿAlī ʿĀshūr. Beirut: Dār Iḥyāʾ al-Turāth al-ʿArabī, 2000.
McDermott, Martin J. 'A debate between al-Mufīd and al-Bāqillānī'. In *Recherches d'Islamologie: Recueil d'articles offert à Georges C. Anawati et Louis Gardet par leurs collègues et amis*, 223–35. Louvain: Peeters, 1977.
McDermott, Martin J. *The Theology of al-Shaikh al-Mufīd (d. 413/1022).* Beirut: Dār al-Mashriq, 1978.
McGrath, Alister E. *The Genesis of Doctrine: A Study in the Foundations of Doctrinal Criticism.* Vancouver: Regent College Publishing, 1997.
Melchert, Christopher. 'The adversaries of Aḥmad Ibn Ḥanbal'. *Arabica*, 44, no. 2 (1997), 234–53.
Miskawayh, Abū ʿAlī Aḥmad b. Muḥammad. *Tajārib al-umam wa-taʿāqub al-himam.* Edited by Abū al-Qāsim Imāmī. Tehran: Surūsh, 2001–2.
Modarressi, Hossein. *Crisis and Consolidation in the Formative Period of Shīʿite Islam: Abū Jaʿfar ibn Qiba al-Rāzī and His Contribution to Imāmite Shīʿite Thought.* Princeton, NJ: Darwin Press, 1993.
Modarressi, Hossein. 'Early debates on the integrity of the Qurʾān: A brief survey'. *Studia Islamica*, 77 (1993), 5–39.
Modarressi, Hossein. *An Introduction to Shīʿī Law: A Bibliographical Study.* London: Ithaca Press, 1984.
Modarressi, Hossein. *Tradition and Survival: A Bibliographical Survey of Early Shīʿite Literature.* Oxford: Oneworld, 2003.
Momen, Moojan. *An Introduction to Shiʿi Islam: The History and Doctrines of Twelver Shiʿism.* New Haven, CT: Yale University Press, 1985.
Mottahedeh, Roy. *Loyalty and Leadership in an Early Islamic Society.* Princeton, NJ: Princeton University Press, 1980.
Mufīd, al-Shaykh Muḥammad b. Muḥammad. *ʿAdam sahw al-Nabī.* Edited by Muḥammad Riḍā Ḥusaynī Jalālī. Beirut: Dār al-Mufīd, 1993.
Mufīd, al-Shaykh Muḥammad b. Muḥammad. *Awāʾil al-maqālāt fī al-madhāhib wa-l-mukhtārāt.* Edited by Ibrāhīm Anṣārī. Beirut: Dār al-Mufīd, 1993.

Mufīd, al-Shaykh Muḥammad b. Muḥammad. *al-Fuṣūl al-mukhtāra min al-ᶜUyūn wa-l-Maḥāsin*. Edited by Mīr ᶜAlī Sharīfī. Beirut: Dār al-Mufīd, 1993.

Mufīd, al-Shaykh Muḥammad b. Muḥammad. *al-Ḥikāyāt*. Edited by Muḥammad Riḍā Ḥusaynī Jalālī. Beirut: Dār al-Mufīd, 1993.

Mufīd, al-Shaykh Muḥammad b. Muḥammad. *al-Ifṣāḥ fī imāmat Amīr al-Muʾminīn*. Beirut: Dār al-Mufīd, 1993.

Mufīd, al-Shaykh Muḥammad b. Muḥammad. *al-Iᶜlām bi-mā ittafaqat ᶜalayhi al-Imāmiyya min al-aḥkām*. Edited by Muḥammad al-Ḥassūn. Beirut: Dār al-Mufīd, 1993.

Mufīd, al-Shaykh Muḥammad b. Muḥammad. *al-Irshād fī maᶜrifat ḥujaj Allāh ᶜalā al-ᶜibād*. Beirut: Dār al-Mufīd, 1993.

Mufīd, al-Shaykh Muḥammad b. Muḥammad. *al-Masāʾil al-Ṣāghāniyya*. Edited by Muḥammad al-Qāḍī. Beirut: Dār al-Mufīd, 1993.

Mufīd, al-Shaykh Muḥammad b. Muḥammad. *al-Masāʾil al-Sarawiyya*. Edited by Ṣāʾib ᶜAbd al-Ḥamīd. Beirut: Dār al-Mufīd, 1993.

Mufīd, al-Shaykh Muḥammad b. Muḥammad. *al-Masāʾil al-ᶜUkbariyya*. Edited by ᶜAlī Akbar Ilāhī Khurāsānī. Beirut: Dār al-Mufīd, 1993.

Mufīd, al-Shaykh Muḥammad b. Muḥammad. *Masʾala fī al-irāda*. Beirut: Dār al-Mufīd, 1993.

Mufīd, al-Shaykh Muḥammad b. Muḥammad. *Rasāʾil fī al-ghayba*. Edited by ᶜAlāʾ Āl Jaᶜfar. Beirut: Dār al-Mufīd, 1993.

Mufīd, al-Shaykh Muḥammad b. Muḥammad. *Risāla fī maᶜnā al-mawlā*. Edited by Mahdī Najaf. Beirut: Dār al-Mufīd, 1993.

Mufīd, al-Shaykh Muḥammad b. Muḥammad. *Taṣḥīḥ Iᶜtiqādāt al-Imāmiyya*. Edited by Ḥusayn Dargāhī. Beirut: Dār al-Mufīd, 1993.

[Pseudo-]Mufīd, Muḥammad b. Muḥammad. *al-Ikhtiṣāṣ*. Edited by ᶜAlī Akbar Ghaffārī. Qum: Manshūrāt Jamāᶜat al-Mudarrisīn fī al-Hawza al-ᶜIlmiyya, n.d.

Mughniyya, Muḥammad Jawād. *al-Shīᶜa fī al-mīzān*. Beirut: Dār al-Shurūq, 1979.

Muhajirani, Abbas. 'Twelve-Imām Shiᶜite theological and philosophical thought'. In *Shiᶜism*, edited by Paul Luft and Colin Turner, 2:175–98. London: Routledge, 2008.

Muḥyī al-Dīn, ᶜAbd al-Razzāq. *Adab al-Murtaḍā min sīratihi wa-āthārihi*. Baghdad: Maṭbaᶜat al-Maᶜārif, 1957.

Murad, Hasan Qasim. '*Jabr* and *qadar* in early Islam: A reappraisal of their political and religious implications'. In *Islamic Studies Presented to Charles J. Adams*, edited by Wael B. Hallaq and Donald P. Little, 117–32. Leiden: Brill, 1991.

Murtaḍā, al-Sharīf ᶜAlī b. al-Ḥusayn al-Mūsawī. *Amālī al-Murtaḍā: Ghurar al-fawāʾid wa-durar al-qalāʾid*. Edited by Muḥammad Abū al-Faḍl Ibrāhīm. Cairo: Dār Iḥyāʾ al-Kutub al-ᶜArabiyya, 1954.

Murtaḍā, al-Sharīf ᶜAlī b. al-Ḥusayn al-Mūsawī. *al-Dhakhīra fī ᶜilm al-kalām*. Edited by Aḥmad Ḥusaynī. Qum: Muʾassasat al-Nashr al-Islāmī, 1990.

Murtaḍā, al-Sharīf ᶜAlī b. al-Ḥusayn al-Mūsawī. *al-Dharīᶜa ilā uṣūl al-sharīᶜa*. Qum: Muʾassasat al-Imām al-Ṣādiq, 2009. Previously published as *al-Dharīᶜa ilā uṣūl al-sharīᶜa*. Edited by Abū al-Qāsim Gurjī. Tehran: Tehran University Publications, 1967. (References are to the 2009 edition, unless otherwise specified.)

Murtaḍā, al-Sharīf ᶜAlī b. al-Ḥusayn al-Mūsawī. *Dīwān al-Sharīf al-Murtaḍā*. Edited by Rashīd al-Ṣaffār. Beirut: Dār al-Balāgha, 1998.

Murtaḍā, al-Sharīf ᶜAlī b. al-Ḥusayn al-Mūsawī. *al-Intiṣār*. Qum: Muᵓassasat al-Nashr al-Islāmī, 1415 H.

Murtaḍā, al-Sharīf ᶜAlī b. al-Ḥusayn al-Mūsawī. *Masāᵓil al-Nāṣiriyyāt* [*sic*]. Edited by Markaz al-Buḥūth wa-l-Dirāsāt al-ᶜIlmiyya. Tehran: Rābiṭat al-Thaqāfa wa-l-ᶜAlāqāt al-Islāmiyya, 1997.

Murtaḍā, al-Sharīf ᶜAlī b. al-Ḥusayn al-Mūsawī. *Mawsūᶜat turāth al-Sayyid al-Murtaḍā fī ᶜilm al-kalām wa-radd al-shubuhāt*. Najaf: al-Markaz al-Islāmī li-l-Dirāsāt al-Istrātījiyya, 2015.

Murtaḍā, al-Sharīf ᶜAlī b. al-Ḥusayn al-Mūsawī. *al-Mūḍiḥ ᶜan jihat iᶜjāz al-Qurᵓān = al-Ṣarfa*. Edited by Muḥammad Riḍā Anṣārī Qummī. Mashhad: Majmaᶜ al-Buḥūth al-Islāmiyya, 2003.

Murtaḍā, al-Sharīf ᶜAlī b. al-Ḥusayn al-Mūsawī. *al-Mulakhkhaṣ fī uṣūl al-dīn*. Edited by Muḥammad Riḍā Anṣārī Qummī. Tehran: Markaz-i Nashr-i Dānishgāhī, 1381 SH.

Murtaḍā, al-Sharīf ᶜAlī b. al-Ḥusayn al-Mūsawī. *al-Muqniᶜ fī al-ghayba*. Edited by Muḥammad ᶜAlī al-Ḥakīm. Qum: Muᵓassasat Āl al-Bayt, 1995.

Murtaḍā, al-Sharīf ᶜAlī b. al-Ḥusayn al-Mūsawī. *Rasāᵓil al-Sharīf al-Murtaḍā*. Edited by Aḥmad Ḥusaynī. Qum: Dār al-Qurᵓān al-Karīm, 1985–90.

Murtaḍā, al-Sharīf ᶜAlī b. al-Ḥusayn al-Mūsawī. *al-Shāfī fī al-imāma*. Edited by ᶜAbd al-Zahrāᵓ al-Ḥusaynī al-Khaṭīb. Tehran: Muᵓassasat al-Ṣādiq, 1986.

Murtaḍā, al-Sharīf ᶜAlī b. al-Ḥusayn al-Mūsawī. *Sharḥ Jumal al-ᶜilm wa-l-ᶜamal*. Edited by Yaᶜqūb Jaᶜfarī Marāghī. Tehran: Dār al-Uswa, 1998.

Murtaḍā, al-Sharīf ᶜAlī b. al-Ḥusayn al-Mūsawī. *Tanzīh al-anbiyāᵓ wa-l-aᵓimma*. Edited by Fāris Ḥassūn Karīm. Qum: Maktab al-Iᶜlām al-Islāmī, 2002.

Muslim b. al-Ḥajjāj al-Naysabūrī. *Ṣaḥīḥ Muslim*. Beirut: Dār al-Fikr, n.d.

Muẓaffar, Muḥammad Riḍā. *ᶜAqāᵓid al-Imāmiyya*. Najaf: Maktabat al-Amīn, 1968.

Najāshī, Aḥmad b. ᶜAlī. *Rijāl al-Najāshī*. Edited by Mūsā Zanjānī. Qum: Muᵓassasat al-Nashr al-Islāmī, 1418 H.

Nashshār, ᶜAlī Sāmī. *Nashᵓat al-fikr al-falsafī fī al-Islām*. Cairo: Dār al-Maᶜārif, 1977.

Nasr, Seyyed Hossein. 'Ithnā ᶜAshariyya'. *Encyclopaedia of Islam, 2nd edn* [= *EI*^{2}], 4 (1978), 277.

Nawas, John A. 'A reexamination of three current explanations for al-Maᵓmun's introduction of the *miḥna*'. *International Journal of Middle East Studies*, 26, no. 4 (1994), 615–29.

Nawbakhtī, al-Ḥasan b. Mūsā. *Firaq al-Shīᶜa*. Edited by Hellmut Ritter. Istanbul: Jamᶜiyyat al-Mustashriqīn al-Almāniyya, 1931.

Naysābūrī, Abū Rashīd. *al-Masāᵓil fī al-khilāf bayn al-Baṣriyyīn wa-l-Baghdādiyyīn*. Edited by Maᶜn Ziyāda and Riḍwān al-Sayyid. Beirut: Maᶜhad al-Inmāᵓ al-ᶜArabī, 1979.

Naẓarī, Ḥamīd ᶜAṭāᵓī. 'Nigarishī bar nigārishhā-yi kalāmī: maṣāᵓib wa maṣāᶜib-i Rasāᵓil-i Murtaḍā'. *Āyina-yi pazhūhish*, 155 (1394 SH), 54–69.

Naẓarī, Ḥamīd ᶜAṭāᵓī. 'Nikātī dar bāb-i sākhtār wa nisbat-i du kitāb al-Mulakhkhaṣ wa l-Dhakhīra-yi Sharīf Murtaḍā'. *Āyina-yi pazhūhish*, 159 (1395 SH), 37–47.

Naẓarī, Ḥamīd ᶜAṭāᵓī. 'Piyvast wa takmila-yi maqāla-yi "Nigarishī bar nigārishhā-yi kalāmī: maṣāᵓib wa maṣāᶜib-i Rasāᵓil-i Murtaḍā"'. *Āyina-yi pazhūhish*, 155 (1394 SH), 74–9.

Newman, Andrew J. *The Formative Period of Twelver Shīʿism: Ḥadīth as Discourse between Qum and Baghdad*. Richmond: Curzon, 2000.

Nielsen, Jørgen S. 'Maẓālim'. *Encyclopaedia of Islam, 2nd edn* [= *EI*²], 6 (1991), 933.

Niʿma, ʿAbdullāh. *Falāsifat al-Shīʿa*. Beirut: Dār Maktabat al-Ḥayāh, 1961.

Niʿma, ʿAbdullāh. *Hishām b. al-Ḥakam*. Beirut: Dār al-Fikr al-Lubnānī, 1985.

Ormsby, Eric. *Theodicy in Islamic Thought: The Dispute over al-Ghazālī's 'Best of All Possible Worlds'*. Princeton, NJ: Princeton University Press, 1984.

Oxford English Dictionary. 2nd edn. Oxford: Oxford University Press, 1989.

Pierce, Matthew. *Twelve Infallible Men: The Imams and the Making of Shiʿism*. Cambridge, MA: Harvard University Press, 2016.

Pingree, David. 'Astrology'. In *Religion, Learning, and Science in the ʿAbbasid Period*, edited by M. J. L. Young, J. D. Latham and R. B. Serjeant, 290–300. Cambridge: Cambridge University Press, 1990.

Pomerantz, Maurice A. 'A political biography of al-Ṣāḥib Ismāʿīl b. ʿAbbād (d. 385/995)'. *Journal of the American Oriental Society*, 134, no. 1 (2014), 1–23.

al-Qāḍī al-Nuʿmān, Abū Ḥanīfa al-Nuʿmān b. Ḥayyūn al-Maghribī. *Daʿāʾim al-Islām*. Edited by Āṣif b. ʿAlī Aṣghar Fayḍī. Cairo: Dār al-Maʿārif, 1963.

al-Qāḍī, Wadād. 'Abū Ḥayyān al-Tawḥīdī: A Sunni voice in the Shiʿi century'. In *Culture and Memory in Medieval Islam*, edited by Farhad Daftari and Josef W. Meri, 128–59. London: I. B. Tauris, 2003.

al-Qāḍī, Wadād. 'An early Fāṭimid political document'. *Studia Islamica*, 48 (1978), 71–108.

Qummī, ʿAlī b. Ibrāhīm. *Tafsīr = Tafsīr al-Qummī*. Edited by Ṭayyib al-Mūsawī al-Jazāʾirī. Qum: Dār al-Kitāb, 1983.

Rabb, Intisar A. '"Reasonable doubt" in Islamic law'. *Yale Journal of International Law*, 40, no. 1 (2015), 41–94.

Rabbānī, Muḥammad Ḥasan. 'Abū Muslim Iṣfahānī-yi'. www.icnc.ir/index.aspx?pid=289&metadataId=44ad7844-5233-4199-aeaf-2fe10fd44a38.

Raḍī, al-Sharīf Muḥammad b. al-Ḥusayn. *Dīwān al-Sharīf al-Raḍī*. Beirut: Dār Ṣādir, 1961.

Raḍī, al-Sharīf Muḥammad b. al-Ḥusayn. *Khaṣāʾiṣ al-aʾimma*. Edited by Muḥammad Hādī Amīnī. Mashhad: Majmaʿ al-Buḥūth al-Islāmiyya, 1406 H.

Raḍī, al-Sharīf Muḥammad b. al-Ḥusayn. *al-Majāzāt al-nabawiyya*. Edited by Ṭaha al-Zaynī. Cairo: Muʾassasat al-Ḥalabī, 1967.

Raḍī, al-Sharīf Muḥammad b. al-Ḥusayn. *Nahj al-balāgha*. Edited by Muḥammad ʿAbduh. Beirut: Dār al-Maʿrifa, n.d.

Rahman, Fazlur. 'Barāhima'. *Encyclopaedia of Islam, 2nd edn* [= *EI*²], Brill Online, 2012.

Rāwandī, Quṭb al-Dīn. *al-Kharāʾij wa-l-jarāʾiḥ*. Qum: Muʾassasat al-Imām al-Mahdī, 1989.

Rāzī, Fakhr al-Dīn Muḥammad b. ʿUmar. *ʿIṣmat al-anbiyāʾ*. Edited by Muḥammad Ḥijāzī. Cairo: Maktabat al-Thaqāfa al-Dīniyya, 1986.

Rāzī, Fakhr al-Dīn Muḥammad b. ʿUmar. *al-Tafsīr al-kabīr = Mafātīḥ al-ghayb*. Cairo: al-Maṭbaʿa al-Bahiyya al-Miṣriyya, 1934–62.

Refudeen, Mohammed Awais. 'Phenomenology versus historicism: The case of Imamate'. *American Journal of Islamic Social Sciences*, 15, no. 2 (1998), 63–73.

Reinhart, A. Kevin. *Before Revelation: The Boundaries of Muslim Moral Thought*. Albany: State University of New York Press, 1995.

Richard, Yann. *Shiᶜite Islam: Polity, Ideology, and Creed*. Translated by Antonia Nevill. Cambridge, MA: Blackwell, 1995.

Rippin, Andrew. 'Literary analysis of Qurᵓān, *Sīra* and *Tafsīr*: The methdologies of John Wansbrough'. In *Approaches to Islam in Religious Studies*, edited by Richard C. Martin, 151–63, 227–32. Oxford: Oneworld, 2001.

Rummānī et al. *Thalāth rasāᵓil fī iᶜjāz al-Qurᵓān*. Edited by Muḥammad Khalafullāh and Muḥammad Zaghlūl Salām. Cairo: Dār al-Maᶜārif, 1976.

Sabra, Abdelhamid I. 'The simple ontology of *kalām* atomism: An outline'. *Early Science and Medicine*, 14, no. 1–3 (2009), 68–78.

Ṣadr, Ḥasan. *Nihāyat al-dirāya*. Edited by Mājid Gharbāwī. Qum: al-Mashᶜar, n.d.

Ṣadr, Ḥasan. *al-Shīᶜa wa-funūn al-Islām*. Sidon: Maṭbaᶜat al-ᶜIrfān, 1912.

Ṣadūq, Muḥammad b. ᶜAlī Ibn Bābawayh. *ᶜIlal al-sharāᵓiᶜ*. Najaf: al-Maktaba al-Ḥaydariyya, 1966.

Ṣadūq, Muḥammad b. ᶜAlī Ibn Bābawayh. *al-Iᶜtiqādāt fī dīn al-Imāmiyya*. Edited by ᶜIṣām ᶜAbd al-Sayyid. Beirut: Dār al-Mufīd, 1994.

Ṣadūq, Muḥammad b. ᶜAlī Ibn Bābawayh. *Kamāl al-dīn wa-tamām al-niᶜma*. Edited by Ḥusayn al-Aᶜlamī. Beirut: Muᵓassasat al-Aᶜlamī li-l-Maṭbūᶜāt, 1991.

Ṣadūq, Muḥammad b. ᶜAlī Ibn Bābawayh. *al-Khiṣāl*. Edited by ᶜAlī Akbar Ghaffārī. Qum: Manshūrāt Jamāᶜat al-Mudarrisīn fī al-Hawza al-ᶜIlmiyya, 1403 H.

Ṣadūq, Muḥammad b. ᶜAlī Ibn Bābawayh. *Maᶜānī al-akhbār*. Edited by ᶜAlī Akbar Ghaffārī. Qum: Intishārāt Islāmī, 1379 H.

Ṣadūq, Muḥammad b. ᶜAlī Ibn Bābawayh. *Man lā yaḥḍuruhu al-faqīh*. Edited by ᶜAlī Akbar Ghaffārī. Qum: Muᵓassasat al-Nashr al-Islāmī, n.d.

Ṣadūq, Muḥammad b. ᶜAlī Ibn Bābawayh. *al-Muqniᶜ*. Qum: Muᵓassasat al-Imām al-Hādī, 1415 H.

Ṣadūq, Muḥammad b. ᶜAlī Ibn Bābawayh. *al-Tawḥīd*. Edited by Hāshim al-Ḥusaynī al-Ṭihrānī. Beirut: Dār al-Maᶜrifa, 1967.

Ṣadūq, Muḥammad b. ᶜAlī Ibn Bābawayh. *ᶜUyūn akhbār al-Riḍā*. Edited by Ḥusayn al-Aᶜlamī. Beirut: Muᵓassasat al-Aᶜlamī, 1984.

Ṣafadī, Ṣalāḥ al-Dīn. *al-Wāfī bi-l-wafayāt*. Edited by Aḥmad al-Arnāᵓūṭ and Turkī Muṣṭafā. Beirut: Dār Iḥyāᵓ al-Turāth al-ᶜArabī, 2000.

Sarmadī, Maḥmūd. 'Abū Muslim Iṣfahānyī-yi Mufassirī'. http://library.tebyan.net/ar/Viewer/Text/78411/1.

Sayyārī, Aḥmad b. Muḥammad. *Revelation and Falsification: The Kitāb al-qirāᵓāt of Aḥmad b. Muḥammad al-Sayyārī*. Edited by Etan Kohlberg and Mohammad Ali Amir-Moezzi. Leiden: Brill, 2009.

al-Sayyid, Riḍwān. *al-Jamāᶜa wa-l-mujtamaᶜ wa-l-dawla*. Beirut: Dār al-Kitāb al-ᶜArabī, 1997.

Schmidtke, Sabine. 'Al-ᶜAllāma al-Ḥillī and Shiᶜite Muᶜtazilite theology'. In *Shiᶜism*, edited by Paul Luft and Colin Turner, 2:151–74. London: Routledge, 2008.

Schmidtke, Sabine. 'Ibn Mattawayh'. *Encyclopaedia of Islam, 3rd edn* [= *EI*3]. Brill Online, 2016.

Schmidtke, Sabine. *The Theology of al-ʿAllāma al-Ḥillī (d. 728/1325)*. Berlin: K. Schwarz, 1991.

Schmidtke, Sabine and Camilla Adang. 'Muʿtazilī discussions of the abrogation of the Torah: Ibn Ḫallād (4th/10th century) and his commentators'. *Arabica*, 60, no. 6 (2013), 701–42.

Schrieke, Bertram, Jamal Eddine Bencheikh, Jan Knappert and Basil W. Robinson. 'Miʿrādj'. *Encyclopaedia of Islam, 2nd edn* [= *EI*^{2}], Brill Online, 2012.

Schwarb, Gregor. 'Short communication: A newly discovered fragment of al-Sharīf al-Murtaḍā's *K. al-Mulakhkhaṣ fī uṣūl al-dīn* in Hebrew script'. *Intellectual History of the Islamicate World*, 2, nos 1–2 (2014), 75–9.

Sellheim, Rudolf. 'Al-Marzubānī'. *Encyclopaedia of Islam, 2nd edn* [= *EI*^{2}], 6 (1991), 634.

al-Shahīd al-Awwal, Muḥammad b. Makkī al-Jizzīnī. *al-Arbaʿūn ḥadīth*^{an}. Qum: Madrasat al-Imām al-Mahdī, 1407 H.

al-Shahīd al-Awwal, Muḥammad b. Makkī al-Jizzīnī. *Dhikrā al-Shīʿa fī aḥkām al-sharīʿa*. Qum: Muʾassasat Āl al-Bayt li-Iḥyāʾ al-Turāth, 1419 H.

al-Shahīd al-Thānī, Zayn al-Dīn b. ʿAlī al-Jubaʿī. *Rasāʾil al-Shahīd al-Thānī*. Qum: lithograph.

Shahrastānī, Muḥammad b. ʿAbd al-Karīm. *al-Milal wa-l-niḥal*. Edited by Aḥmad Fahmī Muḥammad. Beirut: Dār al-Kutub al-ʿIlmiyya, 1992.

Shahrastānī, Muḥammad b. ʿAbd al-Karīm. *Nihāyat al-aqdām fī ʿilm al-kalām*. Edited by Alfred Guillaume. Cairo: Maktabat al-Mutanabbī, 1980.

Shammarī, Raʾūf. 'al-Sharīf al-Murtaḍā mutakallim^{an}'. PhD dissertation, University of Zliten, Libya, 2004.

Shams al-Dīn, Muḥammad Jaʿfar. *Dirāsāt fī al-ʿaqīda al-Islāmiyya*. Beirut: Dār al-Kitāb al-Lubnānī, 1977.

Sharshar, Muḥammad Ḥasan Bayyūmī. *al-Balāgha al-qurʾāniyya wa-l-nabawiyya fī āthār al-Sharīfayn*. Cairo: Zahrāʾ al-Sharq, 2006.

Shihadeh, Ayman. 'The existence of God'. In *The Cambridge Companion to Classical Islamic Theology*, edited by Tim Winter, 197–217. Cambridge: Cambridge University Press, 2008.

Shīrāzī, Ṣadr al-Dīn ʿAlī Ibn Maʿṣūm. *al-Darajāt al-rafīʿa fī ṭabaqāt al-Shīʿa*. Najaf: al-Maṭbaʿa al-Ḥaydariyya, 1962.

Smoor, Pieter. 'Al-Maʿarrī'. *Encyclopaedia of Islam, 2nd edn* [= *EI*^{2}], 5 (1986), 927.

Sourdel, Dominique. 'Dār al-ʿIlm'. *Encyclopaedia of Islam, 2nd edn* [= *EI*^{2}], 2 (1983), 127.

Sourdel, Dominique. 'L'Imamisme vu par le Cheikh al-Mufīd'. *Revue des Études Islamiques*, 40 (1972), 217–96.

Stearns, Justin. *Infectious Ideas: Contagion in Premodern Islamic and Christian Thought in the Western Mediterranean*. Baltimore: Johns Hopkins University Press, 2011.

Strothmann, Rudolf. 'Ḥasan al-Uṭrūsh'. *Encyclopaedia of Islam, 2nd edn* [= *EI*^{2}], 3 (1979), 254.

Stroumsa, Sarah. *Freethinkers of Medieval Islam: Ibn al-Rāwandī, Abū Bakr al-Rāzī, and Their Impact on Islamic Thought*. Leiden: Brill, 1999.

Subḥānī, Jaʿfar. *ʿIṣmat al-anbiyāʾ fī al-Qurʾān al-karīm*. Qum: Muʾassasat al-Imām al-Ṣādiq, 1420 H.

Subḥānī, Jaᶜfar. *Risāla fī al-taḥsīn wa-l-taqbīḥ al-ᶜaqliyyayn*. Qum: Muᵓassasat al-Imām al-Ṣādiq, 1420 H.

[Pseudo-]Sulaym b. Qays. *Kitāb Sulaym b. Qays al-Hilālī*. Edited by Muḥammad Bāqir Anṣārī. Najaf: n.p., n.d.

Ṭabarānī, Sulaymān b. Aḥmad. *al-Muᶜjam al-kabīr*. Edited by Ḥamdī ᶜAbd al-Majīd al-Salafī. Beirut: Dār Iḥyāᵓ al-Turāth al-ᶜArabī, 1983.

Ṭabarī, Muḥammad b. Jarīr b. Rustam. *al-Mustarshid fī imāmat Amīr al-Muᵓminīn ᶜAli b. Abī Ṭālib*. Edited by Aḥmad Maḥmūdī. Qum: Muᵓassasat al-Thaqāfa al-Islāmiyya, 1415 H.

Ṭabāṭabāᵓī, Muḥammad Ḥusayn. *al-Mīzān fī tafsīr al-Qurᵓān*. Beirut: Muᵓassasat al-Aᶜlamī, 1970–4.

Ṭabāṭabāᵓī, Muḥammad Ḥusayn. *al-Shīᶜa fī al-Islām*. Translated by Jaᶜfar Bahāᵓ al-Dīn. Tehran: Manshūrāt Qism al-Dirāsāt al-Islāmiyya.

Ṭabrisī, Aḥmad b. ᶜAlī. *al-Iḥtijāj*. Edited by Muḥammad Bāqir al-Kharsān. Najaf: Dār al-Nuᶜmān, 1966.

Ṭabrisī, al-Faḍl b. al-Ḥasan. *Majmaᶜ al-bayān fī tafsīr al-Qurᵓān*. Beirut: Muᵓassasat al-Aᶜlamī, 1995.

Takim, Liyakat N. *The Heirs of the Prophet: Charisma and Religious Authority in Shiᶜite Islam*. Albany: State University of New York Press, 2006.

Tanūkhī, al-Muḥassin b. ᶜAlī. *al-Faraj baᶜd al-shidda*. Edited by ᶜAbbūd al-Shāljī. Beirut: Dār Ṣādir, 1978.

Tanūkhī, al-Muḥassin b. ᶜAlī. *Nishwār al-muḥāḍara wa-akhbār al-mudhākara*. Edited by ᶜAbbūd al-Shāljī. Beirut: Dār Ṣādir, 1995.

Tawḥīdī, Abū Ḥayyān ᶜAlī b. Muḥammad. *Akhlāq al-wazīrayn*. Edited by Muḥammad al-Ṭanjī. Beirut: Dār Ṣādir, 1992.

Tawḥīdī, Abū Ḥayyān ᶜAlī b. Muḥammad. *al-Baṣāᵓir wa-l-dhakhāᵓir*. Edited by Wadād al-Qāḍī. Beirut: Dār Ṣādir, 1988.

Tawḥīdī, Abū Ḥayyān ᶜAlī b. Muḥammad. *al-Hawāmil wa-l-shawāmil*. Edited by Aḥmad Amīn and al-Sayyid Aḥmad Ṣaqr. Cairo: al-Hayᵓa al-ᶜĀmma li-Quṣūr al-Thaqāfa, 2001.

Thaᶜālibī, Abū Manṣūr ᶜAbd al-Malik. *Fiqh al-lugha wa-sirr al-ᶜarabiyya*. Edited by Fāᵓiz Muḥammad. Beirut: Dār al-Kitāb al-ᶜArabī, 1996.

Thaᶜālibī, Abū Manṣūr ᶜAbd al-Malik. *Yatīmat al-dahr fī maḥāsin ahl al-ᶜaṣr*. Edited by Mufīd Qumayḥa. Beirut: Dār al-Kutub al-ᶜIlmiyya, 1983.

Thomas, David. 'Miracles in Islam'. In *The Cambridge Companion to Miracles*, edited by Graham Twelftree, 199–215. Cambridge: Cambridge University Press, 2011.

Tirmidhī, Muḥammad b. ᶜĪsā. *Sunan al-Tirmidhī*. Edited by ᶜAbd al-Wahhāb ᶜAbd al-Laṭīf. Beirut: Dār al-Fikr, 1983.

Tor, Deborah. 'ᶜAyyār'. *Encyclopaedia of Islam, 3rd edn* [= *EI*[3]]. Brill Online, 2016.

Tottoli, Roberto. 'Shuᶜayb'. *Encyclopaedia of the Qurᵓān* [= *EQ*]. Brill Online, 2012.]

Tucker, William F. *Mahdis and Millenarians: Shiᶜite Extremists in Early Muslim Iraq*. New York: Cambridge University Press, 2008.

Ṭūsī, Muḥammad b. al-Ḥasan. *al-Amālī*. Qum: Dār al-Thaqāfa, 1993.

Ṭūsī, Muḥammad b. al-Ḥasan. *al-Fihrist*. Edited by Muḥammad Ṣādiq Baḥr al-ᶜUlūm. Qum: Manshūrāt al-Sahrīf al-Raḍī, n.d.

Ṭūsī, Muḥammad b. al-Ḥasan. *al-Ghayba*. Edited by ᶜIbādullāh Ṭihrānī and Aḥmad Nāṣiḥ. Qum: Muᵓassasat al-Maᶜārif al-Islāmiyya, 1411 H.

Ṭūsī, Muḥammad b. al-Ḥasan. *al-Iqtiṣād al-hādī ilā sabīl al-rashād*. Qum: Maṭbaᶜat al-Khayyām, 1400 H.

Ṭūsī, Muḥammad b. al-Ḥasan. *al-Khilāf*. Qum: Muᵓassasat al-Nashr al-Islāmī, 1407 H.

Ṭūsī, Muḥammad b. al-Ḥasan. *al-Mabsūṭ*. Edited by Muḥammad Taqī Kashfī. Tehran: al-Maktaba al-Murtaḍawiyya, 1387 H.

Ṭūsī, Muḥammad b. al-Ḥasan. *al-Rasāᵓil al-ᶜashr*. Edited by Muḥammad Taqī Dānishpazhūh et al. Qum: Muᵓassasat al-Nashr al-Islāmī, n.d.

Ṭūsī, Muḥammad b. al-Ḥasan. *Rijāl al-Ṭūsī*. Edited by Jawād Qayyūmī Iṣfahānī. Qum: Muᵓassasat al-Nashr al-Islāmī, 1415 H.

Ṭūsī, Muḥammad b. al-Ḥasan. *Talkhīṣ al-Shāfī*. Edited by Ḥusayn Baḥr al-ᶜUlūm. Najaf: Maṭbaᶜat al-Ādāb, 1963.

Ṭūsī, Muḥammad b. al-Ḥasan. *al-Tibyān fī tafsīr al-Qurᵓān*. Edited by Aḥmad Ḥabīb Qaṣīr. Qum: Maktab al-Iᶜlām al-Islāmī, 1989.

Ṭūsī, Muḥammad b. al-Ḥasan. *al-ᶜUdda fī uṣūl al-fiqh*. Edited by Muḥammad Riḍā Anṣārī Qummī. Qum: al-Muḥaqqiq, 1997.

Tustarī, Asadullāh al-Kāẓimī. *Kashf al-qināᶜ ᶜan wujūh ḥujjiyyat al-ijmāᶜ*. Qum: Muᵓassasat Āl al-Bayt, 1400 H.

ᶜUthmān, ᶜAbd al-Karīm. *Naẓariyyat al-taklīf: Ārāᵓ al-Qāḍī ᶜAbd al-Jabbār al-kalāmiyya*. Beirut: Muᵓassasat al-Risāla, 1971.

van den Bergh, Simon. 'Ghazali on "gratitude towards God" and its Greek sources'. *Studia Islamica*, 7 (1957), 77–98.

van Ess, Josef. 'Early development of *kalām*'. Reprinted in *Islamic Philosophy and Theology*, edited by Ian Richard Netton, 1:175–94. London: Routledge, 2007.

van Ess, Josef. *The Flowering of Muslim Theology*. Translated by Jane Marie Todd. Cambridge, MA: Harvard University Press, 2006.

van Ess, Josef. 'Ḳadariyya'. *Encyclopaedia of Islam, 2nd edn* [= *EI*²]. Brill Online, 2012.

van Ess, Josef. 'The logical structure of Islamic theology'. In *Logic in Classical Islamic Culture*, edited by Gustave E. von Grunebaum, 21–50. Wiesbaden: Harrassowitz, 1970.

van Ess, Josef. 'Political ideas in early Islamic religious thought'. *British Journal of Middle Eastern Studies*, 28, no. 2 (2001), 151–64.

van Ess, Josef. 'Tas̲h̲bīh wa-Tanzīh'. *Encyclopaedia of Islam, 2nd edn* [= *EI*²]. Brill Online, 2012.

van Ess, Josef. *Theologie und Gesellschaft im 2. und 3. Jahrhundert Hidschra: Eine Geschichte des religiösen Denkens im frühen Islam*. Berlin: Walter de Gruyter, 1991–7.

Vasalou, Sophia. 'The miraculous eloquence of the Qur'an: General trajectories and individual approaches'. *Journal of Qur'anic Studies*, 4, no. 2 (2002), 23–53.

Vasalou, Sophia. *Moral Agents and Their Deserts: The Character of Muᶜtazilite Ethics*. Princeton, NJ: Princeton University Press, 2008.

Vasalou, Sophia. 'Subject and body in Baṣran Muᶜtazilism, or: Muᶜtazilite *kalām* and the fear of triviality'. *Arabic Sciences and Philosophy*, 17, no. 2 (2007), 267–98.

von Stietencron, Heinrich. 'Theology'. *The Brill Dictionary of Religion*. Edited by Kocku von Stuckrad. Brill Online, 2016.

Wāᵓilī, Aḥmad. *Huwiyyat al-tashayyuᶜ*. Beirut: Dār al-Ṣafwa, 1994.

Wiegers, Gerard A., Eilert Herms, Ingrid Schoberth and Karl Ernst Nipkow. 'Doctrine'. *Religion Past and Present*. Edited by Hans Dieter Betz et al. Brill Online, 2016.

Wisnovsky, Robert. 'Avicenna and the Avicennian tradition'. In *The Cambridge Companion to Arabic Philosophy*. Edited by Peter Adamson and Richard C. Taylor, 92–136. Cambridge: Cambridge University Press, 2005.

Wisnovsky, Robert. *Avicenna's Metaphysics in Context*. Ithaca, NY: Cornell University Press, 2003.

Wolfson, Harry Austryn. *The Philosphy of the Kalam*. Cambridge, MA: Harvard University Press, 1976.

Yāqūt b. ᶜAbdullāh al-Ḥamawī. *Muᶜjam al-buldān*. Beirut: Dār Iḥyāᵓ al-Turāth al-ᶜArabī, 1979.

Yāqūt b. ᶜAbdullāh al-Ḥamawī. *Muᶜjam al-udabāᵓ*. Edited by Iḥsān ᶜAbbās. Beirut: Dār al-Gharb al-Islāmī, 1993.

Zadeh, Travis. '"Fire cannot harm it": Mediation, temptation and the charismatic power of the Qur'an'. *Journal of Qur'anic Studies*, 10, no. 2 (2008), 50–72.

Zayn al-ᶜĀbidīn, ᶜAbd al-Salām. *Murājaᶜāt fī ᶜiṣmat al-anbiyāᵓ*. Beirut: n.p., 2000.

Zilio-Grandi, Ida. 'The gratitude of man and the gratitude of God: Notes on *šukr* in traditional Islamic thought'. *Islamochristiana*, 38 (2012), 45–61.

Zayna, Ḥusnī. *al-ᶜAql ᶜind al-Muᶜtazila*. Beirut: Dār al-Āfāq al-Jadīda, 1978.

Zinser, Hartmut. 'Group, religious'. *The Brill Dictionary of Religion*. Edited by Kocku von Stuckrad. Brill Online, 2016.

Ziriklī, Khayr al-Dīn. *al-Aᶜlām*. Beirut: Dār al-ᶜIlm li-l-Malāyīn, 1980.

INDEX

ᶜAbd al-Jabbār, 9, 21, 194
  circle of, 56, 88, 89, 109, 129, 154, 184, 213, 213–15
  critique of Imamism by, 7, 26–7, 163, 169, 172, 184, 187
  views of, 53–4, 55–6, 57, 72, 106–7, 111, 112, 135, 138, 184
  see also Basran Muᶜtazilism
Abraham, 203
abrogation, 117, 199–202
Abū Aḥmad al-Ḥusayn b. Mūsā (father of Murtaḍā), 18, 217
Abū Rashīd al-Naysābūrī, 9
Abū al-Ṣalāḥ al-Ḥalabī, 21, 198
accidents (sing. *ᶜaraḍ*), 61
acquisitionism, 134–5
acts, 61, 69
  classification of, 88–96
  creation (*khalq*) of, 133, 214
  dependency on agents of, 59, 67, 133–4
  moral value of, 55, 60, 88–97, 99, 109, 110, 137–8, 185
agency, human, 63, 128–9, 132–4, 144
agents, 59, 63, 89–90, 105, 107, 110, 132, 203; *see also* deserts; moral obligation
alerts, divine (sing. *khāṭir*), 140
ᶜAlī b. Abī Ṭālib, Imama of, 160–2, 163–4, 166–7, 168
Amālī (Murtaḍā), 22, 24
animals, 104, 105, 106, 107
anthropomorphism, 52–3
apostasy, 112
Ashᶜaris, 70–1, 87, 112, 115, 134, 189
astrology, 190
atoms (sing. *jawhar*), 61, 62
Attribute of Essence, God's, 74–5, 78
attributes (sing. *ṣifa*), 61, 62–3, 92
  of essence vs of act, 62, 63, 72, 75–6, 77
  see also God: attributes of
Attributist position on God, 70–1, 73–4, 213, 214

*badā*ʾ, 201–2, 213–14
Baghdadi Muᶜtazilism, 3, 56, 66, 73, 79, 99–100, 102, 104, 111, 119, 126n150, 154, 215
  Mufīd agreeing with, 56, 66, 73, 79, 104, 120, 126n150
Balkhī, Abū al-Qāsim, 6–7, 24, 154, 195
Barāhima, 116, 118, 186
Basran Muᶜtazilism, 9, 71, 75, 87, 95
  Murtaḍā agreeing with, 52–3, 60, 62, 66, 75, 77–8, 79, 99–100, 102, 106, 109, 116, 120, 131, 133, 136, 144, 159, 214, 216
  Murtadā disagreeing with, 67, 95, 111–13, 119, 204, 213–14, 215–16
  see also ᶜAbd al-Jabbār: circle of
Baṣrī, Abū al-Ḥusayn, 23, 27, 44n132, 69, 138
best interest (*al-aṣlaḥ*), 99, 103, 215
bodies (sing. *jism*), 61
  origination of, 66–8
Būyids and Imamism, 16–17, 18, 154, 163, 171, 219

causes (sing. *ᶜilla*), 59–60, 64–6, 92–3, 97–8
cautionary prudence (*taqiyya*), 164, 167
Companions, 162, 168–9, 191
compensation (*ᶜiwaḍ*), 104–7, 110, 136, 214
compulsion and coercion, 89
consensus, probative, 156, 157, 161, 162, 219
contagion, 65–6
corruption (*mafsada, istifsād*), 98, 101–2
creation, 135–7; *see also* acts: creation (*khalq*) of

deserts, 88–90, 95–6, 97–8, 103, 109, 112–13, 141
deserved treatments, 97–8, 104, 107–15, 141; *see also* compensation (*ᶜiwaḍ*); praise and blame; punishment; reward
determinants (sing. *sabab*), 64, 92
determinism, 128, 132–3, 134–5, 143, 197
Devil, 101
Dhakhīra (Murtaḍā), 24–5
Dharīᶜa (Murtaḍā), 26
divine assistance (*luṭf*), 98–101, 117, 214, 215–16, 217
  and the Imama, 100, 154–5, 216
  and moral obligation, 98–101, 139–40
  and pain, 102, 103–4
  and prophethood, 185
doctrine, meaning of, 4, 12
dreams, revelatory, 203

entities (sing. *maᶜnā*), 61, 92–3
essence, divine, 70–1; *see also* God: attributes of
essences (sing. *dhāt*), 58, 61, 62, 63, 64, 97–8
evidence, 53, 57–8, 59, 65
evidencing from the known to the unknown, 59–60, 75, 79, 90–2, 94, 99–100, 102–3, 106
existence, as attribute, 62

fear
  of authority, 156, 185, 186
  of punishment, 111–12, 140–1, 143

Ghadīr Khumm tradition, 163–4
gnosticism, 129, 130, 132, 165–6, 203
God
  attributes of, 52, 63, 70–6, 77–8, 138, 214
  existence of, 66–7, 69, 134
  freedom to act of, 98, 113, 135–7, 139–40
  justice of, 87, 100, 101, 106, 155, 214, 216
  omnipotence of, 100, 103–4, 114, 119, 141
  pain inflicted by, 102–3, 106
  will of, 72, 75–6, 138
  see also divine assistance

harm *see* compensation (*ᶜiwaḍ*); pain
ḥayāt, 130, 131
Ḥillī, ᶜAllāma, 76
Hishām b. al-Ḥakam, 70, 130, 211–12
history, sacred vs ordinary, 152, 166, 168–9
  and the Imama, 159, 160–1, 165, 170, 216–17
  and previous prophets, 183, 184, 200–1
  and the Qurʾān, 192, 198
human beings, 129–32, 137, 214; *see also* agency; agents; *rūḥ*
Ḥusayn, 167

Ibn Abī al-Hadīd, 26, 27, 44n134, 220
Ibn Mattawayh, 9, 138
Ibn Qiba, 168, 169, 173
Ibn al-Rāwandī, 68
Imama, Shiᶜi theory of
  compatibility with Muᶜtazilism of, 52–3, 153, 154, 157, 158, 171, 186
  in defining Imamism, 6, 151–3, 165, 170, 173
  and divine assistance, 100, 153, 154–5, 170, 215–16, 217
  Muᶜtazili critiques of, 1, 7, 163, 169, 187
  rational arguments for, 26, 154–6, 161–2, 216
  revelational arguments for, 26, 154, 156, 161, 162–3
  see also Imams
Imami Shiᶜsm and Muᶜtazilism
  nature of relation of, 2–3, 6–7, 153
  tension in Murtaḍā's thought between, 53, 57, 77, 112, 113, 129, 154, 158, 183–4, 186, 189, 201–2, 215
Imamis, sociopolitical situation of, 16–17, 163, 169, 218, 219
Imams
  identification of, 158, 163, 164–5, 189; *see also* ᶜAlī b. Abī Ṭālib, Imama of
  infallibility of, 153, 155, 156, 157–8, 160, 161–2, 164–5, 167, 172–3, 213, 214, 216
  moral superiority of, 57, 155, 157, 184

Imams (*cont.*)
necessity of, 153, 154–7, 172–3, 212, 213, 216
number of, 166, 214
occultation of, 169–71, 173, 214, 216–17, 218
political powerlessness of, 155, 161, 164, 165–6, 168, 215
qualifications of, 154, 157–60, 172, 173, 203, 217
as source of authority, 53, 77, 156, 211–12
vis-à-vis prophets, 155, 182–4, 186–7, 188, 203–4
see also Imama, Shiᶜi theory of
impostors, 101, 114
infallibility *see* Imams: infallibility of; prophets: infallibility of
infinite regression, 68–9, 73
initiated benevolence, 90, 97, 136, 139
injustice, 91, 93, 107
inquisition (*miḥna*), 76–7
intention, 89–90
intercession, 112–13, 213
investigation, 53, 55, 57–8, 60, 134, 140, 141, 203
Ismaᶜilis, 165

Jāḥiẓ, 1–2, 219–20
Jubbāʾīs, 27, 61, 94, 100, 137, 190, 194
judgements (sing. *ḥukm*), 58
justice, divine *see* God: justice of
Juwaynī, 120n6, 133

kalām, 4, 63–4
Karājikī, Abū al-Fatḥ, 21, 27, 34
Karbalāʾ, 167
knowledge (*ᶜilm*), 53–6
necessary vs acquired, 54–6, 60, 67–8, 91–2, 93–4, 107, 133–4
reason as source of, 56–7, 60, 93, 109, 141–2, 154, 156, 157–8, 185–6, 212, 214

language, 5, 78, 79
leadership, Imama as, 154–6
lying, 92, 93, 113–14, 119, 187

Maᶜarrī, Abū al-ᶜAlāʾ, 20
Mānkdīm, 9, 138, 146n45
messengers, 184–5, 204; *see also* prophets
Method of Negation, 58–9, 79, 94, 193
miracles, 57, 59, 78, 158, 171, 172, 188–90, 204
Qurʾān as instance of, 192–8, 202, 204
moral obligation, 137–43
and divine assistance, 98–101, 139–40, 216
justification for, 98, 101, 102, 109–10, 116–18, 137–9, 215
and religious experience, 140–2
requiring Imams/prophets, 142, 154–5, 156, 166, 185–6, 216
subjects of, 94–5, 129, 130, 131–2, 138, 203
thanksgiving as, 114–15, 139
morality, rational vs revelational
judgements of, 105, 110, 111, 113, 139
relationship between, 93, 97, 99, 111, 116–18, 141–2, 185–6
see also acts: moral value of; deserts; moral obligation; reason (*ᶜaql*)
Muᶜammar b. ᶜAbbād al-Sulamī, 130
Mufīd, 6–7, 23, 69, 113, 126n150, 130–1, 142, 212, 218
Murtaḍā agreeing with, 57, 133, 142, 143, 144, 156, 170, 173, 191, 213
Murtaḍā diverging from, 56, 62, 66, 71, 72–3, 75, 76, 78–80, 104, 105, 106, 119–20, 129, 131–2, 133, 136, 142, 143, 144, 157, 167, 170, 171, 173, 184, 185, 187, 198, 201, 203, 204, 212, 214
Mughnī (ᶜAbd al-Jabbār), 7, 26, 120n3
Muḥammad, 183
family of, 161–2
illiteracy of, 202
miracles of, 189–90, 192–4, 195, 196
Mulakhkhaṣ (Murtaḍā), 24–5, 120n3, 121n23
Murtaḍā
biography of, 18–21, 217, 219
jurisprudence of, 22, 219
Muᶜtazilism of, 23, 52–3, 79, 216
thought of *see* individual topics
writings, 22–3, 28–38; *see also* titles of individual works
Muᶜtazilism
divine assistance in, 98–9, 140, 154, 155, 215–16
divine justice in, 87–8, 91, 100, 106, 182
overlap with other affiliations, 3–4, 23
see also Baghdadi Muᶜtazilism; Basran Muᶜtazilism; Imami Shiᶜism and Muᶜtazilism
mutual cancellation, 97, 112, 213

nafs, 130, 131
Nahj al-balāgha (Raḍī), 18
Naẓẓām, 24, 27, 194, 195, 196
non-prevalent reports (*akhbār al-āḥād*), 22, 53, 201

occasionalism, 64

pain, 102–4, 105, 106, 138
pardon, 95–6, 109, 111, 113–14, 119
perseverance (*muwāfāt*), 112, 168
plain-good acts, 90, 91, 95–6; *see also* acts: moral value of
praise and blame, 90, 95–6, 107–8, 114, 115; *see also* deserved treatments
prayer, 99, 116, 118
pre-eternality of God, 73–4
prevalence, 22, 156, 163, 189, 191, 193, 201
prophets
  function of, 184–6, 187–8
  infallibility of, 27, 101, 157, 187–8, 198–9, 203, 204
  necessity of, 142, 185–6
  qualifications of, 186–7, 194
  veracity of, 188–9, 196, 201
  vis-à-vis Imams, 155, 182–4, 186–7, 188, 203–4
punishment
  desert and waiver of, 97, 108, 109–10, 111–13, 137
  fear of, 111–12, 140–1, 143
  moral value of, 95–6

qadariyya, 128–9
Qur'ān
  inimitability of, 192–8, 204, 214
  integrity of, 191–2, 219
  origination of, 76–7, 192, 195, 204, 213–14

Raḍī, al-Sharīf al-, 18, 19, 42n88
rational beings
  and deserved treatments, 109, 114, 143
  imaginary group of, 56, 108, 113, 116, 119, 137, 154
  and necessary knowledge, 55, 56, 93, 110
rationalism, 11–12, 129–30, 132, 133, 187, 211–12
reason (*ʿaql*), 11–12, 53
  knowledge dictated by, 56–7, 93, 99, 109, 116, 141–2, 156, 157–8, 214
  limits of, 111, 113, 118, 119, 144, 158, 185–6, 212
  see also morality, rational vs revelational
repentance (*tawba*), 112–13
revelation *see* morality, rational vs revelational
revisionary ratios, 6, 215, 216
reward, 97–8, 108–10, 112, 113, 136, 137, 138–9; *see also* deserved treatments; punishment
rūḥ, 130–1
Rummānī, 21, 148n70, 196

Ṣadūq, 69, 212, 218
Sallār al-Daylamī, 2, 21, 27, 43n126
ṣarfa, theory of, 192, 195–8, 204, 214
Shāfī fī al-imāma (Murtaḍā), 7, 26–7, 153, 156
simple substance (*jawhar basīṭ*), 130
slavery, 105, 117
speech, 77
states (sing. *ḥāl*), 63, 64, 71–2, 75–6, 96, 97–8
  theory of, 63, 70–1, 72–3, 74, 79, 214
'station between the two stations', 6, 182, 213
syndics, of ʿAlids/Ṭālibids, 17–18

Ṭabāṭabā'ī, Muḥammad Ḥusayn, 76
Tanzīh al-anbiyā' (Murtaḍā), 27, 153, 199
Tawḥīdī, Abū Ḥayyān, 218
thanksgiving, 114–15, 117, 139
theology
  definition of, 4–5, 12
  grand vs subtle, 5, 63, 129
  and Imami historiography, 151–3, 160–1, 162, 164–6, 168–9, 183, 200–1, 216–17
threat, the *see* fear: of punishment; punishment
traditionalists, 52, 66, 70, 129–30, 154, 189, 191, 211–12, 218, 219
Ṭūsī, Muḥammad b. al-Ḥasan, 9, 21, 22, 23, 26, 96
  agreeing with Murtaḍā, 56, 57, 61, 62, 69, 73, 75, 76, 79–80, 90, 120, 132, 136, 142, 144, 170, 185, 192, 201, 213, 214
  diverging from Murtaḍā, 90, 96, 133, 136, 143, 144, 171, 173, 184, 198, 203, 204, 214
tyrants, 105–6

unbelievers, 133, 142–3, 168
  compensation for, 104, 106, 214
  moral obligation of, 94–5, 139

unbelievers (*cont.*)
  possibility of pardon for, 95, 111, 114
  possibility of reward for, 97, 112

vileness, 89, 90, 91, 92–4, 96, 97, 110, 137–8; *see also* acts: moral value of

Wāqifiyya, 2, 164, 217
willing, 72, 75–6, 96–7, 138
worship, 115–16, 117, 139

Zaydis, 161, 164, 171

EU representative:
Easy Access System Europe
Mustamäe tee 50, 10621 Tallinn, Estonia
Gpsr.requests@easproject.com

www.ingramcontent.com/pod-product-compliance
Lightning Source LLC
Chambersburg PA
CBHW051114230426
43667CB00014B/2580
* 9 7 8 1 4 7 4 4 4 1 2 4 7 *